The
Coding Manual for
Qualitative Researchers

SAGE has been part of the global academic community since 1965, supporting high quality research and learning that transforms society and our understanding of individuals, groups and cultures. SAGE is the independent, innovative, natural home for authors, editors and societies who share our commitment and passion for the social sciences.

Find out more at: **www.sagepublications.com**

Second Edition

The
Coding Manual for
Qualitative Researchers

Johnny Saldaña

Los Angeles | London | New Delhi
Singapore | Washington DC

Los Angeles | London | New Delhi
Singapore | Washington DC

SAGE Publications Ltd
1 Oliver's Yard
55 City Road
London EC1Y 1SP

SAGE Publications Inc.
2455 Teller Road
Thousand Oaks, California 91320

SAGE Publications India Pvt Ltd
B 1/I 1 Mohan Cooperative Industrial Area
Mathura Road
New Delhi 110 044

SAGE Publications Asia-Pacific Pte Ltd
3 Church Street
#10-04 Samsung Hub
Singapore 049483

Editor: Jai Seaman
Editorial assistant: Anna Horvai
Production editor: Rachel Eley
Copyeditor: Neville Hankins
Proofreader: Derek Markham
Marketing manager: Ben Sherwood
Cover design: Jennifer Crisp
Typeset by: C&M Digitals (P) Ltd, Chennai, India
Printed by: Henry Ling Limited, at the Dorset
Press, Dorchester, DT1 1HD

First edition published 2009
Reprinted 2009, 2010 (three times), 2011 (twice), 2012 (twice)
This second edition published 2013
Reprinted 2013

Library of Congress Control Number: 2012932600

British Library Cataloguing in Publication data

A catalogue record for this book is available from
the British Library

ISBN 978-1-44624-736-5
ISBN 978-1-44624-737-2 (pbk)

Abbreviated Contents

Contents

About the Author

Johnny Saldaña received his BFA and MFA degrees in Drama Education from the University of Texas at Austin, and is a Professor of Theatre at Arizona State University's (ASU's) School of Theatre and Film in the Herberger Institute for Design and the Arts. He is the author of *Longitudinal Qualitative Research: Analyzing Change through Time* (AltaMira Press), *Fundamentals of Qualitative Research* (Oxford University Press), *Ethnotheatre: Research from Page to Stage* (Left Coast Press), and the editor of *Ethnodrama: An Anthology of Reality Theatre* (AltaMira Press). The first edition of *The Coding Manual for Qualitative Researchers* (Sage Publications) has been cited by scholars and practitioners internationally in such fields as K–12 and higher education, human development, health care, social sciences, business, government, social services, technology, and the arts.

Mr. Saldaña's research in qualitative inquiry and performance ethnography has received awards from the American Educational Research Association – Qualitative Research Special Interest Group, the American Alliance for Theatre & Education, the National Communication Association – Ethnography Division, and the ASU Herberger Institute for Design and the Arts. He has published a wide range of research articles in such journals as *Research in Drama Education, Multicultural Perspectives, Youth Theatre Journal, Journal of Curriculum and Pedagogy, Teaching Theatre, Research Studies in Music Education,* and *Qualitative Inquiry,* and has contributed several chapters to research methods handbooks.

For e-mail correspondence, contact: Johnny.Saldana@asu.edu.

Preface to the Second Edition

The second edition of *The Coding Manual for Qualitative Researchers* includes three new methods profiles (Subcoding, Causation Coding, and Eclectic Coding); enhanced discussions in the Analysis sections; a new chapter that outlines analytic transition processes between First and Second Cycles of coding; additional methods of qualitative data analysis and writing after Second Cycle coding; and a new glossary of the 32 coding methods. References, CAQDAS profiles, and the section on analyzing visual and mediated data have been updated. Emotion Coding's example has been changed, and the criteria for selecting the most appropriate coding method(s) for a study have been expanded. Many new figures have been added throughout the text.

Google Scholar updates, conferences, and e-mail correspondence with students and colleagues over the past four years have informed me how the first edition of *The Coding Manual for Qualitative Researchers* has been utilized in a variety of studies internationally. Just a small sampling of topics addressed by scholars and practitioners include:

K–12 Education

- children's perceptions of climate change
- high school teachers' perceptions of occupational professionalism
- hegemonic masculinity in Portuguese physical education classes
- school reform in Sweden
- emotional and behavioral disability student mainstreaming in Hong Kong

Higher Education

- university faculty professional development assessment
- Black female and Latina careers in higher education
- graduate student teaching assistants' encounters with student aggression
- college leadership competencies
- pre-service teacher professional development in South Africa

The Arts

- content analysis of music lyrics in Mexican *narcocorridos*
- designers' and engineers' thinking and decision-making processes
- lifelong outcomes of participation in high school speech and theatre programs
- art education for people with autism
- music therapy in African prisons

Human Development

- gay and transgender identities
- adolescents' perceptions of religion and spirituality
- civic engagement in young adults
- interpersonal dating and intimacy relationships among the elderly
- retirement dilemmas of people with intellectual disabilities in Australia

Social Sciences

- juvenile correctional officers as advocates
- sociopolitical analysis of being "at risk"
- Latino youth perspectives on immigration
- African American Hurricane Katrina survivors and disaster resilience
- religious affiliation among Canadians

Business

- corporate social responsibility policies
- financial crisis analysis
- European retail barcode systems
- product innovation teams in the Netherlands
- organizational change management and relocation in the UK

Technology

- global organization use of social networking sites
- virtual microscopy in human anatomy courses

- electronic health record chart biopsies
- thematic synthesis in software engineering
- male resistance to women in technical work

Government and Social Services

- humanitarian assistance disaster response
- NASA telescope history
- the Great Lakes Water Quality Agreement between Canada and the USA
- county administration in Sweden
- national forest policy in Finland

Health Care

- self-concept and social functioning of women with breast cancer
- children's perceptions of parental depression
- rural southern African Americans with HIV
- risk behaviors of Slovene injection drug users
- group interpersonal psychotherapy in rural Uganda

I am both humbled and honored that *The Coding Manual for Qualitative Researchers* has been referenced for these types of studies and many others worldwide. Graduate students and their professors have told me how much they appreciate the book's clarity and mentorship tone for their professional development and projects. Yet I must also extend my own thanks and gratitude to the legacy of scholars whose publications provide rich sources for several of the ideas collected in this manual. I give extensive credit where credit is due by quoting, citing, and referencing their works through fair use guidelines.

My primary role as author of this book is to serve as a contemporary archivist of the vast literature on qualitative methods, and to selectively display and explain relevant material about codes and coding. But the amount of books and e-resources on the subject has increased exponentially over the past decade, and I cannot possibly survey everything in the area. I must rely on you to bring your specific disciplinary knowledge base and, of course, your rich personal experiences, to supplement the material included in this resource. I hope that the expanded second edition of *The Coding Manual for Qualitative Researchers* offers readers even more pragmatic guidance for qualitative data analysis.

Johnny Saldaña
Arizona State University

Acknowledgements

Thanks are extended to:

Patrick Brindle of SAGE Publications, London, who initially encouraged me to create this manual.

Anna Horvai, Jai Seaman, and Rachel Eley of SAGE Publications, London, and the anonymous manuscript reviewers for their pre-publication guidance throughout this project.

My qualitative research instructors at Arizona State University: Tom Barone, Mary Lee Smith, Amira De la Garza, and Sarah J. Tracy, for introducing me to the methods and literature of qualitative inquiry.

Harry F. Wolcott, Norman K. Denzin, Yvonna S. Lincoln, Mitch Allen, Joe Norris, and Laura A. McCammon, for their inspiration, mentorship, and collegial support for my own research endeavors.

Katie Desmond of QSR International Pty Ltd/NVivo, Ann Dupuis of ResearchWare, Inc./HyperRESEARCH, Normand Péladeau of Provalis Research/QDA Miner, Thomas Ringmayr of ATLAS.ti, Julia Schehl of VERBI Software/MAXQDA, and David K. Woods of Transana, for their assistance with CAQDAS screenshots and permissions.

AltaMira Press, Elsevier, Oxford University Press, and *Journal of Drug Issues* for permissions to reprint extended excerpts from selected works.

Lisa A. Kramer, Chiara M. Lovio, Laura A. McCammon, Teresa Minarsich, Angie Hines and Matt Omasta for selected data contributions and analytic displays from fieldwork.

Jonothan Neelands and Tony Goode for the formatting ideas.

Jim Simpson for the "shop talk" and support.

And all writers of references listed in this manual whose works, brought together in this collection, provide us with the right tools for the right job.

I code, therefore I am.
(Anonymous, written on a seminar room chalkboard)

ONE

An Introduction to Codes and Coding

CHAPTER SUMMARY

This chapter first presents the purposes and goals of *The Coding Manual for Qualitative Researchers*. It then provides definitions and examples of codes and categories and their roles in qualitative data analysis. The procedures and mechanics of coding follow, along with discussions of analytic software and team collaboration. The chapter concludes with reflections on necessary researcher attributes and the role of method in coding.

Purposes of the Manual

The three primary purposes of the manual are:

- to discuss the functions of codes, coding, and analytic memo writing during the qualitative data collection and analytic processes;
- to profile a selected yet diverse repertoire of coding methods generally applied in qualitative data analysis; and
- to provide readers with sources, descriptions, recommended applications, examples, and exercises for coding and further analyzing qualitative data.

This manual does not address such matters as qualitative research design or how to conduct interviews or participant observation fieldwork. Those topics are already masterfully discussed in other textbooks. The manual is intended as a reference to supplement those existing works. It focuses exclusively on codes and coding and how they play a role in the qualitative data analytic process. For newcomers to qualitative inquiry it presents a repertoire of coding methods in broad brushstrokes. Additional information and extended discussion of the methods can be found in most of the cited sources. Grounded theory (discussed in Chapter Two), for example, is clearly profiled, streamlined, and re-envisioned in Kathy Charmaz's (2006) *Constructing Grounded Theory: A Practical Guide through Qualitative Analysis*, while Graham R. Gibbs' (2007) *Analysing Qualitative Data* provides an elegant survey of basic analytic processes.

The manual does not maintain allegiance to any one specific research genre or methodology. Throughout this book you will read a breadth of perspectives on codes and coding, sometimes purposely juxtaposed to illustrate and highlight the diverse opinions among scholars in the field. The following are just two examples of such professional divergence:

> Any researcher who wishes to become proficient at doing qualitative analysis must learn to code well and easily. The excellence of the research rests in large part on the excellence of the coding. (Strauss, 1987, p. 27)

> But the strongest objection to coding as a way to analyze qualitative research interviews is not philosophical but the fact that it does not and cannot work. It is impossible in practice. (Packer, 2011, p. 80)

No one, including myself, can claim final authority on coding's utility or the "best" way to analyze qualitative data. In fact, there are a few instances where I take moderate liberty with adapting and even renaming prescribed coding methods for clarity or flexibility's sake. This is not intended to standardize terminology within the field, but simply to employ consistency throughout this particular manual.

I must also emphasize at the very beginning that *there are times when coding the data is absolutely necessary, and times when it is most inappropriate for the study at hand.* All research questions, methodologies, conceptual frameworks, and field-work parameters are context specific. Also, whether you choose to code or not depends on your individual value, attitude, and belief systems about qualitative inquiry. For the record, here are mine, from *Fundamentals of Qualitative Research*:

> Qualitative research has evolved into a multidisciplinary enterprise, ranging from social science to art form. Yet many instructors of research methods vary in their allegiances, preferences, and prescriptions for how to conduct fieldwork and how to write about it. I myself take a pragmatic stance toward human inquiry and leave myself open to choosing the right tool for the right job. Sometimes a poem says it best; sometimes a data matrix does. Sometimes words say it best; sometimes numbers do. The more well versed you are in the field's eclectic methods of investigation, the better your ability to understand the diverse patterns and complex meanings of social life. (Saldaña, 2011b, pp. 177–8)

Coding is just *one* way of analyzing qualitative data, not *the* way. Be cautious of those who demonize the method outright. And be equally cautious of those who swear unyielding affinity to codes, or what has been colloquially labeled "coding fetishism." I prefer that you yourself, rather than some presumptive theorist or hardcore methodologist, determine whether coding is appropriate for your particular research project.

I also wrote this manual because I found it problematic (but not difficult) to teach coding in my own qualitative research methods course. I provided students with an array of readings about the process from multiple sources because I had yet to find that single satisfactory book (to me) that focused exclusively on the topic. General introductory texts in qualitative inquiry are so numerous and well written that it becomes difficult not to find the best one to use, but which one of such quality works to select as the primary textbook. This manual supplements introductory works in the subject because most limit their discussions about coding to the writer's prescribed, preferred, or signature methods. I wanted to provide in a single resource a selected collection of various coding methods developed by other researchers (and myself) that provides students and colleagues with a useful reference for classroom exercises and assignments, and for their own independent research for thesis and dissertation fieldwork and future qualitative studies. But by no means is it an exhaustive resource. I deliberately exclude such discipline-specific methods as psychotherapy's Narrative Processes Coding System (Angus, Levitt, & Hardtke, 1999), and such signature methods as the Davis Observation Code system for medical interviews (Zoppi & Epstein, 2002, p. 375). If you need additional information and explanation about the coding methods, check the References.

This manual is intended primarily as a reference work. It is not necessarily meant to be read cover to cover, but it certainly can be if you wish to acquaint yourself with all 32 coding methods profiles and their analytic possibilities. There are, in fact, several principles related to coding matters not discussed in the first two chapters that are unique to some of the profiles. If you choose to review all the contents, read selected sections at a time, not all of them in one sitting, otherwise it can overwhelm you. If you are scanning the manual to see which coding method(s) might be appropriate for your particular study, read the profiles' Description and Applications sections to see if further reading of the profile is merited, or check the glossary in Appendix A. It is doubtful you will use every coding method included in this manual for your particular research endeavors throughout your career, but they are available here on an "as-needed" basis for your unique projects. Like an academic curriculum, the sequential order of the profiles has been carefully considered. They do not necessarily progress in a linear manner from simple to complex, but are clustered generally from the fundamental to the intermediate to the advanced.

What Is a Code?

A code in qualitative inquiry is most often a word or short phrase that symbolically assigns a summative, salient, essence-capturing, and/or evocative attribute for a portion of language-based or visual data. The data can consist of interview transcripts, participant observation field notes, journals, documents, drawings, artifacts, photographs, video, Internet sites, e-mail correspondence, literature, and so on. The portion of data to be coded during First Cycle coding processes can range in magnitude from a single word to a full paragraph to an entire page of text to a stream of moving images. In Second Cycle coding processes, the portions coded can be the exact same units, longer passages of text, analytic memos about the data, and even a reconfiguration of the codes themselves developed thus far. Charmaz (2001) describes coding as the "critical link" between data collection and their explanation of meaning.

Do not confuse the use of *code* in qualitative data analysis with the use of *code* in the field of semiotics, even though there are some slight parallels between the two applications. In semiotics, a code relates to the interpretation of symbols in their specific social and cultural contexts. In qualitative data analysis, a code is a researcher-generated construct that symbolizes and thus attributes interpreted meaning to each individual datum for later purposes of pattern detection, categorization, theory building, and other analytic processes. Just as a title represents and captures a book, film, or poem's primary content and essence, so does a code represent and capture a datum's primary content and essence.

Coding examples

An example of a coded datum, as it is presented in this manual, looks like this when taken from a set of field notes about an inner city neighborhood. The one-word capitalized code in the right column is called a Descriptive Code, which summarizes the primary topic of the excerpt:

> [1] I notice that the grand majority of homes have chain   [1] SECURITY
> link fences in front of them. There are many dogs
> (mostly German shepherds) with signs on fences that
> say "Beware of the Dog."

Here is an example of several codes applied to data from an interview transcript in which a high school senior describes his favorite teacher. The codes are based on what outcomes the student receives from his mentor. Note that one of the codes is taken directly from what the participant himself says and is placed in quotation marks – this is called an In Vivo Code:

> [1] He cares about me. He has never told me but he does.   [1] SENSE OF SELF-WORTH
> [2] He's always been there for me, even when my parents   [2] STABILITY
> were not. He's one of the few things that I hold as a
> constant in my life. So it's nice. [3] I really feel   [3] "COMFORTABLE"
> comfortable around him.

Did you agree with the codes? Did other words or phrases run through your mind as you read the data? It is all right if your choices differed from mine. Coding is not a precise science; it is primarily an interpretive act. Also be aware that a code can sometimes *summarize*, *distill*, or *condense* data, not simply *reduce* them. Madden (2010), in fact, notes that such analytic work does not diminish but "value adds" to the research story (p. 10).

The introductory examples above were kept purposely simple and direct. But depending on the researcher's academic discipline, ontological and epistemological orientations, theoretical and conceptual frameworks, and even the choice of coding method itself, some codes can attribute more evocative meanings to data. In the excerpt below, a mother describes her teenage son's troubled school years. The codes emerge from the perspective of middle- and junior high school years as a difficult period for most youth. They are not specific types of codes; they are "first-impression" phrases derived from an open-ended process called Eclectic Coding:

> [1] My son, Barry, went through a really tough time about,   [1] MIDDLE-SCHOOL
> probably started the end of fifth grade and went into   HELL
> sixth grade. [2] When he was growing up young in school   [2] TEACHER'S PET
> he was a people-pleaser and his teachers loved him to
> death. [3] Two boys in particular that he chose to try to   [3] BAD INFLUENCES
> emulate, wouldn't, were not very good for him. [4] They   [4] TWEEN ANGST
> were very critical of him, they put him down all the
> time, and he kind of just took that and really kind of
> internalized it, I think, for a long time. [5] In that time   [5] THE LOST BOY
> period, in the fifth grade, early sixth grade, they really
> just kind of shunned him all together, and so his
> network as he knew it was gone.

Note that when we reflect on a passage of data to decipher its core meaning, we are *decoding*; when we determine its appropriate code and label it, we are *encoding*. For ease of reference throughout this manual, *coding* will be the sole term used. Simply understand that coding is the transitional process between data collection and more extensive data analysis.

Coding for patterns

In the examples presented thus far, each unit of data was assigned its own unique code. This is due primarily to the short length of the excerpts. In larger and complete data sets, you will find that several to many of the same codes will be used repeatedly throughout. This is both natural and deliberate – natural because there are mostly repetitive patterns of action and consistencies in human affairs, and deliberate because one of the coder's primary goals is to find these repetitive patterns of action and consistencies in human affairs as documented in the data. In the example below, note how the same Process Code (a word or phrase which captures action) is used twice during this small unit of elementary school classroom activity:

> [1] Mrs. Jackson rises from her desk and announces,   [1] LINING UP FOR LUNCH
> "OK, you guys, let's get lined up for lunch. Row
> One." Five children seated in the first row of
> desks rise and walk to the classroom door.
> Some of the seated children talk to each other.
> [2] Mrs. Jackson looks at them and says,   [2] MANAGING BEHAVIOR
> "No talking, save it for the cafeteria.
> [3] Row Two." Five children seated in the   [3] LINING UP FOR LUNCH

second row of desks rise and walk
to the children already standing in line.

Another way the above passage could be coded is to acknowledge that MANAGING BEHAVIOR is not a separate action or an interruption of the routine that disrupts the flow of LINING UP FOR LUNCH, but to interpret that MANAGING BEHAVIOR is an embedded or interconnected part of the larger social scheme that composes LINING UP FOR LUNCH. The coding might appear thusly, using a method called Simultaneous Coding (which applies two or more codes within a single datum):

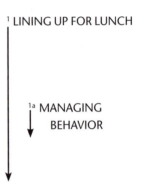

[1] Mrs. Jackson rises from her desk and announces, "OK, you guys, let's get lined up for lunch. Row One." Five children seated in the first row of desks rise and walk to the classroom door. Some of the seated children talk to each other. [1a] Mrs. Jackson looks at them and says, "No talking, save it for the cafeteria. [1] Row Two." Five children seated in the second row of desks rise and walk to the children already standing in line.

[1] LINING UP FOR LUNCH

[1a] MANAGING BEHAVIOR

Take note of some important caveats when it comes to understanding patterns and regularity: idiosyncrasy *is* a pattern (Saldaña, 2003, pp. 118–22) and there can be patterned variation in data (Agar, 1996, p. 10). Sometimes we code and categorize data by what participants talk about. They may all share with you their personal perceptions of school experiences, for example, but their individual value, attitude, and belief systems about education may vary greatly from being bored and disengaged to being enthusiastic and intrinsically motivated. When you search for patterns in coded data to categorize them, understand that sometimes you may group things together not just because they are exactly alike or very much alike, but because they might also have something in common – even if, paradoxically, that commonality consists of differences.

For example, each one of us may have a strong opinion about who should be leading our country. The fact that we each have an individual opinion about that issue is what we have in common. As for *whom* we each believe should be leading the country, that is where the differences and variations occur. Acknowledge that a confounding property of category construction in qualitative inquiry is that data cannot always be precisely and discretely bounded; they are within "fuzzy" boundaries at best (Tesch, 1990, pp. 135–8). That is why a method called Simultaneous Coding is an option we have, when needed. Finally, Hatch (2002) offers that you think of patterns not just as stable regularities but as varying forms. A pattern can be characterized by:

- similarity (things happen the same way)
- difference (they happen in predictably different ways)

- frequency (they happen often or seldom)
- sequence (they happen in a certain order)
- correspondence (they happen in relation to other activities or events)
- causation (one appears to cause another) (p. 155)

Coding filters

The act of coding requires that you wear your researcher's analytic lens. But how you perceive and interpret what is happening in the data depends on what type of filter covers that lens. For example, consider the following statement from an older male: "There's just no place in this country for illegal immigrants. Round them up and send those criminals back to where they came from." One researcher, a grounded theorist using In Vivo Coding to keep the data rooted in the participant's own language, might code the datum this way:

[1] There's just no place in this country for illegal immigrants. Round them up and send those criminals back to where they came from.	[1] "NO PLACE"

A second researcher, an urban ethnographer employing Descriptive Coding to document and categorize the breadth of opinions stated by multiple participants, might code the same datum this way:

[1] There's just no place in this country for illegal immigrants. Round them up and send those criminals back to where they came from.	[1] IMMIGRATION ISSUES

And a third researcher, a critical race theorist employing Values Coding to capture and label subjective perspectives, may code the exact same datum this way:

[1] There's just no place in this country for illegal immigrants. Round them up and send those criminals back to where they came from.	[1] XENOPHOBIA

The collection of coding methods in this manual is a repertoire of possible filters to consider and apply to your approaches to qualitative inquiry. But even before that, your level of personal involvement as a participant observer – as a peripheral, active, or complete member during fieldwork – filters how you perceive, document, and thus code your data (Adler & Adler, 1987). So do the types of questions you ask and the types of responses you receive during interviews (Kvale & Brinkmann, 2009), the detail and structuring of your field notes (Emerson, Fretz, & Shaw, 2011), the gender, social class, and race/ethnicity of your participants – and yourself (Behar & Gordon, 1995; Stanfield & Dennis, 1993), and whether you collect data from adults or children (Greene & Hogan, 2005; Tisdall, Davis, & Gallagher, 2009; Zwiers & Morrissette, 1999).

Merriam (1998) states, "our analysis and interpretation – our study's findings – will reflect the constructs, concepts, language, models, and theories that structured the study in the first place" (p. 48). And it is not only your approach to qualitative inquiry (e.g., case study, ethnography, phenomenology) and ontological, epistemological, and methodological issues that influence and affect your coding decisions (Creswell, 2013; Mason, 2002). Sipe and Ghiso (2004), in their revealing narrative about coding dilemmas for a children's literacy study, note that "All coding is a judgment call" since we bring "our subjectivities, our personalities, our predispositions, [and] our quirks" to the process (pp. 482–3). Like the characters in director Akira Kurosawa's classic film, *Rashômon*, multiple realities exist because we each perceive and interpret social life from different points of view.

Coding as a heuristic   *– aid to discovery*

The majority of qualitative researchers will code their data both during and after collection as an analytic tactic, for coding *is* analysis (Miles & Huberman, 1994, p. 56). Differing perspectives, however, attest that "Coding and analysis are not synonymous, though coding is a crucial aspect of analysis" (Basit, 2003, p. 145). Coding is a heuristic (from the Greek, meaning "to discover") – an exploratory problem-solving technique without specific formulas or algorithms to follow. Coding is only the initial step toward an even more rigorous and evocative analysis and interpretation for a report. Coding is not just labeling, it is *linking*: "It leads you from the data to the idea, and from the idea to all the data pertaining to that idea" (Richards & Morse, 2007, p. 137).

And, coding is a cyclical act. Rarely is the First Cycle of coding data perfectly attempted. The Second Cycle (and possibly the third and fourth cycles, and so on) of recoding further manages, filters, highlights, and focuses the salient features of the qualitative data record for generating categories, themes, and concepts, grasping meaning, and/or building theory. Coffey and Atkinson (1996) propose that "coding is usually a mixture of data [summation] and data complication ... breaking the data apart in analytically relevant ways in order to lead toward further questions about the data" (pp. 29–31).

Dey (1999) posits, though his original intent was to be critical, "With categories we impute meanings, with coding we compute them" (p. 95). To some, *code* is a "dirty four-letter word." A few research methodologists perceive a code as mere shorthand or an abbreviation for the more important category yet to be discovered. Unfortunately, some use the terms *code* and *category* interchangeably and even in combination when they are, in fact, two separate components of data analysis. I advocate that qualitative codes are essence-capturing and essential elements of the research story that, when clustered together according to similarity and regularity (a pattern), they actively facilitate the development of categories and thus analysis of their connections. Ultimately, I like one of Charmaz's (2006) metaphors for the process when she states that coding "generates the bones of your analysis. ... [I]ntegration will assemble those bones into a working skeleton" (p. 45).

Codifying and Categorizing

To codify is to arrange things in a systematic order, to make something part of a system or classification, to categorize. When codes are applied and reapplied to qualitative data, you are codifying – a process that permits data to be "segregated, grouped, regrouped and relinked in order to consolidate meaning and explanation" (Grbich, 2007, p. 21). Bernard (2011) succinctly states that analysis is "the search for patterns in data and for ideas that help explain why those patterns are there in the first place" (p. 338). Coding is thus a method that enables you to organize and group similarly coded data into categories or "families" because they share some characteristic – the beginning of a pattern (see the examples in Pattern Coding and Focused Coding in Chapter Five). You use classification reasoning plus your tacit and intuitive senses to determine which data "look alike" and "feel alike" when grouping them together (Lincoln & Guba, 1985, p. 347).

From codes to categories

For example, in Harry, Sturges, and Klingner's (2005) ethnographic study of the overrepresentation of minorities in special education programs, data initially coded as classroom MATERIALS, COMPUTERS, and TEXTBOOKS were categorized under the major heading **Resources**. As their study continued, another major category emerged labeled **Teacher Skills** with the subcategories *Instructional Skills* and *Management Skills*. The codes subsumed under these subcategories – part of the overall hierarchical "coding scheme" (Lewins & Silver, 2007) – were:

Category: Teacher Skills

Subcategory 1: Instructional Skills

    Code: PEDAGOGICAL
    Code: SOCIO-EMOTIONAL
    Code: STYLE/PERSONAL EXPRESSION
    Code: TECHNICAL

Subcategory 2: Management Skills

    Code: BEHAVIORIST TECHNIQUES
    Code: GROUP MANAGEMENT
    Code: SOCIO-EMOTIONAL
    Code: STYLE (overlaps with instructional style)
    Code: UNWRITTEN CURRICULUM

As another example, in Basit's (2003) study of the aspirations of teenage British Muslim girls, analysis of interview data with the girls, their parents, and their teachers brought forth 23 major categories that clustered under six major themes. One major theme was IDENTITY, and its related categories were **Ethnicity**, **Language**, and **Religion**. Under the theme CAREER ASPIRATIONS, the categories were **Career Choices**, **Unrealistic Aspirations**, and **Career Advice**.

Maykut and Morehouse (1994) refine each category by developing a rule for inclusion in the form of a propositional statement, coupled with sample data. For example, if an emergent category in a case study is labeled **Physical Health**, its rule for inclusion as a propositional statement might read:

> **Physical Health**: The participant shares matters related to physical health such as wellness, medication, pain, etc.: "I'm on 25 milligrams of amitriptyline each night"; "I hate going to the gym."

Emergent categories might also evolve as conceptual processes rather than descriptive topics such as:

> **Inequity**: Participants perceive unfair treatment directed toward themselves and favoritism directed toward others: "I've been working here for over 25 years and some newcomers are making higher salaries than me."

The categories' propositional statements are then compared with each other to discern possible relationships to create an *outcome proposition* based on their combination.

Recoding and recategorizing

Rarely will anyone get coding right the first time. Qualitative inquiry demands meticulous attention to language and deep reflection on the emergent patterns and meanings of human experience. Recoding can occur with a more attuned perspective using First Cycle methods again, while Second Cycle methods describe those processes that might be employed during the second (and third and possibly fourth ...) review of data. Punch (2009), researching childhoods in Bolivia, describes how her codes, categories, and themes (as she defines them) developed and subdivided during her ethnographic fieldwork and concurrent data analysis:

> [O]ne of my initial large codes was 'home'. Everything relating to life at home was coded under this category and then subdivided into three themes: gender roles; child/adult work roles in the household; power and discipline. On reading through this latter category, I realized not only did it concern adult power over children, but also children's strategies for counteracting adult power. After reorganizing these two sub-sections, I decided to split up the theme of children's strategies into different types: avoidance strategies, coping strategies, and negotiation strategies. Finally, on browsing again through the sub-theme of negotiation strategies I found that I could further sub-divide it into child-parent negotiations and sibling negotiations. These data then formed the basis for structuring my findings on children's lives at home. (pp. 94–5)

If you extract the coding scheme described in Punch's narrative above, and transform it into an outline format or a hierarchical tree, it might appear thusly:

I. HOME

    A. **Gender Roles**

    B. **Child/Adult Work Roles in the Household**

    C. **Power and Discipline**

        1. *Adult Power Over Children*

        2. *Children's Strategies for Counteracting Adult Power*

            a. Avoidance Strategies

            b. Coping Strategies

            c. Negotiation Strategies

                i. *Child/Parent Negotiations*

                ii. *Sibling Negotiations*

As you code and recode, expect – or rather, strive for – your codes and categories to become more refined and, depending on your methodological approach, more conceptual and abstract. Some of your First Cycle codes may be later subsumed by other codes, relabeled, or dropped altogether. As you progress toward Second Cycle coding, there may be some rearrangement and reclassification of coded data into different and even new categories. Abbott (2004) cleverly likens the process to "decorating a room; you try it, step back, move a few things, step back again, try a serious reorganization, and so on" (p. 215).

For example, I observed and interviewed fourth- and fifth-grade children to learn the ways they hurt and oppress each other (Saldaña, 2005b). This was preparatory fieldwork before an action research project that attempted to empower children with strategies, learned through improvised dramatic simulations and role-playing, for dealing with bullying in the school environment. I initially categorized their responses into **Physical** and **Verbal** forms of oppression. Some of the codes that fell under these categories were:

Category: Physical Oppression

    Code: PUSHING

    Code: FIGHTING

    Code: SCRATCHING

Category: Verbal Oppression

    Code: NAME-CALLING

    Code: THREATENING

    Code: LAUGHING AT

As coding continued, I observed that a few oppressions were a combination of both physical *and* verbal actions. For example, a child can EXCLUDE others physically from a game by pushing them away, accompanied with a verbal statement such as, "You can't play with us." Hence, a third major category emerged: **Physical and Verbal Oppression**.

As the study continued, more data were collected through other methods, and gender differences in children's perceptions and enactment of oppression became strikingly apparent. To young participants, oppression was not about the body and voice; it was about *"force"* and *"feelings."* The three initial categories were eventually reduced to two during Second Cycle coding, and renamed based on what seemed to resonate with gender-based observations. The new categories and a few sample codes and rearranged subcodes included:

> **Category: Oppression through Physical *Force*** (primarily but not exclusively by boys)
>
> > Code: FIGHTING
> >
> > > Subcode: SCRATCHING
> > > Subcode: PUSHING
> > > Subcode: PUNCHING
>
> **Category: Oppression through Hurting Others' *Feelings*** (primarily but not exclusively by girls)
>
> > Code: PUTTING DOWN
> >
> > > Subcode: NAME-CALLING
> > > Subcode: TEASING
> > > Subcode: TRASH TALKING

Also note how the subcodes themselves are specific, observable types of *realistic* actions related to the codes, while the two major categories labeled **Oppression** are more *conceptual* and *abstract* in nature.

See the Domain and Taxonomic Coding profile in Chapter Three for an extended discussion of this case, the Initial and Focused Coding examples in Chapters Three and Five respectively, and the techniques of Code Mapping and Code Landscaping in Chapter Four to see how a series of codes gets categorized.

From codes and categories to theory

Some categories may contain clusters of coded data that merit further refinement into subcategories. And when the major categories are compared with each other and consolidated in various ways, you begin to transcend the "reality" of your data and progress toward the thematic, conceptual, and theoretical. As a very basic process, codifying usually follows the ideal and streamlined scheme illustrated in Figure 1.1.

Keep in mind that the actual act of reaching theory is much more complex and messy than illustrated. Richards and Morse (2007) clarify that "categorizing is how we get 'up' from the diversity of data to the shapes of the data, the sorts

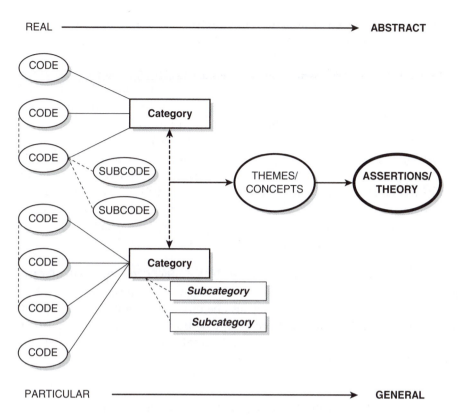

Figure 1.1 A streamlined codes-to-theory model for qualitative inquiry

of things represented. *Concepts* are how we get up to more general, higher-level, and more abstract constructs" (p. 157). Our ability to show how these themes and concepts systematically interrelate lead toward the development of theory (Corbin & Strauss, 2008, p. 55), though Layder (1998) contends that pre-established sociological theories can inform, if not drive, the initial coding process itself. The development of an original theory is not always a necessary outcome for qualitative inquiry, but acknowledge that pre-existing theories drive the entire research enterprise, whether you are aware of them or not (Mason, 2002).

In the example above of children's forms of oppression, there were two major categories that emerged from the study: **Oppression through Physical *Force***, and **Oppression through Hurting Others' *Feelings***. So, what major themes or concepts can be developed from these categories? An obvious theme we noticed was that, in later childhood, *peer oppression is gendered*. One higher-level concept we constructed – an attempt to progress from the real to the abstract – was *child stigma*, based on the observation that children frequently label those who are perceived different in various ways "weird," and thus resort to oppressive actions (Goffman, 1963). We could not, in confidence, formulate a formal theory from this study due to the limited amount of fieldwork time in the classrooms. But a key assertion (Erickson, 1986) – a statement that proposes a summative, interpretive observation of the local contexts of a study – that we did develop and put forth was:

> To artist and activist Augusto Boal, adult participation in theatre for social change is "rehearsal for the revolution." With ages 9–11 children, however, their participation in theatre for social change seems more like an "audition" for pre-adolescent social interaction. The key assertion of this study is: *Theatre for social change overtly reveals the interpersonal social systems and power hierarchies within an elementary school classroom microculture, because the original dramatic simulations children create authentically reflect their statuses and stigmas.* It diagnostically shows which children are leaders, followers, resisters, and targets; who is influential and who is ignored; which children may continue to assert dominance in later grade levels; and which children may succumb to those with more authority in later grade levels. (Adapted from Saldaña, 2005b, p. 131)

This key assertion, like a theory, attempts to progress from the particular to the general by inferring *transfer* – that what was observed in just six elementary school classrooms at one particular site may also be observed in comparable elementary school classrooms in other locations. This assertion also progresses from the particular to the general by *predicting patterns* of what may be observed and what may happen in similar present and future contexts.

The differences between codes and themes

Several qualitative research texts recommend that you initially "code for themes." That, to me, is misleading advice because it muddies the terminology waters. A theme is an *outcome* of coding, categorization, or analytic reflection, not something that is, in itself, coded (that is why there is no "Theme Coding" method in this manual, but there *are* references to thematic analysis and a section called Themeing the Data). A datum is initially and, when needed, secondarily coded to discern and label its content and meaning according to the needs of the inquiry. Rossman and Rallis (2003) explain the differences: "think of a category as a *word or phrase* describing some segment of your data that is *explicit*, whereas a theme is a *phrase or sentence* describing more *subtle and tacit* processes" (p. 282, emphasis added). As an example, SECURITY can be a code, but DENIAL MEANS A FALSE SENSE OF SECURITY can be a theme.

Qualitative researchers are not algorithmic automatons. If we are carefully reading and reviewing the data before and as we are formally coding them, we cannot help but notice a theme or two (or a pattern, trend, or concept) here and there. Make a note of it in an analytic memo (see Chapter Two) when it happens, for it can sometimes guide your continued coding processes. A set of themes is a good thing to emerge from analysis, but at the beginning cycles there are other rich discoveries to be made with specific coding methods that explore such phenomena as participant processes, emotions, and values.

What Gets Coded?

Richards and Morse (2007) humorously advise for analytic work, "If it moves, code it" (p. 146). But what exactly *gets* coded in the data?

Units of social organization

Lofland, Snow, Anderson, and Lofland (2006) note that social life happens at four coordinates, "the intersection of one or more *actors* [participants] engaging in one or more *activities* (behaviors) at a particular *time* in a specific *place*" (p. 121, emphasis in original). The authors first outline major *units* of social organization into:

1 cultural practices (daily routines, occupational tasks, microcultural activity, etc.);
2 episodes (unanticipated or irregular activities such as divorce, championship games, natural disasters, etc.);
3 encounters (a temporary interaction between two or more individuals such as sales transactions, panhandling, etc.);
4 roles (student, mother, customer, etc.) and social types (bully, tight-ass, geek, etc.);
5 social and personal relationships (husband and wife, party-goers, etc.);
6 groups and cliques (gangs, congregations, families, jocks, etc.);
7 organizations (schools, fast-food restaurants, prisons, corporations, etc.);
8 settlements and habitats (villages, neighborhoods, etc.); and
9 subcultures and lifestyles (the homeless, skinheads, gay leather bears, etc.)

But you will not find in this manual any coding methods based on the major units outlined above such as "Encounter Coding," "Organization Coding," or "Lifestyle Coding." When the units above are combined with *aspects* listed below, they then become topics for study *and coding*. Lofland et al.'s aspects include:

1 cognitive aspects or meanings (e.g., ideologies, rules, self-concepts, identities);
2 emotional aspects or feelings (e.g., sympathy in health care, road rage, workplace satisfaction);
3 hierarchical aspects or inequalities (e.g., racial inequality, battered women, high school cliques)

Aside from examining the magnitude and frequency of social life outlined above, Lofland et al. also recommend examining how participant agency interacts and interplays with structures and processes, plus causes and consequences observed in the data (2006, pp. 144–67).

Aspects *in combination with* units lend themselves to such First Cycle coding methods (see Chapter Three) as Emotion Coding, Values Coding, and Versus Coding. Structures and processes can be discerned through Descriptive Coding, Process Coding, and Domain and Taxonomic Coding, while causes and consequences can be discerned through Causation Coding, Pattern Coding or grounded theory's Second Cycle coding methods (see Chapter Five, and Maxwell, 2004).

The coded researcher

In the coding examples profiled in Chapters Three through Five, you will notice that the interviewer's questions, prompts, and comments are not coded. This is because the researcher's utterances are more functional than substantive *in these particular cases* and do not merit a code. Also, I prioritize the participants' data when it comes to analyzing interviews since I am studying their perceptions, not mine. My interpretations of their narratives via coding is my contribution to the meaning-making enterprise.

But if the exchanges between an interviewer and interviewee are more than just information gathering – if the interactions are significant dialogic exchanges of issues and jointly constructed meanings – then the researcher's contributions could be appropriately coded alongside the participant's. Certainly, the researcher's participant observation field notes, authored from a first-person perspective, merit codes since they both document naturalistic action and include important interpretations of social life and potentially rich analytic insights.

Amounts of data to code

One related issue with which qualitative research methodologists disagree is the amount of the data corpus – the total body of data – that should be coded. Some (e.g., Friese, 2012; Lofland et al., 2006; Strauss, 1987; cf. Wolcott, 1999) feel that every recorded fieldwork detail is worthy of consideration, for it is from the patterned minutiae of daily, mundane life that we might generate significant social insight. Others (e.g., Guest, MacQueen, & Namey, 2012; Morse, 2007; Seidman, 2006), if not most, feel that only the most salient portions of the corpus related to the research questions merit examination, and that even up to one-half to two-thirds of the total record can be summarized or "deleted," leaving the remainder for intensive data analysis.

The potential hazard is that the portions deleted might contain the as yet unknown units of data that could pull everything together, or include the negative or discrepant case that motivates a rethinking of a code, category, theme, concept, assertion, or theory. Postmodern perspectives on ethnographic texts consider all documentation and reports partial and incomplete anyway, so the argument for maintaining and coding a full or condensed data corpus seems moot. Amount notwithstanding, insure that you have not just sufficient qualitative but sufficient *quality* data with which to work that have been appropriately transcribed and formatted (see Poland, 2002).

I have learned from years of qualitative data analysis that, only with experience, I now feel more secure knowing and feeling what is important in the data record and what is not, and thus code only what rises to the surface – "relevant text" as Auerbach and Silverstein (2003) label it. Sullivan (2012) identifies his significant passages of data from the corpus as "key moments," and the reconstructed assembly of same-topic interview passages from different participants as "cherry-picked" dialogic "sound bites" for intensive thematic or discourse analysis. Everything else, like in a traditional film editing studio, falls to the cutting room floor.

The beginning of my fieldwork career was a major learning curve for me, and I coded anything and everything that was collected. I advise the same for novices to qualitative research. You, too, will eventually discover from experience what matters and what does not in the data corpus. (Of course, there will always be brief passages of minor or trivial consequence scattered throughout interviews and field notes. Code these N/A – Not Applicable.)

So, what *gets* coded? Slices of social life recorded in the data – participant activities, perceptions, and the tangible documents and artifacts produced by them. Your own reflective data in the form of analytic memos (discussed in Chapter Two) and observer's comments in field notes are also substantive material for coding. The process does not have to be approached as if it were some elusive mystery or detective story with deeply hidden clues and misleading red herrings scattered throughout. If "human actions are based upon, or infused by, social or cultural meanings: that is, by intentions, motives, beliefs, rules, discourses, and values" (Hammersley & Atkinson, 2007, p. 7), then why not just code these actions and social meanings directly (assuming they are represented in your data and your inferential skills are working at an optimum)? The entire process *and products* of creating data about the data in the form of codes, categories, analytic memos, and graphical summaries are "metadata activities" (MacQueen & Guest, 2008, p. 14).

The Mechanics of Coding

Preparing data for coding gives you a bit more familiarity with the contents and initiates a few basic analytic processes. It is comparable to "warming up" before more detailed work begins.

Data layout

As you prepare text-based qualitative data for manual (i.e., paper and pencil) coding and analyzing, lay out printed interview transcripts, field notes, and other researcher-generated materials in double-spaced format on the left half or left two-thirds of the page, keeping a wide right-hand margin for writing codes and notes. Rather than keeping your data running together as long unbroken passages, separate the text into short paragraph-length units with a line break in between them whenever the topic or subtopic appears to change (as best as you can, because in real life "social interaction does not occur in neat, isolated units" (Glesne, 2011, p. 192)). Gee, Michaels, and O'Connor (1992) call these unit breaks and their rearrangement into poetic-like verses for discourse analysis "stanzas" of text, and emphasize that "formatting choices are a part of the analysis and may reveal or conceal aspects of meaning and intent" (p. 240). Unit divisions will also play a key role in formatting data for CAQDAS (Computer-Assisted Qualitative Data Analysis Software) programs (discussed later).

Below is an excerpt from a word-processed interview transcript without any breaks in the text. The participant is a White male PhD student interviewed midway through his doctoral program of study:

> PARTICIPANT: I'm 27 years old and I've got over $50,000 in student loans that I have to pay off, and that scares the hell out of me. I've got to finish my dissertation next year because I can't afford to keep going to school. I've got to get a job and start working.
> INTERVIEWER: What kind of job do you hope to get?
> PARTICIPANT: A teaching job at a university someplace.
> INTERVIEWER: Any particular part of the country?
> PARTICIPANT: I'd like to go back to the east coast, work at one of the major universities there. But I'm keeping myself open to wherever there's a job. It's hard listening to some of the others [in the current graduating class] like Jake and Brian interviewing for teaching jobs and being turned down. As a white male, that lessens my chances of getting hired.
> INTERVIEWER: I think most employers really do look for the best person for the job, regardless of color.
> PARTICIPANT: Maybe. If I can get some good recs [letters of recommendation], that should help. My grades have been real good and I've been getting my name out there at conferences.
> INTERVIEWER: All of that's important.
> PARTICIPANT: The prospectus is the first step. Well, the IRB [Institutional Review Board approval] is the first step. I'm starting the lit review this summer, doing the interviews and participant observation in the fall, writing up as I go along, and being finished by spring.
> INTERVIEWER: What if more time is needed for the dissertation?
> PARTICIPANT: I've got to be finished by spring.

An unformatted excerpt such as the above could be entered into a CAQDAS program as is. But for manual coding, and even for some preliminary formatting for selected CAQDAS programs, the interview text can be divided into separate units or stanzas when a topic or subtopic shift occurs. Each stanza, with a noticeable line break in between, could conceivably become a unit that will receive its own code. Other necessary formatting, such as truncating names or placing non-coded passages in brackets, can be taken care of at this layout stage of data preparation:

> P: I'm 27 years old and I've got over $50,000 in student
> loans that I have to pay off, and that scares the hell out
> of me. I've got to finish my dissertation next year because

I can't afford to keep going to school. I've got to get a
job and start working.

[I: What kind of job do you hope to get?]
P: A teaching job at a university someplace.
[I: Any particular part of the country?]
P: I'd like to go back to the east coast, work at one of the
major universities there. But I'm keeping myself open to
wherever there's a job.

It's hard listening to some of the others [in the current
graduating class] like Jake and Brian interviewing for
teaching jobs and being turned down. As a white male,
that lessens my chances of getting hired.
[I: I think most employers really do look for the best
person for the job, regardless of color.]
P: Maybe.

If I can get some good recs [letters of recommendation],
that should help. My grades have been real good and I've
been getting my name out there at conferences.
[I: All of that's important.]

P: The prospectus is the first step. Well, the IRB
[Institutional Review Board approval] is the first step.
I'm starting the lit review this summer, doing the
interviews and participant observation in the fall,
writing up as I go along, and being finished by spring.
[I: What if more time is needed for the dissertation?]
P: I've got to be finished by spring.

The interview excerpt above will be coded and analyzed in Chapter Four's profile, Eclectic Coding.

Pre-coding

In addition to coding with words and short phrases, never overlook the opportunity to "pre-code" (Layder, 1998) by circling, highlighting, bolding, underlining,
or coloring rich or significant participant quotes or passages that strike you – those
"codable moments" worthy of attention (Boyatzis, 1998). Creswell (2013, p. 205)
recommends that such quotes found in data contained in a CAQDAS program file
can be simultaneously coded *as* QUOTES with their other codes to enable later

retrieval. Selected programs have areas dedicated to storing intriguing quotations for later access. These data can become key pieces of the evidentiary warrant to support your propositions, assertions, or theory, and serve as illustrative examples throughout your report (Booth, Colomb, & Williams, 2003; Erickson, 1986; Lofland et al., 2006). The codes or quotes may even be so provocative that they become part of the title, organizational framework, or through-line of the report. For example, in my study of theatre of the oppressed (i.e., theatre for social change) with elementary school children, I was puzzled why young people continually employed combative tactics during improvisational dramatic simulations to resolve imbalanced power issues, when I was trying to teach them proactive peace-building efforts. A fourth-grade girl poignantly provided the answer when we discussed my concerns by explaining to me, "Sometimes, you can't be nice to deal with oppression" (Saldaña, 2005b, p. 117). The quote was so powerful that it began my final research report as a datum that would both capture the reader's interest and later explain the through-line of the study.

Bernard and Ryan (2010) recommend that rich text features of word processing software can also enable initial coding and categorization *as* data are transcribed. In a health study related to participants talking about their experiences with the common cold, "*Signs and symptoms are tagged with italics*; <u>treatments and behavioral modifications are tagged with underlining</u>; and **diagnosis is tagged with bold type**" (p. 91, rich text features added). Field notes can also employ rich text features for "at a glance" separation before coding and analytic review:

Descriptive, narrative passages of field notes are logged in regular font.

"Quotations, things spoken by participants, are logged in bold font."

OC: Observer's Comments, such as the researcher's subjective impressions or analytic jottings, are set in italics.

Preliminary jottings

Start coding *as* you collect and format your data, not after all fieldwork has been completed. When you are writing up field notes, transcribing recorded interviews, or filing documents you gathered from the site, jot down any preliminary words or phrases for codes on the notes, transcripts, or documents themselves, or as an analytic memo or entry in a research journal for future reference. They do not have to be accurate or final at this point, just ideas for analytic consideration while the study progresses. Be wary of relying on your memory for future writing. Get your thoughts, however fleeting, documented in some way.

Also make certain that these code jottings are distinct in some way from the body of data – bracketed, capitalized, italicized, bolded, etc. Liamputtong and Ezzy (2005, pp. 270–3) recommend formatting pages of data into three columns rather than two. The first and widest column contains the data themselves – interview transcripts, field notes, etc. The second column contains space for preliminary code notes and jottings, while the third column lists the final codes. The second column's ruminations or first impressions may help provide a transitional link between the raw data and codes:

COLUMN 1 Raw Data	COLUMN 2 Preliminary Codes	COLUMN 3 Final Code
[1] The closer I get to retirement age, the faster I want it to happen. I'm not even 55 yet and I would give anything to retire now.	*"retirement age"*	[1] RETIREMENT ANXIETY
But there's a mortgage to pay off and still a lot more to sock away in savings before I can even think of it. I keep playing the	*financial obligations*	
lottery, though, in hopes of winning those millions. No luck yet.	*dreams of early retirement*	

Some of my students, during preliminary stages of analysis, devote the right-hand margin to tentative codes for specific data units, while the left-hand margin includes broader topics or interpretive jottings for later analytic memo writing (see Chapter Two).

Virtually all methodologists recommend initial and thorough readings of your data while writing analytic memos or jotting in the margins tentative ideas for codes, topics, and noticeable patterns or themes. Write your code words or phrases completely rather than abbreviating them to mnemonics or assigning them reference numbers. Avoid such truncations as "PROC-AN CD" or "122-A," which just make the decoding processes of your brain work much harder than they need to during analysis.

Questions to consider as you code

Auerbach and Silverstein (2003, p. 44) recommend that you keep a copy of your research concern, theoretical framework, central research question, goals of the study, and other major issues on one page in front of you to keep you focused and allay your anxieties because the page focuses your coding decisions. Emerson et al. (2011) advise a general list of questions to consider when coding field notes (in chronological order), regardless of research purpose:

- What are people doing? What are they trying to accomplish?
- How, exactly, do they do this? What specific means and/or strategies do they use?
- How do members talk about, characterize, and understand what is going on?

- What assumptions are they making?
- What do I see going on here?
- What did I learn from these notes?
- Why did I include them? (p. 177)

I would add to this list the question I ask myself during all cycles of coding and data analysis: "What strikes you?" Sunstein and Chiseri-Strater (2007) expand on this by suggesting that fieldworkers, during all stages of a project, ask themselves:

- What surprised me? (to track your assumptions)
- What intrigued me? (to track your positionality)
- What disturbed me? (to track the tensions within your value, attitude, and belief systems) (p. 106)

Coding contrasting data

If you are working with multiple participants in a study, it may help to code one participant's data first, then progress to the second participant's data. You might find that the second data set will influence and affect your recoding of the first participant's data, and the consequent coding of the remaining participants' data. The same may hold true for a coding system applied to an interview transcript first, then to a day's field notes, then to a document. Bazeley (2007) recommends that the second document coded should contrast "in some important way with the first … to maximize the potential for variety in concepts (or in their forms of expression) early in the process" (p. 61). Be aware that, depending on the coding method(s) chosen, some codes may appear more frequently in selected types of data than others. Selected CAQDAS program functions can keep you abreast of the codes and their frequencies as analysis progresses.

The Numbers of Codes

The actual number of codes, categories, themes, and/or concepts you generate for each project will vary and depend on many contextual factors, yet one question students ask most is how often codes "should" get applied to qualitative data. The answer depends on the nature of your data, which particular coding method you select for analysis, and how detailed you want or need to be – in other words, more filters to consider.

"Lumping" and "splitting" the data

For example, the following data excerpt is from a speech by a second-year, inner city, grades K–8 school teacher speaking to pre-service education majors enrolled in a university teaching methods course (Saldaña, 1997). She has just completed several poignant vignettes about some of her most difficult students. Notice that just one In Vivo Code is applied to capture and represent the essence of this entire 145-word excerpt – a broad brush-stroke representation called Holistic Coding:

[1] I'm not telling you this to depress you or scare you but it was a reality for me. I thought I was so ready for this population because I had taught other groups of kids. But this is such a unique situation, the inner city school. No, I should take that back: It's not as much of a unique situation *anymore*. There are more and more schools that are turning into inner city schools. … I really had to learn about the kids. I had to learn about the culture, I had to learn the language, I had to learn the gang signals, I had to learn what music was allowed, what t-shirts they could wear on certain days and not on other days. There was just a lot to learn that I had never even thought about.

[1] "A LOT TO LEARN"

The method above is called "lumper" coding. The opposite is someone who codes as a "splitter," one who splits the data into smaller codable moments (Bernard, 2011, p. 379). Thus, more detailed In Vivo Coding of the exact same passage might appear thusly:

I'm not telling you this to depress you or scare you but it was a [1] reality for me. [2] I thought I was so ready for this population because I had taught other groups of kids. But this is such a [3] unique situation, the inner city school. No, I should take that back: It's not as much of a unique situation *anymore*. There are more and more schools that are turning into [4] inner city schools. … [5] I really had to learn about the kids. I had to learn about [6] the culture, I had to learn the language, I had to learn the gang signals, I had to learn what music was allowed, what t-shirts they could wear on certain days and not on other days. There was just [7] a lot to learn that I had never even thought about.

[1] "REALITY"
[2] "I THOUGHT I WAS SO READY"
[3] "UNIQUE SITUATION"

[4] "INNER CITY SCHOOLS"
[5] "I REALLY HAD TO LEARN"
[6] "THE CULTURE"

[7] "A LOT TO LEARN"

Now this 145-word excerpt is represented with seven codes rather than one. I state the numbers not to suggest that more is better or that less is more, but to highlight that lumping is an expedient coding method (with future detailed sub-coding still possible), while splitting generates a more nuanced analysis from the start. Each approach has its advantages and disadvantages aside from the obvious factors of time and mental energy required. Lumping gets to the essence of categorizing a phenomenon while splitting encourages careful scrutiny of social action represented in the data. But lumping may lead to a superficial analysis if the coder does not employ conceptual words and phrases, while fine-grained splitting of data may overwhelm the analyst when it comes time to categorize the codes. Perspectives vary within the professional literature: Stern (2007) admits, "I never do a line-by-line [coding] analysis because there is so much filler to skip over. Rather, I do a search and seizure operation looking for cream [that rises to the top] in the data" (p. 118). But Charmaz (2008) advises that detailed line-by-line coding promotes a more trustworthy analysis that "reduces the likelihood of imputing your motives, fears, or unresolved personal issues to your respondents and to your collected data" (p. 94).

During Second Cycle coding, you might collapse the original number of First Cycle codes into a smaller number as you reanalyze the data and find that larger segments of text are better suited to just one key code rather than several smaller ones. It is only from experience that you will discover which approach works best for you, your particular study, and your particular research goals.

The quantities of qualities

Friese (2012) prescribes that qualitative research projects should never venture into the thousands for a final number of codes; between 120 and 300 codes total are recommended (p. 73). More modestly, Lichtman (2010) projects that most qualitative studies in education will generate 80–100 codes that will be organized into 15–20 categories and subcategories which eventually synthesize into five to seven major concepts (p. 194). Creswell (2013) begins his analyses with a shortlist of five to six Provisional Codes to begin the process of "lean coding." This expands to no more than 25–30 categories that then combine into five to six major themes (pp. 184–5). Other disciplines and varying approaches to qualitative inquiry may prescribe different sets of numbers as general guidelines for analysis, but MacQueen, McLellan, Kay, and Milstein (2009) observe that "For the most part, coders can only handle 30–40 codes at one time" for a study, especially if they are using a system developed by someone else (p. 218).

The final number of major themes or concepts should be held to a minimum to keep the analysis coherent, but there is no standardized or magic number to achieve. Unlike Lichtman's five to seven central concepts and Creswell's five to six major themes, anthropologist Harry F. Wolcott (1994, p. 10) generally advises throughout his writings that *three* of anything major seems an elegant quantity for reporting qualitative work.

The codebook or code list

Since the number of codes can accumulate quite quickly and change as analysis progresses, keep a record of your emergent codes in a separate file as a codebook – a compilation of the codes, their content descriptions, and a brief data example for reference. CAQDAS programs, by default, will maintain a list of codes you have created for the project and provide space to define them. This can be reviewed periodically – both on the monitor screen and on hard copy – as coding progresses to assess its current contents and possible evolution. Maintaining this list provides an analytic opportunity to organize and reorganize the codes into major categories and subcategories. This management technique also provides a comparative list if you are working with multiple participants and sites. One school site's data, for example, may generate a list of codes significantly different from another school site.

Codebooks or CAQDAS code lists become especially critical as a set of coding standards when multiple team members work together on the same project's data (see Coding Collaboratively below). Bernard and Ryan (2010, p. 99) advise that, for some studies with a more compact number of codes, each item in the codebook can specify its:

- *short description* – the name of the code itself
- *detailed description* – a 1–3 sentence description of the coded datum's qualities or properties
- *inclusion criteria* – conditions of the datum or phenomenon that merit the code
- *exclusion criteria* – exceptions or particular instances of the datum or phenomenon that do not merit the code
- *typical exemplars* – a few examples of data that best represent the code
- *atypical exemplars* – extreme or special examples of data that still represent the code
- *"close, but no"* – data examples that could mistakenly be assigned this particular code

Also note that a codebook differs from an *index*, the latter being a coded composite of the data corpus, organized alphabetically, hierarchically, chronologically, categorically, etc. CAQDAS programs are superior for indexing functions with a qualitative data corpus.

Manual and CAQDAS Coding

Some instructors of statistics and quantitative data analysis require that their students first learn how to "crunch the numbers" manually using only a pocket/hand calculator to provide them with cognitive understanding and ownership of the formulas and results. Once a statistical test has been administered this way, they can then use computers with software specifically designed to calculate numeric data.

Coding and qualitative data analysis have their equivalent trial. I am one of those instructors who requires that my students first perform "manual" coding and qualitative data analysis using paper and pencil on hard copies of data entered and formatted with basic word processing software only. The reason is that each class assignment of data gathering is relatively small scale and thus a manageable project to analyze in this manner. But if a student's dissertation project or my own independent research studies require multiple participant interviews or extended fieldwork and extensive field note taking, then CAQDAS becomes a vital and indispensable tool for the enterprise.

Basit (2003) compared personal experiences between manual and electronic coding and concluded, "the choice will be dependent on the size of the project, the funds and time available, and the inclination and expertise of the researcher" (p. 143). I would add to this the research goals of the enterprise and the emergent satisfaction with the electronic coding system. Gallagher (2007) and her research team began a multi-site ethnography with CAQDAS, yet they soon learned that their software choice

> was effective for data management, but inadequate for the nuanced and complex work of data analysis. [The software package] gave us style, but not substance; it sacrificed the attention to, and containment of, complexity we were after. ... In effect, we returned to a manual [coding] system that respected the sheer quantity and complexity of qualitative data and the surrounding contexts. (pp. 71, 73)

Coding collaboratively with hard-copy data is difficult enough for a research team. The task exponentially increases in complexity if CAQDAS files are shared and accessed at different times among individual team members.

Coding manually

Trying to learn the basics of coding and qualitative data analysis simultaneously with the sometimes complex instructions and multiple functions of CAQDAS programs can be overwhelming for some, if not most. Your mental energies may be more focused on the software than the data. I recommend that for first-time or small-scale studies, code on hard-copy printouts first, not via a computer monitor (cf. Bazeley, 2007, p. 92). There is something about manipulating qualitative data on paper and writing codes in pencil that give you more control over and ownership of the work. Perhaps this advice stems from my admitted lack of technological expertise and old-fashioned ways of working that have become part of my "codus" operandi.

But for those with software literacy, a few of Microsoft Word's basic functions can code directly onto word-processed data. Some will select a passage of text and insert a COMMENT, which contains the code for the datum. Others might insert a vertical TEXT BOX running along the right-hand margin and insert the codes aligned with the data (see Figure 1.2).

One of my mixed methods survey projects employed Microsoft Excel as a repository for the database because there were 234 surveys returned, and the software provided excellent organization with individual cells holding thousands of entries and their accompanying codes (see Figure 1.3). Each row represented an individual participant's survey data, while each column held the responses to a specific survey question. An additional row below each individual respondent contained the codes for his or her data. Excel also enabled me to calculate survey ratings into means and to conduct *t*-tests for subgroup comparisons. The software's CONCATENATE function merges qualitative data from cells you specify, making the extraction of codes a speedy task.

the physical and the emotional and the mind all engaged in creating character relationships. (running out of time) Thank you for all your hard work today. I will see you next week with the scripts. [89]Please put the desks back in place as you leave.

[90]Students return desks to rows and start to leave. Ian goes up to Ms B and shares the suggestion he didn't get to share. Ms B's back is turned to me so I don't get to hear how she responds. Ian leaves.

[92]*OC: really want to discuss Ian with Ms B at a later point. Must ask how she responded to his suggestion shared after the class ended. Also would like to know if she is aware of him raising his hand when her back is turned. Is there a history with the class and Ian that would explain the hostility they seem to have towards him? How does she handle this?*

I thank Ms. B for letting me observe and leave the classroom and head back to my car.

Right-margin text box:

89 – class – routines

90 – transitions
91 – Ian – interactions w/ Ms B

92 – Ms B – future inquiry

Figure 1.2 A Microsoft Word field notes document with codes in a right-margin text box (courtesy of Teresa Minarsich)

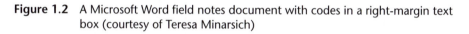

Figure 1.3 A Microsoft Excel spreadsheet with mixed methods data and codes in its cells

Nevertheless, there is something to be said for a large area of desk or table space with each code written on its own index card or "sticky note," or multiple pages or strips of paper, spread out and arranged into appropriate clusters to see the smaller pieces of the larger puzzle – a literal perspective not always possible on

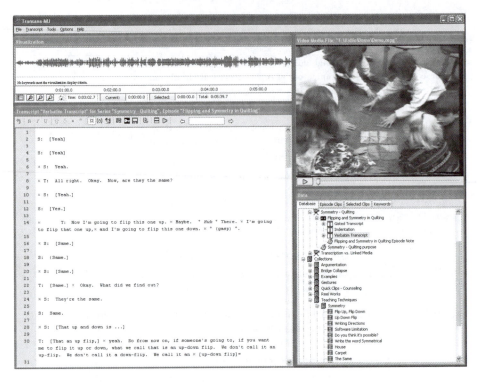

Figure 1.4 A Transana v. 2.42 screenshot of audio transcription and video analysis (courtesy of Transana, www.transana.org)

a computer monitor screen. After you feel the codes are fairly well set from your initial hard-copy work, then transfer your codes onto the electronic file. But first, "Touch the data. ... Handling the data gets additional data out of memory and into the record. It turns abstract information into concrete data" (Graue & Walsh, 1998, p. 145). Even proponents of CAQDAS recommend that hard-copy printouts of code lists and coded data be generated occasionally to permit you to work with traditional writing materials such as red pens and highlighters to explore data in fresh ways.

Coding electronically

After you have gained some experience with hard-copy coding and have developed a basic understanding of the fundamentals of qualitative data analysis, apply that experiential knowledge base by working with CAQDAS. Keep in mind that CAQDAS itself does not actually code the data for you; that task is still the responsibility of the researcher. The software efficiently stores, organizes, manages, and reconfigures your data to enable human analytic reflection. Some specialty programs, like Transana, enable coding of digital audio and video documents stored in their files (see Figure 1.4). I advise that you work with a smaller portion of your data first, such as a day's field notes or a single interview transcript, before importing the data corpus into the program. As with all word-processed work on a computer, back up your original files as a precautionary measure.

Several major CAQDAS programs to explore, whose websites provide online tutorials or demonstration software/manual downloads of their most current versions, are:

- AnSWR: www.cdc.gov/hiv/topics/surveillance/resources/software/answr
- ATLAS.ti: www.atlasti.com
- HyperRESEARCH: www.researchware.com
- MAXQDA: www.maxqda.com
- NVivo: www.qsrinternational.com
- QDA Miner: www.provalisresearch.com
- Qualrus: www.qualrus.com
- Transana: www.transana.org (for audio and video data materials)
- Weft QDA: www.pressure.to/qda/

Selected CAQDAS programs, such as AnSWR and Weft QDA, are available free of charge. Refer to Bazeley (2007), Edhlund (2011), Friese (2012), Lewins and Silver (2007), and Richards (2009) for accompanying literature on the major commercial programs. Also see Hahn (2008) and La Pelle (2004) for qualitative data analysis with basic word processing software and office suites; Brent and Slusarz (2003) and Meyer and Avery (2009) for advanced computational strategies with software; Davidson and di Gregorio (2011) for Web 2.0 tools like DiscoverText (www.discovertext.com) and CAT, the Coding Analysis Toolkit (http://cat.ucsur. pitt.edu/); and Richards and Morse (2007, pp. 85–90) for what selected CAQDAS programs can and cannot do. Many CAQDAS programs are discussed and reviewed at an online forum for users: http://caqdas.soc.surrey.ac.uk/.

It is impractical to advise or prescribe which software program is "best" for particular qualitative studies and even for individual researchers. You are the best judge of your own software needs for your data and your personal preferences, so explore several of the programs available to you on your own at the web addresses provided above to make an informed decision. I have learned, however, that peer and instructor mentorship with a CAQDAS program is vital and more effective than just reading its software manual on your own. If you are able to enroll in workshops or classes in CAQDAS facilitated by master teachers, I highly recommend them.

At the time of this writing, a variety of technological tools exclusively designed or adaptable for qualitative data management and analysis seems to appear more and more frequently. It becomes virtually impossible to keep up with all the electronic, software, and Internet resources available to researchers. My only recommendation is to gain as much general technological literacy as you can to make yourself aware of all your options, but to select your final tools wisely so that they help, rather than hinder, your analytic efforts.

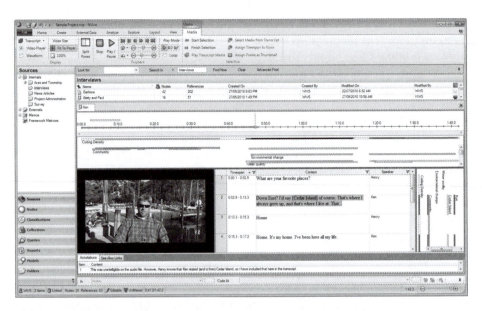

Figure 1.5 A Video Coding screenshot from NVivo 9 (NVivo 9 is designed and developed by QSR International Pty Ltd. NVivo is a trademark or registered trademark of QSR International. www.qsrinternational.com)

Data formatting for CAQDAS

The heading and paragraph formats of qualitative data such as field notes and, in particular, interview transcripts need to conform consistently with the particular software package's prescriptions for text layout. This becomes vital for its coding and retrieval functions to work consistently and reliably. ATLAS.ti, MAXQDA, and NVivo all import and handle documents saved in rich text format, enabling you to employ supplemental "cosmetic" coding devices such as colored fonts, bolding, and italicizing in your data (Lewins & Silver, 2007, p. 61). MAXQDA, for example, can directly import .doc and .docx files.

One of the best features of some CAQDAS programs is their ability to display code labels themselves in various colors for "at a glance" reference and visual classification. Figure 1.5 illustrates a sample screenshot from the most current version of NVivo. Note how the video data and transcript are accompanied with codes and "coding stripes," which delineate which portion of data is assigned a particular code.

Programs like MAXQDA include a user-assigned color coding feature – a highlighting function that changes the text's background color to align with its code's color. Reviewing similarly color-coded data during Second Cycle coding makes it easier to refine First Cycle codes and to create new or revised categories.

Coding capabilities with CAQDAS

Selected qualitative data analysis programs permit you to do what you can do manually, such as: apply more than one code to the same passage or sequential

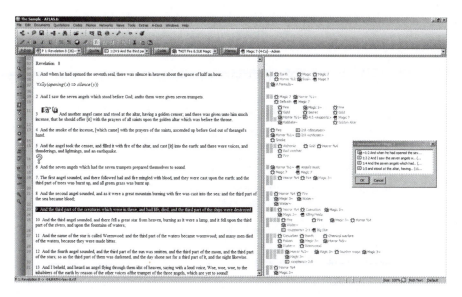

Figure 1.6 A screenshot excerpt from ATLAS.ti v. 6.2 (courtesy of ATLAS.ti, www.atlasti.com)

passages of text (variously labeled in the methods literature as "simultaneous coding," "double coding," "co-occurrence coding," "multiple coding," or "overlap coding"); code a smaller portion of text within a larger portion of coded text ("subcoding," "embedded coding," or "nested coding"); and subsume several similarly coded passages under one larger code ("pattern coding," "meta coding," "umbrella coding," or "hierarchical coding"); along with the ability to instantly and conveniently insert comments or analytic memos related to a specific datum or code. Each CAQDAS program will employ its own distinct set of terms for its coding functions and operations, so refer to the user's manual for specific ways of working.

CAQDAS, unlike the human mind, can maintain and permit you to organize evolving and potentially complex coding systems into such formats as hierarchies and networks for "at a glance" user reference. Figure 1.6 illustrates a sample window excerpt from the most recent version of ATLAS.ti, which lists each simultaneous code by name assigned to each single datum.

Though I stated above that software does not code for you, there is a utilitarian function called "auto coding" available in most CAQDAS programs, which can alleviate some of the repetitiveness of manually coding similar passages of text, especially those gathered from surveys or structured interviews. Passages have to be formatted in prescribed ways and contain the same root word or phrase, however, for this function to work accurately. The ATLAS.ti handbook strongly recommends a manual review after auto coding has been performed to verify the software's coding assignments, and Lewins and Silver (2007) suggest that researchers should not feel "compelled to make use of auto coding just because it is available" (p. 21).

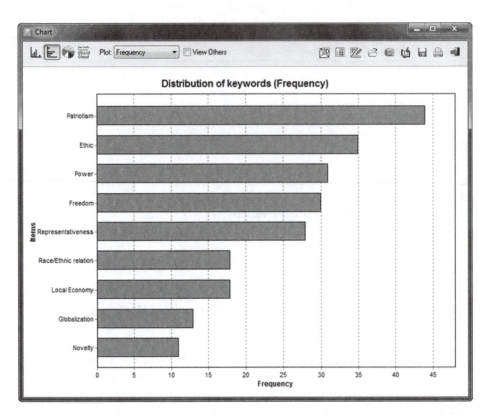

Figure 1.7 A code frequency bar chart from QDA Miner v. 3.2 (courtesy of Provalis Research, www.provalisresearch.com)

Searches and queries with CAQDAS

Another one of CAQDAS's advantages over manual paper and pencil coding and analysis is its search and querying abilities to quickly collect and display key words and phrases and similarly coded data for examination. For example, Figure 1.7 illustrates code frequencies in the form of a bar chart from QDA Miner 3.2 software.

Searches or queries of coded passages can even find where particular codes co-occur, overlap, appear in a sequence, or lie in proximity to each other. These search functions can perform such actions as retrieve, filter, group, link, and compare, enabling the researcher to perform such human actions as infer, make connections, identify patterns and relationships, interpret, and build theory with the data (Lewins & Silver, 2007, p. 13). Figure 1.8 illustrates a sample MAXQDA 10 Code Relations Browser window, which enables you to determine *possible* interrelationships among coded data (Kuckartz, 2007). The varying sizes of the squares within the matrix indicate the relative frequency of such matches. Double clicking one of the squares inside the Code Relations Browser brings up all the text segments with overlapping codes.

CAQDAS also permits the researcher to shift quickly back and forth between multiple analytic tasks such as coding, analytic memo writing, and exploring patterns in progress. Add to this the software's ability to recode, uncode, rename, delete, move,

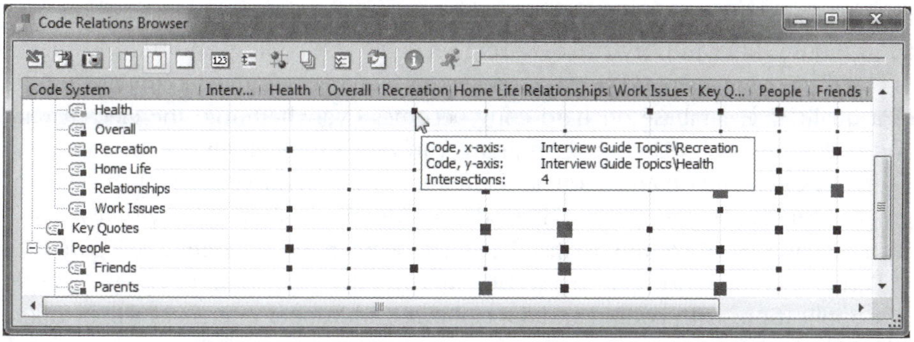

Figure 1.8 A Code Relations Browser screenshot from MAXQDA 10 (courtesy of MAXQDA – The Art of Text Analysis. Verbi Software-Consult-Research GmbH. © 1989–2012, Marburg, Berlin, Germany. Web: www.maxqda.com)

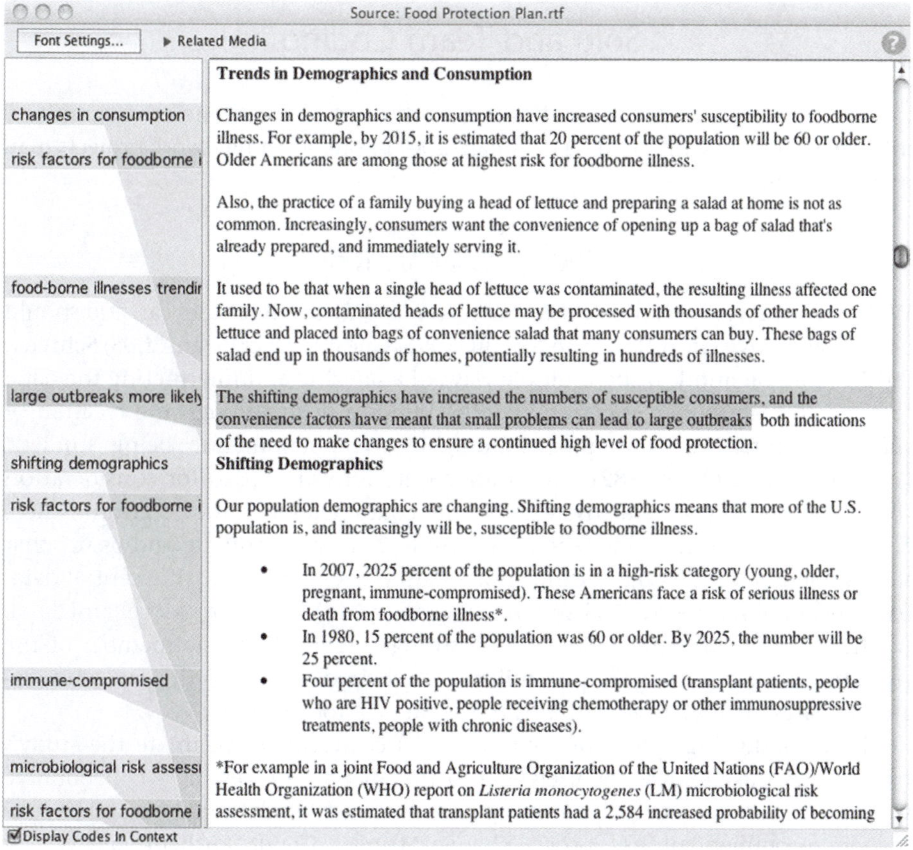

Figure 1.9 A HyperRESEARCH 3.0 Codes in Context display (courtesy of ResearchWare, Inc., www.researchware.com)

merge, group, and assign different codes to shorter and longer passages of text with a few mouse clicks and keystrokes during Second Cycle coding, and the advantages of CAQDAS over paper and pencil soon become apparent. And when the magnitude of a qualitative database on hard copy becomes overwhelming, the elegant data and coding displays of selected programs can provide the analyst with a sense of necessary order and organization, and enhance one's cognitive grasp of the work in progress, such as HyperRESEARCH's Codes in Context display, which visually "fans" each code in the left column to its related data segment on the right (see Figure 1.9).

Rather than presenting in this section an extended discussion of CAQDAS's specific applications with coding and data analysis, additional references will be made on an "as relevant" basis throughout the rest of this manual. Since most readers of this book are more than likely newcomers to qualitative data analysis, I assume that manual coding will be the first method you employ. Thus, I present the coding profiles with that assumption in mind. Those with experience or expertise in CAQDAS programs can adapt the coding principles described in this manual into their particular software package's active files and documents.

Solo and Team Coding

Coding in most qualitative studies is a solitary act – the "lone ethnographer" intimately at work with her data (Galman, 2007) – but larger fieldwork projects may involve a team.

Coding collaboratively

Writers of joint research projects advocate that coding in these cases can and should be a collaborative effort (Erickson & Stull, 1998; Guest & MacQueen, 2008; Schreier, 2012). Multiple minds bring multiple ways of analyzing and interpreting the data: "a research team builds codes and coding builds a team through the creation of shared interpretation and understanding of the phenomenon being studied" (Weston et al., 2001, p. 382). Provocative questions are posed for consideration that could possibly generate new and richer codes (Olesen, Droes, Hatton, Chico, & Schatzman, 1994). Ultimately, team members must coordinate and insure that their sometimes individual coding efforts harmonize, particularly if a central database and multi-user CAQDAS system are employed. MacQueen, McLellan-Lemal, Bartholow, and Milstein (2008, p. 132) strongly advise that one member of the team be assigned primary responsibility as "codebook editor" – the one who creates, updates, revises, and maintains the master list for the group.

Those conducting action or community-based research can invite the study's participants/stakeholders themselves into the analytic process as a collaborative venture to provide a sense of ownership and investment in data analysis and its consequent recommendations for social change (Stringer, 1999). Northcutt and McCoy (2004) label focus group development of their own categories of interest "affinities." Children and adolescents, too, can be taught to investigate and analyze issues that relate to their social worlds (Alderson, 2008; Heiligman, 1998; Warren, 2000). Haw and Hadfield (2011), and Heath, Hindmarsh, and Luff (2010), hold "data sessions" in which informed colleagues and sometimes participants themselves are invited to preview and review video fragments from fieldwork to collaboratively interrogate and discuss relevant multiple dimensions of the research issues suggested. This dialogic exchange of ideas in a workshop and collegial atmosphere attunes the research team to new and varying perspectives before more intensive scrutiny and formal analysis of the video are undertaken.

Team members can both code their own and others' data gathered in the field to cast a wider analytic net and provide a "reality check" for each other. For these types of collaborative ventures, *intercoder agreement* or *interpretive convergence* (the percentage at which different coders agree and remain consistent with their assignment of particular codes to particular data) is an important part of the process (for formulas and discussions see Bernard, 2011, pp. 447–9; Boyatzis, 1998, pp. 144–59; DeCuir-Gunby, Marshall, & McCulloch, 2011; Hruschka et al., 2004; and Krippendorff, 2009). There is no standard or base percentage of agreement among qualitative researchers, but the 80–90% range seems a minimal benchmark to those most concerned with an evidentiary statistic. Such measures as the Kappa Coefficient and other coding comparison queries are calculation functions included in MAXQDA 10 and NVivo 9.

Some methodologists question the utility and application of intercoder agreement for qualitative data analysis since the entire process is an interpretive enterprise. Thus, research teams may wish to dispense with such quantitative measures altogether and rely on intensive group discussion, "dialogical intersubjectivity," coder adjudication, and simple group consensus as an agreement goal (Harry et al., 2005, p. 6; Kvale & Brinkmann, 2009, p. 243; Sandelowski & Barroso, 2007, p. 230).

"Coding by committee" can range from a time-saving democratic effort to a frustrating enterprise filled with road blocks, depending on the amount and complexity of data and – to be honest – the researcher personalities involved. Group dynamics suggest that a team meeting regularly to collectively code data should consist of no more than five people. More than five individuals makes problem solving and decision making exponentially more difficult. It may also be wise to develop strategies and contingency plans ahead of time for what to do in case coding progress stalls or if professional disagreements occur and an executive decision needs to be made. I myself prefer to be the "lone wolf coder" when it comes to working with colleagues on a research project, but my team members are given copies of my coded data to review at all stages, and are encouraged to function as rigorous examiners and auditors of my analyses.

Coding solo

If you are working as a lone ethnographer, shop talk with a colleague or mentor about your coding and analysis as you progress through them. Both solo and team coders can even consult the participants themselves during analysis (a process sometimes called "member checking") as a way of validating the findings thus far. Even if you and other members of a research seminar are each working on different projects, sharing coded field note excerpts and discussing your dilemmas about coding and analysis generate peer support and may even help you and others find better connections between categories in progress (Burant, Gray, Ndaw, McKinney-Keys, & Allen, 2007; Strauss, 1987). Discussion not only provides an opportunity to articulate your internal thinking processes, but also presents windows of opportunity for clarifying your emergent ideas and possibly making new insights about the data.

Ezzy (2002, pp. 67–74) recommends several strategies for checking the progress of your analysis while still in the field. Though applicable for team researchers as well, the lone researcher can benefit most from these recommendations to assess the trustworthiness of his or her account: (1) check your interpretations developed thus far with the participants themselves; (2) initially code *as* you transcribe interview data; and (3) maintain a reflective journal on the research project with copious analytic memos.

Necessary Personal Attributes for Coding

Aside from such cognitive skills as induction, deduction, abduction, synthesis, evaluation, and logical and critical thinking, there are seven personal attributes all qualitative researchers should possess, particularly for coding processes.

First, you need to be *organized*. This is not a gift that some people have and others do not. Organization is a set of disciplined skills that can be learned and cultivated as habits. A small-scale qualitative study's word count of data will range in the tens and sometimes hundreds of thousands of words. The multiple codes you generate will need a tightly organized framework for qualitative analysis; in fact, organization *is* analysis. And despite the electronic filing systems of hard drives and CAQDAS, you will still encounter and manipulate many pages of paper in qualitative work. Date and label all incoming data and keep multiple digital and hard copies as backups.

Second, you need to exercise *perseverance*. Virtually every writer of qualitative research methods literature remarks that coding data is challenging and time consuming. Some writers also declare how tedious and frustrating it can be. Take breaks from your work when you need to, of course – this will keep you refreshed and alert. But cultivate a personal work ethic and create an environment and schedule that enable you to sustain extended periods of time with analytic tasks requiring your full concentration.

Third, you need to be able to *deal with ambiguity*. The acts of coding and codifying are not precise sciences with specific algorithms or procedures to follow. Yes, occasionally answers may suddenly and serendipitously crystallize out of nowhere. But at other times, a piece of the analytic puzzle may be missing for days or weeks or even months. Rich ideas need time to formulate, so have trust and faith in yourself that these may emerge in due time. But remember that you can accelerate the process through analytic memo writing.

Fourth, you will need to exercise *flexibility.* Coding is a cyclical process that requires you to recode not just once but twice (and sometimes even more). Virtually no one gets it right the first time. If you notice that your initial methods choices may not be working for you or not delivering the emergent answers you need, be flexible with your approach and try a modified or different method altogether. Virtually all researcher-developed coding schemes are never fixed from the beginning – they evolve as analysis progresses.

Fifth, you need to be *creative.* There is a lot of art to social science. Noted ethnographer Michael H. Agar (1996) asserts that the early stages of analysis depend on "a little bit of data and a lot of right brain" (p. 46). We generally advocate that qualitative researchers remain close to and deeply rooted in their data, but every code and category you construct or select are choices from a wide range of possible options. Creativity also means the ability to think visually, to think in metaphors, and to think of as many ways as possible to approach a problem. Creativity is essential for your data collection, data analysis, and even for your final written report.

Sixth, you need to be *rigorously ethical.* Honesty is perhaps another way to describe this, but I deliberately choose the phrase because it implies that you will always be: rigorously ethical with your participants and treat them with respect; rigorously ethical with your data and not ignore or delete those seemingly problematic passages of text; and rigorously ethical with your analysis by maintaining a sense of scholarly integrity and working hard toward the final outcomes.

The seventh and arguably most important skill you need for coding is an *extensive vocabulary.* Quantitative research's precision rests with numeric accuracy. In qualitative research, our precision rests with our word choices. For example, there are subtle interpretive differences between something that "may," "could," "can," "probably," "possibly," and "seemingly" happen and a wide interpretive difference between something that happens "frequently," "usually," and "often" (Hakel, 2009). Is a custard pie thrown in somebody's face on a television situation comedy episode to be coded JUVENILE VIOLENCE or SLAPSTICK COMEDY? An unabridged dictionary and thesaurus become vital reference tools to find just the right words for your codes, categories, themes, concepts, assertions, and theories. Explore the origins of key words in an unabridged dictionary to find surprising new meanings (e.g., did you know that the root word of *hypocrite* is "actor"?). A thesaurus review of a key word chosen as a code or category may introduce you to an even better – and more precise – word for your analysis.

For an applied introduction to the cognitive skills and personal attributes necessary for coding and qualitative data analysis, see Appendix D's exercises and simulations.

On Method

Thorough – even cursory – descriptions about the researcher's code development and coding processes rarely make it into the methods section of a final report (but a dissertation writer should consider including his or her codebook as an appendix to the study). The majority of readers would most likely find the discussion tedious or irrelevant compared to the more important features, such as the major categories and findings. Also, scholarly journals place length restrictions on article manuscripts, so some components of the research story must be left out and, more often than not, codes and coding fall by the wayside. But in all honesty, I do not think most of the academic community minds (cf. Stewart, 1998). I am not advocating that published research should include what most feel is a behind-the-scenes matter. Just acknowledge that the long time and rigorous effort you put into, and joyous personal analytic growth you experience through, coding and analytic memo writing are private affairs between you and your data (cf. Constas, 1992). When you invite important guests to your home for dinner, you do not ask them to appear two or three hours before the scheduled serving time to watch you cook in the kitchen. They arrive just before the meal to feast on and enjoy what you have worked so hard to prepare.

Yet, analogy aside, please do not refer to or consider this manual a "cookbook" for your raw data. That suggests that the methods profiled here are like tested recipes guaranteed to produce successful dishes every time. Method "is just a way of ordering our capacity for insight – but does not produce it" (Ruthellen Josselson, in Wertz et al., 2011, p. 321). Most methodologists concur that coding schemes are customized to the specific contexts of a study; your data are unique, as are you and your creative abilities to code them. I do not have the answers to your questions, but you and your data do. In good faith, I guarantee you some guidance and, if we are both lucky, perhaps some insight.

(I jokingly mused to myself whether this manual might be disparagingly tagged by some as "the *Cliff's Notes* of qualitative data analysis" or *Coding for Dummies*. Either way, as a pragmatist I will take that as a *compliment* about the work.)

Critiques against coding

There have been some legitimate critiques against coding, some of them philosophical and some of them methodological. Yet when I hear these criticisms I am inclined to think that my colleagues' reservations originate from what used to be earlier, post-positivist approaches to coding – mechanical and technical paradigms that did indeed make the enterprise sheer drudgery and the outcomes often little more than topic-driven lists. Below are some of the most frequent criticisms I have heard against coding and my responses to those perceptions:

"Coding is reductionist": Coding is what you perceive it to be. If you see it as reductionist, then that is what it will be for you. But recall that my definition of coding approaches the analytic act as one that assigns rich symbolic meanings through essence-capturing and/or evocative attributes to data. The 32 coding profiles in this book present an array of methods. And by design or necessity, a few are indeed meant to assist with nothing more complicated than descriptive, topical indexing, and even fewer are formulaic and prescriptive because that is how their developers intended them. But most of these methods are geared toward discovering a participant's voice, processes, emotions, motivations, values, attitudes, beliefs, judgments, conflicts, microcultures, identities, life course patterns, etc. These are not "reductionist" outcomes but multi-dimensional facets about the people we study.

"*Coding tries to be objective*": Somewhat and no. This could become an extended discussion about the ontological, epistemological, and methodological assumptions of inquiry, but let me bypass those in favor of a quick response. Intercoder agreement in team coding does indeed seem as if "objectivity" is the driving analytic force due to the need for two or more researchers to independently corroborate on the meaning of each datum. But in reality, the process is not so much being objective as it is simply achieving similar results between two or more people.

For the individual researcher, assigning symbolic meanings (i.e., a code) to data is an act of personal signature. And since we each most likely perceive the social world differently, we will therefore experience it differently, interpret it differently, document it differently, code it differently, analyze it differently, and write about it differently. "Objectivity" has always been an ideal yet contrived and virtually impossible goal to achieve in quantitative research. So why should qualitative inquiry carry its baggage? We do not claim to be objective because the notion is a false god.

"*Coding distances you from your data*": If you are doing your job right as a qualitative researcher, nothing could be further from the truth. Coding *well* requires that you reflect deeply on the meanings of each and every datum. Coding *well* requires that you read and reread and reread yet again as you code, recode, and recode yet again. Coding *well* leads to total immersion in your data corpus with the outcome being exponential and intimate familiarity with its details, subtleties, and nuances. When you can quote verbatim by memory what a participant said from your data corpus and remember its accompanying code, I do not understand how that action has "distanced" you from your work.

"*Coding is nothing more than counting*": In traditional content analysis studies, counting the number of times a particular set of codes occurs is indeed an important measure to assess the frequency of items or phenomena. But one of the caveats I propose later in this manual is that frequency of occurrence is not necessarily an indicator of significance. The analytic approaches for most of these coding methods do not ask you to count; they ask you to ponder, to scrutinize, to interrogate, to experiment, to feel, to empathize, to sympathize, to speculate, to assess, to organize, to pattern, to categorize, to connect, to integrate, to synthesize, to reflect, to hypothesize, to assert, to conceptualize, to abstract, and – if you are really good – to theorize. Counting is easy; thinking is hard work.

"*Coding is 'dangerous,' 'violent,' and 'destructive'*": I have difficulty understanding why word choices such as these have been used to describe the act of coding. I associate these words with natural disasters, criminals, and war, not with qualitative data analysis. I feel these monikers are sensationalist hyperbole in a culture of fear, and I question their legitimacy and accuracy for describing their critics' intended concerns. In other words, these are, to me, poor word choices for an argument. And poor word choosers make bad coders.

"*There's more to data analysis than just coding*": I absolutely agree. The more than 40 analytic approaches documented in Appendix B alone support this perception. This manual advocates that coding is a heuristic – a method of discovery that hopefully stimulates your *thinking* about the data you have been given and have collected. And in case you have forgotten two very important principles I stated at the beginning of this chapter, here they are again:

- Coding is just *one* way of analyzing qualitative data, not *the* way.
- There are times when coding the data is absolutely necessary, and times when it is most inappropriate for the study at hand.

Coding as craft

I am very well aware of the interpretivist turn in qualitative inquiry and the movements toward narrative presentation and emancipatory social action through ethnographic fieldwork (Denzin & Lincoln, 2011). My own qualitative research projects, in fact, have ranged from the realist to the literary and from the confessional to the critical (van Maanen, 2011). But as a theatre practitioner, my discipline acknowledges that we must attend to both the art *and craft* of what we do to make our stage production work successful. And as a teacher educator, it is my job to teach how to teach. Hence, I must have an attunement to various methods of classroom practice because my professional responsibilities require that I do. Some methods are organizational, managerial, time efficient, and related to carefully planned curriculum design. Yet I emphasize to my students that such processes as the creative impulse, trusting your instincts, taking a risk, and just being empathetically human in the classroom are also legitimate methods of teaching practice. Education is complex; so is social life in general and so is qualitative inquiry in particular.

This heightened, ever-present awareness of craft, of "how to," transfers into my research work ethic. I have become both humbly and keenly aware not only of what I am doing but why I am doing it. A metacognition of method, even in an emergent, intuitive, inductive-oriented, and socially conscious enterprise such as qualitative inquiry, is vitally important. This awareness comes with time and experience (and trial and error), but development can be accelerated if you have some preparatory knowledge of "how to." I hope this manual smoothes your learning curve a bit and assists with your professional and personal growth as a qualitative researcher.

This introduction focused on codes and coding. There is an accompanying heuristic with this process – writing analytic memos, the subject of the next chapter.

TWO

Writing Analytic Memos

> **CHAPTER SUMMARY**
>
> This chapter first reviews the purposes and goals of analytic memo writing, then discusses 11 recommended topics for reflection during data collection and analysis. A section is included on the related processes of grounded theory methodology, followed by suggestions for the analysis of visual data.

The Purposes of Analytic Memo Writing

The purposes of analytic memo writing are to document and reflect on: your coding processes and code choices; how the process of inquiry is taking shape; and the emergent patterns, categories and subcategories, themes, and concepts in your data – all possibly leading toward theory. Codes written in the margins of your hard-copy data or associated with data and listed in a CAQDAS file are nothing more than labels until they are analyzed. Your private and personal written musings before, during, and about the entire enterprise is a question-raising, puzzle-piecing, connection-making, strategy-building, problem-solving, answer-generating, rising-above-the-data heuristic. Robert E. Stake (1995) muses, "Good research is not about good methods as much as it is about good thinking" (p. 19). And Valerie Janesick (2011) wisely observes that, in addition to systematic analysis, "the qualitative researcher should expect to uncover some information through informed hunches, intuition, and serendipitous occurrences that, in turn, will lead to a richer and more powerful explanation of the setting, context, and participants in any given study" (p. 148).

What is an Analytic Memo?

Analytic memos are somewhat comparable to researcher journal entries or blogs – a place to "dump your brain" about the participants, phenomenon, or process under investigation by thinking and thus writing and thus thinking even more about them: "Memos are sites of conversation with ourselves about our data" (Clarke, 2005, p. 202). Think of a code not just as a significant word or phrase you applied to a datum, but as a prompt or trigger for written reflection on the deeper and complex meanings it evokes. The objective is researcher reflexivity on the data corpus, "thinking critically about what you are doing and why, confronting and often challenging your own assumptions, and recognizing the extent to which your thoughts, actions and decisions shape how you research and what you see" (Mason, 2002, p. 5). Coding and analytic memo writing are concurrent qualitative data analytic activities, for there is "a reciprocal relationship between the development of a coding system and the evolution of understanding a phenomenon" (Weston et al., 2001, p. 397).

Let me clarify that I use *analytic* memo as my term of choice because, to me, all memos are analytic regardless of content. Some methodologists recommend that you label, classify, and keep separate different types of memos according to their primary purpose: a coding memo, theoretical memo, research question memo, task memo, etc. But I have found it difficult in my own work to write freely and analytically within the bounded parameters of an artificial memo category as a framing device. Kathy Charmaz advises in her grounded theory workshops, "Let your memos read like letters to a close friend. There's no need for stodgy academic prose." I simply write what is going through my mind, *then* determine what type of memo I have written to title it and thus later determine its place in the data corpus. Yes, memos are data; and as such they, too, can be coded, categorized, and searched with CAQDAS programs. Dating each memo helps keep track of the evolution of your study. Giving each memo a descriptive title and evocative subtitle enables you to classify it and later retrieve it through a CAQDAS search. Depending on the depth and breadth of your writing, memos can even be woven as substantive portions into the final written report.

Also important to note here is the difference between analytic memos and field notes. Field notes, as I distinguish them, are the researcher's written documentation of participant observation, which may include the observer's personal and subjective responses to and interpretations of social action encountered. Field notes may contain valuable comments and insights that address the recommended categories for analytic memo reflection described below. Thus, personal field notes are potential sites in which rich analysis may occur. I recommend extracting these memo-like passages from the corpus and keeping them in a separate file devoted exclusively to analytic reflection.

Virtually every qualitative research methodologist agrees: whenever *anything* related to and significant about the coding or analysis of the data comes to mind, stop whatever you are doing and write a memo about it immediately. The goal is not to summarize the data but to reflect and expound on them. Future directions, unanswered questions, frustrations with the analysis, insightful connections, and anything about the researched and the researcher are acceptable content for memos. Most CAQDAS programs enable the researcher to instantly insert and link an analytic memo (or comment or annotation) to a specific datum or code. But sometimes "ah-ha" moments of insight occur at unexpected and inopportune times – in the shower, while driving, eating lunch, etc. So, keep a small paper notepad and something to write with, or a digital audio recorder or other handheld device, nearby at all times for brief jottings or reminders in lieu of computer access. Do not rely on "mental notes to self."

Examples of Analytic Memos

Despite the open-ended nature of analytic memo writing in qualitative inquiry, there are some general and recommended categories for reflection. Below is one of the coding examples from Chapter One. Examples of analytic memo content related to the excerpt follow:

[1] My son, Barry, went through a really tough time about, probably started the end of fifth grade and went into sixth grade. [2] When he was growing up young in school he was a people-pleaser and his teachers loved him to death. [3] Two boys in particular that he chose to try to emulate, wouldn't, were not very good for him. [4] They were very critical of him, they put him down all the time, and he kind of just took that and really kind of internalized it, I think, for a long time. [5] In that time period, in the fifth grade, early sixth grade, they really just kind of shunned him all together, and so his network as he knew it was gone.	[1] MIDDLE-SCHOOL HELL [2] TEACHER'S PET [3] BAD INFLUENCES [4] TWEEN ANGST [5] THE LOST BOY

Extensive memo writing, as illustrated below, over just one small passage of coded data, such as that above, is most unlikely. The example is kept deliberately brief to show how the same piece of data can be approached from multiple angles for analytic memo writing.

Analytic memos can reflect on the following (in no particular order of importance):

Reflect on and write about how you personally relate to the participants and/or the phenomenon. Establish connections between yourself and the social world you are studying. Sympathize and empathize with the participants' actions to understand their perspectives and worldviews. In what ways are you similar to them? Examine your own emotions, relationship, and values, attitudes, and beliefs about the phenomenon you are exploring. An analytic memo, based on the data excerpt above, might read:

11 November 2011
PERSONAL RELATIONSHIP TO THE STUDY: LIVING [PREADOLESCENT] HELL
 I can relate. Just change the grade levels to seventh and eighth and Barry's story is my own. I, too, was the teacher's pet, the best little boy in the world. Some of my peers were such bullying bastards that they made junior high school a living hell for

me. I wasn't made bad by the bad-ass influences around me. They just, sigh, put me down all the time, too. School became a place where I dreaded going. Barry probably dreaded it, too. When you're bullied, fear is the major emotion at work.

Reflect on and write about your study's research questions. Focusing on your a priori (determined beforehand) articulated research questions, purposes, and goals as analysis progresses will keep you on track with the project. Start by writing the actual question itself then elaborate on answers in progress. An analytic memo might read:

12 November 2011
RESEARCH QUESTION: FACTORS THAT INFLUENCE AND AFFECT

This study addresses: What factors in Barry's past influenced and affected his current condition? Five years after the time frame of the mother's story, he's still loved by his teachers; and yes, he is still a "people pleaser" – very popular among his crowd. His tween years, as he himself put it in another retrospective interview, were "a dead period." And when you lose your friends, it's hell. This middle school dead period seemed to have influenced and affected his moody entry into high school, but he overcame it. So now, the task is learning what happened to Barry beginning in ninth grade that changed him for the better.

Reflect on and write about your code choices and their operational definitions. Define your codes and rationalize your specific choices for the data. This is an internal "reality check" of your thinking processes, and reflection may generate other possible codes or more refined coding methods (see Eclectic Coding in Chapter Four). Glaser (1978) reminds us that, through "writing memos on codes, the analyst draws and fills out analytic properties of the descriptive data" (p. 84). Code management systems in most CAQDAS programs will permit you to enter a more concise definition for each code you generate, while CAQDAS memo systems provide more space to reflect and expand on the codes' meanings. An analytic memo might read:

13 November 2011
CODE DEFINITION: TWEEN ANGST

Since Barry is in sixth grade, he's a "tween." The word "tween" is almost limbo-like: in-between; not quite a child, not quite a teen – you're a "tween." This almost has a condescending tone to it. When you're in-between, you're in parentheses. When you're in-between, you're neither here nor there. It's a transition, a phase, a stage, a place where you can get lost, where you can lose yourself if you're not careful.

Angst, the second part of the code phrase, is another choice that is my own word. The mother did not say it directly, but that is what it seems her son experienced. Angst – or anxious tension – is what so many adolescents go through, but I wonder if they are ever taught that word? Will knowing that what they are going through has a label ease the pain or make it any better? To be rejected is one of the most devastating acts for a tween (and a child and a teenager and an adult). Was he rejected because he was a "people pleaser"? I know I was. It sucks to be good – at least when you are a tween.

Use TWEEN ANGST whenever Barry experienced this state, as described by himself or his mother, during his sixth through eighth grade school years.

Reflect on and write about emergent patterns, categories, themes, concepts, and assertions. Remember that individual codes eventually become part of a broader scheme of classification. Reflection on how the codes tentatively get placed into categories and/or subcategories, suggest a theme, evoke a higher-level concept, or stimulate an assertion, may begin to create a sense of order to your analysis thus far. An analytic memo might read:

14 November 2011
EMERGENT PATTERNS, CATEGORIES, THEMES, CONCEPTS, AND ASSERTIONS: MIDDLE-SCHOOL HELL

MIDDLE-SCHOOL HELL seems to be an umbrella code for TWEEN ANGST and THE LOST BOY. Barry says in another interview that those years were a "DEAD PERIOD" for him – an evocative In Vivo Code. But I think I focus on the particular by using MIDDLE-SCHOOL HELL to represent many students within that age range.

However, don't discount "DEAD PERIOD" as a major theme or concept at this time. As I continue analysis, that code may be more conceptual than I think at this point in the study. Something in me does not want to let it go. A "DEAD PERIOD" can occur during any portion of a person's life, while TWEEN ANGST is limited to a specific age range.

Reflect on and write about the possible networks (links, connections, overlaps, flows) among the codes, patterns, categories, themes, concepts, and assertions. One of the most critical outcomes of qualitative data analysis is to interpret how the individual components of the study weave together. The actual integration of key words from the coding into the analytic memo narrative – a technique I call *codeweaving* – is a practical way of insuring that you are thinking how the puzzle pieces fit together. First-draft diagrams of network relationships between and among concepts are also possible as analytic memo content (see Chapter Four for an extended example). Networking makes you think of possible hierarchies, chronological flows, and influences and affects (i.e., cause and effect). The codes just from the data excerpt above are: MIDDLE-SCHOOL HELL, TEACHER'S PET, BAD INFLUENCES, TWEEN ANGST, and THE LOST BOY. An analytic memo might read:

15 November 2011
NETWORKS: CODEWEAVING ABOUT MIDDLE-SCHOOL HELL

A codeweaving attempt with this data excerpt to compose an assertion is: "Bad influences can turn teacher's pets into lost boys, resulting in tween angst in the limbo of middle-school hell." Another version is: "Middle-school hell is a site of tween angst: teacher's pets can become lost boys by bad influences." Peer influence, according to the developmental literature, becomes very strong during these preadolescent years. "His network as he knew it was gone" suggests that when friendships decay, children become lost (my term).

A preliminary sketch of this codewoven process appears in Figure 2.1.

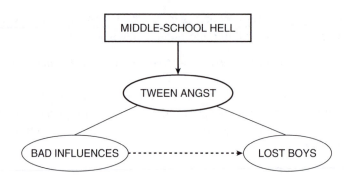

Figure 2.1 An analytic memo sketch on codeweaving

Reflect on and write about an emergent or related existing theory. Transcend the local and particular of your study, and reflect on how your observations may apply to other populations, to the bigger picture, to the generalizable, even to the universal. Explore possible metaphors and symbols at work in your data that suggest transferability. Speculate on how your theory predicts human action and explains why those actions occur. Integrate existing literature and theories into or compare them with your own particular study's data. An analytic memo might read:

16 November 2011
THEORY: HUMAN NETWORKS AND POSITIONING THEORY
    Who *hasn't* faced rejection at some point in his or her life, especially during the adolescent years? I was particularly struck by the mother's observation, "his network as he knew it was gone." When we lose our "networks," we lose our connections, our links. Like qualitative data analysis, we become isolated "bins" or "nodes" awaiting placement in the overall scheme of things, but risk being discarded or renamed or subsumed if we don't contribute something. Who *hasn't* felt "leftover" or "miscellaneous" at some point in his or her life? Once lost, we go inward; once lost, we hide to protect ourselves.
    Positioning theory from the 1980s and 1990s might be relevant here. Reflexive and interactive positioning are the dynamics at work within Barry and among him and his peers. But also check out the human development literature, as what is happening here may simply be "classic" alignment with typical adolescent social and emotional trends.

Reflect on and write about any problems with the study. Opportunities to reflect on fieldwork or analytic "glitches" by writing about them may generate solutions to your dilemmas. The act is also a way to raise provocative questions for continued reflection (or "refraction" – musings on complex and ambiguous "blurry moments" (O'Connor, 2007, p. 4)), to expand on the complexity of the social worlds you are observing, or to vent any personal frustrations you may be feeling about the study. An analytic memo might read:

17 November 2011
PROBLEM: THINKING OUTSIDE THE CHRONOLOGICAL BOX

I find I'm locking myself into the traditional human development schema: early childhood, middle childhood, adolescence, adulthood, etc. The trajectory of Barry's life course is falling into the same old patterns of elementary, middle, and high school. Not that there's anything wrong with that, but perhaps I should be thinking of other phase/ stage systems for plotting his life course. By default we attribute portions of our lives as "the elementary school years," "the high school years," etc. Maybe I should divide what I'm finding thus far into "turning points" or "milestones" schemas, regardless of grade level?

Reflect on and write about any personal or ethical dilemmas with the study. Ethical issues of varying magnitude arise in virtually every study with human participants. Most of these dilemmas are usually unforeseen, based on what participants unexpectedly bring to interviews or what the researcher observes in the field that counters his or her value, attitude, and belief systems. Reflection keeps you attuned to these matters and may help you brainstorm possible solutions. An analytic memo might read:

18 November 2011
ETHICS: WHAT CAN/SHOULD I ASK?

I'm still hesitant to ask Barry to talk more about that "dead period" in middle school. He seems evasive about it, looks downward whenever it's brought up. Even his teachers seem to tiptoe around the issue – they drop hints but don't say anything outright. I don't want to cause him any emotional distress, but at the same time I feel I need to find out more about that time period in his life. Maybe asking his mother to talk about those years rather than Barry will get the info to help me plot his life course? Barry knows that I'm interviewing her, so it's no secret.

Reflect on and write about future directions for the study. Each qualitative research project is unique and cumulative in nature. The more you interview participants and observe them in natural social settings, the more ideas you generate for possible future research action. As data collection and analysis progress, you may discover missing elements or a need for additional data. You may even reconceptualize your entire initial approach and find inspiration from a new insight about the phenomenon or process under investigation. An analytic memo might read:

19 November 2011
FUTURE DIRECTIONS: ADDITIONAL TEACHER PARTICIPANTS

If possible, track down some of Barry's teachers from middle school and see if I can get IRB [Institutional Review Board] and their principal's permission to interview them about Barry. It would be interesting to hear what they remember about him from educators' perspectives. Also interesting would be for me to ask them about the TWEEN ANGST code and see how they react.

One of the things I'm learning is how little I really know about middle- and junior high school students. Since I work with elementary and high school youth for my labs, I have a pretty good handle on them. But the tween years are elusive to me. Find a site and get back in touch with what happens from sixth through eighth grades.

Reflect on and write about the analytic memos generated thus far. Corbin and Strauss (2008) note that beginning memo writing tends to start off simply and descriptively, while later writings become more substantive and abstract (p. 108). Though this may happen on its own accord, the researcher will also have to consciously achieve it. It is worthwhile to periodically review the stock of analytic memos developed thus far to compose "metamemos" that tactically summarize, integrate, and revise what has been observed and developed to date. This method also provides the researcher with a "reality check" of the study and analysis in progress. An analytic memo might read:

20 November 2011
METAMEMO: IN-BETWEEN
After scanning the analytic memos thus far, I notice recurring themes about "tween," "middle," "lost." I recall a lecture I heard about human beings caught "in parentheses" as a significant transitional state. Barry at this stage is also in many transitions: from elementary to high school, from child to adolescent, from teacher's pet to lost boy. There's that "betwixt and between" phrase that sticks in my head, but it seems so trite. Barry on the classic "hero's journey" is another metaphor that comes to mind – the protagonist who must undergo severe trial and loss of self to find oneself again. Perhaps my attempt to systematically categorize these data is proving useful for what could become an evocative narrative analysis instead? Like Barry, I too feel caught in parentheses and IN-BETWEEN something as this analysis progresses. That can be a good thing, though – a place for inward reflection, deep introspection – before that breakthrough moment – I hope.

Reflect on and write about the final report for the study. Extended analytic memos can become substantive "think pieces," suitable for integration into the final report of your study. As you "write out loud," you may find yourself composing passages that can easily be edited and inserted directly into the finished text. Or, you might use analytic memo writing as a way to ponder the organization, structure, and contents of the forthcoming final report. An analytic memo might read:

21 November 2011
FINAL REPORT: TWO VOICES
Make certain to cite the mother's observation, "His network as he knew it was gone" as an introductory quote for the section on Barry's "dead period."
Barry's mother is becoming quite a prominent figure in this study. At first she was a supplemental participant, interviewed primarily to gather additional info on Barry's

life course. But I now see how her influences and affects on her son's life course have played very major roles. Barry speaks quite fondly of her and considers her a tremendous nurturer of who he is and who he is becoming. It would be interesting to edit and piece together portions of their separate interviews into a two-voice narrative – one providing commentary on the other:

BARRY: In elementary school I was always picked on a lot, so I was always trying to fit in.

SANDY: Barry went through a really tough time about, probably started the end of fifth grade and went into sixth grade. When he was growing up young in school he was a people-pleaser and his teachers loved him to death. Two boys in particular that he chose to try to emulate were not very good for him. They were very critical of him, they put him down all the time, and he kind of just took that and really kind of internalized it, I think, for a long time. In that time period, in the fifth grade, early sixth grade, they really just kind of shunned him all together, and so his network as he knew it was gone.

BARRY: It's kind of a dead period.

SANDY: At Lakewood Middle School he had a really tough time, real tough. The first day of school in seventh grade, some – I'll use the term "gang-banger," but I don't know – was picking on a little kid. And Barry said,

BARRY
AND SANDY: "Hey man, get off his case."

SANDY: And from that moment on, all of the tension was focused on him. From the time he entered Lakewood to the time he left Lakewood, he was a target by the bad guys. That was a very tough time for him.

Selected CAQDAS manuals recommend that memos can be viewed by multiple research team members to share information and exchange emergent ideas about the study as analysis progresses.

To recap, analytic memos are opportunities for you to reflect on and write about:

- how you personally relate to the participants and/or the phenomenon
- your study's research questions
- your code choices and their operational definitions
- emergent patterns, categories, themes, concepts, and assertions
- the possible networks (links, connections, overlaps, flows) among the codes, patterns, categories, themes, concepts, and assertions
- an emergent or related existent theory
- any problems with the study
- any personal or ethical dilemmas with the study
- future directions for the study
- the analytic memos generated thus far
- the final report for the study

Birks, Chapman, and Francis (2008) provide a clever mnemonic for remembering the overall purposes of analytic memo writing, simply labeled "MEMO":

- **M** – Mapping research activities (documentation of the decision-making processes of research design and implementation as an audit trail)
- **E** – Extracting meaning from the data (analysis and interpretation, concepts, assertions, theories)
- **M** – Maintaining momentum (researcher perspectives and reflexivity throughout the evolutionary journey of the study)
- **O** – Opening communication (for research team member exchanges)

Reflection and refraction

It was noted above that an intriguing way to conceptualize the contemplation of qualitative data is not just as reflection but as *refraction* (O'Connor, 2007), a perspective that acknowledges mirrored reality and the researcher's lens as

> dimpled and broken, obscured in places, operating as a concave or at other times a convex lens. As such, it throws unexpected and distorted images back. It does not imitate what looks into the mirror but deliberately highlights some things and obscures others. It is deliciously ... unpredictable in terms of what might be revealed and what might remain hidden. (p. 8)

Writing *about* the problematic, the ambiguous, and the complex is no guarantee that crystal clarity will evolve, but the approach is a heuristic that may lead to deeper awareness of the multifaceted social world, and serve as an initiating tactic to refocus the blurry.

Ultimately, analytic memo writing is the transitional process from coding to the more formal write-up of the study (see Chapter Six). Your reflections and refractions on the topics listed above collectively generate potential material for formulating a set of core ideas for presentation. Substantive analytic memos may also contribute to the quality of your analysis by rigorous reflection on the data. Stern (2007) proposes, "If data are the building blocks of the developing theory, memos are the mortar" (p. 119), while Birks and Mills (2011) consider memos the "lubricant" of the analytic machine, and "a series of snapshots that chronicle your study experience" (pp. 40–1).

Coding and Categorizing Analytic Memos

Analytic memos themselves from the study can be coded and categorized according to their content. The descriptive titles in the examples above enable you to group related memos by reflections on NETWORKS; EMERGENT PATTERNS, CATEGORIES, THEMES, CONCEPTS, AND ASSERTIONS; ETHICS; METAMEMOS; etc. The subtitles function as subcodes or themes and enable you to subcategorize the contents into more study-specific groupings – for example, analytic memos about specific participants, specific code groups, specific theories in progress, etc. CAQDAS programs provide these classification functions for organized review and reflection.

Analytic memos generate codes and categories

One principle I stress throughout selected profiles in later chapters is that, even after you have coded a portion of your data and categorized the codes into various lists, *analytic memo writing serves as an additional code- and category-generating method*. By memo writing about the specific codes you have applied to your data, you may discover even better ones. By memo writing about your puzzlement and loss for a specific code for a particular datum, the perfect one may emerge. By memo writing about how some codes seem to cluster and interrelate, a category for them may be identified. Codes and categories are found not just in the margins or headings of interview transcripts and field notes – they are also embedded *within* analytic memos. Corbin and Strauss (2008) provide meticulous and in-depth examples of this procedure in their third edition of *Basics of Qualitative Research*.

The cyclical collection, coding, and analytic memo writing of data are not distinct linear processes but "should blur and intertwine continually, from the beginning of an investigation to its end" (Glaser and Strauss, 1967, p. 43). This is one of the major principles developed by grounded theory's premiere writers, Barney G. Glaser and Anselm L. Strauss, and elaborated in future writings by Juliet Corbin, Kathy Charmaz, Adele E. Clarke, and Janice Morse. Bryant and Charmaz's (2007) edited volume, *The Sage Handbook of Grounded Theory*, is perhaps the most authoritative collection of extended essays on the methodology.

Grounded Theory and its Coding Canon

Briefly, grounded theory, developed in the 1960s, is generally regarded as one of the first methodologically systematic approaches to qualitative inquiry. The process usually involves meticulous analytic attention by applying specific types of codes to data through a series of cumulative coding cycles that ultimately lead to the development of a theory – a theory "grounded" or rooted in the original data themselves.

In this coding manual, six particular methods are considered part of grounded theory's coding canon (though they can all be used in other non-grounded-theory studies): In Vivo, Process, Initial, Focused, Axial, and Theoretical Coding. (In earlier publications, Initial Coding was referred to as "Open" Coding, and Theoretical Coding was referred to as "Selective" Coding.)

In Vivo, Process, and Initial Coding are First Cycle methods – coding processes for the beginning stages of data analysis that fracture or split the data into individually coded segments. Focused, Axial, and Theoretical Coding are Second Cycle methods – coding processes for the latter stages of data analysis that both literally and metaphorically constantly compare, reorganize, or "focus" the codes into categories, prioritize them to develop "axis" categories around which others revolve, and synthesize them to formulate a central or core category that becomes the foundation for explication of a grounded theory. Categories also have "properties" and "dimensions" – variable qualities that display the range or distribution within similarly coded data.

Each of these six coding methods will be profiled in later chapters, but the thing to note here is the coding processes' ongoing interrelationship with analytic memo writing, and the memos' reorganization and integration into the final report of the study. Gordon-Finlayson (2010) emphasizes that "coding is simply a structure on which reflection (via memo-writing) happens. *It is memo-writing that is the engine of grounded theory, not coding*" (p. 164, emphasis in original). Glaser and Holton (2004) further clarify that "Memos present hypotheses about connections between categories and/or their properties and begin to integrate these connections with clusters of other categories to generate the theory" (n.p.).

Figure 2.2 presents a very reduced and elemental model of developing "classic" grounded theory for reference. Note how analytic memo writing is a linked component of the major stages leading toward the development of theory.

I minimize the number of analytic memo examples in the coding profiles that follow because I myself find reading extensive ones in research methods textbooks too case specific and somewhat fatiguing. If you wish to see how a trail of analytic memos progresses from First through Second Cycles of coding with the same data excerpt, see the profiles for Initial, Focused, Axial, and Theoretical Coding.

Analytic Memos on Visual Data

A slippery issue for some is the analysis of visual data such as photographs, documents, print materials (magazines, brochures, etc.), Internet websites, video/film, children's drawings, television broadcasts, and other items in addition to the physical environments and artifacts of fieldwork (room décor, architecture, participant dress and accessories, etc.). Despite some pre-existing coding frameworks for visual representation, I feel the best approach to analyzing visual data is a holistic, interpretive lens guided by intuitive inquiry and strategic questions. Rather than one-word or short phrase codes (which are still possible if desired for such approaches as content analysis), the researcher's careful scrutiny of and reflection on images, documented through field notes and analytic memos, generate language-based data that *accompany* the visual data. Ironically, we must use words to articulate our "take" on pictures and imagery. So any descriptors and interpretations we use for documenting the images of social life should employ rich, dynamic words. Gee (2011) proposes that the methods we use for discourse analysis of written texts are just as valid for analyzing visual materials (p. 188).

If you do choose to code visual data for particular reasons, I recommend a strategic selection from Grammatical, Elemental, and Affective Methods (see Chapter Three) when conducting such genres of research as traditional ethnography or

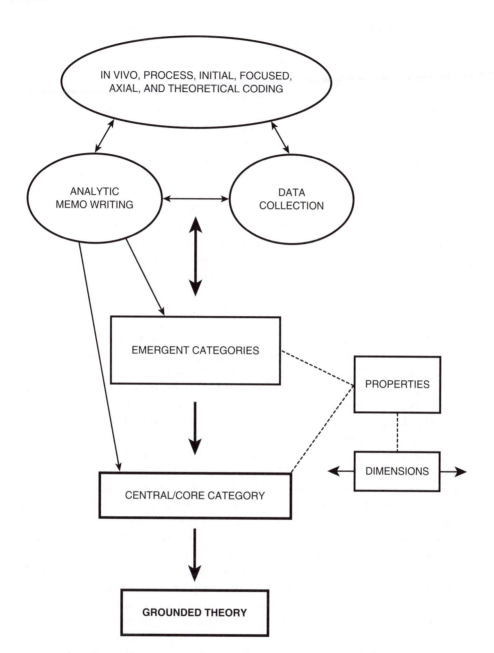

Figure 2.2 An elemental model for developing "classic" grounded theory

content analysis, which generally prescribe systematic counting, indexing, and categorizing of elements. But repeated viewings and analytic memo writing about visual data documented in field notes or maintained in a repository are more appropriate approaches to qualitative inquiry because they permit detailed yet selective attention to the elements, nuances, and complexities of visual imagery, and a broader interpretation of the compositional totality of the work. Clark (2011, p. 142) ruminates that participant-developed visual artifacts such as photos, drawings, collages, and other artistic products should not be considered "nouns" (i.e., things analyzed by a researcher *after* their production) but as "verbs" – processes co-examined with participants *during* the artistic product's creation, followed by participants' reflections on the interpretations and meanings of their own work.

Just as no two people most likely interpret a passage of text the same way, no two people will most likely interpret a visual image the same way. Each of us brings our background experiences, values system, and disciplinary expertise to the processing of the visual, and thus our personal reactions, reflections, and refractions. Spencer (2011) advocates that readings of the visual should adopt a sociological lens with a critical filter through "thick description" analytic narratives: "the 'craft' of visual research requires a balance between inductive forces – allowing the collected data to speak for itself, and deductive forces – structuring, ordering principles derived from theoretical models and concepts" (p. 132).

Documents and artifacts

For example, documents are "social products" that must be examined critically because they reflect the interests and perspectives of their authors (Hammersley & Atkinson, 2007, p. 130) and carry "values and ideologies, either intended or not" (Hitchcock & Hughes, 1995, p. 231). Official documents in particular are "a site of claims to power, legitimacy, and reality" (Lindlof & Taylor, 2011, p. 232). When I analyze hard-copy materials such as teacher-prepared handouts with my research methods students, I propose to them, "Tell me something about the person who created this document, based on what you infer from the document's appearance and content." I have knowledge of who created the material, but my students do not. I assess from their responses whether they can tell me such things as the writer's gender ("What leads you to believe that the person who created this document is male/female?"), level of education ("What do the vocabulary and narrative style tell you about the individual?"), values system ("What do you infer is important to him/her?"), and ways of working ("What do such things as the layout, organization, color choices, and font/type styles tell you about this person's work ethic?"). Students are remarkably perceptive to inductively, abductively, and deductively reading the document's "clues" to closely profile the personality of its creator.

If you subscribe to the theory that the products we create embody who we are, then the environments we establish for ourselves may also embody who we are. Personal settings such as a work area, office, and home contain material items or artifacts that its user/owner has collected, created, inherited, and/or purchased. Each artifact has a history of how it got there and a reason or meaning for its presence. Spaces have a macro "look" and "feel" to them based on the collective assembly of its micro details of specific items, organization, maintenance, cleanliness, lighting, color, and other design elements. If I am walking into a new space, the primary analytic task that runs through my mind is, "Tell me something about the person or people who work/live here." Certainly we can learn much more about a space's occupants and its artifacts by having participants give us a guided tour accompanied with questions and answers about significant items that attract our visual attention. If we have permission to digitally photograph parts of the setting, the visual documentation later permits more reflection and meaning-making through analytic memoing. We need not conduct an extensive written inventory of each and every single item in a space, but the guiding principle I apply to my own visual analysis is, "What's the first and general impression I get about this environment, and what details within it lead me to that impression?"

Live and video recorded action

Many times in fieldwork we document the visual through textual narratives. As an example, below is a set of field notes about a young actor's on-stage performance work – three-dimensional, kinetic visual data – in one of his high school play productions of a modern farce. Unlike the observation of natural social life, observation of live or video-recorded theatrical performance takes into account both planned and spontaneous action by the actor's body and voice:

> Compared to other actors, Barry's movements are sharp, crisp, economic. He maintains still poses in compositions, does not steal focus. His voice is clear, good volume, articulate, wide variety, range. He is dynamic, has good energy, believable in his dialogue. Even when there's an error with a rope (as part of the set that falls) he covers well. Unlike other actors, he does not "foot-fudge," wander, or rock. The others overact, miss the comic timing, speech is sometimes sloppy, difficult to hear. Barry has a leading man quality about him, a presence. He looks handsome, blonde hair cut close – had it long recently – sturdy build, the physique of a beginning football player.

Rather than coding this documented set of visual (and verbal) data in the margin, an analytic memo about this field note set focuses on the visual discourses:

10 November 2011
VISUAL DATA: BARRY'S PHYSICALITY

A good actor needs what Howard Gardner calls "kinesthetic intelligence." Barry, as a high school actor, displays a heightened awareness of it on stage, though in everyday life his physicality is relaxed, even "dumpy." This intelligence comes from metacognition and technique, an attunement to and consciousness of everything your body is doing during performance. Not everyone has this skill, even university actors.

The majority of male Hollywood celebrities are handsome, well-built, and their fan base is drawn to their physical appearance. The beautiful, even in everyday life, also tend to be the popular. In the classroom, I notice girls surrounding Barry before class begins. His "leading man" presence not only means playing a lead role in a play, but leading others who are willing to follow in organized activity. Though he is aware of his body, he is not arrogant about it, which perhaps adds even more to his charisma and appeal. In high school (and adulthood), when you've got looks, you've got an advantage. His I would label/code: COMFORTABLE CONFIDENCE.

The still image of a digital photo permits nuanced visual analysis, but Walsh et al. (2007) note that digital video data of action can be coded multiple times for in-depth detail by replaying the file while focusing on different aspects with each "pass." Heath et al. (2010), however, advise against coding and categorization of video and instead support an analytic inductive approach that favors "the ways in which social action and interaction involve the interplay of talk, visible and material conduct" (p. 9). Short video fragments are microanalyzed through a combination of conversation analysis transcription (running vertically down a page) with descriptive documentation of the visual record (running horizontally across a page) such as facial expressions, focal points, gestures, whole body movements, and manipulation of objects/artifacts.

Coding systems for a video/film, if used, could include not just the content but the filmmaking techniques employed to assess its artistic impact (e.g., HANDHELD, ZOOM, HARD CUT, DISSOLVE, VOICE-OVER). Walsh et al. (2007), and Lewins and Silver (2007), profile several software programs (e.g., Transana, The Observer) that can code digital video, but they also note each one's limitations such as cost, currency, and user-friendliness. Several CAQDAS programs (e.g., ATLAS.ti and NVivo) can access or store digital video and photographs for coding in addition to text.

Overall, a researcher's video analysis is comparable to a video camera's and player's functions. Your eyes can zoom in and out to capture the big picture as well as the small details. When necessary, you can freeze the frame, play a portion in slow motion, or loop a section to replay continuously in order to scrutinize the details and nuances of action. Your written analysis of video is like the translation subtitles or DVD soundtrack commentary that accompanies the original footage.

Recommended guidance

Adele E. Clarke's (2005) "Mapping visual discourses" chapter in her text *Situational Analysis* presents a thorough list of questions to consider from the perspectives of aesthetic accomplishment ("How does the variation in color direct your attention within the image?") to contextual and critical readings ("What work is the image doing in the world? What is implicitly and explicitly normalized?") (pp. 227–8). Thomson (2008), and Freeman and Mathison (2009, pp. 156–63), provide excellent guidelines and questions for the analysis of children's drawings and participant-produced photographs and media ("How does the image relate to bigger ideas, values, events, cultural constructions?"). Altheide (1996) provides rich data collection protocols for and conceptual approaches to media analyses of print and electronic documents. Kozinets (2010) sharply attunes readers to the visual components of "netnography" or online research such as web page layout, font styles, graphical representations, and links to YouTube video clips. Berger (2009) superbly reviews how everyday objects and artifacts can be analyzed from sociological, psychological, anthropological, and other perspectives to interpret the meanings and values of our personal possessions and material culture. Berger (2012) also uses these lenses and filters for media analyses of films, television programs, video games, print advertising, cell phone communications, and so on. Hammersley and Atkinson (2007) provide rich guidance for analyzing indoor environments from an ethnographic perspective. And Heath et al. (2010) offer valuable guidelines for all facets of working with and inductively analyzing video recordings.

As a theatre practitioner I was trained to design for the stage, so visual literacy is a "given" in my ethnographic ways of working. Today's mediated and visual cultures seem to indoctrinate and endow all of us by default with visual literacy – heightened awareness of images and their presentation and representation. From my readings of various systematic methods for analyzing visual data, I have yet to find a single satisfactory approach that rivals the tacit and visceral capabilities of human reflection and interpretation. Trust your intuitive, holistic impressions when analyzing and writing about visual materials.

The next chapter begins with an overview of how to use this manual to guide you through its First Cycle coding methods profiles, and how to select the most appropriate one(s) for your particular qualitative research study.

THREE

First Cycle Coding Methods

CHAPTER SUMMARY

This chapter first reviews the multiple factors to consider when selecting one or more particular coding methods for your analytic work. Then, 25 First Cycle coding methods are profiled. Each profile contains the following: Sources, Description, Applications, Example, Analysis, and Notes.

The Coding Cycles

In theatre production of original works, a folk saying goes, "Plays are not written – they're *re*written." A comparable saying for qualitative researchers is, "Data are not coded – they're *re*coded." Some methodologists label the progressive refinement of codes in a study as "stages," "levels," or "feedback loops." But to me, the reverberative nature of coding – comparing data to data, data to code, code to code, code to category, category to category, category back to data, etc. – suggests that the qualitative analytic process is cyclical rather than linear.

The coding methods in this manual are divided into two main sections: First Cycle and Second Cycle coding methods, with one hybrid method that lies in between them (see Figure 3.1).

First Cycle methods are those processes that happen during the initial coding of data and are divided into seven subcategories: Grammatical, Elemental, Affective, Literary and Language, Exploratory, Procedural, and a final profile entitled Themeing the Data. Each subcategory's major characteristics will be explained in brief introductions later in this chapter and descriptions can also be found in Appendix A. Most First Cycle methods are fairly simple and direct.

Second Cycle methods (see Chapter Five) are a bit more challenging because they require such analytic skills as classifying, prioritizing, integrating, synthesizing, abstracting, conceptualizing, and theory building. If you have taken ownership of the data through careful First Cycle coding (and recoding), the transition to Second Cycle methods becomes easier. But be aware that codes are not the only method you should employ, as noted anthropologists George and Louise Spindler (1992) attest: "only the human observer can be alert to divergences and subtleties that may prove to be more important than the data produced by any predetermined

---

FIRST CYCLE CODING METHODS

Grammatical Methods
Attribute Coding
Magnitude Coding
Subcoding
Simultaneous Coding

Elemental Methods
Structural Coding
Descriptive Coding
In Vivo Coding
Process Coding
Initial Coding

Affective Methods
Emotion Coding
Values Coding
Versus Coding
Evaluation Coding

Literary and Language Methods
Dramaturgical Coding
Motif Coding
Narrative Coding
Verbal Exchange Coding

Exploratory Methods
Holistic Coding
Provisional Coding
Hypothesis Coding

Procedural Methods
Protocol Coding
OCM (Outline of Cultural
    Materials) Coding
Domain and Taxonomic Coding
Causation Coding

Themeing the Data

FIRST TO SECOND CYCLE CODING METHOD
Eclectic Coding

SECOND CYCLE CODING METHODS
Pattern Coding
Focused Coding
Axial Coding
Theoretical Coding
Elaborative Coding
Longitudinal Coding

Figure 3.1   First Cycle and Second Cycle coding methods (see Appendix A for descriptions)

categories of observation or any instrument. ... The categories of happenings repeat themselves endlessly in human affairs, yet each event is unique" (pp. 66–7). Thus, memo writing before, during, and after you code becomes a critical analytic heuristic (see Chapter Two).

Selecting the Appropriate Coding Method(s)

Which coding method(s) – and notice the plural option – is appropriate for your particular study? Permit me to offer the sage yet tiresome advice we say too often in qualitative inquiry: "It depends." Noted methodologist Michael Quinn Patton (2002) rationalizes this by noting, "Because each qualitative study is unique, the analytical approach used will be unique" (p. 433). And, as I noted at the beginning of this manual, no one, including myself, can claim final authority on the "best" way to code qualitative data.

Depending on the nature and goals of your study, you may find that one coding method alone will suffice, or that two or more are needed to capture the complex processes or phenomena in your data (see Eclectic Coding in Chapter Four). Most of the coding methods profiled in this manual are not discrete and a few even overlap slightly in function; some can be "mixed and matched" when needed. Be cautious of muddying the analytic waters, though, by employing too many methods for one study (such as 10 First Cycle coding methods) or integrating incompatible methods (such as an Exploratory Method with a Procedural Method).

Let me offer an array of different answers for the various contexts of beginning qualitative researchers.

Various perspectives on coding decisions

Which coding method(s) is appropriate for your particular study? Some feel coding must be prefaced and accompanied with careful reading and rereading of your data as your subconscious, not just your coding system, develops connections that lead to flashes of insight (DeWalt & DeWalt, 2011). Some feel that more than one coding method and at least two different analytic approaches should be explored in every study to enhance accountability and the depth and breadth of findings (Coffey & Atkinson, 1996; Leech & Onwuegbuzie, 2005; Mello, 2002). Some research genres, such as discourse analysis, may not employ coding at all but rely instead on detailed transcription notation and extensive analytic memos about the data (Gee et al., 1992). Some forgo coding of data altogether to rely on phenomenological interpretations of the themes in and meanings of texts (van Manen, 1990; Wertz et al., 2011). Some perceive coding as an abhorrent act incompatible with newer interpretivist qualitative research methodologies such as performance ethnography and narrative inquiry (Hendry, 2007; Lawrence-Lightfoot & Davis, 1997). Some believe prescribed methods of coding are altogether aconceptual, mechanistic, futile, purposeless (Dey, 1999), and even "destructive" and "violent" toward meaning-making (Packer, 2011, pp. 79, 325). Others, like me, believe in the necessity and payoff of coding for selected qualitative studies, yet wish to keep themselves open during initial data collection and review before determining which coding method(s) – if any – will be most appropriate and most likely to yield a substantive analysis. I label this personal stance "pragmatic eclecticism."

Research question alignment

Which coding method(s) is appropriate for your particular study? The nature of your central and related research questions – and thus the answers you seek – will influence the specific coding choice(s) you make. Trede and Higgs (2009) review how research question framing should harmonize with ontological, epistemological, and other stances: "Research questions embed the values, world view and direction of an inquiry. They also are influential in determining what type of knowledge is going to be generated" (p. 18).

For example, ontological questions address the nature of participants' realities, so aligned research questions might begin with: "What is the nature of …?" "What are the lived experiences of … ?" and "What is it like being … ?" These types of questions suggest the exploration of personal, interpretive meanings found within the data. Selected coding methods that may catalog and better reveal these ontologies include: In Vivo, Process, Emotion, Values, Dramaturgical, and/or Focused Coding, plus Themeing the Data.

Epistemological questions address theories of knowing and an understanding of the phenomenon of interest. Aligned research questions might begin with: "How does … ?" "What does it mean to be … ?" and "What factors influence … ?" These types of questions suggest the exploration of participant actions/processes and perceptions found within the data. Selected coding methods that may catalog and better reveal these epistemologies include: Descriptive, Process, Initial, Versus, Evaluation, Dramaturgical, Domain and Taxonomic, Causation, and/or Pattern Coding, plus Themeing the Data.

These are all, of course, merely a few coding suggestions based on the initiating words of hypothetical and incomplete question prompts. The point here is to carefully consider which coding method(s) may generate the *types* of answers you need, based on the *forms* of questions you pose.

Paradigmatic, conceptual, and methodological considerations

Which coding method(s) is appropriate for your particular study? Specific coding methods decisions may happen before, during, and/or after an initial review of the data corpus. One study with young people I conducted (Saldaña, 2005b) primarily used In Vivo Coding to honor children's voices and to ground the analysis from their perspectives (In Vivo Codes use the direct language of participants as codes rather than researcher-generated words and phrases). This choice was determined *beforehand* as part of the critical ethnographic research design. Thus, the coding decision was based on the *paradigm* or *theoretical approach* to the study. But another project I conducted with teachers (Hager, Maier, O'Hara, Ott, & Saldaña, 2000) applied Versus Coding – phrases that capture the actual and conceptual conflicts within, among, and between participants, such as TEACHERS VS. ADMINISTRATORS – to the data *after* I noticed that interview transcripts and field notes were filled with tensions and power issues. Thus, the coding decision was based on an *emergent conceptual framework* for the study. Still another longitudinal ethnographic study I conducted (Saldaña, 1997) "mixed and matched" various coding methods at the beginning – Eclectic Coding – because I was not quite sure what was happening and thus what I was looking for. What eventually emerged as the primary method was Descriptive Coding since I had multiple types of data (interview transcripts, field notes, documents, etc.) collected over a 20-month period, *and* I required a Longitudinal Coding system that would enable me to analyze participant change across time. Thus, the coding decisions were based on the *methodological needs* of the study.

Coding and a priori goals

Which coding method(s) is appropriate for your particular study? Some methodologists advise that your choice of coding method(s) and even a provisional list of codes should be determined beforehand to harmonize with your study's conceptual framework or paradigm, and to enable an analysis that directly answers your research questions and goals (see Structural, Provisional, Hypothesis, Protocol, and Elaborative Coding). If your goal is to develop *new* theory about a phenomenon or process, then classic or re-envisioned grounded theory and its accompanying coding methods – In Vivo, Process, Initial, Focused, Axial, and Theoretical Coding – are your recommended but not required options. (In the Examples and Analyses portions of these coding profiles, I stay with the same participant and her data to show how one particular case progresses from First through Second Cycle coding methods.)

But some well-intended research goals can emerge as quite problematic. For example, *identity* is a concept (or construct, process, phenomenon, etc.) that has multiple approaches to and definitions of it, depending on the discipline – if not the individual. The fields of psychology, sociology, anthropology, human development, education, feminist studies, cultural studies, queer studies, visual studies, etc., each have their own body of scholars, literature, theories, and oral traditions about what *identity* means and consists of. In my multidisciplinary readings, I have observed that there seems to be a diversity of perspectives and an "almost but not quite there" grasp on this very complex concept. Pre-established codes that relate to attributes (gender, age, ethnicity, etc.), culture, values, attitudes, and beliefs, for example, are most likely essential to studies about identity.

But what becomes more and less important after that depends on who is being researched and who the researcher is. Some will say identity is a state of being; others will say it is a state of becoming. Some say identity is the accumulation of one's past; others say it is how we envision ourselves in the present and future. Some say identity is your individual sense of self; others say it is how you are similar to and different from other people. Some say identity is composed of the personal stories you tell; others say it is composed of the interpersonal relationships you have. Some say identity is what you do; some say it is what you value and believe; some say it is how you perform; and others say it is what you own and consume. Some say identity can be categorized; some say it is holistic; and others say it is composed of multiple and shifting forms in different social contexts. Some say identity is cultural; some say it is political; some say it is psychological; and others say it is sociological. Still others will say it is all of the above; and still others will say it is some of that but it is also something more. The point here is that *identity exists by how it is defined*. So if you are using a priori codes, you need to do some very deep thinking about what identity means before you start applying its related codes to your data.

Coding in mixed methods studies

Which coding method(s) is appropriate for your particular study? Depending on the qualitative coding method(s) you employ, the choice may have numeric conversion and transformation possibilities. Mixed methods studies (Creswell & Plano Clark, 2011; Tashakkori & Teddlie, 2003) currently explore how qualitative data can sometimes be "quantitized" for statistical analysis – descriptive measures such as frequencies and percentages – or for survey instrument development. Major codes or even significant quotes from participant interviews might serve as stimuli for writing specific survey instrument items that ask respondents to assign a numeric rating of some kind. In this manual, Magnitude Coding is a method that applies numbers or other symbols to data and even to codes themselves that represent values on a scale such as: 3 = HIGH, 2 = MEDIUM, and 1 = LOW. There are some methodological purists who object to combining qualitative data with quantitative measurement. But I feel that as researchers we should keep ourselves open to numeric representation – when appropriate – as a supplemental heuristic to analysis. Magnitude Coding may even be used concurrently with such Affective Methods as Values, Emotion, and Evaluation Coding, and with the Exploratory Method of Hypothesis Coding.

Most CAQDAS programs include such statistical capabilities as word frequency counts (e.g., ATLAS.ti's "Word Cruncher" function), code frequency counts, the matrix display of "quantitized" qualitative data in Excel spreadsheets, and even the transfer of converted qualitative data into quantitative data analysis programs such as SPSS (see www.ibm.com). Microsoft Excel can also perform selected statistical analyses such as *t*-tests and analysis of variance (ANOVA). Some CAQDAS programs can also import and associate quantitative data with the qualitative data set, enabling mixed methods analysis. Remember that word frequency in the data corpus does not necessarily suggest significance, but it is nevertheless worth exploring as a query (as featured in NVivo, for example) to explore any emergent but as yet undetected patterns.

Exploratory coding

Which coding method(s) is appropriate for your particular study? Several of my students have explored variations of coding based on hunch-driven queries. One student wrote in an analytic memo that an interview transcript excerpt was coded twice – once with Descriptive Coding, then a second time on a clean copy with Versus Coding – just "to see what would happen." He learned that applying the two coding methods *sequentially* gave him a richer perspective on the same data set. Another student took advantage of available margin space by coding one page of an interview transcript on the left-hand side with Versus Coding, and on the right-hand side with In Vivo Coding, again, just to explore what the two outcomes might suggest. He learned that In Vivo Coding gave him heightened awareness of the individual's unique circumstances, while Versus Coding enabled him to transcend the particulars of the case and transfer more conceptual ideas to a broader population. These were forms of Simultaneous Coding, triggered by nothing more than researcher curiosity to explore "what if … ?" And if they had taken it one step further and made deliberate choices for a Second Cycle of analysis, they may have ventured into Eclectic Coding (profiled in Chapter Four).

"Generic" coding methods

Which coding method(s) is appropriate for your particular study? An instructor familiar with the methods profiled in this manual and your particular project can offer specific recommendations and guidance. In lieu of mentorship, I suggest starting with a combination of these basic coding methods in the order listed as a "generic" approach to your data and analysis, but remain open to changing them if they are not generating substantive discoveries for you:

First Cycle coding methods

1 Attribute Coding (for all data as a management technique)
2 Structural Coding or Holistic Coding (for all data as a "grand tour" overview)
3 Descriptive Coding (for field notes, documents, and artifacts as a detailed inventory of their contents)
4 In Vivo Coding, Initial Coding, and/or Values Coding (for interview transcripts as a method of attuning yourself to participant language, perspectives, and worldviews)

Second Cycle coding methods

1 Eclectic Coding (for refining your First Cycle choices)
2 Pattern Coding and/or Focused Coding (for categorization of your coded data as an initial analytic strategy)

New and hybrid coding schemes

Which coding method(s) is appropriate for your particular study? The 32 coding methods profiled in this manual are not the only ones available to you. For example, an elementary school reading teacher coded transcripts of her student's responses during literature discussion groups using Bloom's taxonomy of the cognitive domain – KNOWLEDGE, COMPREHENSION, APPLICATION, ANALYSIS, SYNTHESIS, and EVALUATION (Hubbard & Power, 1993, p. 79). One of my longitudinal case study's symbolic "volumes" and "tempos" of selected stages from his tumultuous adolescence were arts-based coded with musical dynamics (a form of Magnitude Coding) such as ADAGIO, MEZZO FORTE, ALLEGRETTO, and ANDANTE. You can develop new or hybrid coding methods or adapt existing schemes, customized to suit the unique needs and disciplinary concerns of your study. Templates are provided to document them after the First and Second Cycle coding methods have been profiled.

General criteria for coding decisions

Which coding method(s) is appropriate for your particular study? Flick (2009, p. 378) offers an excellent checklist for considering and selecting an analytic method to apply in a qualitative research study, which I have adapted below for purposes of this coding manual. Notice, though, that most of these criteria cannot be addressed until you have done some preliminary coding on a portion of your data. Thus, pilot test your initial choices with a few pages of field notes and/or interview transcripts. Also examine the recommended Applications in the methods profiles and Appendices A and B in this manual for options, guidance, and direction, but not as mandates, restrictions, or limitations. Glesne (2011) reassures researchers, "Learn to be content ... with your early, simple coding schemes, knowing that with use they will become appropriately complex" (p. 191). As a review and summary, here are the general principles and factors discussed thus far, plus additional criteria that may influence and affect your coding method(s) choice(s).

Foundation principles

- Because each qualitative study is unique, the analytic approach you use will be unique – which may or may not utilize coding.
- Some methodologists advise that your choice of coding method(s) and even a provisional list of codes should be determined beforehand (deductive) to harmonize with your study's conceptual framework, paradigm, or research goals. But emergent, data-driven (inductive) coding choices are also legitimate.
- If needed, you can develop new or hybrid coding methods or adapt existing schemes, customized to suit the unique needs and disciplinary concerns of your study.

Initial decision making

- Keep yourself open during initial data collection and review before determining which coding method(s) – if any – will be most appropriate and most likely to yield a substantive analysis.
- In lieu of mentorship, start with a combination of "generic" coding methods as a beginning approach to your data and analysis, but remain open to changing them if they are not generating substantive discoveries for you.
- If your goal is to develop new theory about a phenomenon or process, then classic or re-envisioned grounded theory and its accompanying coding methods (In Vivo, Process, Initial, Focused, Axial, and Theoretical Coding) are your recommended but not required options.
- Pilot test your coding choice(s) on a few pages of data to assess their possibilities.

Coding compatibility

- Carefully consider which coding method(s) may generate the types of answers you need, based on the forms of research questions you pose.
- Insure that the particular data forms (e.g., interview transcripts, participant observation field notes) lend themselves to the chosen coding method(s).
- Depending on the nature and goals of your study and forms of data, you may find that one coding method alone will suffice, or that two or more are needed to capture the complex processes or phenomena in your data.
- Be cautious of mixing incompatible methods; choose each one purposefully.
- Depending on the qualitative coding method(s) you employ, the choice may have numeric conversion and transformation possibilities for basic descriptive statistics or mixed methods studies.

- Coding methods choices may happen not just before but even during and after an initial review of the data corpus, based on emergent or new conceptual frameworks and methodological needs of the study.
- Explore variations of coding based on hunch-driven queries, triggered by nothing more than researcher curiosity to explore "what if… ?"
- Data are not coded – they're *re*coded. Be willing to change your method(s) if your initial choice(s) is not working.

Coding outcomes

- After an initial "breaking in" period has passed, you should feel more comfortable and confident applying the codes to your data.
- The analytic pathway should feel as if you are grasping specificity and complexity – not complication.
- As you are applying the coding method(s) to the data and writing analytic memos, you should feel as if you are making new discoveries, insights, and connections about your participants, their processes, and/or the phenomenon under investigation.

On overwhelming fear

One of the most frequent concerns from my own students when they begin their qualitative data analytic assignments is feeling overwhelmed by the vast array of coding methods from which to choose. And even though we have explored selected approaches and conducted in-class exercises with some depth, there is still that initial fear when they begin to code their own collected data by themselves. I acknowledge their "overwhelming fear," for I remember it quite well when I first coded my first day's set of field notes almost 20 years ago – wondering if I was doing it right and puzzled by the purpose of it all.

Like many first-time ventures with new ways of working, there is an initial anxiety that may lead to hesitation or, at worst, paralysis from starting the task. But do not let overwhelming fear stop you. Acknowledge that it is a common feeling among many novice (and even expert) researchers; you are not alone. Simply take qualitative data analysis one datum at a time. There may be a few bumps in the road here and there, but coding gets easier and goes faster as you continue to learn and practice this craft.

Overview of First Cycle Coding Methods

First Cycle coding methods are organized into seven broad subcategories, but remember that several of these individual methods overlap slightly and can be compatibly "mixed and matched" or Eclectically Coded for application in one particular study. For example, coding of an interview transcript might employ an amalgam of In Vivo, Initial, Emotion, Values, and Dramaturgical Coding. As another example, a single code can be both Descriptive *and* Holistic for qualitative metasynthesis (see Themeing the Data).

Grammatical Methods are techniques for enhancing the organization, nuances, and texture of qualitative data. *Elemental Methods* are foundation approaches to coding qualitative texts. *Affective Methods* investigate participant emotions, values, and other subjective qualities of human experience. *Literary and Language Methods* draw on aspects of written and oral communications for codes. *Exploratory Methods* are those that permit open-ended investigation, while *Procedural Methods* are, for lack of a better term, "standardized" ways to code data. The final section, *Themeing the Data*, acknowledges that extended passages of code in the form of sentences can also capture the essence and essentials of participant meanings.

The Coding Methods Profiles

Each coding method profiled in the manual is outlined as follows.

Sources

Credit is given here to those writers whose works provide information or inspiration for the coding method. The authors' titles can be found in the References section of the manual. A listing does not always mean that the source will contain further information about the particular coding procedure. In a few cases, a reference may have utilized or described the methodological foundations for a particular code without necessarily outlining procedures for applying it.

Description

A short description of the code and its function is provided. Somewhat complex coding methods will include an extended discussion for clarification. Also see Appendix A for a more condensed review of the method and its applications.

Applications

The general purpose and projected outcome of the coding method is briefly described here. A description of possible studies that might (not must) incorporate the coding method is also provided. These recommendations may include particular research methodologies (e.g., grounded theory, narrative inquiry), disciplines (e.g., education, communication), outcomes (e.g., generating a list of themes, learning about participant agency), and appropriateness (e.g., a coding method better suited for interview transcripts rather than field notes).

Example

Excerpts of varying length from field notes, interview transcripts, and documents provide material for coding demonstrations. All authentic data included were collected from independent or class research projects approved by my university's Institutional Review Board (which included participants' permission to publish collected data), previously published research, outdoor public observations, and public documents. Pseudonyms replace actual participant names, and the settings have been changed to protect participant confidentiality. A few examples are fictional data composed solely for illustrative purposes. The content ranges from the mundane to the explicit and covers a number of subject areas (e.g., teaching, human development, health care, workplace organization, interpersonal relationships). Most examples are deliberately brief and straightforward to assist with comprehension.

As you have seen thus far, codes are presented in capital letters toward the right-hand margin next to the data with superscript numbers linking the data excerpt to its specific code:

Driving west along the highway's access road and up Main St. to Wildpass Rd. there were [1] abandoned	[1] BUILDINGS
warehouse buildings in disrepair, [2] spray painted gang	[2] GRAFFITI
graffiti on walls of several occupied and unoccupied buildings. I passed a [3] Salvation Army Thrift Store,	[3] BUSINESSES
Napa Auto Parts store, a tire manufacturing plant, old houses in-between industrial sites, an auto glass store, Market/Liquors, Budget Tire, a check cashing service.	
[4] More spray paint was on the walls.	[4] GRAFFITI

This visual strategy is intended as an easy "at a glance" manual reference, but your own coding process does not have to follow this system. If you are working on hard copy (highly recommended for first-time and small-scale qualitative research projects), you can circle, underline, or highlight a passage of data and connect it with a line to your penciled code written in the margin. If you are using CAQDAS (highly recommended for large-scale or long-term qualitative research projects), employ its prescribed methods for selecting the text and type in or select from the evolving menu its accompanying code.

Keep in mind that no two qualitative researchers think and, most likely, code alike. Your ideas for codes may be different – even better – than the ones I present in the examples. It is all right if you interpret the data differently than me.

Analysis

Depending on the method, some examples merit a brief discussion of the consequent analysis after coding. This section presents the possible directions researchers might progress toward, recommendations for extended data analysis, and cautionary advice. Again, the cited Sources will provide a more thorough discussion of what follows the particular coding process.

A list of recommended – not mandated or all-inclusive – analytic and representational strategies for further consideration is included in this section, and suggests such modalities as: research genres (e.g., phenomenology, portraiture), analytic methods (e.g., frequency counts, content analysis), graphic representations (e.g., matrices, displays), next cycle coding processes, and others. The References will provide excellent detailed methods for enhancing your qualitative work. See Appendix B for a glossary of these analytic recommendations.

Notes

Concluding or supplemental comments about the coding method are provided in this section.

Grammatical Methods

Grammatical coding methods refer not to the grammar of language but to the basic grammatical principles of a technique.

Attribute Coding logs essential information about the data and demographic characteristics of the participants for future management and reference. Virtually all qualitative studies will employ some form of Attribute Coding.

Magnitude Coding applies alphanumeric or symbolic codes and/or subcodes to data, when needed, to describe their variable characteristics such as intensity or frequency. Magnitude Codes add adjectival or statistical texture to qualitative data and assist with mixed methods or quantitative studies.

Subcoding assigns a second-order tag after a primary code to detail or enrich the entry. The method is appropriate when general code entries will later require more extensive indexing, categorizing, and subcategorizing into hierarchies or taxonomies, or for nuanced qualitative data analysis.

Simultaneous Coding occurs when two or more codes are applied to or overlap with a qualitative datum to detail its complexity. CAQDAS lends itself well to this method since the programs can display and manage multiple code assignments simultaneously.

Attribute Coding
Sources

Bazeley, 2003; DeWalt & DeWalt, 2011; Gibbs, 2002; Lofland et al., 2006

Description

(Miles & Huberman (1994) and Richards (2009) refer to this type of coding grammar as "Descriptive Coding," but that term will be used in a different context in this manual. Also, Bogdan & Biklen (2007) classify this type of coding grammar as "Setting/Context Codes." Attribute Coding is chosen as the term for this manual to harmonize with CAQDAS language.)

Attribute Coding is the notation, usually at the beginning of a data set rather than embedded within it, of basic descriptive information such as: the fieldwork setting (e.g., school name, city, country), participant characteristics or demographics (e.g., age, gender, ethnicity, health status), data format (e.g., interview transcript, field note, document), time frame (e.g., 2010, May 2012, 8:00–10:00 a.m.), and other variables of interest for qualitative and some applications of quantitative analysis. CAQDAS programs enable you to enter Attribute Codes for data sets in related files.

Applications

Attribute Coding is appropriate for virtually all qualitative studies, but particularly for those with multiple participants and sites, and studies with a wide variety of data forms (e.g., interview transcripts, field notes, journals, documents, diaries, correspondence, artifacts, video). Altheide (1996, p. 28) prescribes documenting the generic attributes of media for analysis, such as a news story's medium (newspaper, magazine, Internet site, TV (live, video-tape, local, national), etc.), date of broadcast/ print, length of report, title, main topic, themes, and so on.

Attribute Coding is good qualitative data management and provides essential participant information and contexts for analysis and interpretation. Mason (1994) calls this process giving data various "addresses" for easy location within the corpus. Lofland et al. (2006) recommend that "folk/setting-specific" information be included as codes that identify the types of activities and behaviors that appear in the data set for future categorization and explorations of interrelationship.

Examples

Any data set might include the following sample Attribute Codes and descriptors for each participant in a standardized format established by the researcher:

PARTICIPANT (PSEUDONYM): BARRY
AGE: 18
GRADE LEVEL: 12
GPA: 3.84
GENDER: MALE
ETHNICITY: WHITE
SEXUAL ORIENTATION: HETEROSEXUAL

SOCIAL CLASS: LOWER-MIDDLE
RELIGION: METHODIST
DATA FORMAT: INTERVIEW 4 OF 5
TIME FRAME: MARCH 2011

A set of participant observation field notes might include these types of Attribute Codes:

PARTICIPANTS: 5th GRADE CHILDREN
DATA FORMAT: P.O. FIELD NOTES/SET 14 OF 22
SITE: WILSON ELEMENTARY SCHOOL, PLAYGROUND
DATE: 6 OCTOBER 2010
TIME: 11:45 a.m.–12:05 p.m.
ACTIVITIES INDEX [a list of the field notes' major contents]:
    RECESS
    BOYS PLAYING SOCCER
    BOYS ARGUING
    GIRLS IN CONVERSATION
    GIRLS PLAYING FOUR-SQUARE
    TEACHER MONITORING
    DISCIPLINE

Analysis

CAQDAS programs can maintain and link Attribute Codes (which in programming language may be called Attributes, Properties, Values, etc.) with data and provide the researcher with opportunities to query and compare First and Second Cycle coded data in tables and matrices by such demographic variables as age, grade level, gender, ethnicity, religion, geographic location, and others. Unanticipated patterns of interrelationship (i.e., correlation), influences and affects (i.e., causation), cultural themes, and longitudinal trends may emerge from the systematic investigation of data or even hunch-driven queries according to selected characteristic combinations of interest (Bazeley, 2003). Quantitative transformation of selected Attribute Codes is also possible to analyze them as nominal data and their possible correlations with other data sets (e.g., ATTRIBUTE ABSENT = 0, ATTRIBUTE PRESENT = 1; for gender coding, MALE = 1, FEMALE = 2).

Rubin and Rubin (2012) advise that seemingly mundane attribute references *within* the data themselves, such as dates, time frames, and the names of people and programs, can be coded as events or topical markers that may reveal organizational, hierarchical, or chronological flows from the data, especially if multiple participants with differing perspectives are involved.

Attribute Coding is intended as a *coding grammar*, a way of documenting descriptive "cover" information about participants, the site, and other related components of the study.

Some recommended ways to further analyze Attribute Codes are (see Appendix B):

- case studies (Merriam, 1998; Stake, 1995)
- content analysis (Krippendorff, 2003; Schreier, 2012; Weber, 1990; Wilkinson & Birmingham, 2003)
- cross-cultural content analysis (Bernard, 2011)
- frequency counts (LeCompte & Schensul, 1999)
- graph-theoretic techniques for semantic network analysis (Namey, Guest, Thairu, & Johnson, 2008)
- illustrative charts, matrices, diagrams (Miles & Huberman, 1994; Morgan, Fellows, & Guevara, 2008; Northcutt & McCoy, 2004; Paulston, 2000)
- longitudinal qualitative research (Giele & Elder, 1998; McLeod & Thomson, 2009; Saldaña, 2003, 2008)
- mixed-methods research (Creswell, 2009; Creswell & Plano Clark, 2011; Tashakkori & Teddlie, 2003)
- qualitative evaluation research (Patton, 2002, 2008)
- survey research (Fowler, 2001; Wilkinson & Birmingham, 2003)
- within-case and cross-case displays (Gibbs, 2007; Miles & Huberman, 1994; Shkedi, 2005)

Notes

Educational qualitative studies (e.g., Greig, Taylor, & MacKay, 2007) should make concerted efforts to separate and compare boys' and girls' data. For example, recent research in brain-based learning suggests marked differences between the ways children of both genders process information. Multicultural/multiethnic studies and projects in critical race theory should also separate and compare data gathered from participants of different racial/ethnic backgrounds. See Rebekah Nathan's (2005) ethnography, *My Freshman Year*, for an example of how Attribute Coding of university students by gender and ethnicity enabled her to observe how their on-campus dining patterns countered the school's goals of achieving "community and diversity" (pp. 61–6, 171–2).

Magnitude Coding

Sources

Miles & Huberman, 1994; Weston et al. 2001

Description

Magnitude Coding consists of and adds a supplemental alphanumeric or symbolic code or subcode to an existing coded datum or category to indicate its intensity, frequency, direction, presence, or evaluative content. Magnitude Codes can be qualitative, quantitative, and/or nominal indicators to enhance description.

Applications

Magnitude Coding is appropriate for descriptive qualitative studies that include basic statistical information such as frequencies or percentages, and qualitative studies in social science and health care disciplines that also support quantitative measures as evidence of outcomes.

Some methodologists object to combining qualitative and quantitative applications. Mixed-methods research, however, is a method gaining currency in qualitative inquiry (Creswell & Plano Clark, 2011; Tashakkori & Teddlie, 2003). Magnitude Coding is supplemental shorthand to add texture to codes, subcodes, and categories. Sometimes words say it best; sometimes numbers do; and sometimes both can work in concert to compose a richer answer and corroborate each other.

Examples

Magnitude Codes can consist of words or abbreviations that suggest intensity:

STRONGLY (STR)
MODERATELY (MOD)
NO OPINION (NO)

or words or abbreviations that suggest frequency:

OFTEN (O)
SOMEWHAT (S)
NOT AT ALL (N)

Magnitude Codes can consist of numbers in lieu of descriptive words to indicate intensity or frequency, as well as such continua as weight or importance:

3 = HIGH
2 = MEDIUM
1 = LOW
0 = NONE OR N/A
47 INSTANCES
16 EXCHANGES
87%

Fielding (2008) recommends that coding can suggest "direction" of a particular process, phenomenon, or concept:

POSITIVE SELF-IMAGE
NEGATIVE SELF-IMAGE

Magnitude Codes can also suggest direction through symbols representing conceptual ideas or opinions:

← = BACK TO BASICS EDUCATION
→ = PROGRESSIVE EDUCATIONAL CHANGE
↓ = MAINTAIN STATUS QUO IN THE SCHOOLS
↔ = MIXED RECOMMENDATIONS FOR EDUCATION

Magnitude Codes can apply symbols to indicate the presence or absence of something within a category:

+ = PRESENT
Ø = ABSENT
? = UNKNOWN OR UNCLEAR
Y = YES
N = NO
M = MAYBE

Magnitude Codes can consist of words or numbers that suggest evaluative content:

POS = POSITIVE
NEG = NEGATIVE
NEU = NEUTRAL
MIX = MIXED

In the example below, a patient describes the differences between and merits of his primary care and sleep medicine physicians. Descriptive Coding indicates the subjects he addresses about each of them, and the numeric ratings added afterward are the researcher's interpretation of the quality of care received. The rating system used for this example of Magnitude Coding is:

3 = HIGH QUALITY
2 = SATISFACTORY QUALITY
1 = LOW QUALITY
[blank] = NO EVALUATIVE COMMENT

Interview words and phrases that suggest and support the assigned ratings have been bolded for reference:

[1] Dr Lucas-Smith's office, she's my main doctor, is **very organized**, the receptionists are **friendly** and the nursing staff acts **very professionally**. [2] But Dr Johnson's office staff seems like interns **in training** – and *bad* ones, at that. Sometimes you feel like they **haven't got a clue** about what's going on, you know?

[1] DR LS STAFF: 3

[2] DR J STAFF: 1

Now, [3] Dr Lucas-Smith is a bit **cold**, maybe *too* "**professional**," but [4] she's relatively fresh out of med school so her **knowledge is state-of-the-art**. That's what **I like** about her: she was **able to clear up** two health problems of mine – a cyst under my left arm and a superficial blood clot on my leg – that previous doctors didn't know what to do about.

[3] DR LS DECORUM: 2
[4] DR LS EXPERTISE: 3

Dr Johnson is kind of old-school but [5] he **knows his stuff**. [6] My office visits with him are **OK** but [7] he does **so much small-talk** that I wanna tell him, "Just treat me so I can get outta here, I've already been waiting an hour for you."

[5] DR J EXPERTISE: 3
[6] DR J DECORUM: 2
[7] DR J WAIT TIME: 1

[8] With Dr Lucas-Smith, it's **efficient** – in and outta there, probably because she's so **popular** and has **lots of patients** she needs to see. You **don't feel rushed**, but you do feel like you're **there for a purpose**, so let's get to it.

[8] DR LS WAIT TIME: 3

Analysis

Magnitude Codes can be placed in a summary table or matrix for at-a-glance analysis (see Figure 3.2).

DR QUALITY:	DR LS	DR J
STAFF	3	1
DECORUM	2	2
EXPERTISE	3	3
WAIT TIME	3	1
TOTALS	11	7

Figure 3.2 Magnitude Codes in a summary table

CAQDAS programs and Microsoft Excel can generate selected statistics culled from Magnitude Codes. The MAXQDA program, for example, permits you to see the "weight" of a coded segment of text or a code itself in comparison to others, providing another measure of magnitude for analysis. Excel includes calculation functions for both descriptive and inferential statistics such as the mean, *t*-test, chi-square distributions, etc. And Wheeldon and Åhlberg (2012, pp. 138–42) offer the "salience score" as a mixed methods statistic for recording the frequency or presence of individual variables throughout data collection, ranging from 0 (not salient) to 9 (extremely salient).

Grounded theory coding methods recommend the search for a property's or category's *dimensions* such as intensity and frequency. Magnitude Coding can be used as subcodes during First Cycle stages to tentatively plot the ranges observed in the data for these dimensions. In the coding example above, the doctors' degrees of professionalism can range from 1 (low quality) to 3 (high quality). Later coding cycles will shift the emphasis away from specific people and onto abstract concepts. Thus, PROFESSIONALISM becomes the new coded property with its dimensions ranging from "low" to "high" or, using In Vivo Code language, from "OLD SCHOOL" to "STATE-OF-THE-ART."

Numbers and words, or quantities and qualities, can sometimes work in conjunction rather than opposition. There were occasions when I needed to visit an urgent care facility for health matters, and was asked by nurses during my initial examinations: "On a scale of *one* to *ten*, how much pain are you in, with *one* being 'none at all,' to *ten* being 'extremely agonizing' pain?" My self-reported number – a quantitative indicator – to the nurse, informed her of my perception of discomfort/quality with my body, and suggested to her the most appropriate action to take. The culturally constructed "1 to 10 scale" uses a finite range of numbers to express the magnitude of a quality. It is interesting to observe how most people, when a number such as "3" or "8" is uttered on a scale of 1 to 10, seem to share a tacit understanding about the inferred quality suggested by that number.

Magnitude Coding is intended as a *coding grammar*, a way of "quantitizing" and/or "qualitizing" a phenomenon's intensity, frequency, direction, presence, or evaluative content (Tashakkori & Teddlie, 1998). It is most often refinement or specification of a code during First Cycle coding methods but can also be applied during Second Cycle coding for assessing variability and dimensions of a code, subcode, or category.

Some recommended ways to further analyze Magnitude Codes are (see Appendix B):

- Hypothesis Coding and Pattern Coding
- assertion development (Erickson, 1986)
- content analysis (Krippendorff, 2003; Schreier, 2012; Weber, 1990; Wilkinson & Birmingham, 2003)
- data matrices for univariate, bivariate, and multivariate analysis (Bernard, 2011)
- descriptive statistical analysis (Bernard, 2011)
- frequency counts (LeCompte & Schensul, 1999)
- graph-theoretic techniques for semantic network analysis (Namey, Guest, Thairu, & Johnson, 2008)

- illustrative charts, matrices, diagrams (Miles & Huberman, 1994; Morgan, Fellows, & Guevara, 2008; Northcutt & McCoy, 2004; Paulston, 2000; Wheeldon & Åhlberg, 2012)
- longitudinal qualitative research (Giele & Elder, 1998; McLeod & Thomson, 2009; Saldaña, 2003, 2008)
- mixed methods research (Creswell, 2009; Creswell & Plano Clark, 2011; Tashakkori & Teddlie, 2003)
- qualitative evaluation research (Patton, 2002, 2008)
- quick ethnography (Handwerker, 2001)
- splitting, splicing, and linking data (Dey, 1993)
- survey research (Fowler, 2001; Wilkinson & Birmingham, 2003)
- within-case and cross-case displays (Gibbs, 2007; Miles & Huberman, 1994; Shkedi, 2005)

Notes

It is very difficult to sidestep quantitative representation and suggestions of magnitude in any qualitative research study. Phrases such as "*most* participants," "happened *often*," or "*extremely* important" appear *frequently* in our work. Such descriptors are not a liability, but instead an asset to enhance the "approximate accuracy" and texture of the prose.

Magnitude Codes can be applied to Values Codes, Emotion Codes, Hypothesis Codes, and Evaluation Codes that may contain continua of intensity, frequency, direction, presence, and/or evaluative content. Faherty (2010), for example, differentiates between the codes ANGER1 and ANGER2 as *mild* anger and *extreme* anger, respectively (p. 63).

Subcoding

Sources

Gibbs, 2007; Miles & Huberman, 1994

Description

(The methods literature uses various terms when referring to a primary code tagged with another: "embedded coding," "nested coding," "secondary coding," "joint coding," etc. Subcoding, as the most frequent term, will be used in this manual.)

A Subcode is a second-order tag assigned after a primary code to detail or enrich the entry, depending on the volume of data you have or specificity you may need for categorization and data analysis (Miles & Huberman, 1994, p. 61). Gibbs (2007) explains that the most general code is called the "parent" while its subcodes are the "children"; subcodes that share the same parent are "siblings" in a hierarchy (p. 74).

Applications

Subcoding is appropriate for virtually all qualitative studies, but particularly for ethnographies and content analyses, studies with multiple participants and sites, and studies with a wide variety of data forms (e.g., interview transcripts, field notes, journals, documents, diaries, correspondence, artifacts, video). Subcoding is also appropriate when general code entries will later require more extensive indexing, categorizing, and subcategorizing into hierarchies or taxonomies, for example, or for nuanced qualitative data analysis as a "splitter" rather than "lumper."

Subcoding could be employed after an initial yet general coding scheme has been applied (such as Holistic Coding) and the researcher realizes that the classification scheme may have been too broad. For example, data first coded as SCHOOLS could be later subcoded into SCHOOLS-CLASSROOMS, SCHOOLS-PLAYGROUNDS, SCHOOLS-CAFETERIAS, SCHOOLS-FRONT OFFICES, etc. Subcodes might also be added to primary codes if the analyst has noticed particular emergent qualities or interrelationships such as: SCHOOLS-FAILING, SCHOOLS-BUSINESSLIKE, SCHOOLS-AUTONOMOUS, SCHOOLS-A+.

Example

An ethnographer's field notes describe an inner city, lower-income neighborhood in a large metropolitan area. The italicized "*OC*" sections in these notes are Observer's Comments (Bogdan & Biklen, 2007, pp. 163–4), subjective impressions or memos embedded within the factual description, which also merit consideration for codes and subcodes. Major things for observation thus far have included RESIDENTS, BUSINESSES, and GRAFFITI, but this portion of notes focuses on HOUSES (a simple Descriptive Code which functions as the parent code) with attached subcodes (children) that detail the primary code:

[1] Some houses, because of their disrepair, look abandoned. But the things seen through the window and in the yard clue you that someone still lives there.	[1] HOUSES-DISREPAIR
[2] One house has a picture portrait of Jesus and a cross on its front wall. I notice TV antennas on several roofs.	[2] HOUSES-DÉCOR
OC: [3] *No cable TV – a luxury; can't afford it; not a priority.*	[3] HOUSES-ECONOMICS
[4] Laundry hangs in the back yards of several homes on a clothesline.	[4] HOUSES-YARDS
[5] There's a house with a small statue of the Virgin Mary in front, [6] "Beware of the Dog/*Perro*" signs.	[5] HOUSES-DÉCOR [6] HOUSES-SECURITY

⁷ Desk chairs, worn upholstered furniture are
in the front yards of some homes.

⁷ HOUSES-YARDS

OC: ⁸ *It's all we've got.*

⁸ HOUSES-ECONOMICS

Analysis

Later data retrieval will collect everything coded with HOUSES into a general category, and more specific subcategories can be composed with the subcodes. Thus, everything subcoded with YARDS will be reassembled into one bin, DÉCOR into another, etc. These contents may be organized even further, if needed, to enable more fine-grained analysis of the data corpus. The subcodes for data coded HOUSES might be collected and ordered thusly, which could even serve as an outline for a written ethnographic account of the topic (see Descriptive Coding):

I. HOUSES

    A. ECONOMICS

        1. YEARS BUILT
        2. DISREPAIR
        3. AVAILABLE UTILITIES

    B. DÉCOR

        1. OUTDOOR SURFACES
        2. ART WORK
        3. RELIGIOUS ARTIFACTS

    C. YARDS

        1. FRONT YARDS
        2. SIDE AND BACK YARDS

    D. SECURITY

        1. FENCES AND GATES
        2. SIGNAGE
        3. DOGS

Subcoding is intended as a *coding grammar*, a way of initially detailing and organizing data into preliminary categories, subcategories, hierarchies, taxonomies, and indexes. Some recommended ways to further analyze Subcodes are (see Appendix B):

- content analysis (Krippendorff, 2003; Schreier, 2012; Weber, 1990; Wilkinson & Birmingham, 2003)
- cross-cultural content analysis (Bernard, 2011)
- descriptive statistical analysis (Bernard, 2011)

- domain and taxonomic analysis (Schensul et al., 1999b; Spradley, 1979, 1980)
- frequency counts (LeCompte & Schensul, 1999)
- interrelationship (Saldaña, 2003)
- qualitative evaluation research (Patton, 2002, 2008)
- splitting, splicing, and linking data (Dey, 1993)
- within-case and cross-case displays (Gibbs, 2007; Miles & Huberman, 1994; Shkedi, 2005)

Notes

Use subcoding only when detailed data analysis or indexing is necessary. It may be confounding for first-time ventures of manual (hard-copy) coding, but very easy for CAQDAS programs to log and later retrieve. For additional examples of Subcoding, see the profiles for Magnitude, Initial, Evaluation, Protocol, Domain and Taxonomic, and Longitudinal Coding. See Code Landscaping in Chapter Four for a method of manually organizing codes, subcodes, and sub-subcodes into categories based on frequency.

Subcoding differs from Simultaneous Coding. A Subcode relates directly to its primary code (e.g., HOUSES-DISREPAIR), while Simultaneous Codes – two or more significant codes assigned to the same datum – may differ in inferential meaning (e.g., HOUSES and POVERTY).

Simultaneous Coding

Source

Miles & Huberman, 1994

Description

(The methods literature uses various terms when referring to two or more codes applied to the same passage or sequential passages of text: "simultaneous coding," "double coding," "co-occurrence coding," "multiple coding," "overlap coding," "subcoding," "embedded coding," "nested coding," etc. Simultaneous Coding, as the simpler term, will be used in this manual.)

Simultaneous Coding is the application of two or more different codes to a single qualitative datum, or the overlapped occurrence of two or more codes applied to sequential units of qualitative data.

Applications

Simultaneous Coding is appropriate when the data's content suggests multiple meanings that necessitate and justify more than one code since complex "social interaction does not occur in neat, isolated units" (Glesne, 2011, p. 192). Miles and Huberman (1994) advise that simultaneous coding "is warranted if a segment is both descriptively and inferentially meaningful" (p. 66). Be aware that some may attribute indecisiveness on the researcher's part if Simultaneous Coding is used excessively. This may also suggest that there is no clear or focused research purpose and thus a clear lens and filter for analyzing the data. If Simultaneous Coding is used, justify the rationale for its use.

Examples

A public school teacher is interviewed on how holding an advanced graduate degree affects her salary. Her MFA (Master of Fine Arts) required 30 more credit hours than an MA (Master of Arts), yet the district does not acknowledge the legitimacy of her degree. In this first example, note how *the entire unit* merits two codes because the researcher perceives two separate issues at work within the teacher's story. Another code is applied later that refers to the "cultural shock and adaptation" processes employed for the study's conceptual framework. This code *overlaps* with the two major unit codes:

I: Did completing your MFA degree affect your pay scale or status of employment?

NANCY: [1a & 1b] Not one bit. But I fought. I wrote a couple of letters to the district human resources director explaining that I have an MFA which is 60 credit hours, and they stipulated an *MA* degree for a pay raise. And my degree was like getting 30 more credit hours of schooling which would be the "Master's plus 24," which is the next pay line. And we went over it and over it and she wouldn't give me the extra pay raise. And then I explained that I have 96 graduate credit hours now, so I have far above the 30 credit hours for a master's, and they still wouldn't give it to me. And so it's kind of a moot issue, they just won't do it.

[1a] INEQUITY
[1b] SCHOOL DISTRICT BUREAUCRACY

I: Are you going to continue to pursue it or just …

NANCY: [2] No, I'm going to let it be because I know I won't win like that, you know? I just know it. Um, so I'm just gonna drop it and I probably won't reach the "Master's plus 24" while I'm here because that's like a whole 'nother degree for me. So I'll just stick to what I'm at right now.

[2] ACCULTURATION

As a second example from field notes, a school fundraising event is described. The *entire unit* is assigned the descriptive Process Code FUNDRAISING, but within this unit there are four separate yet related Process Codes that identify the actions at work. These could be perceived in this particular example as *nested codes* within the primary *hierarchical code*:

Today is Valentine's Day and flowers can be seen carried by students and teachers through the hallways. Nancy is dressed in a red sweater top, blue jean shorts, and red glittered earrings.

[1] At 8:00 a.m. I enter Nancy's classroom. A very large cardboard box and two plastic tubs with carnations are by the platform. Nancy tells a student, "Aren't they pretty this year? They're prettier than last year." The flowers cost $150 and the goal is to make $150 profit on them. Nancy drove to a mall floral shop yesterday to get them.	[1] FUNDRAISING
[1a] She tells three girls who take flowers to sell, "OK, one dollar apiece, guys. And I don't have any change, guys. [1b] We're gonna have so much fun today." The girls leave with the flowers. Nancy goes into the hall and says to a student, [1c] "Hey Mike, how are you? … They're gonna sell them in the cafeteria. … Yeah, they're in there now."	[1a] DELEGATING [1b] MOTIVATING [1c] PROMOTING
[1d] Two junior high students come in and look at the flowers. Boy: "Do you want one, Elena?" Elena: "Yeah." Boy: "What color?" Elena: "Red." The Boy gives Nancy a dollar, waves the flower above Elena's head and says laughingly, "Here, here!"	[1d] TRANSACTING

Analysis

The first example above displays a case that occasionally occurs in qualitative data when the richness or complexity of an event or participant's story makes it difficult for a researcher to assign only one major code to the datum. And if the researcher's focus for the study includes several areas of interest, and if a single datum captures or illustrates points related to more than one of those areas, Simultaneous Coding can be applied. The method can also serve as a means of investigating interrelationship. If passages coded INEQUITY are consistently coupled with such codes as SCHOOL DISTRICT BUREAUCRACY, STAFF AUTHORITY, PRINCIPAL'S LEADERSHIP, and ACCULTURATION, emergent patterns can be explored and tested.

The second example (FUNDRAISING) shows how a particular coded phenomenon or process can be broken down into its constituent elements through Simultaneous Coding. Such detail work can support and lead to Process Coding, Domain and Taxonomic Coding, or Causation Coding. This type of coding may also help you see both "the bigger picture" and "the trees in the forest" at work in the data.

Logistically, Simultaneous Coding should be used sparingly if there are massive amounts of data and especially if they will be coded manually. CAQDAS programs are better equipped to manage extensive Simultaneous Coding (Bazeley, 2007, pp. 71–3; Lewins & Silver, 2007, p. 11). Van de Ven and Poole (1995) transformed coded qualitative data into quantitative dichotomous variables for longitudinal statistical analysis, but they first layered a "track" of up to five different codes for a single key incident across time. Qualitative codes on this track consisted of such items as the people involved with the incident, their relationships within their organization, and an assessment of their outcomes. The coding was not only simultaneous, but also *multi-dimensional*. CAQDAS programs such as NVivo can apply multiple codes to the same passage of text, which later enables the computer to process "intersections" – the generation of associations, links, and matrices (Bazeley, 2007).

Simultaneous Coding is intended as a *coding grammar*, a way of applying multiple codes and/or coding methods, if and when needed, to complex passages of qualitative data.

Some recommended ways to further analyze Simultaneous Codes are (see Appendix B):

- content analysis (Krippendorff, 2003; Schreier, 2012; Weber, 1990; Wilkinson & Birmingham, 2003)
- graph-theoretic techniques for semantic network analysis (Namey et al., 2008)
- illustrative charts, matrices, diagrams (Miles & Huberman, 1994; Morgan et al., 2008; Northcutt & McCoy, 2004; Paulston, 2000; Wheeldon & Åhlberg, 2012)
- interrelationship (Saldaña, 2003)
- situational analysis (Clarke, 2005)
- splitting, splicing, and linking data (Dey, 1993)

Notes

Simultaneous Coding differs from the process of Subcoding. A Subcode relates directly to its primary code (e.g., HOUSES-DISREPAIR), while Simultaneous Codes may differ in assigned meaning (e.g., HOUSES and POVERTY).

Elemental Methods

Elemental coding methods are primary approaches to qualitative data analysis. They have basic but focused filters for reviewing the corpus and they build a foundation for future coding cycles.

Structural Coding applies a content-based or conceptual phrase representing a topic of inquiry to a segment of data to both code and categorize the data corpus. Structural Codes are generally foundation work for further detailed coding.

Descriptive Coding assigns basic labels to data to provide an inventory of their topics. Many qualitative studies employ Descriptive Codes as a first step in data analysis.

In Vivo Coding and Process Coding are foundation methods for grounded theory, though they are applicable to other analytic approaches. In Vivo Coding draws from the participant's own language for codes. Process Coding uses gerunds exclusively for codes. These techniques are employed in other grounded theory methods: Initial, Focused, Axial, and Theoretical Coding.

Initial Coding is the first major stage of a grounded theory approach to the data. The method is truly open-ended for a researcher's first review of the corpus, and can incorporate In Vivo and Process Coding.

Structural Coding

Sources

Guest et al., 2012; MacQueen et al., 2008; Namey et al., 2008

Description

(A colloquial term for this method is "Utilitarian Coding," referring to its categorization functions. In this manual, Structural Coding will be the term used since its Sources have labeled it as such.)

Structural Coding applies a content-based or conceptual phrase representing a topic of inquiry to a segment of data that relates to a specific research question used to frame the interview (MacQueen et al., 2008, p. 124). The similarly coded segments are then collected together for more detailed coding and analysis.

Applications

Structural Coding is appropriate for virtually all qualitative studies, but particularly for those employing multiple participants, standardized or semi-structured data-gathering protocols, hypothesis testing, or exploratory investigations to gather topics lists or indexes of major categories or themes.

Structural Coding is a question-based code that "acts as a labeling and indexing device, allowing researchers to quickly access data likely to be relevant to a particular analysis from a larger data set" (Namey et al., 2008, p. 141). Structural Coding both codes and initially categorizes the data corpus to examine comparable segments' commonalities, differences, and relationships. The Sources suggest that Structural Coding is perhaps more suitable for interview transcripts than other data such as researcher-generated field notes, but open-ended survey responses are also appropriate with this method.

Example

A mixed methods study is conducted to survey and interview participants who currently smoke about their habit. One particular area of inquiry focuses on the smokers' past cessation attempts (if any) to investigate their choices of techniques and their success and/or non-success with them.

In the example below, an interviewer asks a middle-aged adult male about his smoking history and habits. Note how these segments of data are preceded by the particular research question from the study, followed by its related Structural Code. Since Structural Coding does not rely on margined entries, the examples will scan across the entire page. Note that the participant's responses and the interviewer's questions, probes, and follow-ups are included in the coded segments:

Research Question: What types of smoking cessation techniques (if any) have participants attempted in the past?

Structural Code: [1] UNSUCCESSFUL SMOKING CESSATION TECHNIQUES

> [1] I: Have you ever tried to quit smoking?
>
> PARTICIPANT: Yeah, several times.
>
> I: Were any of them successful?
>
> PARTICIPANT: Only for a short while. Then I started back up again.
>
> I: What kinds of stop-smoking techniques have you tried in the past?
>
> PARTICIPANT: The nicotine lozenges seemed to work best, and I was doing pretty well on those for about two or three weeks. But then life stuff got in the way and the work stress was too much so I started smoking again.
>
> I: What other techniques have you tried?
>
> PARTICIPANT: A long time ago I tried cold turkey. I just kept myself busy doing stuff around the house to keep my mind off of smoking. But then my car got broken into a couple of days later and the window got busted, so the stress just got to me and I started smoking again.
>
> I: Are there any other ways you've tried to stop smoking?
>
> PARTICIPANT: Mm. *(pause)* No. Those were my only two attempts. Both of them failed, though.

Research Question: What factors lead to participants' unsuccessful smoking cessation attempts?

Structural Code: [2] REASONS FOR UNSUCCESSFUL SMOKING CESSATION

> [2] I: You said that "stress got to" you as a reason to start smoking again.
>
> PARTICIPANT: Yeah, and not, it wasn't the stress of not smoking that got to me, it was life stress – the car break-in, work – it just got to be too much for me and I broke down and needed a cigarette, *really* needed one.
>
> I: What was it about work that made you want to smoke again?
>
> PARTICIPANT: There was a lot of responsibility and expectations riding on me. I was worried that, well, at that time I was worried that things weren't going to turn out the way they needed to, whether I would have enough

personnel, deadlines to meet, just too much stress. And I knew this was coming so maybe I just picked the wrong time to quit.

I: And what is "life stuff"? *(PARTICIPANT chuckles)* What does that –

PARTICIPANT: Life stuff – laundry, ironing, grocery shopping, uh, feeding the cats, cleaning their litter boxes, running around to do this and that with barely any time to do it.

I: I can relate to that. Now, when you went "cold turkey," how did you cope? …

Analysis

"Structural Coding generally results in the identification of large segments of text on broad topics; these segments can then form the basis for an in-depth analysis within or across topics" (MacQueen et al., 2008, p. 125). The coding method can be kept at a basic level by applying it as a categorization technique for further qualitative data analysis. But depending on the research study's goals, quantitative applications are also possible.

Namey et al. (2008) "suggest determining frequencies on the basis of the number of individual participants who mention a particular theme, rather than the total number of times a theme appears in the text. … [A] code frequency report can help identify which themes, ideas, or domains were common and which rarely occurred" (p. 143). In the study profiled above, other participants' similarly coded interview segments would be collected together, then further coded and/or subcoded to extract data related to the specific research questions. UNSUCCESSFUL SMOKING CESSATION TECHNIQUES for this particular group might include such coded items and their frequency counts in descending order as:

Technique	Number of Participants	
PRESCRIPTION MEDICATION	19	
"COLD TURKEY"	8	
Keep Busy		3
Thoughts of Saving Money		2
Exercise		2
Try Not to Think About It		1
NICOTINE PATCHES	8	
SUPPORT NETWORK	6	
Friends		4
Partner/Spouse		2
NICOTINE GUM	5	
NICOTINE LOZENGES	4	
GRADUAL WITHDRAWAL	4	
COUNSELING	2	
HYPNOSIS	1	
AVERSION THERAPY	1	

An "at a glance" scan of the above data would suggest that the category **Counseling Intervention** (COUNSELING, HYPNOSIS, AVERSION THERAPY) was the least used technique with this particular group, with PRESCRIPTION MEDICATION as the most frequent **Medicinal Intervention**. Graph-theoretic data reduction techniques, "also referred to as semantic network analyses, may be used to identify complex semantic relationships in bodies of texts" through tables and matrices (Namey et al., 2008, p. 146). The data in this study can be analyzed by gender, for example, to investigate any differences between men's and women's choices of smoking cessation measures. Advanced statistical techniques such as hierarchical clustering and multi-dimensional scaling can identify associations, co-occurrence, distance and proximity, dimension, and other quantitative aspects of qualitative data. In the example above, **Nicotine Substitutes** (PATCHES, GUM, LOZENGES) might statistically associate in hierarchical clustering analysis. CAQDAS programs and their transfer of converted data to quantitative software programs are indispensable for such analytic work.

Quantitative follow-up, however, is not always necessary. Other qualitative methods, such as thematic analysis and grounded theory, are also applicable with structurally coded data.

Some recommended ways to further analyze Structural Codes are (see Appendix B):

- First Cycle coding methods
- content analysis (Krippendorff, 2003; Schreier, 2012; Weber, 1990; Wilkinson & Birmingham, 2003)
- frequency counts (LeCompte & Schensul, 1999)
- graph-theoretic techniques for semantic network analysis (Namey et al., 2008)
- illustrative charts, matrices, diagrams (Miles & Huberman, 1994; Morgan et al., 2008; Northcutt & McCoy, 2004; Paulston, 2000; Wheeldon & Åhlberg, 2012)
- interrelationship (Saldaña, 2003)
- quick ethnography (Handwerker, 2001)
- splitting, splicing, and linking data (Dey, 1993)
- survey research (Fowler, 2001; Wilkinson & Birmingham, 2003)
- thematic analysis (Auerbach & Silverstein, 2003; Boyatzis, 1998; Smith & Osborn, 2008)
- within-case and cross-case displays (Gibbs, 2007; Miles & Huberman, 1994; Shkedi, 2005)

Notes

Structural Coding is an analytic cousin of Holistic Coding. The latter, however, is more exploratory and even tentative in nature, while the former is framed and driven by a specific research question and topic.

Descriptive Coding

Sources

Miles & Huberman, 1994; Saldaña, 2003; Wolcott, 1994

Description

(This method is also called "topic coding" in some of the literature, but Descriptive Coding will be used in this manual to align with Wolcott's terminology.)

Descriptive Coding summarizes in a word or short phrase – most often as a noun – the basic topic of a passage of qualitative data. To clarify, Tesch (1990) differentiates that "it is important that these [codes] are identifications of the *topic*, not abbreviations of the *content*. The topic is what is talked or written *about*. The content is the substance of the message" (p. 119).

Applications

Descriptive Coding is appropriate for virtually all qualitative studies, but particularly for beginning qualitative researchers learning how to code data, ethnographies, and studies with a wide variety of data forms (e.g., interview transcripts, field notes, journals, documents, diaries, correspondence, artifacts, video).

Many ethnographic studies usually begin with such general questions as "What is going on here?" and such reflective questions as "What is this a study about?" Descriptive Coding is just one approach to analyzing the data's basic topics to assist with answering these types of questions. Turner (1994) calls this cycle the development of a "basic vocabulary" of data to form "bread and butter" categories for further analytic work (p. 199). Description is the foundation for qualitative inquiry, and its primary goal is to assist the reader to see what you saw and to hear what you heard in general (Wolcott, 1994, pp. 55, 412), rather than scrutinize the nuances of people in social action. Descriptive Codes from data collected across various time periods and charted in matrices are essential for assessing longitudinal participant change (Saldaña, 2003, 2008). The coding method is also appropriate for documenting and analyzing the material products and physical environments of ethnographic fieldwork (Hammersley & Atkinson, 2007, pp. 121–39).

Example

An ethnographer walks through an inner city, lower-income neighborhood in a large metropolitan area and takes field notes describing the setting. The field notes are written descriptively – that is, factually and objectively as much as possible. The italicized *"OC"* sections interspersed throughout are Observer's Comments (Bogdan & Biklen, 2007, pp. 163–4), subjective impressions or memos embedded within the factual description, which also merit consideration for codes. Note how several Descriptive Codes repeat as the topics shift:

Driving west along the highway's access road and up Main St. to Wildpass Rd. there were [1] abandoned warehouse buildings in disrepair, [2] spray painted gang graffiti on walls of several occupied and unoccupied buildings. I passed a [3] Salvation Army Thrift Store,	[1] BUILDINGS [2] GRAFFITI [3] BUSINESSES

Napa Auto Parts store, a tire manufacturing plant, old houses in-between industrial sites, an auto glass store, Market/Liquors, Budget Tire, a check cashing service. [4] More spray paint was on the walls.

[4] GRAFFITI

OC: [5] *There seems to be an abundance of car-oriented businesses in the neighborhood. Industrial looking atmosphere – no "showroom" qualities. Here is where "repair" is more important than sales.*

[5] BUSINESSES

I parked on Turquoise Rd. and walked along the periphery of an elementary school lot. [6] The majority of the homes had dirt front yards; the only vegetation growing were weeds. Maybe one house per block had what would be called a lawn. The majority seem unattended, not cared for. The homes look like they were built in the 1930s, 1940s at the latest. [7] I saw spray paint on the "No Trespassing" sign of the elementary school and smaller gang symbols on it. [8] A beer bottle and beer can were against the fence of the school. [9] Surfaces on the houses vary – maybe one per block looks fairly well painted. The majority are peeling in paint, rotted wood, various materials (wood, stucco, tin) on the same house.

[6] HOUSES

[7] GRAFFITI

[8] TRASH
[9] HOUSES

OC: *Priorities, energies, financial resources do not go into the appearance of homes. There are more important things to worry about.*

[10] I notice that the grand majority of homes have chain link fences in front of them. There are many dogs (mostly German shepherds) with signs on fences that say "Beware of the Dog."

[10] SECURITY

OC: *There's an attempt to keep things at home safe. Protection from robbers, protection of property. Keep your distance – this is mine.*

Analysis

Descriptive Coding leads primarily to a categorized inventory, tabular account, summary, or index of the data's contents. It is essential groundwork for Second Cycle coding and further analysis and interpretation (Wolcott, 1994, p. 55). In the example above, all qualitative data passages coded with HOUSES, for example, would be extracted from the main body of field notes and reassembled together in a separate file for an organized and categorized narrative portrait of the environment for further analysis:

> Priorities, energies, and financial resources of this neighborhood's residents do not go into the appearance of their homes (there are more important things to worry about).

Houses appear to have been built in the 1930s through 1940s. I notice TV antennas (rather than cable) on several roofs. Surfaces on the houses vary. Maybe one per block looks fairly well painted. But the majority's exteriors have peeling paint, rotting wood, and an assembly of wood, stucco, and tin on the same house. Some, because of their disrepair, look unattended and abandoned. But look in the yards and inside the homes through their windows: people still live here.

Laundry hangs on clotheslines in the back yards of several homes. The majority have dirt front yards where the only vegetation growing is weeds. Maybe one house per block has what would be called a lawn; other front yards contain desk chairs and worn upholstered furniture. There's a house with a small statue of the Virgin Mary in front. Another house has a picture portrait of Jesus and a cross on its front wall.

Berger (2009), Clarke (2005), and Hammersley and Atkinson (2007) emphasize that fieldwork and field notes should place particular importance on interpreting the meanings of artifacts and physical environments of our social worlds. Everything from maintenance to design of homes, businesses, schools, recreation areas, streets, and so forth is inference laden. A home is not merely a structure but "a site of symbolic ordering … a physical embodiment of [its residents'] identity," biography, and values (Hammersley & Atkinson, 2007, p. 136). Descriptive Coding is one approach to documenting from rich field notes the tangible products that participants create, handle, work with, and experience on a daily basis.

Some recommended ways to further analyze Descriptive Codes are (see Appendix B):

- Subcoding, Hypothesis Coding, Domain and Taxonomic Coding, Pattern Coding, and Focused Coding
- content analysis (Krippendorff, 2003; Schreier, 2012; Weber, 1990; Wilkinson & Birmingham, 2003)
- cross-cultural content analysis (Bernard, 2011)
- domain and taxonomic analysis (Schensul et al., 1999b; Spradley, 1979, 1980)
- frequency counts (LeCompte & Schensul, 1999)
- graph-theoretic techniques for semantic network analysis (Namey et al., 2008)
- grounded theory (Bryant & Charmaz, 2007; Charmaz, 2006; Corbin & Strauss, 2008; Glaser & Strauss, 1967; Stern & Porr, 2011; Strauss & Corbin, 1998)
- mixed methods research (Creswell, 2009; Creswell & Plano Clark, 2011; Tashakkori & Teddlie, 2003)
- qualitative evaluation research (Patton, 2002, 2008)
- quick ethnography (Handwerker, 2001)
- thematic analysis (Auerbach & Silverstein, 2003; Boyatzis, 1998; Smith & Osborn, 2008)
- within-case and cross-case displays (Gibbs, 2007; Miles & Huberman, 1994; Shkedi, 2005)

Notes

Descriptive Coding is a straightforward method for novices to qualitative research, particularly for those first using CAQDAS programs. The method categorizes data at a basic level to provide the researcher with an organizational grasp of the study. Coding with simple descriptive nouns alone, however, may not enable more complex and theoretical analyses as the study progresses.

In Vivo Coding

Sources

Charmaz, 2006; Corbin & Strauss, 2008; Glaser, 1978; Glaser & Strauss, 1967; Strauss, 1987; Strauss & Corbin, 1998

Description

(In Vivo Coding has also been labeled "literal coding," "verbatim coding," "inductive coding," "indigenous coding," and "emic coding" in selected methods literature. In this manual, In Vivo Coding will be used since it is the most well-known label.)

In vivo's root meaning is "in that which is alive," and as a code refers to a word or short phrase from the actual language found in the qualitative data record, "the terms used by [participants] themselves" (Strauss, 1987, p. 33).

Folk or indigenous terms are participant-generated words from members of a particular culture, subculture, or microculture. Folk terms indicate the existence of the group's cultural categories (McCurdy, Spradley, & Shandy, 2005, p. 26). For example, some homeless youth say that they "sp'ange" (ask passers-by for "spare change"). In Vivo Coding a subculture's unique vocabulary or argot is one method of extracting these indigenous terms (and refer to Domain and Taxonomic Coding for more specific categorization guidelines).

Applications

In Vivo Coding is appropriate for virtually all qualitative studies, but particularly for beginning qualitative researchers learning how to code data, and studies that prioritize and honor the participant's voice. In Vivo Coding is one of the methods to employ during grounded theory's Initial Coding but can be used with several other coding methods in this manual.

In Vivo Coding is particularly useful in educational ethnographies with youth. The child and adolescent voices are often marginalized, and coding with their actual words enhances and deepens an adult's understanding of their cultures and worldviews. In Vivo Coding is also quite applicable to action and practitioner research (Coghlan & Brannick, 2010; Fox, Martin, & Green, 2007; Stringer, 1999) since one of the genre's primary goals is to frame the facilitator's interpretations of terms "that participants use in their everyday lives, rather than in terms derived from the academic disciplines or professional practices" (Stringer, 1999, p. 91).

Example

An adult female interviewer talks to Tiffany, a 16-year-old teenage girl, about her friendships at high school. Note how all In Vivo Codes are placed in quotation marks, and how virtually each line of data gets its own code:

I [1] hated school last year.	[1] "HATED SCHOOL"
[2] Freshman year, it was awful,	[2] "FRESHMAN YEAR AWFUL"
I hated it. And [3] this year's a lot better	[3] "THIS YEAR'S BETTER"
actually. Um, I [4] don't know why. I	[4] "DON'T KNOW WHY"
guess, over the summer I kind of	
[5] stopped caring about what other	[5] "STOPPED CARING"
people thought and I don't know.	
It's [6] hard to explain. I [7] found stuff out	[6] "HARD TO EXPLAIN"
about myself, and so I went back, and	[7] "FOUND STUFF OUT"
all of a sudden I found out that when	
I [8] wasn't trying so hard to [9] have people like	[8] "WASN'T TRYING SO HARD"
me and to do [10] what other people wanted,	[9] "HAVE PEOPLE LIKE ME"
people [11] liked me more. It was [12] kind of	[10] "WHAT OTHER PEOPLE WANTED"
strange. Instead of [13] trying to please	[11] "LIKED ME MORE"
them all the time, they liked me more	[12] "KIND OF STRANGE"
when I [14] wasn't trying as hard. And,	[13] "TRYING TO PLEASE THEM"
I don't know, like every-, everybody might,	[14] "WASN'T TRYING AS HARD"
um, people who are just, kind of, [15] friends	[15] "FRIENDS GOT CLOSER"
got closer to me. And people who didn't	
really know me [16] tried to get to know me.	[16] "TRIED TO KNOW ME"
[17] I don't know.	[17] "I DON'T KNOW"

Analysis

As you read interview transcripts or other documents that feature participant voices, attune yourself to words and phrases that seem to call for bolding, underlining, italicizing, highlighting, or vocal emphasis if spoken aloud. Their salience may be attributed to such features as impacting nouns, action-oriented verbs, evocative word choices, clever or ironic phrases, similes and metaphors, etc. If the same words, phrases, or variations thereof are used often by the participant (such as "I don't know" in the example above), and seem to merit an In Vivo Code, apply it. In Vivo Codes "can provide a crucial check on whether you have grasped what is significant" to the participant, and may help "crystallize and condense meanings" (Charmaz, 2006, p. 57).

Thus, keep track of codes that are participant inspired rather than researcher generated by always putting In Vivo Codes in quotation marks: "HATED SCHOOL".

Key writers of grounded theory advocate meticulous work and that an In Vivo (or other) Code should appear next to every line of data. Depending on your goals, In Vivo Codes can be applied with less frequency, such as one word or phrase for every three to five sentences. In the interview excerpt above, rather than 17 In Vivo Codes I could have limited the number to 4:

I hated school last year. [1] Freshman year,   [1] "FRESHMAN YEAR AWFUL"
it was awful, I hated it. And this year's
a lot better actually. Um, I don't know why.
I guess, over the summer I kind of stopped caring
about what other people thought and
cared more about, just, I don't know. It's hard to
explain. I [2] found stuff out about myself, and so I   [2] "FOUND STUFF OUT"
went back, and all of a sudden I found out that
when I [3] wasn't trying so hard to have people   [3] "WASN'T TRYING SO HARD"
like me and to do what other people wanted,
people liked me more. It was kind of strange.
Instead of trying to please them all the time,
they liked me more when I wasn't trying as hard.
And, I don't know, like every-, everybody
might, um, people who are just, kind of, [4] friends   [4] "FRIENDS GOT CLOSER"
got closer to me. And people who didn't really
know me tried to get to know me. I don't know.

But do not infer that there is a fixed rule or formula for an average number of codes per page or a recommended ratio of codes to text. Trust your instincts with In Vivo Coding. When something in the data appears to stand out, apply it as a code. Researcher reflection through analytic memo writing, coupled with Second Cycle coding, will condense the number of In Vivo Codes and provide a reanalysis of your initial work. Strauss (1987, p. 160) also recommends that researchers examine In Vivo Codes not just as themes but as possible *dimensions* of categories – that is, the continuum or range of a property.

Remember that memos are a critical component of grounded theory's coding processes, and *memo writing also serves as a code- and category-generating method*. An analytic memo excerpt based on the coding example above reads as follows (and note that In Vivo Codes and participant quotes are included throughout):

25 May 2011
CODE: "I DON'T KNOW"
    Tiffany is genuinely puzzled ("DON'T KNOW WHY", "HARD TO EXPLAIN") by a paradox of sustaining quality friendships: "when I wasn't trying so hard to have people like me and to do what other people wanted, people liked me more." At

age 16, she is learning "about myself" – who she is and wants to become, rather than what others want or expect from her. Just as there is documented and developmental *emotional ambivalence* in middle childhood, perhaps adolescence has its equivalent stage called SOCIAL AMBIVALENCE, concurrent with the individual's IDENTITY WORK.

In Vivo Codes capture "behaviors or processes which will explain to the analyst how the basic problem of the actors is resolved or processed" (Strauss, 1987, p. 33) and "help us to preserve participants' meanings of their views and actions in the coding itself" (Charmaz, 2006, p. 55).

In Vivo Codes can also provide imagery, symbols, and metaphors for rich category, theme, and concept development, plus evocative content for arts-based interpretations of the data. Using some of Tiffany's own language, a poetic reconstruction (called "found poetry" or "poetic transcription") of the above vignette's codes and transcript excerpts might read:

Freshman year:
   awful,
   hated school. ...
Over the summer:
   stopped caring about what others thought,
   found stuff out about myself. ...
This year's better:
   friends got closer,
   tried to know me,
   liked me more. ...
Don't know why:
   kind of strange,
   hard to explain. ...
This year's better. (Saldaña, 2011b, p. 129)

Playwright and verbatim theatre performer Anna Deavere Smith purports that people speak in "organic poems" through everyday discourse. Thus, In Vivo Coding is one strategy for getting at the organic poetry inherent in a participant.

In Vivo Codes could be used as the sole coding method for the First Cycle of data analysis, and the sole method of choice for small-scale studies, but that may limit the researcher's perspective on the data, a perspective that can contribute to more conceptual and theoretical views about the phenomenon or process. Sometimes the participant says it best; sometimes the researcher does. Be prepared and willing to mix and match coding methods as you proceed with data analysis.

CAQDAS programs such as NVivo, MAXQDA, and ATLAS.ti make In Vivo Coding easy by permitting the analyst to select a word or small phrase from the data, clicking a dedicated icon, and assigning the selected text *as* an In Vivo Code. But be aware that some CAQDAS functions will retrieve multiple text units only if they share the *exact* same code you have applied to them. In Vivo Coded data most often are so unique that they will require careful review and self-categorization into an NVivo node, for example. Also, selected CAQDAS programs may not permit the use of quotation marks to accompany and indicate an In Vivo Code entry. Thus, find an alternative format for the code (e.g., all CAPS) in lieu of quotation marks, if necessary.

Some recommended ways to further analyze In Vivo Codes are (see Appendix B):

- Second Cycle coding methods
- action and practitioner research (Altrichter, Posch, & Somekh, 1993; Coghlan & Brannick, 2010; Fox, Martin, & Green, 2007; Stringer, 1999)
- case studies (Merriam, 1998; Stake, 1995)
- discourse analysis (Gee, 2011; Rapley, 2007; Willig, 2008)
- domain and taxonomic analysis (Schensul et al., 1999b; Spradley, 1979, 1980)
- frequency counts (LeCompte & Schensul, 1999)
- grounded theory (Bryant & Charmaz, 2007; Charmaz, 2006; Corbin & Strauss, 2008; Glaser & Strauss, 1967; Stern & Porr, 2011; Strauss & Corbin, 1998)
- interactive qualitative analysis (Northcutt & McCoy, 2004)
- memo writing about the codes/themes (Charmaz, 2006; Corbin & Strauss, 2008; Glaser, 1978; Glaser & Strauss, 1967; Strauss, 1987)
- metaphoric analysis (Coffey & Atkinson, 1996; Todd & Harrison, 2008)
- narrative inquiry and analysis (Clandinin & Connelly, 2000; Coffey & Atkinson, 1996; Cortazzi, 1993; Coulter & Smith, 2009; Daiute & Lightfoot, 2004; Holstein & Gubrium, 2012; Murray, 2003; Riessman, 2008)
- phenomenology (Butler-Kisber, 2010; Giorgi & Giorgi, 2003; Smith, Flowers, & Larkin, 2009; van Manen, 1990; Wertz et al., 2011)
- poetic and dramatic writing (Denzin, 1997, 2003; Glesne, 2011; Knowles & Cole, 2008; Leavy, 2009; Saldaña, 2005a, 2011a)
- polyvocal analysis (Hatch, 2002)
- portraiture (Lawrence-Lightfoot & Davis, 1997)
- qualitative evaluation research (Patton, 2002, 2008)
- thematic analysis (Auerbach & Silverstein, 2003; Boyatzis, 1998; Smith & Osborn, 2008)

Notes

Researchers new to coding qualitative data often find In Vivo Coding a safe and secure method with which to begin. But be wary of overdependence on the strategy because it can limit your ability to transcend to more conceptual and theoretical levels of analysis and insight.

See Carolyn Lunsford Mears' (2009) outstanding book on interviewing and transcript analysis, *Interviewing for Education and Social Science Research: The Gateway*

Approach, which extracts and arranges the essentialized verbatim texts of participants into poetic mosaics.

Process Coding

Sources

Bogdan & Biklen, 2007; Charmaz, 2002, 2008; Corbin & Strauss, 2008; Strauss & Corbin, 1998

Description

(Process Coding has also been labeled "action coding" in selected methods literature. In this manual, Process Coding will be used since it implies broader concepts.)

Process Coding uses gerunds ("-ing" words) exclusively to connote action in the data (Charmaz, 2002). Simple observable activity (e.g., reading, playing, watching TV, drinking coffee) and more general conceptual action (e.g., struggling, negotiating, surviving, adapting) can be coded as such through a Process Code. The processes of human action can be "strategic, routine, random, novel, automatic, and/or thoughtful" (Corbin & Strauss, 2008, p. 247). Processes also imply actions intertwined with the dynamics of time, such as those things that emerge, change, occur in particular sequences, or become strategically implemented through time (Hennink, Hutter, & Bailey, 2011, p. 253; Saldaña, 2003).

Applications

Process Coding is appropriate for virtually all qualitative studies, but particularly for those that search for "ongoing action/interaction/emotion taken in response to situations, or problems, often with the purpose of reaching a goal or handling a problem" (Corbin & Strauss, 2008, pp. 96–7). Processes are also embedded within "psychological concepts such as prejudice, identity, memory [and] trust" because these are things "people do rather than something people *have*" (Willig, 2008, p. 164). For grounded theory, Process Coding happens simultaneously with Initial Coding, Focused Coding, and Axial Coding, and a search for *consequences* of action/interaction is also part of the process. *Sub*processes are usually "the individual tactics, strategies, and routine actions that make up the larger act" (Strauss & Corbin, 1998, p. 169).

Like In Vivo Coding, Process Coding is not necessarily a specific method that should be used as the sole coding approach to data, though it can be with small-scale projects.

Example

An adult female interviewer talks to a teenage girl about rumors. Note how the codes are all gerund based (and note that the interviewer's questions and responses are not coded – just the participant's responses):

TIFFANY: Well, [1] that's one problem, that [my school is] pretty small, so [2] if you say one thing to one person, [3] and then they decide to tell two people, [4] then those two people tell two people, and [5] in one period everybody else knows. [6] Everybody in the entire school knows that you said whatever it was. So … .

[1] PROBLEMIZING SCHOOL SIZE
[2] SAYING ONE THING
[3] TELLING OTHERS
[4] TELLING OTHERS
[5] EVERYBODY KNOWING
[6] KNOWING WHAT YOU SAID

I: Have you ever had rumors spread about you?

TIFFANY: Yeah, [7] it's just stupid stuff, completely outlandish things, too. [8] I, I don't really want to repeat them.

[7] REJECTING RUMORS
[8] NOT REPEATING WHAT WAS SAID

I: That's OK, you don't have to.

TIFFANY: [9] They were really, they were ridiculous. [10] And the worst thing about rumors, [11] I don't really care if people think that, because obviously they're pretty stupid to think that in the first place. But [12] the thing I care about is, like, last year, especially freshman year, was a really horrible year school-wise. And, [13] I guess it was good in a way that you find out who your real friends are, because [14] some of them turned on me and [15] then started to say that those things were true and, like, [16] then people thought, "Well that person's her friend, so they must know." And so, [17] it just made the entire thing worse. And [18] you really learn a lot about people and, uh, and [19] who your real friends are. LuAnn's [20] probably the only person who's really stuck by me this entire time, and [21] just laughed at whatever they said.

[9] REJECTING RIDICULOUSNESS
[10] CRITICIZING RUMORS
[11] NOT CARING WHAT PEOPLE THINK
[12] REMEMBERING A HORRIBLE YEAR
[13] FINDING OUT WHO YOUR REAL FRIENDS ARE
[14] TURNING ON YOU
[15] SAYING THINGS ARE TRUE
[16] ASSUMING BY OTHERS
[17] MAKING THINGS WORSE
[18] LEARNING A LOT ABOUT PEOPLE
[19] LEARNING WHO YOUR FRIENDS ARE
[20] STICKING BY FRIENDS
[21] LAUGHING AT WHAT OTHERS SAY

Analysis

Charmaz (2008) wisely observes that "When you have studied a process, your categories will reflect its phases [or stages]" (p. 106). The conventions of storyline are used in analytic memo writing when reviewing data for process – for example, the first step, the turning point, the second step, the third step, subsequently, thus, and so on. Participant language with transitional indicators such as "if," "when," "because," "then," "and so," etc., clue the researcher to a sequence or process in action. These sequences or processes can be ordered as a numeric series of actions, listed as a bullet-pointed set of outcomes, or graphically represented with first-draft illustrations as a flow diagram. Simple examples based on the interview above include:

Narrative – Spreading Rumors:

1 [I]f you say one thing to one person,
2 and then they decide to tell two people,
3 then those two people tell two people,
4 and in one period everybody else knows.

Coded Process – Spreading Rumors:

1 SAYING ONE THING
2 TELLING OTHERS
3 TELLING OTHERS
4 EVERYBODY KNOWING

See Figure 3.3 for an illustrated process of spreading rumors.

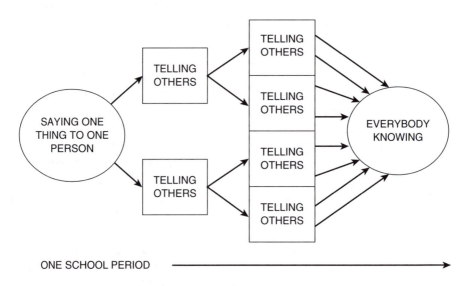

Figure 3.3 An illustrated process for spreading rumors

Consequences of Rumors [the Process Codes that led to the outcomes are listed for reference]:

False accusations (SAYING THINGS ARE TRUE, ASSUMING BY OTHERS)

Confrontation (TURNING ON YOU)

Hurt feelings (MAKING THINGS WORSE, CRITICIZING RUMORS)

Bad memories (NOT REPEATING WHAT WAS SAID, REMEMBERING A HORRIBLE YEAR)

Reinforcement of loyalties (FINDING OUT WHO YOUR REAL FRIENDS ARE, LEARNING WHO YOUR FRIENDS ARE, STICKING BY FRIENDS)

Social awareness (LEARNING A LOT ABOUT PEOPLE)

"High road" personal growth (REJECTING RUMORS, REJECTING RIDICULOUSNESS, CRITICIZING RUMORS, NOT CARING WHAT PEOPLE THINK, LAUGHING AT WHAT OTHERS SAY)

Bernard and Ryan (2010, pp. 131–2) recommend charting participant process in a horizontal matrix, so that the first cell describes the *historic context*, followed by the *triggers* that initiate the *main event*. Next, the *immediate reaction* is outlined, concluding with the *long-term consequences*.

Researcher reflection through analytic memo writing, coupled with Second Cycle coding, will condense the number of Process Codes and provide a reanalysis of your initial work. Dey (1993) encourages consideration of the complex interplay of factors that compose a process and how we can "obtain a sense of how events originate and evolve, and their shifting significance for those involved. Process refers to movement and change over time. In place of a static description, we can develop a more dynamic account of events" (p. 38). CAQDAS program linking functions enable you to mark the trail of participant process throughout the data corpus. Refer to the Analytic Storylining section in Chapter Six for process-oriented vocabulary to employ in analytic memos and write-ups.

Some recommended ways to further analyze Process Codes are (see Appendix B):

- Causation Coding
- Second Cycle coding methods
- action and practitioner research (Altrichter, Posch, & Somekh, 1993; Coghlan & Brannick, 2010; Fox, Martin, & Green, 2007; Stringer, 1999)
- case studies (Merriam, 1998; Stake, 1995)
- cognitive mapping (Miles & Huberman, 1994; Northcutt & McCoy, 2004)
- decision modeling (Bernard, 2011)
- discourse analysis (Gee, 2011; Rapley, 2007; Willig, 2008)
- grounded theory (Bryant & Charmaz, 2007; Charmaz, 2006; Corbin & Strauss, 2008; Glaser & Strauss, 1967; Stern & Porr, 2011; Strauss & Corbin, 1998)
- illustrative charts, matrices, diagrams (Miles & Huberman, 1994; Morgan et al., 2008; Northcutt & McCoy, 2004; Paulston, 2000; Wheeldon & Åhlberg, 2012)
- logic models (Knowlton & Phillips, 2009; Yin, 2009)

- memo writing about the codes/themes (Charmaz, 2006; Corbin & Strauss, 2008; Glaser, 1978; Glaser & Strauss, 1967; Strauss, 1987)
- splitting, splicing, and linking data (Dey, 1993)
- thematic analysis (Auerbach & Silverstein, 2003; Boyatzis, 1998; Smith & Osborn, 2008)
- vignette writing (Erickson, 1986; Graue & Walsh, 1998)

Notes

To appreciate the breadth and depth of Corbin and Strauss's (2008) discussion of Process Coding, readers are referred to their book, *Basics of Qualitative Research*, for a full explanation and thorough examples of memo writing that capture process, and how micro- and macro-levels of analysis can be projected onto the data.

Also refer to Dramaturgical Coding for a comparable approach to analyzing a participant's tactics and strategies, and Causation and Longitudinal Coding for links between phases, stages, and cycles of process and action.

Initial Coding

Sources

Charmaz, 2006; Corbin & Strauss, 2008; Glaser, 1978; Glaser & Strauss, 1967; Strauss, 1987; Strauss & Corbin, 1998

Description

(Earlier publications in grounded theory refer to Initial Coding as "Open Coding." Charmaz's (2006) term will be used in this manual since it implies an initiating procedural step in harmony with First Cycle coding processes.)

Initial Coding is breaking down qualitative data into discrete parts, closely examining them, and comparing them for similarities and differences (Strauss & Corbin, 1998, p. 102). The goal of Initial Coding, particularly for grounded theory studies, is "to remain open to all possible theoretical directions indicated by your readings of the data" (Charmaz, 2006, p. 46). It is an opportunity for you as a researcher to reflect deeply on the contents and nuances of your data and to begin taking ownership of them. Initial Coding is not necessarily a specific formulaic method. It is a First Cycle, open-ended approach to coding the data with some recommended general guidelines.

Initial Coding can employ In Vivo Coding or Process Coding, for example, or other selected methods profiled in this manual. At times you may notice that elements of a possible or developing category are contained within the data. If so, code them during the initial cycle.

Applications

Initial Coding is appropriate for virtually all qualitative studies, but particularly for beginning qualitative researchers learning how to code data, ethnographies, and studies with a wide variety of data forms (e.g., interview transcripts, field notes, journals, documents, diaries, correspondence, artifacts, video).

Initial Coding is intended as a starting point to provide the researcher with analytic leads for further exploration and "to see the direction in which to take [this] study" (Glaser, 1978, p. 56). But Clarke (2005) recommends a period of "digesting and reflecting" on the data before beginning Initial Coding ventures (p. 84). All proposed codes during this cycle are tentative and provisional. Some codes may be reworded as analysis progresses. The task can also alert the researcher that more data are needed to support and build an emerging theory.

Charmaz (2006) advises that detailed, line-by-line Initial Coding (as it is outlined below) is perhaps more suitable for interview transcripts than for researcher-generated field notes. But Clarke (2005), in her postmodern approach to grounded theory, stresses the need to examine the non-human material elements of our social world that *will* be found in field notes and artifacts. She also prescribes that for initial visual discourse/materials analysis, coding is not important but interpreting and analytic memo writing are critical. It is thus the memos themselves – the researcher's narratives – that are coded for further analysis.

Example

An adult female interviewer asks a 16-year-old girl about her social friendships (note that the interviewer's questions, responses, and comments are not coded – just the participant's responses). It is not required during Initial Coding, but since one of the eventual goals of grounded theory is to formulate categories from codes, I occasionally include not only a Process Code (e.g., LABELING), but also subcode it with specific referents (e.g., LABELING: "GEEKY PEOPLE"; LABELING: "JOCKS"). These referents may or may not later evolve into categories, dimensions, or properties of the data as analysis continues:

[I: Last week you were talking about the snobby girls at lunchroom. And then you just were talking about that you didn't like some people because they were cliquish. So what kind of, who are your friends? Like, what kind of people do you hang out with?]

TIFFANY: [1] I hang out with everyone. Really, [2] I choose. Because I've been [living] here for so long, you get,

[1] "HANGING OUT WITH EVERYONE"
[2] "CHOOSING" WHO YOU HANG OUT WITH

[3] I can look back to kindergarten, and at some point I was [4] best friends with everybody who's been here, [5] practically.

[I: You mean in choir?]

TIFFANY: [6] Almost everybody in my grade. No, in school. And so there are [7] certain people that I've just been [8] friends with since forever. And then it's [9] not fair of me to stereotype either, like, say, "Oh well, like, the [10] really super popular pretty girls are all mean and [11] they're all snobby and they all talk about each other," [12] 'cause they don't. Some of them, some of them don't. And [13] those are the ones I'm friends, friends with. And then there are the, there are the [14] geeky people. [15] Some of them though, the geeks at our school, aren't like harmless geeks. They're like [16] strange-psycho-killer-geek-people-who-draw-swastikas-on-their-backpacks [17] kind of geeks.

[I: So are they like Colorado … ?]

TIFFANY: Yeah, [18] some of them are kind of, it's really scary. [19] But then again [20] there's not the complete stereotype. Some of the, [21] not all of them are completely, like, wanna kill all the popular people. So, [22] I'm friends with those people. And then the [23] jocks, [24] not all of the guys are idiots, so [25] I'm friends with the ones who can carry on a conversation.

[I: (laughs) So, so you wouldn't put yourself in any of the …]

TIFFANY: [26] I'm friends with someone because of who they are, [27] not because of what group they, they hang out in basically. 'Cause I think [28] that's really stupid to be, like, [29] "What would people think if they saw me walking with this

[3] RECALLING FRIENDSHIPS
[4] "BEST FRIENDS WITH EVERYBODY"
[5] QUALIFYING: "PRACTICALLY"

[6] QUALIFYING: "ALMOST"
[7] FRIENDS WITH "CERTAIN PEOPLE"
[8] FRIENDS WITH "SINCE FOREVER"
[9] "NOT FAIR TO STEREOTYPE"
[10] LABELING: "REALLY SUPER POPULAR PRETTY GIRLS"
[11] IDENTIFYING STEREOTYPES
[12] DISPELLING STEREOTYPES
[13] CHOOSING FRIENDS: "SUPER POPULAR PRETTY GIRLS"
[14] LABELING: "GEEKY PEOPLE"
[15] QUALIFYING: "SOME OF THEM"
[16] LABELING: "STRANGE-PSYCHO-KILLER-GEEK"
[17] QUALIFYING: "KIND OF"

[18] QUALIFYING: "SOME OF THEM"
[19] QUALIFYING: "BUT THEN…"
[20] DISPELLING STEREOTYPES
[21] QUALIFYING: "NOT ALL OF THEM"
[22] CHOOSING FRIENDS: "GEEKS"
[23] LABELING: "JOCKS"
[24] DISPELLING STEREOTYPES
[25] CHOOSING FRIENDS: JOCKS "WHO CAN CARRY ON A CONVERSATION"

[26] CRITERIA FOR FRIENDSHIP: "WHO THEY ARE"
[27] CRITERIA FOR FRIENDSHIP: NOT GROUP MEMBERSHIP
[28] ETHICS OF FRIENDSHIP

person?" or something.

[I: So you wouldn't define yourself with any specific group?]

TIFFANY: [30] No.

[I: Do you think anyone else would define you as ...]

TIFFANY: I think people, [31] people define me as popular. Mainly because I would rather hang out with someone who's [32] good hearted but a little slow, compared to someone [33] very smart but very evil (chuckle).

[29] NOT CONCERNED WITH WHAT OTHERS THINK

[30] MAINTAINING INDIVIDUALITY

[31] DEFINING SELF THROUGH OTHERS: "POPULAR"
[32] CRITERIA FOR FRIENDSHIP: "GOOD HEARTED BUT SLOW"
[33] CRITERIA FOR FRIENDSHIP: NOT THOSE "VERY SMART BUT VERY EVIL"

Analysis

Though you are advised to code quickly and spontaneously, pay meticulous attention to the rich dynamics of data through line-by-line coding – a "microanalysis" of the corpus (Strauss & Corbin, 1998, p. 57) or what is colloquially referred to as data "splitting." Selected writers of grounded theory acknowledge that such detailed coding is not always necessary, so sentence-by-sentence or even paragraph-by-paragraph coding is permissible depending on your research goals and analytic work ethic. Codes in parentheses or accompanied with question marks can be part of the process for analytic follow-up or memo writing and recoding.

One major facet of Initial Coding to grounded theory methodologists is the search for *processes* – participant actions that have antecedents, causes, consequences, and a sense of temporality. CHOOSING FRIENDS and DISPELLING STEREOTYPES (the "-ing" codes) are two such active processes culled from Initial Coding in the example above that may or may not be developed further during Second Cycle coding.

Also during this or later cycles of grounded theory coding, there will be a search for the *properties* and *dimensions* of categories – conceptual ideas that bring together similarly coded and related passages of data. In the example above, the process of CHOOSING FRIENDS has the categories GEEKS and JOCKS, each with selected properties or CRITERIA FOR FRIENDSHIP – for example, JOCKS "WHO CAN CARRY ON A CONVERSATION". These categories and their properties may or may not be developed further during Second Cycle coding.

A personal debriefing or "reality check" by the researcher is critical during and after the initial coding of qualitative data, thus an analytic memo is written to reflect on the process thus far. Notice that *memo writing also serves as a code- and category-generating method*. Since range and variance are "givens" when looking at a property's dimensions, reflect on why the range and variance are there to begin with. An analytic memo excerpt based on the coding example above reads:

30 May 2011
CODE: DISCRIMINATING

   Adolescence seems to be a time of contradictions, especially when it comes to choosing your friends. Tiffany is aware of the cliques, their attributed labels, and their accompanying stereotypes at school. Though she herself labels a group in broad terms ("super popular pretty girls," "geeks," "jocks"), she acknowledges that there are subcategories within the group and exceptions to the stereotypes. Though she states she chooses friends for "who they are" and does not care what others think of her for the friends she "hangs out" with, she has explicit criteria for who from the stereotyped group she's friends with. She thinks others define her as "popular" and, as such, is aware of the stereotypical attributes from others that come with being part of that group. Her language is peppered with qualifiers: "some of them," "not all of them," "kind of," "practically," "almost," etc. Developmentally, as an adolescent she seems right on target for *discriminating* – DISCRIMINATING cognitively the exceptions to stereotypes, while being SOCIALLY DISCRIMINATE about her own friendships.

Strauss and Corbin (1998) advise that at least 10 interviews or observations with detailed coding are necessary for building a grounded theory (p. 281), but other methodologists have recommended a minimum of 20, 30, or 40 separate interviews. Though the First Cycle process is labeled "initial" or "open," suggesting a wide variance of possibilities, Glaser (1978) recommends that the codes developed at this stage somehow relate to each other (p. 57). Strauss and Corbin (1998) also recommend that a separate list of all emerging codes be kept as analysis continues to help the researcher visualize the work in progress and to avoid duplication. CAQDAS code lists will help immensely with this.

Some recommended ways to further analyze Initial Codes are (see Appendix B):

- Second Cycle coding methods, particularly Focused Coding and Axial Coding
- grounded theory (Bryant & Charmaz, 2007; Charmaz, 2006; Corbin & Strauss, 2008; Glaser & Strauss, 1967; Stern & Porr, 2011; Strauss & Corbin, 1998)
- memo writing about the codes/themes (Charmaz, 2006; Corbin & Strauss, 2008; Glaser, 1978; Glaser & Strauss, 1967; Strauss, 1987)
- situational analysis (Clarke, 2005)
- thematic analysis (Auerbach & Silverstein, 2003; Boyatzis, 1998; Smith & Osborn, 2008)

Notes

Initial Coding can range from the descriptive to the conceptual to the theoretical, depending on what you observe in and infer from the data, and depending on your personal knowledge and experiences you bring to your reading of the phenomena – "experiential data" that should be integrated into your analytic memo writing, yet not the central focus of it.

For a closely aligned First to Second Cycle method, see Eclectic Coding in Chapter Four.

Affective Methods

Affective coding methods investigate subjective qualities of human experience (e.g., emotions, values, conflicts, judgments) by directly acknowledging and naming those experiences. Some researchers may perceive these methods as lacking objectivity or rigor for social science inquiry. But affective qualities are core motives for human action, reaction, and interaction and should not be discounted from our investigations of the human condition.

Emotion Coding and Values Coding tap into the inner cognitive systems of participants. Emotion Coding, quite simply, labels the feelings participants may have experienced. Values Coding assesses a participant's integrated value, attitude, and belief systems at work.

Versus Coding acknowledges that humans are frequently in conflict, and the codes identify which individuals, groups, or systems are struggling for power. Critical studies lend themselves to Versus Codes.

Evaluation Coding focuses on how we can analyze data that judge the merit and worth of programs and policies.

Emotion Coding

Sources

Goleman, 1995; Prus, 1996

Description

Emotion Codes label the emotions recalled and/or experienced by the participant, or inferred by the researcher about the participant. Goleman (1995) defines an emotion as "a feeling and its distinctive thoughts, psychological and biological states, and range of propensities to act" (p. 289).

Applications

Emotion Coding is appropriate for virtually all qualitative studies, but particularly for those that explore intrapersonal and interpersonal participant experiences and actions.

Since emotions are a universal human experience, our acknowledgement of them in our research provides deep insight into the participants' perspectives, worldviews, and life conditions. Virtually everything we do has an accompanying emotion(s): "One can't separate emotion from action; they are part of the same flow of events, one leading into the other" (Corbin & Strauss, 2008, p. 7). Your abilities to read non-verbal cues, to infer underlying affects, and to sympathize and empathize with your participants, are critical for Emotion Coding. Kozinets (2010) reinforces that we should attend to the "non-rational" and emotional lives of both participants and ourselves. Ethnographic accounts become richer by "keeping emotions in the foreground of field notes and cultural interactions, by not depriviliging feeling in favour of reason, and by not enforcing an orderly and 'objective' categorization scheme upon lived cultural experience" (p. 168).

Example

An older female in an interview about her pets shares a recent story about one of her cat's illnesses. The Emotion Codes are a combination of In Vivo Codes and emotional states and reactions. Also note that the transcript has been partitioned into units or stanzas (see Chapter One) since that will play a role in its analysis. The coder's choices were based not just on the written transcript's contents, but also on inferences from the recording's vocal nuances and field notes that documented what emotions were witnessed/recalled during the interview itself:

[1] When I first learned that my cat had diabetes, I felt like I was in this surrealistic dream. The news was given to me over the phone by my vet, and it was said with compassion but urgency, and [2] I was in a whirlwind. I had to give them info on my pharmacy so they could call in an order for insulin and syringes. [3] I remember asking the assistant, "Do you mean a human pharmacy or an animal pharmacy?"	[1] "SURREALISTIC DREAM" [2] "WHIRLWIND" [3] CONFUSION
[4] I also asked the vet about the costs associated with it, the cat's longevity, and what came next. I made an appointment so I could learn how to administer insulin shots to my cat. [5] That scared the hell out of me. I've never given shots before, and [6] the thought of hurting my cat or, even worse, doing it wrong and hurting him was tearing me apart. [7] I was trying to keep a brave face for, in front of the vet, and [8] it wasn't as hard as I thought it would be.	[4] FOREBODING [5] "SCARED" [6] "TEARING ME APART" [7] "BRAVE FACE" [8] FEAR DISPELLED

9 So, the first three days were just tension, tension, tension, making sure I was filling the syringe right, giving it to him correctly, making sure there was no bad reactions to the medication. 10 He took them well – his name's Duncan, by the way – took them like nothing's wrong. 11 I was trying to be clinical about it so I could ease some of the tension, but it became routine by the third day. 12 He's doing fine, same as he always was, 13 but I always keep that possibility that in, in the back of my head that he could react badly.

9 "TENSION"

10 MILD SURPRISE

11 DETACHMENT

12 RELIEF
13 DOUBT

14 (long pause; eyes become watery)
[I: That's OK. I'm a cat person, too.]
15 God, this is so hard. They're just like kids, you know?

14 MILD CRYING

15 PARENTAL
CONCERN-LOVE

Analysis

Hundreds of words exist to describe human emotion, and thus the repertoire of potential codes is vast. But what the English language contributes in diversity and accuracy can also become a source of frustration for the researcher attempting to find just the right word to describe, and thus code, a participant's emotional experiences. The participant is also challenged in emotional recall because *some* "affective experiences are fleeting and not available to [accurate] introspection once the feeling has dissipated" (Schwarz, Kahneman, & Xu, 2009, p. 159).

One analytic strategy with Emotion Codes is to track the *emotional journey* or *storyline* of the codes – the structural arc they follow as certain events unfold. From the example above, each stanza's codes are clustered together and consist of:

- First Stanza: "SURREALISTIC DREAM", "WHIRLWIND", CONFUSION
- Second Stanza: FOREBODING, "SCARED", "TEARING ME APART", "BRAVE FACE", FEAR DISPELLED
- Third Stanza: "TENSION", MILD SURPRISE, DETACHMENT, RELIEF, DOUBT
- Fourth Stanza: MILD CRYING, PARENTAL CONCERN-LOVE

Analytic memoing explores what each stanza's Emotion Codes have in common, or what emotional story-within-a-stanza is observed as the entire vignette is analyzed:

11 June 2011
PATTERNS: THE EMOTIONAL JOURNEY WITH A PET'S ILLNESS

The affection this woman has toward her pet is comparable to PARENTAL LOVE ("They're just like kids, you know?"). So when an owner first receives bad news about a pet's major illness – specifically, a diagnosis of diabetes – reality seems suspended as CONFUSION scatters her thoughts. A sense of FOREBODING generates FEAR as consultation with a veterinarian is made to review new medical treatments. The client, though, may be hiding her true feelings about the matter as a coping mechanism.

A sustained period of TENSION follows (layered, perhaps, with a tint of denial) as the owner adjusts to new caretaking and health maintenance responsibilities with her pet. Throughout this negative journey are a few optimistic peaks or niches when one realizes – indeed, is SURPRISED – when things are easier than you thought they'd be, and go smoother than you thought they would. And though adaptation may eventually lead to a new routine and a sense of RELIEF, lingering DOUBT about the pet's continued health remains. I've heard that CRYING is "nature's reset button" for humans. Maybe CRYING is not a downer but a necessary peak to reach occasionally during ongoing TENSION so you can purge the bad out of you and move on.

Overall, this experience is not the proverbial "roller coaster" of emotions – for this participant, it's more like a tense ride through the unknowns of a haunted house.

When the phenomenon is fairly complex (such as treatment for cancer), highly contextual (such as experiencing a divorce), or occurs across a relatively lengthy time period (such as one's personal university education experiences), Emotion Codes could be subcoded or categorized in such a way that permits the analyst to discern which emotion(s) occurs with which specific period or experience – for example: Which emotions are present during the decision to divorce? Which emotions are present during child custody hearings? Which emotions are present during the signing of legal paperwork related to divorce? In this case, an Emotion Code could be preceded by (or Simultaneously Coded with) a Descriptive or Process Code to place the emotional experience in context:

DECISION TO DIVORCE – PERSONAL FAILURE
CUSTODY HEARING – HATRED
SIGNING PAPERS – REVENGEFUL

Dobbert and Kurth-Schai (1992) also alert researchers to the possible variation and intensity of a single emotion (p. 139). A revengeful or retaliatory action, for example, could be conducted coolly, spitefully, or maliciously. If nuance is critical for the analysis, consider subcoding the primary emotion further or applying Magnitude Coding. Also acknowledge that emotional states are very complex, and single experiences can include multiple or conflicting emotions. Thus, Simultaneous Coding and/or Versus Coding (e.g., MOURNING VS. RELIEF) can be used concurrently with Emotion Coding. And since emotional responses are intricately woven with our value, attitude, and belief systems, Values Coding also becomes a critical concurrent method.

If an ANGER, ANGRY, MAD, or comparable Emotion Code is present, be aware that anger is a consequential emotion and that a triggering emotion precedes it, such as EMBARRASSMENT, ANXIETY, or SHAME. "Anger results from a demeaning offense against the self, guilt from transgressing a moral imperative, and hope from facing the worst but yearning for better" (Salovey, Detweiler-Bedell, Detweiler-Bedell, & Mayer, 2008, p. 537). During data collection, explore the participant emotions before anger, and scan your data during analysis when an ANGER code is present to determine the triggering emotion and its appropriate code. CAQDAS will enable you to link this emotional trail of data. Though it may be stating the obvious, where there is frustration or anger, there is tension or conflict. Thus, explore not just the emotions but the *actions* that initiated them (Back, Küfner, & Egloff, 2010; Bernard & Ryan, 2010, pp. 35–6).

Developmentally, middle childhood (approximately ages 8–9) is a period of *emotional ambivalence* in which children experience new emotions but do not necessarily have the vocabulary to describe them. Some young people (and adults) may use metaphors and similes to explain their feelings (e.g., "a floating kind of happy," "like I was in the Twilight Zone"). Researchers may opt to apply In Vivo Codes during the first cycle of coding ("THE TWILIGHT ZONE"), then more standard labels during the next cycle for the emotions experienced by the participant (SURREAL). But if a metaphoric phrase seems to evocatively – if not more accurately – capture the experience, consider keeping it as the code of choice. Eatough and Smith (2006) strongly recommend careful attunement to the participant's *language* use in his or her accounts since individuals "give emotional performances that tell us not about their emotional experience, but about the discursive skills and rules of emotion that they have acquired through language" (p. 117).

Even in adulthood not everyone, particularly heterosexual men (Schwalbe & Wolkomir, 2002), is capable of expressing their emotions, comfortable discussing them, or able to label them accurately. Some may also be quite adept at emotion/impression management, deception, and emotional denial (which could also be coded as such). An inability to articulate what or how one feels, however, should not always be perceived as a deficit: "we should respect people's confusion and indecision and not represent their meanings as more coherent or stable than they are" (Miller, Hengst, & Wang, 2003, p. 222). Researchers may find themselves making several inferences about the subtextual emotional experiences of some participants in selected settings and contexts. Stay particularly attuned to participant body language and the nuances of voice.

If you are not trained in counseling, be wary of playing amateur psychologist during fieldwork, and exercise ethical caution and empathetic and sympathetic support when interviewing people about sensitive or traumatic matters which may generate strong and distressing emotions in recall (McIntosh & Morse, 2009; Morse, Niehaus, Varnhagen, Austin, & McIntosh, 2008).

Each major discipline (psychology, sociology, human communication, human development, education, etc.) will approach and apply in different ways research on emotions. The subject is intricately complex, so explore the literature from various fields of study to assess the conceptual frameworks, operating definitions, and theories regarding emotions. Yet, I myself resonate not just with scientific paradigms but with a piece of folk wisdom: "Life is 20 percent what happens to you, and 80 percent how you react to it." This suggests that we explore not just the actions but, with more emphasis, the emotional *re*actions and *inter*actions of individual people to their particular circumstances.

Some recommended ways to further analyze Emotion Codes are (see Appendix B):

- First Cycle coding methods
- action and practitioner research (Altrichter et al., 1993; Coghlan & Brannick, 2010; Fox et al., 2007; Stringer, 1999)
- cognitive mapping (Miles & Huberman, 1994; Northcutt & McCoy, 2004)
- frequency counts (LeCompte & Schensul, 1999)
- interrelationship (Saldaña, 2003)
- life course mapping (Clausen, 1998)
- metaphoric analysis (Coffey & Atkinson, 1996; Todd & Harrison, 2008)
- narrative inquiry and analysis (Clandinin & Connelly, 2000; Coffey & Atkinson, 1996; Cortazzi, 1993; Coulter & Smith, 2009; Daiute & Lightfoot, 2004; Holstein & Gubrium, 2012; Murray, 2003; Riessman, 2008)
- phenomenology (Butler-Kisber, 2010; Giorgi & Giorgi, 2003; Smith et al., 2009; van Manen, 1990; Wertz et al., 2011)
- poetic and dramatic writing (Denzin, 1997, 2003; Glesne, 2011; Knowles & Cole, 2008; Leavy, 2009; Saldaña, 2005a, 2011a)
- portraiture (Lawrence-Lightfoot & Davis, 1997)
- situational analysis (Clarke, 2005)

Notes

See Arlie Russell Hochschild's (2003) *The Managed Heart: Commercialization of Human Feeling* for her groundbreaking sociological work and theories on "emotional labor" among airline flight attendants, and the possible transfer of these theories to other service and helping professions.

Values Coding

Sources

Gable & Wolf, 1993; LeCompte & Preissle, 1993

Description

Values Coding is the application of codes onto qualitative data that reflect a participant's values, attitudes, and beliefs, representing his or her perspectives or worldview. Though each construct has a different meaning, Values Coding, as a term, subsumes all three.

Briefly, a *value* is the importance we attribute to oneself, another person, thing, or idea. "The greater the personal meaning [of something to someone], the greater the personal payoff; the greater the personal payoff, the greater the personal value" (Saldaña, 1995, p. 28). An *attitude* is the way we think and feel about ourselves, another person, thing, or idea. Attitudes are part of "a relatively enduring system of evaluative, affective reactions based upon and reflecting the evaluative concepts or beliefs, which have been learned" (Shaw & Wright, 1967, p. 3). A *belief* is part of a system that includes our values and attitudes, plus our personal knowledge, experiences, opinions, prejudices, morals, and other interpretive perceptions of the social world. "Beliefs are embedded in the values attached to them" (Wolcott, 1999, p. 97) and can be considered "rules for action" (Stern & Porr, 2011, p. 28).

Applications

Values Coding is appropriate for virtually all qualitative studies, but particularly for those that explore cultural values, identity, intrapersonal and interpersonal participant experiences and actions in case studies, appreciative inquiry, oral history, and critical ethnography.

There is complex interplay, influence, and affect between and among all three constructs that manifest themselves in thought, feeling, and action, but Values Coding does not necessarily have to code for all three or differentiate between them unless the study's goals include determining participant motivation, agency, causation, or ideology. Values Codes can be determined a priori (beforehand) as Provisional Codes, or constructed during coding of the data.

Values Coding is applicable not only to interview transcripts, but also to field notes in which naturalistic participant actions are documented. Using both sources, in fact, corroborates the coding and enhances trustworthiness of the findings (LeCompte & Preissle, 1993, pp. 264–5). What a participant states are his or her values, attitudes, and beliefs may not always be truthful or harmonize with his or her observed actions and interactions.

Example

The types of Values Codes in the example below are distinguished through the use of V: (Value), A: (Attitude), and B: (Belief), though it can sometimes be a slippery task to determine which participant statement is which type. Barry, a high school senior and gifted actor, is asked what he wants to do with his life after he graduates (Saldaña, 1998, p. 108):

Well, I'm struggling with that right now. [1] College is a very scary thing for me to think about. You know,	[1] A: COLLEGE IS "SCARY"
[2] it's hard to get into theatre except through the universities. So my tentative game plan – [3] in fact a	[2] B: THEATRE IS EXCLUSIVE
	[3] B: FUTURE OPTIONS

couple different ways it could go – one, I may go to college and [4] major in theatre and minor in choral music and then come out and look for a job, look for a place to work as an actor.

[5] The thing that scares me the most about that is [6] my parents both had big dreams. My mom wanted to be an actress, my dad wanted to be a politician, you know they both had big dreams. Both went to college, got a degree and they're both teachers now. They teach about what it was that they wanted to do, and [7] I don't want to do that. I don't want to give myself that "out." I don't wanna have that crutch to be able to say, "Oh, this is hard looking for a job in theatre, so I'm just gonna go be a teacher," or "I'm gonna go do this or that" or whatever. [8] I don't wanna be able to give up my dream that easily.

What I would love to do is to get out of high school, work around town for a bit like, I don't know, [9] just some crap job to get the money, go to New York or Chicago, and [10] try to make it big. You know, every actor's dream: to go to one of the big towns and try to be [11] famous, to get my big break. And [12] I know that it's not likely that it will even happen, but there's a part of me, I guess it's the [13] romantic side of me again that says [14] if I want it bad enough, I'll get it. And that's what separates me from other people who are out there, starving artists, that [15] drive, is that I want it more than anything, more than life itself, I want, [16] I want this.

[4] V: FINE ARTS

[5] A: FUTURE IS SCARY
[6] B: UNOBTAINED DREAMS
   ARE POSSIBLE

[7] V: PURSUING PERSONAL
   DREAM

[8] V: MAINTAINING
   PERSONAL DREAM

[9] A: NON-THEATRE WORK
   IS MENIAL
[10] V: SUCCESS
[11] V: FAME
[12] B: REALISTIC CAREER
   EXPECTATIONS
[13] A: "ROMANTIC"
[14] B: PERSEVERANCE NETS
   SUCCESS

[15] A: "DRIVE"
[16] V: PROFESSIONAL
   ACTING CAREER

Analysis

If you have coded units according to values, attitudes, and beliefs, the next step is to categorize them and reflect on their collective meaning, interaction, and interplay, working under the premise that the three constructs are part of an interconnected system. With the above data we get:

Values

   FINE ARTS
   PURSUING PROFESSIONAL DREAM

MAINTAINING PERSONAL DREAM
SUCCESS
FAME
PROFESSIONAL ACTING CAREER

Attitudes

COLLEGE IS "SCARY"
FUTURE IS SCARY
NON-THEATRE WORK IS MENIAL
"ROMANTIC"
"DRIVE"

Beliefs

THEATRE IS EXCLUSIVE
FUTURE OPTIONS
UNOBTAINED DREAMS ARE POSSIBLE
REALISTIC CAREER EXPECTATIONS
PERSEVERANCE NETS SUCCESS

Analytic reflection through memoing and assertion development weaves the three constructs' most salient codes together:

> Barry possesses the passion and perseverance to transcend realistic yet mundane career options to pursue his dream as a professional actor in a business that makes no guarantees of success. Theatre is an imaginary world – a dream world – and those aspiring performers slumbering in its fearless fantasy know that they should wake up to confront reality, but prefer the art form's illusory lures of possibility and fame: "I know that it's not likely that it will even happen, but there's a part of me, I guess it's the romantic side of me ... that says if I want it bad enough, I'll get it."

Conceptual values, attitudes, and beliefs may not always be directly stated by participants. Phrases such as "It's important that," "I like," "I love," or "I need" alert you to what may be valued, believed, thought, or felt, along with such obvious cluing phrases as "I think," "I feel," and "I want." Participant observation in natural social settings relies more on researcher inferences of values, attitudes, and beliefs. But sometimes the most direct way to find out what someone values, thinks, feels, and believes is to simply ask him or her, "What do you value?", "What's important to you?", "What matters to you most?", "What do you think and feel about ...?"

Values within an individual are influenced and affected by the social and cultural networks to which he or she belongs. *Differential association*, for example, is a sociological "theory that suggests that people's values are influenced by the groups they interact with most intensively" (Rubin & Rubin, 2012, p. 132). Gubrium and Holstein (2009, p. 70) remind us that values are shaped by the individual's specific biography and historic period of existence, while Chang (2008, p. 96) notes that personal values are also reflected through the activities in which we engage, and in the material items we possess. Analysis and analytic memos generated from Values Coding might explore the origins of the participant's value, attitude, and belief systems derived from such individuals, institutions, and phenomena as parents, peers, school, religion, media, and age cohort, as well as the participant's personal and unique experiences, development, and self-constructed identities from social interaction and material possessions.

Questionnaires and survey instruments, such as Likert scales and semantic differentials, are designed to collect and measure a participant's values, attitudes, and beliefs about selected subjects (Gable & Wolf, 1993). The quantitative data, however, transform meaning into numbers for statistical analysis, yet still have their place in such fields as psychology, opinion research, evaluation research, and organizational studies. Also, these quantitative scales assume direction and intensity of a value, attitude, and belief, necessitating a fixed, linear *continuum* of response (e.g., less to more, strongly agree to strongly disagree) rather than a three-dimensional *ocean* allowing for diverse responses and varying levels of depth (Saldaña, 2003, pp. 91–2). Qualitative inquiry provides richer opportunities for gathering and assessing, in language-based meanings, what the participant values, believes, thinks, and feels about social life.

Values Coding also requires a paradigm, perspective, and positionality. If a participant states, "I really think that marriage should only be between one man and one woman," the researcher is challenged to code the statement any number of ways depending on the *researcher's own* systems of values, attitudes, and beliefs. Thus, is this participant's remark to be coded: V: TRADITIONAL MARRIAGE, B: HETERONORMATIVITY, or A: HOMOPHOBIC? If the goal is to capture the participant's worldview or personal ideology, then the first and second codes are more grounded in his or her perspective. But if the study is critical ethnography, for example, then the latter code may be more appropriate. Values Coding is values laden.

Some recommended ways to further analyze Values Codes are (see Appendix B):

- action and practitioner research (Altrichter et al., 1993; Coghlan & Brannick, 2010; Fox et al., 2007; Stringer, 1999)
- assertion development (Erickson, 1986)
- case studies (Merriam, 1998; Stake, 1995)
- content analysis (Krippendorff, 2003; Schreier, 2012; Weber, 1990; Wilkinson & Birmingham, 2003)
- cross-cultural content analysis (Bernard, 2011)
- discourse analysis (Gee, 2011; Rapley, 2007; Willig, 2008)
- framework policy analysis (Ritchie & Spencer, 1994)
- frequency counts (LeCompte & Schensul, 1999)
- interactive qualitative analysis (Northcutt & McCoy, 2004)
- life course mapping (Clausen, 1998)
- longitudinal qualitative research (Giele & Elder, 1998; McLeod & Thomson, 2009; Saldaña, 2003, 2008)

- narrative inquiry and analysis (Clandinin & Connelly, 2000; Coffey & Atkinson, 1996; Cortazzi, 1993; Coulter & Smith, 2009; Daiute & Lightfoot, 2004; Holstein & Gubrium, 2012; Murray, 2003; Riessman, 2008)
- phenomenology (Butler-Kisber, 2010; Giorgi & Giorgi, 2003; Smith et al., 2009; van Manen, 1990; Wertz et al., 2011)
- political analysis (Hatch, 2002)
- portraiture (Lawrence-Lightfoot & Davis, 1997)
- qualitative evaluation research (Patton, 2002, 2008)
- survey research (Fowler, 2001; Wilkinson & Birmingham, 2003)
- thematic analysis (Auerbach & Silverstein, 2003; Boyatzis, 1998; Smith & Osborn, 2008)

Notes

Since Values Coding can reflect a participant's needs and wants, and emotions are intricately interwoven with one's values system, see Dramaturgical and Emotion Coding for comparable or complementary methods.

Versus Coding

Sources

Altrichter et al., 1993; Hager et al., 2000; Wolcott, 2003

Description

Versus Codes identify in dichotomous or binary terms the individuals, groups, social systems, organizations, phenomena, processes, concepts, etc., in direct conflict with each other. Wolcott (2003) describes a moiety (from the French, meaning "half") as one of two – and only two – mutually exclusive divisions within a group. He observed in *Teachers versus Technocrats* that this social division extends throughout educator subculture during times of stress rather than daily business (pp. 116, 122–7). Moieties exist in many facets of social life, and there is generally an asymmetrical power balance between them, a duality that manifests itself as an X VS. Y code (e.g., TEACHERS VS. PARENTS, REPUBLICANS VS. DEMOCRATS, WORK VS. PLAY).

Applications

Versus Coding is appropriate for policy studies, evaluation research, critical discourse analysis, and qualitative data sets that suggest strong conflicts or competing goals within, among, and between participants.

In selected methodologies such as critical ethnography, the researcher may deliberately "take sides" with a group and its issue. For other genres such as action research (Altrichter et al., 1993; Stringer, 1999) and practitioner research (Fox et al., 2007), discerning the conflicting power issues among constituents and stakeholders is an important diagnostic for initiating and facilitating positive social change. Agar (1996) notes that a contemporary ethnographer "looks for patterns of social domination, hierarchy, and social privilege. He or she examines the power that holds patterns in place, how people accept or struggle against them. The focus is on patterns that reveal injustice" (p. 27).

Example

In a study of teachers responding to state-developed fine arts standards for educational achievement (Hager et al., 2000), there were distinct moieties that emerged as teachers reflected on and grappled with recent policies influencing and affecting their practice. Strong conflicts were evident in the data as participants openly shared their perspectives. One e-mail response reads:

[1] My mentor teacher took one look at the standards when they came out, said "What a load of crap," and dismissed them. [2] She thinks the standards are often impossible to achieve and that you would have to be a superteacher with superstudents to even come close to covering all the material. [3] I don't use the state standards either. I believe that my lessons incorporate many of the standards, but [4] I do not design them around the standards. I design them around the needs of students in my classes. I tend to personalize projects for the students. [5] I grade them individually based on self-improvement rather than a comparison to other students. I think in many ways [6] the standards expect students to be automatons with the same skills and don't allow for variances.	[1] TEACHER VS. STANDARDS [2] "IMPOSSIBLE" VS. REALISTIC [3] TEACHER VS. STANDARDS [4] STANDARDS VS. STUDENT NEEDS [5] CUSTOM VS. COMPARISON [6] STANDARDIZATION VS. "VARIANCES"

Analysis

Conflicting personnel, perspectives, policies, philosophies, curricula, practices, etc., when present in the data corpus from the study illustrated above, were coded as dichotomies, ranging from the actual to the conceptual:

STATE VS. DISTRICT
GRADUATION REQUIREMENT VS. ELECTIVE
IVORY TOWER VS. INNER CITY
PRESCRIPTION VS. AUTONOMY
PRODUCT VS. PROCESS

In Vivo Codes were used occasionally when teachers' statements were highly illustrative or difficult to reduce to a single word or phrase:

> OWNERSHIP VS. "WHO WROTE THESE?"
> "FUN" VS. "TEACH TO THE TEST"

Though not necessary for all studies, Versus Coding may lead to three major moieties: the primary stakeholders, how each side perceives and acts toward the conflict, and the central issue at stake – the latter of which could emerge as a central theme, core category, key assertion, etc. In the study profiled in the example above, the three final moiety categories that subsumed all other Versus Codes were:

Us [teachers] **vs. Them** [all other personnel, such as principals, school districts, the state department of education, state universities, etc.]

Your Way [mandated yet poorly written state standards] **vs. Our Way** [experienced educators working at the local level who know their art and their students]

Con-form [conformity to prescribed and standardized curricula] **vs. Art-Form** [creative expression in the subject area and its practice]

Note that the latter category is a fairly creative construct, one not directly stated by participants but one generated by the research team during discussion about the study. When this conceptual category was uttered, it felt like an "Ah-ha!" moment, cluing us that we had captured the central theme from our fieldwork.

Categorize all codes from your data into one of the three major categories (Stakeholders, Perceptions/Actions, Issues) as an initial analytic tactic, but leave yourself open to reorganizing the codes into other emergent categories, and not just limited to three. Analytic memo writing can focus on what Gibson and Brown (2009) posit as "the reasons why the opposition exists; to try to explain how the two oppositional characteristics may exist in the same empirical space" (p. 141). Analysis should also consider the "mistakes" people make that lead to or sustain the conflict, and if and how they are resolved (p. 134).

Social change theory by Augusto Boal (1995) suggests that humans are rarely in conflict with abstract concepts (e.g., PARTICIPANT VS. RELIGION), but rather with other humans or themselves (e.g., PARTICIPANT VS. CHURCH LEADERSHIP, PARTICIPANT VS. PERSONAL LOSS OF FAITH). Ground your initial Versus Coding in actual, observable conflicts. Abstract moiety categories can emerge during Second Cycle coding and later stages of analysis. For grounded theory studies, however, Charmaz (2009) recommends looking for conceptual tensions or "metaphors of opposition" at whatever cycle they emerge – for example, STRUGGLE VS. SURRENDER, SOCIAL IDENTIFICATIONS VS. SELF-DEFINITIONS (p. 157).

A related technique is "dilemma analysis," coined by Richard Winter, who applied the method in educational action research (Altrichter et al., 1993, pp. 146–52). Data are reviewed to find and juxtapose inconsistencies and contradictions that inhibit professional practice and decision making. These dilemmas are listed as sentences that alternate with "On the one hand" and "On the other hand." For example:

- On the one hand, standards legitimize the merit and worth of dance in the schools.
- On the other hand, dance is an elective rather than required course in the schools.

Sentence couplings such as these can be categorized appropriately and examined by practitioners for reflection and action, or converted to Versus Codes for categorization and analysis. For example, the above coupling might be coded LEGITIMATE VS. ELECTIVE or "MERIT AND WORTH" VS. OPTIONAL FRILL. CAQDAS programs can conveniently and effectively link two different passages of data whose content or perspectives contradict each other for Versus Coding (Lewins & Silver, 2007, p. 63). Another effective model for practitioner research is "force field analysis," which can list the opposing stakeholders' perspectives and use directional arrows of varying sizes to illustrate the conflicting forces between change and the status quo (Fox et al., 2007, pp. 37–8, 172–6).

Some recommended ways to further analyze Versus Codes are (see Appendix B):

- action and practitioner research (Altrichter et al., 1993; Coghlan & Brannick, 2010; Fox et al., 2007; Stringer, 1999)
- assertion development (Erickson, 1986)
- discourse analysis (Gee, 2011; Rapley, 2007; Willig, 2008)
- framework policy analysis (Ritchie & Spencer, 1994)
- grounded theory (Bryant & Charmaz, 2007; Charmaz, 2006; Corbin & Strauss, 2008; Glaser & Strauss, 1967; Stern & Porr, 2011; Strauss & Corbin, 1998)
- interactive qualitative analysis (Northcutt & McCoy, 2004)
- narrative inquiry and analysis (Clandinin & Connelly, 2000; Coffey & Atkinson, 1996; Cortazzi, 1993; Coulter & Smith, 2009; Daiute & Lightfoot, 2004; Holstein & Gubrium, 2012; Murray, 2003; Riessman, 2008)
- political analysis (Hatch, 2002)
- polyvocal analysis (Hatch, 2002)
- qualitative evaluation research (Patton, 2002, 2008)
- situational analysis (Clarke, 2005)
- within-case and cross-case displays (Gibbs, 2007; Miles & Huberman, 1994; Shkedi, 2005)

Notes

The protagonist versus antagonist paradigm of Versus Coding does not necessarily suggest that there is a clear-cut hero and villain evident in the data. Conflicts are contextual, nuanced, and each side has its own story to tell. Clarke (2005) reinforces "that there are not 'two sides' but rather N sides or multiple perspectives in any discourse" (p. 197). Nevertheless, Versus Coding makes evident the power issues at hand as humans often perceive them – as binaries or dichotomies. See Harré and van Langenhove (1999) for a discussion of "positioning theory" in interpersonal interactions.

The description of Code Mapping in Chapter Four utilizes the codes from the study illustrated in Versus Coding.

Evaluation Coding

Sources

Patton, 2002, 2008; Rallis & Rossman, 2003

Description

Evaluation Coding is the application of (primarily) non-quantitative codes to qualitative data that assign judgments about the merit, worth, or significance of programs or policy (Rallis & Rossman, 2003, p. 492). Program evaluation is "the systematic collection of information about the activities, characteristics, and outcomes of programs to make judgments about the program, improve program effectiveness, and/or inform decisions about future programming. Policies, organizations, and personnel can also be evaluated" (Patton, 2002, p. 10). To Rallis and Rossman, evaluation data describe, compare, and predict. Description focuses on patterned observations or participant responses of attributes and details that assess quality. Comparison explores how the program measures up to a standard or ideal. Prediction provides recommendations for change, if needed, and how those changes might be implemented.

Applications

Evaluation Coding is appropriate for policy, critical, action, organizational, and (of course) evaluation studies, particularly across multiple sites and extended periods of time. Appreciative inquiry may also be an approach that finds utility with Evaluation Coding.

Evaluation Coding can emerge from the evaluative perspective of the researcher or from the qualitative commentary provided by participants. Selected coding methods profiled in this manual can be applied to or supplement Evaluation Coding (e.g., Magnitude Coding, Descriptive Coding, Values Coding, and grounded theory coding methods), but Evaluation Coding is also customized for specific studies since "the coding system must also reflect the questions that initiated and structured the evaluation in the first place" (Pitman & Maxwell, 1992, p. 765).

Example

The stewards of a community church surveyed its congregational membership to gather written data on their perceptions of worship services and programming. Selected individuals were interviewed for more in-depth response. A 45-year-old male who had recently left the church talks to a steward about his experiences.

The Evaluation Coding example below employs Eclectic Coding (discussed further in Chapter Four) – an amalgam of Magnitude Coding (to note whether the participant makes a positive [+] or negative [–] comment), Descriptive Coding (to note the topic) and Subcoding or In Vivo Coding (to note the specific qualitative evaluative comment), plus a recommendation coding tag (REC) with a specific memo/action for follow-up. Since Evaluation Coding should reflect the nature and content of the inquiry, all codes relate to specific personnel and programs:

[1] I stopped going to Valley View [Community Church] because it just got so boring. [2] Services were two hours long, sometimes longer. [3] I know that some people are OK with that, but not me. Ninety minutes top for services – an hour's even better. *(laughs)* [4] Opening music just went on and on, and if the pastor got on a roll, [5] the music would just keep going on and on.

[I: What do you mean, "on a roll"?]

[6] I mean, he'd "let the spirit move him," and so he'd keep singing and singing and encouraging the choir to keep singing and singing, and it just made me so frustrated. I wanted things to move on.

[I: Anything else?]

[7] His sermons also got too "folksy." [8] When I first came, the [9] sermons were powerful, provocative, intelligent, made me think of things I hadn't thought of before, and I had been a church-goer for over two decades. [10] But over the past few months it got to be, not repetitive, but it seemed like it because there was just nothing new to hear. [11] It's like he didn't prepare for them like he used to. It's like he was making them up as he went along. [12] I don't think it's me that got above the sermons, he just started dumbing them down. [13] I fell asleep so many times during them, and that never used to happen. So, I quit going there. [14] There was just no more inspiration for me there, you know what I mean?

[1] – SERVICES: "BORING"
[2] REC: SHORTER SERVICES
[3] REC: SURVEY CONGREGATION ON SERVICE LENGTH
[4] – OPENING MUSIC: TOO LONG
[5] REC: DISCUSS SERVICE LENGTH WITH MUSIC DIRECTOR

[6] REC: PASTOR – BALANCE PERSONAL WITH CONGREGATIONAL NEEDS

[7] – SERMONS: "TOO FOLKSY"
[8] REC: PASTOR – REFLECT ON FORMER SERMON PREP & CONTENT
[9] + SERMONS: USED TO BE "POWERFUL"
[10] – SERMONS: "NOTHING NEW"
[11] – SERMONS: SEEM UNPREPARED
[12] – SERMONS: "DUMBED DOWN"
[13] REC: PASTOR – OBSERVE CONGREGATION DURING SERMONS
[14] – SERVICES: UNINSPIRING

Analysis

Patton (2008, p. 478) notes that four distinct processes are used in making sense of evaluation findings: analysis of the data for its patterns; interpretation of their significance; judgment of the results; and recommendations for action. "In the simplest terms, evaluations are said to answer three questions: What? So what? Now what?" (p. 5)

Clients and constituents for evaluation research most often want to know first: what is working and what is not. Hence, the + and − Magnitude Codes receive priority for quick categorization by the researcher, followed by the specific topic, subtopic, and comment. For example, from the data above:

Positive Comments

> SERVICES: USED TO BE "POWERFUL"

Negative Comments

> SERVICES: "BORING", UNINSPIRING
> OPENING MUSIC: "TOO LONG"
> SERMONS: "NOTHING NEW", SEEM UNPREPARED, "TOO FOLKSY",
> "DUMBED DOWN"

Categorizing REC codes by personnel or area helps organize the flow of the evaluator's recommendations and follow-up.

For inductive work, "the evaluator analyst looks for changes in participants, expressions of change, program ideology about outcomes and impacts, and ways that people make distinctions between" those who do and do not receive the desired outcomes (Patton, 2002, p. 476). Types of change to examine are shifts in participant skills, attitudes, feelings, behaviors, and knowledge. The example above can be analyzed at the micro-level for Valley View Community Church's exclusive use to reflect on and possibly change its worship service's format and content after a sufficient number of individuals have been interviewed for comparison. But the analysis can also extend to the macro-level by utilizing grounded theory coding to explore how today's institutional church systems may or may not be serving the needs of their congregants, or how an individual's faith is influenced and affected by church leadership and rituals.

Evaluation data can derive from individual interviews, focus groups, participant observation, surveys, and documents. Individuals each have their own opinions, so expect to find, and thus analyze and present, a wide range of responses, not just an overall assessment. There are many forms of evaluation: outcome, implementation, prevention, summative, formative, etc. See Patton (2008) for an authoritative and full description of approaches, particularly for processual evaluation, and Stringer (1999) for the facilitation and implementation of change as part of action research projects.

Some recommended ways to further analyze Evaluation Codes are (see Appendix B):

- action and practitioner research (Altrichter et al., 1993; Coghlan & Brannick, 2010; Fox et al., 2007; Stringer, 1999)
- assertion development (Erickson, 1986)
- case studies (Merriam, 1998; Stake, 1995)
- decision modeling (Bernard, 2011)
- discourse analysis (Gee, 2011; Rapley, 2007; Willig, 2008)
- framework policy analysis (Ritchie & Spencer, 1994)
- frequency counts (LeCompte & Schensul, 1999)
- graph-theoretic techniques for semantic network analysis (Namey et al., 2008)
- grounded theory (Bryant & Charmaz, 2007; Charmaz, 2006; Corbin & Strauss, 2008; Glaser & Strauss, 1967; Stern & Porr, 2011; Strauss & Corbin, 1998)
- illustrative charts, matrices, diagrams (Miles & Huberman, 1994; Morgan et al., 2008; Northcutt & McCoy, 2004; Paulston, 2000; Wheeldon & Åhlberg, 2012)
- interactive qualitative analysis (Northcutt & McCoy, 2004)
- logic models (Knowlton & Phillips, 2009; Yin, 2009)
- longitudinal qualitative research (Giele & Elder, 1998; McLeod & Thomson, 2009; Saldaña, 2003, 2008)
- memo writing about the codes/themes (Charmaz, 2006; Corbin & Strauss, 2008; Glaser, 1978; Glaser & Strauss, 1967; Strauss, 1987)
- mixed methods research (Creswell, 2009; Creswell & Plano Clark, 2011; Tashakkori & Teddlie, 2003)
- political analysis (Hatch, 2002)
- polyvocal analysis (Hatch, 2002)
- qualitative evaluation research (Patton, 2002, 2008)
- situational analysis (Clarke, 2005)
- splitting, splicing, and linking data (Dey, 1993)
- thematic analysis (Auerbach & Silverstein, 2003; Boyatzis, 1998; Smith & Osborn, 2008)
- within-case and cross-case displays (Gibbs, 2007; Miles & Huberman, 1994; Shkedi, 2005)

Notes

Evaluation research may have political and hidden agendas depending on how it is contracted between the client and analyst. It is not possible to be an "objective" evaluator, but it is possible to be systematic in your collection and analysis of data to assess merit and worth. Rely primarily on what the participants themselves – the primary stakeholders – say and do. Evaluation research is a context-specific enterprise dependent on how (and whose) values and standards are employed. As Stake (1995) notes, "All evaluation studies are case studies" (p. 95).

Literary and Language Methods

Literary and language coding methods borrow from established approaches to the analysis of literature, and a contemporary approach to the analysis of oral communication.

Dramaturgical Coding, Motif Coding, and Narrative Coding draw from various literary traditions for their unique coding assignments to explore underlying sociological, psychological, and cultural constructs.

Dramaturgical Coding approaches cultural life as performance and its participants as characters in social dramas. Motif Coding applies folk literature's symbolic elements as codes for an evocative approach to analysis. Narrative Coding incorporates literary terms as codes to discover the structural properties of participants' stories. Though these methods appear highly systematic, they can lead toward rich arts-based presentations.

Verbal Exchange Coding is H. L. (Bud) Goodall, Jr.'s signature ethnographic approach to analyzing conversation through reflecting on social practices and interpretive meanings.

Dramaturgical Coding

Sources

Berg, 2001; Feldman, 1995; Goffman, 1959; Saldaña, 2005a, 2011a

Description

Dramaturgical Coding approaches naturalistic observations and interview narratives as "social drama" in its broadest sense. Life is perceived as "performance," with humans interacting as a cast of characters in conflict. Interview transcripts become monologue, soliloquy, and dialogue. Field notes and video of naturalistic social action represent improvised scenarios with stage directions. Environments, participant dress, and artifacts are viewed as scenery, costumes, and hand properties.

Dramaturgical Codes apply the terms and conventions of character, play script, and production analysis to qualitative data. For character, these terms include such items as:

1 participant–actor *objectives*, motives in the form of action verbs: OBJ;
2 *conflicts* or *obstacles* confronted by the participant–actor which prevent him or her from achieving his or her objectives: CON;
3 participant–actor *tactics* or *strategies* to deal with conflicts or obstacles and to achieve his or her objectives: TAC;
4 participant–actor *attitudes* toward the setting, others, and the conflict: ATT;
5 *emotions* experienced by the participant–actor (see Emotion Coding): EMO;
6 *subtexts*, the participant–actor's unspoken thoughts or impression management, in the form of gerunds (see Process Coding): SUB

These six elements of character are what a playwright, director, and actor attempt to realize through theatrical performance. Bogdan and Biklen (2007) refer to the above as "Strategy Codes."

Applications

Dramaturgical Coding is appropriate for exploring intrapersonal and interpersonal participant experiences and actions in case studies, particularly those leading toward narrative or arts-based presentational forms (Cahnmann-Taylor & Siegesmund, 2008; Knowles & Cole, 2008; Leavy, 2009).

Dramaturgical Coding attunes the researcher to the qualities, perspectives, and drives of the participant. It also provides a deep understanding of how humans in social action, reaction, and interaction interpret and manage conflict. Lindlof and Taylor (2011) note that "The ways in which participants articulate their own motives are central to many communication studies" (p. 206) and "The *drama* frame is well suited for studies concerned with communication as performance" (p. 270). Lincoln and Denzin (2003) concur, noting that culture is "an ongoing performance, not a noun, a product, or a static thing. Culture is an unfolding production, thereby placing performances and their representations at the center of lived experience" (p. 328). Feldman (1995) adds that while "dramaturgical analysis is generally used to explicate very public performances such as organizational rituals, it can also be used to understand relatively private performances such as the execution of parental roles" (p. 41).

Dramaturgical Coding is best applied to self-standing, inclusive vignettes, episodes, or stories in the data record. One could even subdivide the storied data into stanzas as "scenes," which may include such plotting devices as a curtain-raising prologue and climax (Riessman, 2008, pp. 110–11). Dramaturgical Coding is also applicable to field note data in which two or more participants act, react, and interact in daily routines or are observed in conflict with each other. Comparing and contrasting their individual objectives and tactics as actions and reactions cyclically progress deepens your understanding of power relationships and the processes of human agency.

Example

A female researcher interviews a veteran female high school teacher about her practice by asking, "How do you deal with conflict and discipline in the classroom?" The teacher responds with a personal anecdote and then describes her general ways of working:

(chuckles) [1] I laugh because this last week has been a big discipline week for me. [2] Why is it our freshmen are so unruly and disrespectful? ... Anyways, how do I deal with discipline? [3] I am very forward, straight, and	[1] ATT: IRONIC [2] SUB: BURNING OUT [3] TAC: "UP-FRONT" [4] TAC: "DON'T TAKE

up-front. So, [4] I don't take crap from anybody. And [5] I call kids on their behavior. And this happened today in class as [6] a kid sat there and rolled his eyes at me – [7] again. And [8] I just stopped him and I said, [9] "When you roll your eyes, you are basically saying "F You" to the person you're talking to, and that is disrespectful and not acceptable in my room. [10] So you either be gone or get written up for disrespect and dis-, insubordination." Here on campus it's [11] two days suspension off campus.

So, here [12] we are very, um, disciplined on the basis of respect as a number one issue. And so, [13] I enforce that and [14] I teach that in my classroom every day by being [15] honest and calling kids. Now, [16] some kids get freaked out but eventually they get used to [17] my style and they appreciate it, and they always come back and say, "Wow. I never looked at it that way." So, it's a cool thing. But it's funny you bring it up because [18] this week has just been a nightmare week and I don't know why. [19] Isn't that weird?

CRAP"
[5] TAC: ACCOUNTABILITY
[6] CON: DISRESPECT
[7] EMO: FRUSTRATION
[8] OBJ: CONFRONT
[9] TAC: ADMONISH
[10] TAC: ULTIMATUM
[11] TAC: SUSPENSION

[12] OBJ: DISCIPLINE
[13] OBJ: "I ENFORCE"
[14] OBJ: TEACH RESPECT
[15] TAC: HONESTY
[16] CON: STUDENT "FREAK OUT"
[17] TAC: "MY STYLE"
[18] EMO: FRAZZLED
[19] ATT: IRONIC

Analysis

After a series of vignettes, episodes, or stories have been collected, separate coded data into the six categories of character analysis by listing and reflecting on the Objectives, Conflicts/Obstacles, Tactics/Strategies, Attitudes, Emotions, and Subtexts:

OBJECTIVES: CONFRONT, DISCIPLINE, "I ENFORCE", TEACH RESPECT
CONFLICTS: DISRESPECT, STUDENT "FREAK OUT"
TACTICS: "UP FRONT", "DON'T TAKE CRAP", ACCOUNTABILITY, ADMONISH, ULTIMATUM, SUSPENSION, HONESTY, "MY STYLE"
ATTITUDES: IRONIC, IRONIC
EMOTIONS: FRUSTRATION, FRAZZLED
SUBTEXTS: BURNING OUT

Take note of the types of actions (objectives and tactics/strategies) taken in response to the types of conflicts/obstacles the participant–actor confronts. String the related codes together to discern storylines of actions, reactions, and interactions:

CON: DISRESPECT > EMO: FRUSTRATION > OBJ: CONFRONT > TAC: ADMONISH > TAC: ULTIMATUM

Also acknowledge that an Objective might include not just what the participant–actor wants but what she wants *other* people to do. The attitudes, emotions, and subtexts clue you to the internal perspectives of the participant–actor during these situations. A provocative question to answer as you reflect on the overall dramaturgical elements about a participant–actor is, "What kind of trouble is this person in?" Write a vignette (Erickson, 1986; Graue & Walsh, 1998) as a first-person or omniscient narrative revealing the inner thoughts of the participant–actor, or create a descriptive profile of the participant–actor highlighting her personality characteristics (or, in dramaturgical parlance, her characterization in social performance).

One can even extend the dramaturgical approach to qualitative data analysis and presentation by transforming an interview transcript into a stage monologue or adaptation into stage dialogue (Saldaña, 2011a). The researcher/ethnodramatist envisions a participant–actor's performance and recrafts the text into a more aesthetic form by editing unnecessary or irrelevant passages, rearranging sentences as necessary for enhancing the structure and flow of the story, and recommending appropriate physical and vocal action through italicized stage directions. The 230-word verbatim transcript above (excerpted from a 310-word passage) has been transformed into a 121-word monologue below for an actor to portray in front of an audience, and deliberately includes references to the participant's Objectives, Conflicts/Obstacles, Tactics/Strategies, Attitudes, Emotions, and Subtexts:

> *(to the audience, as she cleans up her classroom after a long day)*
> DIANNE: Why are freshmen so unruly and disrespectful? One of my students today rolled his eyes at me – *again*. I stopped him and said,
> *(as if talking to the student)*
> "When you roll your eyes at me, you are basically saying 'fuck you' to the person you're talking to. And that is disrespectful and not acceptable in my room."
> *(to the audience)*
> I don't take crap from anybody. At this school, *respect* is the number one issue. I enforce that and I teach that in my classroom every day by being *honest*. Now, some kids get freaked out by that, but they eventually get used to my style and they appreciate it. They always come back to me and say,
> *(as if portraying a dense student)*
> "Wow, I never looked at it that way."
> *(as herself, shakes her head, sighs and chuckles)*
> Isn't that weird? (Adapted from Saldaña, 2010, p. 64)

Another dramaturgical character concept is the *superobjective* – the overall or ultimate goal of the participant in the social drama. Respect – exhibited both in the classroom and for the teacher herself – may be the participant's superobjective in the monologue profiled above. But additional stories culled from interviews and observations, coded appropriately, may reinforce that superobjective as the primary theme or reveal a different one at work within her.

Goffman (1963) notes that we tend to assign a person we first meet with categories and attributes that impute a "social identity." Reciprocally, that person is implicitly requesting of others that the impression – the managed presentation of self – fostered before them is a "character [who] actually possesses the attributes he appears to possess" (Goffman, 1959, p. 17). These first impressions change as fieldwork continues and we come to know the character of our participant's "character." And if enough rapport has been developed between the researcher and participant–actor, the latter will reveal "backstage" knowledge of him- or herself that discloses what is genuine behind the managed impression of self.

Acknowledge that inferences about others' actions and motives are from the perspective of researcher as audience member of the social drama. These inferences can sometimes be incorrect, and a follow-up interview with the participant–actor may be necessary for confirmation. Psychology cautions us, however, that humans do not always understand their own motives for action, and they cannot always rationalize and articulate why they acted and reacted in certain ways.

Some recommended ways to further analyze Dramaturgical Codes are (see Appendix B):

- case studies (Merriam, 1998; Stake, 1995)
- discourse analysis (Gee, 2011; Rapley, 2007; Willig, 2008)
- narrative inquiry and analysis (Clandinin & Connelly, 2000; Coffey & Atkinson, 1996; Cortazzi, 1993; Coulter & Smith, 2009; Daiute & Lightfoot, 2004; Holstein & Gubrium, 2012; Murray, 2003; Riessman, 2008)
- performance studies (Madison, 2012; Madison & Hamera, 2006)
- phenomenology (Butler-Kisber, 2010; Giorgi & Giorgi, 2003; Smith et al., 2009; van Manen, 1990; Wertz et al., 2011)
- poetic and dramatic writing (Denzin, 1997, 2003; Glesne, 2011; Knowles & Cole, 2008; Leavy, 2009; Saldaña, 2005a, 2011a)
- portraiture (Lawrence-Lightfoot & Davis, 1997)
- vignette writing (Erickson, 1986; Graue & Walsh, 1998)

Notes

Since Dramaturgical Coding can reflect a participant's needs and wants, also see Values Coding. For complementary methods related to dramaturgical analysis, see Narrative Coding and Lieblich, Zilber, and Tuval-Mashiach's (2008) model of "agency, structure, communion, and serendipity."

Eclectic Coding, a method profiled in Chapter Four, illustrates another example of Dramaturgical Coding as a follow-up to initial data analysis of an interview transcript.

Motif Coding

Sources

Mello, 2002; Narayan & George, 2002; S. Thompson Motif-Index of Folk Literature, http://www.ruthenia.ru/folklore/thompson/index.htm; Thompson, 1977

Description

For this profile, Motif Coding is the application to qualitative data of previously developed or original index codes used to classify types and elements of folk tales, myths, and legends. A motif as a *literary device* is an element that sometimes appears several times within a narrative work, and in Motif Coding the motif or element might appear several times or only once within a data excerpt.

A *type* refers to the complete tale and can include such general titles as "Superhuman Tasks," "Religious Stories," and "Stories about Married Couples." "A type is a traditional tale that has an independent existence. It may be told as a complete narrative and does not depend for its meaning on any other tale" (Thompson, 1977, p. 415). A *motif* is "the smallest element in a tale" that has something unique about it, such as: characters (fools, ogres, widows, etc.), significant objects or items in the action of the story (a castle, food, strange customs, etc.), and single incidents of action (hunting, transformation, marriage, etc.) (pp. 415–16). An alphanumeric example of a Thompson Motif-Index of Folk Literature mythological motif reads: "P233.2 Young hero rebuked by his father." The index contains thousands of detailed entries such as these.

Applications

Motif Coding is appropriate for exploring intrapersonal and interpersonal participant experiences and actions in case studies, particularly those leading toward narrative or arts-based presentational forms (Cahnmann-Taylor & Siegesmund, 2008; Knowles & Cole, 2008; Leavy, 2009), plus identity studies and oral histories. If a particular element, incident, characteristic, trait, action, or unique word/phrase reoccurs throughout a data set, consider Motif Coding as one possible application to the patterned observations.

Motif Coding may be better applied to story-based data extracted from interview transcripts or participant-generated documents such as journals or diaries. Each story analyzed should be a self-standing unit of data – a vignette or episode – with a definite beginning, middle, and end. The same story (with variants) that has become canonized among various individuals may lend itself to Motif Coding – for example, each participant sharing where he or she was and how he or she first heard the news of what happened in the USA on September 11, 2001. Narrative inquiry and analysis have also discerned particular types or genres of stories that may each include their own unique motifs – for example, *chaos narratives* with motifs of illness, multiple setbacks, futile efforts to regain control, and an unresolved ending (Frank, 2012, p. 47).

Thompson's Motif-Index is a specialized system primarily for folklorists and anthropologists, but the website is worth browsing by researchers from other disciplines to acquaint themselves with the breadth of topics about the human experience.

Example

A young adult male describes his strained relationship with his alcoholic father. Motif Coding using the Thompson Motif-Index has been applied to classify the tale type and several significant elements of this story (although original researcher-generated Motif Codes or even Vladimir Propp's folk tale functions could also have been applied). For reference only, the Thompson Motif-Index alphanumeric codes have been added after the phrases:

TALE TYPE/MAJOR MOTIF – TRANSFORMATION: MAN TO OGRE [D94]

[1] We've never been all that close. [2] He used to be an alcoholic and he smoked pot. [3] And, he was actually busted a couple of years back. And as part of his, the charges were dropped, but he had to go to drug rehab. And up until that point I really didn't get along with my father, [4] he was really a jerk, especially when he was drunk, he was really a jerk. [5] And then he sobered up, and for a while nothing changed, and then things changed and everything was cool again. And, I don't know, [6] my grandpa was not an expressive man and was hardly ever home or anything like that, and so [7] my dad doesn't handle emotions very well. And what he does is, when he's upset he'll blow up and then go away, cool off, and then come back and it's as if nothing happened. He got it all out of his system, he's cool with that. [8] I'll do that sometimes, but I have enough of my mom in me that I brood on things. [9] So when he blows up and says things he doesn't mean, comes back and pretends like nothing ever happened, I just assume that those things that he said are to be held as true from that moment on. So he and I don't get along very well.

[1] FATHER AND SON [P233]
[2] TABU: DRINKING [C250]
[3] PUNISHMENT: IMPRISONMENT [Q433]

[4] CRUEL FATHER [S11]

[5] TRANSFORMATION: MAN TO DIFFERENT MAN [D10]
[6] CRUEL GRANDFATHER [S42]
[7] VIOLENCE OF TEMPER [W185]

[8] MOTHER AND SON [P231]

[9] NOT DARING TO CURSE FATHER DIRECTLY, SON DOES SO INDIRECTLY [P236.3]

Analysis

Whether using an established index or your original creations for Motif Coding, the goal is to label both ordinary and significant elements of a story that have the potential for rich symbolic analysis. The work of Jerome Bruner's narrative universals, Joseph Campbell and his "Hero's Journey," or Carl Jung's discussions of archetypes, dreams, and symbols, are worth reviewing for understanding the mythic properties at work in a story's motifs in addition to Stith Thompson's writings on folklore. One could even refer to Bruno Bettelheim's (1976) classic treatise, *The Uses of Enchantment*, to discern how a contemporary participant's story, coded and analyzed with classic folk tale motifs, possesses deep psychological meaning. The young man's story in the example above, according to Bettelheim, is comparable to a classic folk tale whose content represents an essential experience for adolescent development: "threatening as the parent may seem at some time, it is always the child who wins out in the long run, and it is the parent who is defeated. ... The child not only survives the parents but surpasses them" (p. 99). As an analytic tactic, one might even consider what moral or life lesson has been learned from the participant's story.

Shank (2002) outlines how the participant's story and the researcher's retelling of it can be structured as a myth, fable, folk tale, and legend (pp. 148–52), while Poulos (2008) illustrates the use of archetypal themes and mythically informed autoethnographic writing for narrative inquiry (pp. 143–73). Berger (2012) explores how Vladimir Propp's folk tale functions (e.g., violation, trickery, rescue, victory, punishment) can be utilized for media analyses of TV programs (pp. 22–7), but the method is also quite applicable to interview transcripts and participant-generated written narratives.

Motif Coding is a creative, evocative method that orients you to the timeless qualities of the human condition, and represents contemporary, even mundane, social life with epic qualities. The "ogres" in our lives range from demanding bosses to abusive spouses to violent bullies on the playground. We "transform" ourselves on occasion, not just from one human type to another, but from human to animal-like personas. Motifs are part literary element and part psychological association, and their inclusion in a particular tale type crystallizes "an ethos or a way of being" (Fetterman, 2010, p. 65). These symbolic representations are layered with meaning, revealing values and "insight into the secular and sacred and the intellectual and emotional life of a people" or an individual case study (p. 65).

Some recommended ways to further analyze Motif Codes are (see Appendix B):

- Narrative Coding and Focused Coding
- case studies (Merriam, 1998; Stake, 1995)
- life course mapping (Clausen, 1998)
- metaphoric analysis (Coffey & Atkinson, 1996; Todd & Harrison, 2008)
- narrative inquiry and analysis (Clandinin & Connelly, 2000; Coffey & Atkinson, 1996; Cortazzi, 1993; Coulter & Smith, 2009; Daiute & Lightfoot, 2004; Holstein & Gubrium, 2012; Murray, 2003; Riessman, 2008)
- phenomenology (Butler-Kisber, 2010; Giorgi & Giorgi, 2003; Smith et al., 2009; van Manen, 1990; Wertz et al., 2011)

- poetic and dramatic writing (Denzin, 1997, 2003; Glesne, 2011; Knowles & Cole, 2008; Leavy, 2009; Saldaña, 2005a, 2011a)
- portraiture (Lawrence-Lightfoot & Davis, 1997)
- thematic analysis (Auerbach & Silverstein, 2003; Boyatzis, 1998; Smith & Osborn, 2008)
- vignette writing (Erickson, 1986; Graue & Walsh, 1998)

Notes

Stith Thompson's alphanumeric Motif-Index of Folk Literature was a groundbreaking work, but selected future scholars found the massive indexing system unwieldy, incomplete, and unrepresentative of the diverse canons of the world's folk literature. Additional indexing systems developed after his can be found in reference libraries and websites. One of the best descriptions of Thompson's system can be accessed from: http://www.talesunlimited.com/STmotifsearchhelp.asp.

For related methods, see Narrative, Protocol, and OCM (Outline of Cultural Materials) Coding. Narrative Coding in particular will illustrate a repetitive motif within the data example.

Narrative Coding

Sources

Andrews, Squire, & Tamboukou, 2008; Cortazzi, 1993; Coulter & Smith, 2009; Daiute & Lightfoot, 2004; Gubrium & Holstein, 2009; Holstein & Gubrium, 2012; Murray, 2003, 2008; Polkinghorne, 1995; Riessman, 2002, 2008

Description

Andrews et al. (2008) emphasize that not only are there "no overall rules about suitable materials or modes of investigation, or the best level at which to study stories," there is not even a consensual definition of "narrative" itself (p. 1). In this profile, Narrative Coding applies the conventions of (primarily) literary elements and analysis to qualitative texts most often in the form of stories. "Stories express a kind of knowledge that uniquely describes human experience in which actions and happenings contribute positively and negatively to attaining goals and fulfilling purposes" (Polkinghorne, 1995, p. 8). Narrative Coding – and analysis – blends concepts from the humanities, literary criticism, and the social sciences since the coding and interpretation of participant narratives can be approached from literary, sociological/sociolinguistic, psychological, and anthropological perspectives (Cortazzi, 1993; Daiute & Lightfoot, 2004).

Some methodologists assert that the process of narrative analysis is "highly exploratory and speculative" (Freeman, 2004, p. 74), and its "interpretive tools are designed to examine phenomena, issues, and people's lives holistically" (Daiute & Lightfoot, 2004, p. xi). Nevertheless, there may be occasions when the researcher wishes to code participant narratives from a *literary* perspective as a preliminary approach to the data to understand its storied, structured forms, and to potentially create a richer aesthetic through a retelling.

Applications

Narrative Coding is appropriate for exploring intrapersonal and interpersonal participant experiences and actions to understand the human condition through story, which is justified in and of itself as a legitimate way of knowing: "some … stories should be sufficiently trusted to be left unaccompanied by critique or theory" (Hatch & Wisniewski, 1995, p. 2).

Riessman (2008) notes that narrative analysis includes diverse methods (e.g., thematic, structural, dialogic, performative). Narrative analysis is particularly suitable for such inquiries as identity development; psychological, social, and cultural meanings and values; critical/feminist studies; and documentation of the life course – for example, through oral histories. Nuances of narrative can become richly complex when the researcher explores the participant's subject positioning and presentation of self (Goffman, 1959), works with the participant in therapeutic contexts (Murray, 2003, 2008), or experiments with arts-based presentational and representational forms (Cahnmann-Taylor & Siegesmund, 2008; Knowles & Cole, 2008; Leavy, 2009).

Example

A mother reflects on her son's difficult preadolescent years. She is somewhat performative in her retelling of this story, and her close relationship with her child allows her to disclose openly the trials of the time. Prosaic, poetic, and dramatic elements are used as codes to highlight the structure and properties of this narrative excerpt. Also note how the data are divided into small stanzas for analysis:

GENRE: A MODERN-DAY GREEK TRAGEDY; THE WITNESS (MOTHER) RECOUNTS
THE HERO'S (HER SON'S) OFF-STAGE EVENTS THROUGH EPISODES:

Then he went through the time of [1] [*makes a "blow-off" face to illustrate*], I don't wanna say anti-social, he was never [2] anti-social, but making the statement, [3] the way he dressed, the way he looked, everything was making a [4] statement.	[1] VISUAL CHARACTERIZATION: FACIAL EXPRESSION [2] MOTIF: "ANTI-SOCIAL" [3] REPETITIVE PHRASE [4] MOTIF: "STATEMENT"
[5] And that was OK, too. In fact, [6] some of his middle school teachers would call me and say, [7] "I noticed that he's hanging out with some unsavory characters and I think …," you know, that kind of stuff. [8] And I'd	[5] UNIT TRANSITION [6] FLASHBACK [7] VOCAL MIMICRY-PARODY

say, "Well, actually I think his changes are real healthy 'cause he's finally determining what he likes."

⁸ DIALOGUE: TEACHER & MOTHER'S RESPONSE

⁹ From that, and he had a really tough time at Lakewood Middle School ¹⁰ real tough. ¹¹ The first day of school in seventh grade, some – ¹² I'll use the term "gang-banger," but I don't know – was picking on a little kid. And my son said, ¹³ "Hey man, get off his case." ¹⁴ And from that moment on, all of the tension was focused on him. ¹⁵ From the time he entered Lakewood to the time he left Lakewood, ¹⁶ he was a target by the bad guys. That was a very ¹⁷ tough time for him.

⁹ UNIT TRANSITION
¹⁰ MOTIF: "REAL TOUGH"
¹¹ FLASHBACK
¹² ASIDE
¹³ HIGH POINT
¹⁴ COMPLICATION
¹⁵ TIME FRAME
¹⁶ SON AS HERO VS. "BAD GUYS"
¹⁷ MOTIF: "TOUGH"

¹⁸ [*slight laugh*]

¹⁸ CODA-PATHOS

Analysis

Through Narrative Coding of the above example, the genre of the story – a modern-day Greek tragedy – emerged after the application of and reflection upon its structures and properties. This might lead the researcher to continue exploring the mother's stories about her son through the lens of classical drama or even Greek mythology, which might then structure the narrative retelling as a series of grief tales. (The mother's closure – a moral in the form of an analogy with a folk saying – later in the transcript reads, "It was kind of like teaching the dog not to run in the street by getting hit by a car. It was a horrible, painful, awful time, and yet, if it doesn't kill you it'll make you stronger. That's what's happened to him.")

Patterson (2008) elegantly describes one of the most classic approaches to narrative analysis: the six-part Labovian model. Clauses from transcripts are classified into one of six elements, purported as a nearly universal story structure when humans provide an oral narrative:

1 ABSTRACT – what is the story about?
2 ORIENTATION – who, when, where?
3 COMPLICATING ACTION – then what happened?
4 EVALUATION – so what?
5 RESULT – what finally happened?
6 CODA – a "sign off" of the narrative (p. 25)

The mother's transcript example above could have been coded instead with the six Labovian elements, and there would have been close alignment with this classic structure. But Patterson notes that in her work and the work of other researchers, verbatim narratives are not always temporally ordered, and many contain nuances, densities, and complexities that rival traditional story grammars and paradigmatic coding systems.

Polkinghorne (1995) differentiates between *paradigmatic* and *narrative* cognition. The former may include such approaches as grounded theory, which seeks the inductive development of categories from the data, particularly if large collections of stories are available for analyzing patterns (Cortazzi, 1993, p. 7). But these types of findings are "abstractions from the flow and flux of experience" (Polkinghorne, 1995, p. 11); instead, narrative cognition seeks to understand individual and unique human action. And among postmodernists, the process of narrative inquiry is not a solitary research act but a collaborative venture between the researcher and participants.

Gubrium and Holstein (2009) advise that researchers analyzing narrative texts should consider not just the psychological but the sociological contexts of stories collected from fieldwork: "stories operate *within* society as much as they are about society" (p. 11). Environments such as close relationships, local culture, jobs, and organizations influence and affect the individual's telling of personal tales: "Approach the big and little stories as reflexively related, not categorically distinct, dimensions of narrativity" (p. 144).

The frequent use of motifs in the participant's telling of her stories might also be woven into the recrafted narrative as motifs for literary impact. Introspective memory work (Grbich 2007; Liamputtong, 2009; McLeod & Thomson, 2009), conducted by an individual or a group, generates not just many personal stories but possibly their recurring motifs, and thus their connected meanings and through-line – essentials for the structural arcs of extended narrative retellings. When I conducted my own memory work about my student life and teaching career, I was intrigued to discover how many times "red ink" appeared as a significant motif in my recollections of learning and teaching vignettes from childhood onward. I concluded that the red ink I applied to correct student papers was symbolic of my masculinist need to fix things, to bring more color to my perceived colorless life, and to reinforce that I value answers more than questions. As I advise for a life course, oral history, or autoethnographic study, "Don't connect someone's 'dots' – connect his or her *motifs*."

"The unit of analysis is often big gulps of text – entire stories" (Daiute & Lightfoot, 2004, p. 2). To most narrative inquirers, insight into the meanings of participant stories depends on deep researcher reflection through careful reading of the transcripts and extensive journaling. Clandinin and Connelly (2000) attest that they adhere to "*fluid inquiry*, a way of thinking in which inquiry is not clearly governed by theories, methodological tactics, and strategies" (p. 121). Their approach to narrative inquiry is to "find a form to represent … storied lives in storied ways, not to represent storied lives as exemplars of formal categories" (p. 141). The write-up requires rich descriptive detail and a three-dimensional rendering of the participant's life, with emphasis on how participant transformation progresses through time. The ultimate goal is to create a stand-alone story as research representation that may depict "how and why a particular outcome came about" (Polkinghorne, 1995, p. 19), but other approaches to narrative inquiry might also deliberately stress open-ended structures to the researcher's recrafted narratives, structures that leave the reader with evocative closure and provocative questions rather than fixed answers (Barone, 2000; Poulos, 2008).

Bamberg (2004) notes, "it simply is not enough to analyze narratives as units of analysis for their structure and content, though it is a good starting point" (p. 153). Just some of the many prosaic, poetic, and dramatic elements available as coding and subcoding schemes for Narrative Coding include:

- **Story Type** (survivor narrative, epiphany narrative, quest narrative, confessional tale, coming-out story, *testimonio*, etc.)
- **Form** (monologue, soliloquy, dialogue, song, etc.)
- **Genre** (tragedy, comedy, romance, melodrama, satire, etc.)
- **Tone** (optimistic, pessimistic, poignant, rant, etc.)
- **Purpose** (historical, cautionary, persuasive, emancipatory, therapeutic, etc.)
- **Setting** (locale, environment, local color, artifacts, etc.)
- **Time** (season, year, order, duration, frequency, etc.)
- **Plot** (episodic, vignette, chapter, scene, prologue, subplot, etc.)
- **Storyline** (chronological, Labovian, conflict/complication, turning point, rising action, climax, etc.)
- **Point of View** (first-person, third-person, omniscient, witness, etc.)
- **Character Type** (narrator, protagonist, antagonist, composite, secondary, choral, trickster, *deus ex machina*, etc.)
- **Characterization** (gender, ethnicity, physical description, status, motivations, change/transformation, etc.)
- **Theme** (moral, life lesson, significant insight, theory, etc.)
- **Literary Elements** (foreshadowing, flashback, flashforward, juxtaposition, irony, motif, imagery, symbolism, allusion, metaphor, simile, coda, etc.)
- **Spoken Features** (volume, pitch, emphasis/stress, fluency, pausing, parsing, dialect, etc.)
- **Conversation Interactions** (greetings, turn-taking, adjacency pairs, questions, response tokens, repair mechanisms, etc.)

Just as symbols and rituals are forms of "cultural shorthand" (Fetterman, 2008, p. 290), the combined and sometimes unconscious use of selected prosaic, poetic, and dramatic elements above in our everyday and structured communication patterns are our stylistic signatures of individual identity and values – "voiceprints" as they are called in theatre performance practice.

Narrative researchers should also be attuned to story structures from the non-European canons and how that influences and affects a retelling. For example, the use of symbolism in Mexican stories from a Eurocentric perspective might be perceived as "overt," "heavy-handed," or "exotic," whereas from Mexican perspectives the symbolic associations are "bold," "strong," and "brave."

Some recommended ways to further analyze Narrative Codes are (see Appendix B):

- case studies (Merriam, 1998; Stake, 1995)
- discourse analysis (Gee, 2011; Rapley, 2007; Willig, 2008)
- life course mapping (Clausen, 1998)
- metaphoric analysis (Coffey & Atkinson, 1996; Todd & Harrison, 2008)

- narrative inquiry and analysis (Clandinin & Connelly, 2000; Coffey & Atkinson, 1996; Cortazzi, 1993; Coulter & Smith, 2009; Daiute & Lightfoot, 2004; Holstein & Gubrium, 2012; Murray, 2003; Riessman, 2008)
- performance studies (Madison, 2012; Madison & Hamera, 2006)
- phenomenology (Butler-Kisber, 2010; Giorgi & Giorgi, 2003; Smith et al., 2009; van Manen, 1990; Wertz et al., 2011)
- poetic and dramatic writing (Denzin, 1997, 2003; Glesne, 2011; Knowles & Cole, 2008; Leavy, 2009; Saldaña, 2005a, 2011a)
- polyvocal analysis (Hatch, 2002)
- portraiture (Lawrence-Lightfoot & Davis, 1997)
- thematic analysis (Auerbach & Silverstein, 2003; Boyatzis, 1998; Smith & Osborn, 2008)
- vignette writing (Erickson, 1986; Graue & Walsh, 1998)

Notes

Narrative inquiry ranges from systematic methods to open-ended explorations of meaning. Rather than trying to find the "best" way to approach your own narrative analysis, acquaint yourself with the breadth of methodologies available, then choose selectively from the literature.

See *NTC's Dictionary of Literary Terms* (Morner & Rausch, 1991) as a reference for prosaic, poetic, and dramatic elements; Goodall (2008) for pragmatic advice on structuring written narratives; Poulos (2008) for evocative autoethnographic writing; Gibbs (2007) for a concise overview of narrative forms; and Holstein and Gubrium (2012) for an eclectic collection of approaches to narrative analysis. Also see Crossley (2007) for a superb autobiographical (and biographical) interview protocol for narrative analysis in psychology. For supplementary methods related to Narrative Coding, see Dramaturgical and Motif Coding, and Themeing the Data.

Verbal Exchange Coding

Source

Goodall, 2000

Description

Verbal Exchange Coding is the verbatim transcript analysis and interpretation of the types of conversation and personal meanings of key moments in the exchanges. To Goodall (2000), coding is determining the "generic type" of conversation; reflection examines the meaning of the conversation. The goal is to develop fundamental analytic skills to create an *"evocative representation* of the fieldwork experience," the "writing of a *story of culture"* (p. 121, emphasis in original).

Coding begins with a precise transcription of the verbal exchange (which includes non-verbal cues and pauses) between the speakers. The coder then draws from a typology/continuum of five forms of verbal exchange to identify the unit(s):

1 *Phatic Communion* or *Ritual Interaction,* a "class of routine social interactions that are themselves the basic verbal form of politeness rituals used to express social recognition and mutuality of address"; an example is:

   A: Hey.
   B: Morning.
   A: How's it going?
   B: OK. You?

   Simple exchanges such as these can communicate such cultural patterns as status, gender, race, class differences, etc.

2 *Ordinary Conversation,* "patterns of questions and responses that provide the interactants with data about personal, relational, and informational issues and concerns, as well as perform the routine 'business' of ... everyday life".

3 *Skilled Conversation,* which represents "a 'higher' or 'deeper' level of information exchange/discussion" between individuals, and can include such exchanges as debates, conflict management, professional negotiations, etc.

4 *Personal Narratives,* consisting of "individual or mutual self-disclosure" of "pivotal events in a personal or organizational life".

5 *Dialogue,* in which conversation "transcends" information exchange and the "boundaries of self," and moves to higher levels of spontaneous, ecstatic mutuality (Goodall, 2000, pp. 103–4).

Selected questions assist the ethnographer in coding, interpreting, and reflecting on the content and meaning of the verbal exchange. Sample questions include: What is the nature of the relationship? What are the influences of fixed positionings (gender, race/ethnicity, social class, etc.)? What are the rhythms, vocal tones, and silences contributing to the overall meaning? (pp. 106–7).

The second level of Verbal Exchange Coding's categorization and analysis explores the personal meanings of key moments by first examining such facets as speech mannerisms, non-verbal communication habits, and rich points of cultural knowledge (slang, jargon, etc.). The categorization then proceeds to examine the *practices* or the *"cultural performances* of everyday life" (p. 116):

1 *Routines and Rituals* of structured and symbolically meaningful actions during our day.

2 *Surprise-and-Sense-Making Episodes* of the unanticipated or unexpected.

3 *Risk-Taking Episodes* and *Face-Saving Episodes* of conflict-laden exchanges.

4 *Crises* in a verbal exchange or as an overarching pattern of lived experience.

5 *Rites of Passage,* or what is done that significantly "alters or changes our personal sense of self or our social or professional status or identity" (pp. 116–19).

Applications

Verbal Exchange Coding is appropriate for a variety of human communication studies and studies that explore cultural practices. Verbal Exchange Coding can also be applied to pre-existing (secondary data) ethnographic texts such as autoethnographies.

The guidelines listed above should not suggest an overly systematic approach to analyzing verbal exchanges. Goodall's "coding" is a narrative rather than margined words and phrases. Goodall's text evocatively explores "the new ethnography" – storied accounts grounded in the data that weave "the personal experience of the researcher into meaning in ways that serve as analyses of cultures" (p. 127). Verbal Exchange Coding is intended as an introductory approach for novices to closely examine the complexity of talk through focused parameters of conversation types and everyday cultural practices. Interpretive meaning through extensive written reflection (comparable to an analytic memo) rather than traditional margined coding methods is encouraged.

Example

A junior high school play production class in an inner city fine arts magnet program has just read a scripted adaptation of a traditional Mexican American folk tale, *La llorona (The Weeping Woman)*. Nancy, the teacher/director, wants to have her Hispanic students improvisationally create, then write, a modern-day adaptation of the story for public performance. The verbatim transcript below is an excerpt from the first brainstorming session about the updated version. Since Verbal Exchange Coding does not rely on margined entries, the example will scan across the entire page. The coding narrative follows:

NANCY: OK, how can we take the story, this is the old version, how can we update it character-wise and word-wise to also updating it with the rap? Like, how would you say if Maria was beautiful? How would you say that in slang?

GIRL: She's *fine*!

NANCY: OK, so that's what we need to have the words say. We need the updated word and the use of the rap together. I mean, where would you have this take place?

BOY: She's walking down McKinley and she shoots her kids.

GIRL: A drive-by. *(laughter from group)*

NANCY: In a blue Pontiac. So that's what you need to start thinking about, how can we keep the same story intact, of what happens, but we need to convert it into something that's modern.

BOY: She overdosed her kids.

NANCY: Does she take them to the lake or do they find them in a canal?

BOY: Yeah, they find them in a canal with bullet holes in their head.

NANCY: Guys, think about that, don't get too gruesome, that's not our objective to make this into this gross massacre death thing, like finding that body that was burning in the dumpster, that's not what our goal is. Our goal is to update the story into your, how would you say it in today's language?

GIRL: And there were two *locos*... .

(*NANCY explains the costumes in the updated version, such as jeans*)

BOY: G-string? (*laughter from group*)

NANCY: That's Domingo in college. (*laughter from group*) So, you're gonna be wearing the big old baggy pants, big old flannel shirts, platform shoes.

GIRL: We're not in the '70s.

NANCY: I want everyone to come in with something written down for the rap version by Friday. It needs to be your version – it doesn't have to be the whole product, it just has to be the very beginning.

BOY: (*rapping*) Once upon a time, there was a *chica*. (*laughter from group*) She pushed them in the river and along came the fuzz. (*laughter*) ...

(*NANCY asks where the setting for the modern version could be*)

BOY: Long Beach, California.

BOY: You been hanging around with that guy too much. (*boys laugh*)

GIRL: No, instead of drowning them, she gave them drugs.

BOY: Let's do it like the lady did it, she threw them in a car and drove into the river.

GIRL: And then she lied about it later.

GIRL: No cuss words.

CODING: This classroom verbal exchange is mostly *ordinary conversation* (that ever so slightly peaks toward *skilled conversation* before it) to accomplish the business of creative work. A white female teacher facilitates the development of an original play with a class of Hispanic youth who toss out occasional *caló* (language of the street) such as "*locos*" and "*chica*." There are several rich points of cultural knowledge exchanged between them: "McKinley" (a nearby street, noted for its seediness)," "blue Pontiac" (a local in-joke about the stereotypical drive-by car), "that body that was burning in the dumpster" (a neighborhood news story about a recent murder), "that guy" (a notorious local gang member from California), points that would completely elude someone who did not live in the immediate school neighborhood.

The *routine* of the day is drama class in preparation for the *ritual* of performing theatre. Students create *risk-taking episodes* by tossing out their original ideas and, in turn, create a few *surprise-making episodes* through irreverent humor – even black humor when they laugh at a "drive-by" shooting reference. Not included in the transcript are those sly looks and glances given by all speakers, including the teacher, as if to suggest and validate insider and "we-really-shouldn't-be-talking-about-this-but-we-are" knowledge. Laughter is prominent throughout, evoked by both Nancy and her students, during this moderately fast-paced "brainstorming" session.

REFLECTION [excerpts]: Be careful what you ask for – you just might get it. Nancy asked her students, encouraged them in fact, to create a modern-day version of a violent folk tale. She said, "Our goal is to update the story," which is exactly what the class was doing. But in her role as public school educator she had to limit (read: censor) their ideas to what would be acceptable for a public audience (read: parents) on stage.

Communication of the adolescent voice, the inner city voice, the Hispanic voice, is what progressive multicultural education is all about. But because we are dealing with inner city minors (some of whom have seen more gang activity and violence than most white adults), there is a border we cannot cross. Well, like "illegal" immigrants we can cross it anyway, but there is always a risk. So the teacher, like a border patrol officer, has to stop these Hispanic youth from crossing the line. (But I am playing the race card here. Lots of high school theatre programs in white suburban communities have faced the same censorship dilemma.)

Nevertheless, as an Hispanic whose voice is frequently dismissed, discounted, and negated by my white colleagues at work, it burns me to see and hear young people told, "I want to hear and honor your voice, but you can't say *that* on the stage," when I have heard them say much worse in the hallways as they move from one class to the next. The teacher is asking them to adapt a traditional folk tale into modern-day contexts for the purpose of creating art. These junior high schoolers' lives are surrounded by violence (sadly), so that is what they are weaving into their work.

Analysis

Goodall states that "analysis and coding of conversations and practices – as well as interpretive reflections on the meaning of them – are really parts of the overall process of finding patterns that are capable of suggesting a story, an emerging story of your interpretation of a culture" (2000, p. 121). Continued reflection on the meanings of the classroom verbal exchanges documented above addresses such aspects as the culture of the school, theatre classroom culture, Hispanic culture, adolescent culture, the culture of violence, gang subculture, and their complex interrelationships and overlaps.

Goodall's introductory interpretive approach to the analysis of talk is just one of many extensive and systematic approaches to conversation and discourse analysis (see Agar, 1994; Drew, 2008; Gee, 2011; Gee et al., 1992; Jones, Gallois, Callan, & Barker, 1999; Lindlof & Taylor, 2011; Rapley, 2007; Silverman, 2006), which include detailed notation systems for transcription that indicate such speech patterns as pauses, word stress, overlapping dialogue, and other facets of conversation.

Some recommended ways to further analyze Verbal Exchange Codes are (see Appendix B):

- action and practitioner research (Altrichter et al., 1993; Coghlan & Brannick, 2010; Fox et al., 2007; Stringer, 1999)

- discourse analysis (Gee, 2011; Rapley, 2007; Willig, 2008)
- metaphoric analysis (Coffey & Atkinson, 1996; Todd & Harrison, 2008)
- narrative inquiry and analysis (Clandinin & Connelly, 2000; Coffey & Atkinson, 1996; Cortazzi, 1993; Coulter & Smith, 2009; Daiute & Lightfoot, 2004; Holstein & Gubrium, 2012; Murray, 2003; Riessman, 2008)
- performance studies (Madison, 2012; Madison & Hamera, 2006)
- phenomenology (Butler-Kisber, 2010; Giorgi & Giorgi, 2003; Smith et al., 2009; van Manen, 1990; Wertz et al., 2011)
- poetic and dramatic writing (Denzin, 1997, 2003; Glesne, 2011; Knowles & Cole, 2008; Leavy, 2009; Saldaña, 2005a, 2011a)
- thematic analysis (Auerbach & Silverstein, 2003; Boyatzis, 1998; Smith & Osborn, 2008)
- vignette writing (Erickson, 1986; Graue & Walsh, 1998)

Notes

Other evocative methods of analyzing talk and text exist. Gilligan, Spencer, Weinberg, & Bertsch (2006), "in response to the uneasiness and growing dissatisfaction with the nature of coding schemes typically being used [in the 1980s] to analyze qualitative data" (p. 254), developed the *Listening Guide*, "a method of psychological analysis that draws on voice, resonance, and relationship as ports of entry into the human psyche" (p. 253). The four-step reading and notation of verbatim text examines plot, first-person references as poetic structures, and contrapuntal voices (e.g., melodic signatures, silence), followed by an interpretive synthesis based on the research question of interest. See Sorsoli and Tolman (2008) for a clear and detailed example of a case study's transcript analysis using the *Listening Guide*.

Exploratory Methods

Exploratory coding methods are just that – exploratory and preliminary assignments of codes to the data before more refined coding systems are developed and applied. Since qualitative inquiry is an emergent process of investigation, these coding methods use tentative labels as the data are initially reviewed. After they have been analyzed in this manner, researchers might proceed to more specific First Cycle or Second Cycle coding methods (also see Eclectic Coding in Chapter Four).

Holistic Coding applies a single code to each large unit of data in the corpus to capture a sense of the overall contents and the possible categories that may develop.

Provisional Coding begins with a "start list" of researcher-generated codes based on what preparatory investigation suggests might appear in the data before they are analyzed.

Hypothesis Coding applies researcher-developed "hunches" of what might occur in the data before or after they have been initially analyzed. As the corpus is reviewed, the hypothesis-driven codes confirm or disconfirm what was projected, and the process can refine the coding system itself.

Holistic Coding

Source

Dey, 1993

Description

Holistic Coding is an attempt "to grasp basic themes or issues in the data by absorbing them as a whole [the coder as 'lumper'] rather than by analyzing them line by line [the coder as 'splitter']" (Dey, 1993, p. 104). The method is a preparatory approach to a unit of data before a more detailed coding or categorization process through First or Second Cycle methods. A "middle-order" approach, somewhere between holistic and line by line, is also possible as a Holistic Coding method. There are no specific maximum length restrictions for data given a Holistic Code. The coded unit can be as small as one-half a page in length, to as large as an entire completed study.

Applications

Holistic Coding is appropriate for beginning qualitative researchers learning how to code data, and studies with a wide variety of data forms (e.g., interview transcripts, field notes, journals, documents, diaries, correspondence, artifacts, video).

Holistic Coding is applicable when the researcher already has a general idea of what to investigate in the data, or "to 'chunk' the text into broad topic areas, as a first step to seeing what is there" (Bazeley, 2007, p. 67). It is also a time-saving method for those with massive amounts of data and/or a short period for analytic work. But be aware that with less time to analyze often comes a less substantive report. In most cases, Holistic Coding is preparatory groundwork for more detailed coding of the data.

Holistic Coding may be more applicable to what might be labeled self-standing units of data – vignettes or episodes – such as: interview excerpts of a participant's story with a definite beginning, middle, and end; a short one- to two-page document; or a field note excerpt of social life with bounded parameters such as time, place, action, and/or content (e.g., a 15-minute playground recess, a transaction at a sales counter, a congregation's participation during a portion of worship service).

Example

The following guest lecture excerpt is from a second-year, inner city, grades K–8 school teacher talking to education majors enrolled in a university teaching methods course (Saldaña, 1997, p. 44). She has just completed several poignant vignettes about some of her most difficult students:

> [1] I'm not telling you this to depress you or scare you but it was [1] "A LOT TO
> a reality for me. I thought I was so ready for this population   LEARN"
> because I had taught other groups of kids. But this is such a
> unique situation, the inner city school. No, I should take
> that back: It's not as much of a unique situation *anymore*.
> There are more and more schools that are turning into
> inner city schools. … I really had to learn about the kids.
> I had to learn about the culture, I had to learn the language,
> I had to learn the gang signals, I had to learn what music
> was allowed, what t-shirts they could wear on certain
> days and not on other days. There was just a lot to learn
> that I had never even thought about.

The single Holistic Code applied to represent this entire data excerpt was an In Vivo Code: "A LOT TO LEARN". Another possible Holistic Code might be more descriptive in nature: CAUTIONARY ADVICE. If "middle-order" codes or categories are necessary for more detailed analysis, a few that might emerge from the data above for CAUTIONARY ADVICE would read:

PRE-PROFESSIONAL PREPARATION
LEARNING ON-THE-JOB

Analysis

After a first review of the data corpus with Holistic Codes applied, "all the data for a category can be brought together and examined as a whole before deciding upon any refinement" (Dey, 1993, p. 105). Thus, all data coded as "A LOT TO LEARN", PRE-PROFESSIONAL PREPARATION, and LEARNING ON-THE-JOB in the study described above would be collected for closer scrutiny. The researcher might observe that those on-the-job learning curves might be lessened if they were addressed in pre-professional teacher education courses.

Rather than coding datum by datum as soon as transcripts or field notes have been prepared for analysis, it is a worthwhile investment of time and cognitive energy to simply read and reread the corpus to see the bigger picture. Dey (1993) suggests that "time spent becoming thoroughly absorbed in the data early in the analysis may save considerable time in the later stages, as problems are less likely to arise later on from unexpected observations or sudden changes in tack" (p. 110).

Some recommended ways to further analyze Holistic Codes are (see Appendix B):

- First Cycle coding methods
- action and practitioner research (Altrichter et al., 1993; Coghlan & Brannick, 2010; Fox et al., 2007; Stringer, 1999)
- memo writing about the codes/themes (Charmaz, 2006; Corbin & Strauss, 2008; Glaser, 1978; Glaser & Strauss, 1967; Strauss, 1987)
- qualitative evaluation research (Patton, 2002, 2008)
- quick ethnography (Handwerker, 2001)
- thematic analysis (Auerbach & Silverstein, 2003; Boyatzis, 1998; Smith & Osborn, 2008)

Notes

For an inquiry-based method related to Holistic Coding, see Structural Coding.

Provisional Coding

Sources

Dey, 1993; Miles & Huberman, 1994

Description

Provisional Coding establishes a predetermined "'start list' set of codes prior to fieldwork" (Miles & Huberman, 1994, p. 58). These codes can be developed from anticipated categories or types of responses/actions that may arise in the data yet to be collected. The provisional list is generated from such preparatory investigative matters as: literature reviews related to the study, the study's conceptual framework and research questions, previous research findings, pilot study fieldwork, the researcher's previous knowledge and experiences (experiential data), and researcher-formulated hypotheses or hunches. As qualitative data are collected, coded, and analyzed, Provisional Codes can be revised, modified, deleted, or expanded to include new codes.

Applications

Provisional Coding is appropriate for qualitative studies that build on or corroborate previous research and investigations. Miles and Huberman recommend a start list ranging from approximately 12 to 60 codes for most qualitative studies. Creswell (2013) begins with a shorter list of five to six that begins the process of "lean coding." This expands to no more than 25 to 30 categories that then combine into five to six major themes (pp. 184–5).

Layder (1998) encourages the search for "key words, phrases and concepts that spring to mind in thinking about the area under consideration before any data collection or even a literature search has begun" (p. 31). Not only can this list serve as a possible series of Provisional Codes, but the items can be codewoven (see Chapter Two) to explore possible interrelationships related to the phenomenon.

Example

In the field of classroom drama with youth, creative expression by participants is most often realized in one of three ways: non-verbally (through body movement, gesture, pantomime, etc.), verbally (through verbal improvisation, reader's theatre, poetry, etc.), or a combination of both (through choral speaking with gesture, verbal improvisation with pantomime, etc.). These three modes of dramatic expression are "givens" in drama with youth, and can readily become part of the Provisional Code repertoire:

BODY
VOICE
BODY–VOICE

Previous research in the art form with children has focused primarily on language arts development through drama (Wagner, 1998). Provisional Codes might then be developed that focus on such related variables of interest as:

VOCABULARY DEVELOPMENT
ORAL LANGUAGE FLUENCY
STORY COMPREHENSION
DISCUSSION SKILLS

Once in the field, however, a start list of codes generated from previous research may be modified if the researcher observes that the drama facilitator focuses on improvisational drama to develop classroom community and social change with children rather than their language arts skills. ORAL LANGUAGE FLUENCY and DISCUSSION SKILLS might still be observed in the drama classroom and thus the codes can be maintained. But VOCABULARY DEVELOPMENT and STORY COMPREHENSION may be deleted as codes if the instructor's content focuses more on social issues (such as bullying, conflict resolution, peacekeeping skills, etc.) rather than story dramatization and enactment. Hence, new codes might emerge that are more relevant to the fieldwork observations, such as:

COMMUNITY BUILDING
BULLYING – PHYSICAL
BULLYING – VERBAL
CREATING CONFLICT
RESOLVING CONFLICT

Analysis

Other research team members, a colleague not involved with the study, or even the participants themselves can provide the coder with a "reality check" of Provisional Codes as they are initiated and modified. Obviously, when Provisional Codes are first applied to qualitative data, the researcher may soon learn whether each item from the start list has relevance or not.

Researchers should exercise caution with Provisional Codes. A classic fieldwork saying goes, "Be careful: If you go looking for something, you'll find it," meaning that your preconceptions of what to expect in the field may distort your objective and even interpretive observations of what is "really" happening there. If you become too enamored with your original Provisional Codes and become unwilling to modify them, you run the risk of trying to fit qualitative data into a set of codes and categories that may not apply: "Premature coding is like premature closure; it can prevent the investigator from being open to new ideas, alternative ways of thinking about a phenomenon, and divergent – and sometimes quite correct – explanations for events" (LeCompte & Schensul, 1999, p. 97). A willingness to tolerate ambiguity, flexibility, and the ability to remain honest with one's self are necessary personal attributes for researchers and Provisional Coding: "As we encounter more data we can define our categories with greater precision. ... Even an established category set is not cast in stone, but subject to continual modification and renewal through interaction with the data" (Dey, 1993, p. 124).

A small but vital investment of time and energy will go toward the development of Provisional Codes. Preparatory pilot study through participant observation and interviews at the actual fieldwork site may yield a more relevant set of Provisional Codes than previously published research. The context-specific nature of qualitative inquiry suggests customized (or what might be facetiously labeled "designer") coding systems and methods.

CAQDAS programs allow the development and entry of Provisional Codes in their code management systems. As documents are reviewed, a pre-established code from the list can be directly assigned to a selected portion of data. CAQDAS code lists can also be imported from and exported to other projects and users.

Some recommended ways to further analyze Provisional Codes are (see Appendix B):

- content analysis (Krippendorff, 2003; Schreier, 2012; Weber, 1990; Wilkinson & Birmingham, 2003)
- mixed methods research (Creswell, 2009; Creswell & Plano Clark, 2011; Tashakkori & Teddlie, 2003)
- qualitative evaluation research (Patton, 2002, 2008)
- quick ethnography (Handwerker, 2001)
- survey research (Fowler, 2001; Wilkinson & Birmingham, 2003)
- thematic analysis (Auerbach & Silverstein, 2003; Boyatzis, 1998; Smith & Osborn, 2008)

For Second Cycle methods that employ a set of Provisional Codes, see Eclectic and Elaborative Coding.

Notes

For Second Cycle methods that employ a set of Provisional Codes, see Eclectic and Elaborative Coding.

Hypothesis Coding

Sources

Bernard, 2011; Weber, 1990

Description

Hypothesis Coding is the application of a researcher-generated, predetermined list of codes to qualitative data specifically to assess a researcher-generated hypothesis. The codes are developed from a theory/prediction about what will be found in the data before they have been collected or analyzed. "In hypothesis-testing research … you go out to observe armed with a coding scheme worked out in advance. The idea is to record any instances of behavior that conform to the items in the scheme. This allows you to see if your hunches are correct about conditions under which certain behaviors occur" (Bernard, 2011, p. 311). Weber (1990) advocates that the "best content-analytic studies use both qualitative and quantitative operations on texts" (p. 10; cf. Schreier, 2012). The statistical applications can range from simple frequency counts to more complex multivariate analyses.

Applications

Hypothesis Coding is appropriate for hypothesis testing, content analysis, and analytic induction of the qualitative data set, particularly the search for rules, causes, and explanations in the data.

Hypothesis Coding can also be applied midway or later in a qualitative study's data collection or analysis to confirm or disconfirm any assertions or theories developed thus far (see Second Cycle coding methods). Seasoned researchers will often enter a fieldwork setting or approach a body of data with some idea of what will be present and what will most likely be happening. However, this does not necessarily suggest that Hypothesis Coding is warranted. The method is a strategic choice for an efficient study that acknowledges its focused or sometimes narrowly defined parameters of investigation. Ethnographer Martyn Hammersley (1992) admits, "we cannot but rely on constructing hypotheses, assessing them against experience and modifying them where necessary," even when we "adopt a more informal and broader approach in which we sacrifice some of the sharpness of the test in order to allow more of our assumptions to be thrown open to challenge" (p. 169). DeCuir-Gunby et al. (2011) also make the case for the development of predetermined *theory-driven codes* in addition to emergent or *data-driven codes* as a strategy for coding and codebook development.

Example

A mixed methods study (Saldaña, 1992) was conducted to assess how Hispanic and White fourth-grade child audience members would respond to a bilingual play production featuring two characters – one Hispanic and one White. I hypothesized before the study began that Hispanic children would identify and empathize more with their Hispanic counterpart in the play, while White children would be more likely to empathize with both characters but identify more with their White counterpart.

After viewing the production, interviews were conducted with children of similar ethnicity and gender clustered in small focus groups to collect their responses to such questions as: "'John felt that Juan should speak English because they lived in America. But Juan felt that if they wanted to be friends, John would have to learn Spanish. Who was right?' [collect initial response, then ask] 'Why do you feel that way?'" (Saldaña, 1992, p. 8). The research team was trained to expect five types of responses to the first forced-choice question, which were also Hypothesis Codes applied to the transcript data: JOHN, JUAN, BOTH, NEITHER, and NR [NO RESPONSE/"I DON'T KNOW"].

It was predicted that Hispanic children would most likely select JUAN as "right" while White children would be more likely to select BOTH or NEITHER. I predicted this outcome based on the hypothesis that Hispanic children's perceived similarities with Juan's ethnicity and language dilemmas in the play would influence and affect them to deliberately "take sides" with the Spanish-speaking character. Frequency counts moderately supported this hypothesis in terms of likelihood, but there was no *statistically significant* difference between the ethnic groups' choices. Thus, the original hypothesis was not deleted but modified as data analysis continued. (For example, when the data were analyzed by *gender* rather than ethnicity, girls chose Juan's side significantly more than boys.)

As for the follow-up question, "Why do you feel that way?", it was hypothesized that selected types of justifications would emerge *both similar and unique* to each ethnic group of children. Based on common ideologies about language issues in the USA, the following codes (and their inclusive meanings) were developed before analysis began:

RIGHT – We have the right to speak whatever language we want in America
SAME – We need to speak the same language in America – English
MORE – We need to know how to speak more than one language
NR – No Response or "I don't know"

Thus, interview excerpts below were coded according to the hypothesized set of responses:

HISPANIC BOY: [1] John should learn Spanish, and Juan should learn English better.   [1] MORE

WHITE GIRL: [2] It's a free country and you can talk any language you want.   [2] RIGHT

HISPANIC GIRL: [3] Everybody should know more than one language. It wasn't fair enough that John wanted Juan to speak English, and he, he didn't want to speak Spanish.   [3] MORE

No data were coded SAME, most likely due to its perception as a "politically incorrect" perspective to share during interviews. However, as analysis continued, one unanticipated category and thus code emerged – the existence of MANY languages in this country:

HISPANIC BOY: [4] All the people in America speak different languages.   [4] MANY

HISPANIC GIRL: [5] There's a lot of people that speak all kinds of language and they come from all places.   [5] MANY

It was hypothesized that the code MORE (We need to know how to speak more than one language) would appear in both ethnic groups' responses, but RIGHT (We have the right to speak whatever language we want in America) would appear with more frequency among Hispanic children. The results disconfirmed one portion of the hypothesis. Both groups with somewhat equal measure advocated that Americans needed to know how to speak more than one language. Though Hispanics attested with more frequency than Whites that Americans have the right to speak whatever language they wish, the difference was not statistically significant. In fact, it was the unforeseen code MANY (The existence of many languages in America) that was significantly more prominent among Hispanics' responses than Whites. This discovery led to a new observation: although both Hispanic and White youth in this study supported the ideology that one has the right to speak whatever language one chooses in America, Hispanic children were more attuned to speaking a non-English language not just as a "right" but as a pre-existing "given" in the USA.

Analysis

Whether quantitative and/or qualitative, an analysis of Hypothesis Codes is used to test the hypothesis under investigation. Even if you discover, like I did in the study described above, that some of your proposed hypotheses are disconfirmed through discrepant cases or statistical analysis, that in itself is a major learning and forces you to more closely examine the content of your data and thus develop more trustworthy findings. Educational researchers LeCompte and Preissle (1993) promote this as an ongoing process of qualitative inquiry: "ethnographers formulate and systematically test successive hypotheses throughout the research project, generating and verifying successive explanations, both mundane and theoretical, for the behavior exhibited and attitudes held by the people under study" (p. 248).

Hypothesis Coding is a mixed methods approach to data analysis most often applied to content analysis but with some transferability to other qualitative studies. As positivist as the method appears, Weber (1990) assures researchers that "there is no single right way to do content analysis. Instead, investigators must judge what methods are appropriate for their substantive problems" (p. 69). CAQDAS programs are well suited for Hypothesis Coding since the proposed codes can be entered a priori into their code management systems, and their search functions can help the researcher investigate and confirm possible interrelationships among the data.

Some recommended ways to further analyze Hypothesis Codes are (see Appendix B):

- assertion development (Erickson, 1986)
- content analysis (Krippendorff, 2003; Schreier, 2012; Weber, 1990; Wilkinson & Birmingham, 2003)
- data matrices for univariate, bivariate, and multivariate analysis (Bernard, 2011)
- frequency counts (LeCompte & Schensul, 1999)
- logic models (Knowlton & Phillips, 2009; Yin, 2009)
- longitudinal qualitative research (Giele & Elder, 1998; McLeod & Thomson, 2009; Saldaña, 2003, 2008)
- mixed methods research (Creswell, 2009; Creswell & Plano Clark, 2011; Tashakkori & Teddlie, 2003)
- qualitative evaluation research (Patton, 2002, 2008)
- quick ethnography (Handwerker, 2001)

Notes

Hypothesis Coding differs from Protocol Coding in that the former's set of codes is usually developed by the researcher him- or herself, while the latter's set of codes has been developed by other researchers.

Procedural Methods

Procedural coding methods are prescriptive. They consist of pre-established coding systems or very specific ways of analyzing qualitative data. Though some leeway is provided for context- and site-specific studies, the methods profiled in this section contain directed procedures to follow by their developers.

Protocol Coding outlines the general methods, advantages, and disadvantages of following pre-established coding systems developed by other researchers in subject areas related to your own inquiry.

OCM (Outline of Cultural Materials) Coding uses an extensive index of cultural topics developed by anthropologists for the classification of fieldwork data from ethnographic studies. It is a systematic coding system which has been applied to a massive database for the discipline.

Domain and Taxonomic Coding presents some of the signature analytic methods of anthropologist James P. Spradley for the systematic search for and categorization of cultural terms. This method is also primarily for ethnographic studies.

Causation Coding recommends procedures for extracting *attributions* or causal beliefs from participant data about not just how but *why* particular outcomes came about. This method searches for combinations of antecedent and mediating variables that lead toward certain pathways.

Protocol Coding

Sources

Boyatzis, 1998; Schensul, LeCompte, Nastasi, & Borgatti, 1999a; Shrader & Sagot, 2000 (as an exemplar)

Description

A *protocol* in research with human participants refers to detailed and specific procedural guidelines for conducting an experiment, administering a treatment, or, in qualitative inquiry, conducting all aspects of field research and data analysis. Protocol Coding is the collection and, in particular, the coding of qualitative data according to a pre-established, recommended, standardized, or prescribed system. The generally comprehensive list of codes and categories provided to the researcher is applied after his or her own data collection. Some protocols also recommend specific qualitative (and quantitative) data analytic techniques with the coded data.

Applications

Protocol Coding is appropriate for qualitative studies in disciplines with pre-established and field-tested coding systems *if* the researcher's goals harmonize with the protocol's outcomes. Boyatzis (1998) cautions, "the use of prior data and research as the basis for development of a code means that the researcher accepts another researcher's assumptions, projections, and biases" (p. 37). Since standardized ways of coding and categorizing data are provided to the researcher, the coder should insure that all definitions are clear and inclusive of all the possible types of responses to be collected. Some protocols, depending on their transferability and trustworthiness, may also contribute to the reliability and validity (i.e., credibility) of the researcher's new study.

Example

Shrader and Sagot (2000) co-authored a richly detailed qualitative research protocol for the investigation of violence against women with the ultimate goal of developing strategies to improve their conditions – that is, an action research model. Service providers, community members, and women personally affected by family violence are interviewed with a recommended list of questions. Examples asked of women during individual interviews are: "Can you tell me about the violent situation that you are, or were, living with?" (Follow-up: Ask when the violence occurred and what type of violence the respondent has experienced.) Two focus group questions with women are: "Which family members abuse/attack/mistreat other family members?" and "Why does this violence occur?" (pp. 45, 48).

Researchers are provided with a specific series of codes *qua* (in the role of) categories to apply to interview transcripts and documents. After coding, the data are then analyzed through such techniques as matrices, taxonomies, explanatory networks, and decision modeling to assess the outcomes and plan strategic interventions. Shrader and Sagot note that their coding and categorization system was tested in 10 Latin American countries, yet it maintains flexibility for additional categories to be integrated by other researchers. For example, one major code and its cluster of subcodes applied to responses gathered from women affected by family violence include (adapted from Shrader & Sagot, 2000, p. 63):

Category	Code	Definition
Causes of family violence	CAUSES.	Reasons that the respondent perceives as the causes of family violence
	Subcode	*Family violence due to:*
alcohol	.ALCOH	alcoholism or drinking
drugs	.DRUG	drug use
money	.MONEY	lack of money or financial problems
education	.EDUC	lack of education
conditioning	.COND	social conditioning or learned behavior
personality	.PERS	personality of the abuser or the abused
machismo	.MACHO	intrinsic traits of men or "machismo"
control	.CONTR	controlling behavior of the abuser

A woman speculating on the reason behind her husband's abusive behavior might respond, "He was just a sick, twisted man, born that way." This response would receive the code: CAUSES.PERS. Another woman might offer, "Well, his daddy beat his mama, and now he's beating me." This response would be coded: CAUSES.COND.

Analysis

Analytic applications with Protocol Coding should follow the source's specific procedures.

Pre-established research protocols will most often prescribe or recommend specific researcher training, data-gathering, coding, and analytic methods. The protocol may also include such parameters as a required minimum number of participants, a desired statistical range for assessing intercoder reliability, and other guidelines. Depending on the protocol, the procedures and instrumentation may appear inflexible and thus restrictive to certain researchers. But other protocols, such as Shrader and Sagot's, acknowledge the context-specific nature of qualitative inquiry and have built-in allowances for unique settings and cases. Schensul et al. (1999a) recommend using pre-existing or modified coding schemes for team coders when reviewing video-taped data and focus group interview transcripts.

A disadvantage of using others' systems is that the original developers may not always be available to clarify a vague passage in their protocol for you, or to answer unique questions that may arise during the course of your own study. Standardization is often perceived as antithetical to the qualitative paradigm. Protocols provide much of the preparatory work for the new investigator, but he or she should be cautious of accepting every prescription at face value. Assess a protocol critically and, if necessary, adapt the guidelines to suit your own research contexts.

On the plus side, substantive contributions to a specific area of study may be made if your particular study follows a protocol and builds on previous research to confirm and/or disconfirm the original findings, and expands the data and knowledge bases in the subject (see Elaborative Coding). If you yourself develop a research protocol for other qualitative researchers, make certain that all codes are distinctly clear: "If your code is too difficult to learn, other researchers will avoid it" (Boyatzis, 1998, p. 10).

Some works, such as dissertations or longer published journal articles, may not advocate replication of their studies, but if the topic, research questions, or goals of those studies have the potential for transferability to your own investigation, explore the possibilities of adapting their works' suggested protocols.

Since CAQDAS code lists can be imported from and exported to other projects and users, the programs lend themselves well to Protocol Coding.

Notes

Educational research has developed several instruments for the observation, recording, and coding of children's behavior in natural settings and semi-structured participatory activities (Greig, Taylor, & MacKay, 2007; O'Kane, 2000). Mukherji and Albon (2010, p. 110) offer a coding shorthand for children's tasks and social interactions, such as:

SOL – the target child is playing on their own (solitary)
SG – the target child is within a small group (three to five children)

LMM – large muscle movement
PS – problem solving
DB – distress behavior

Other social science fields such as psychology also maintain a series of coding schemes applied to qualitative data for quantitative transformation and analysis (e.g., collecting family narratives to evaluate the transmission of moral values and socialization – see Fiese & Spagnola, 2005). An interesting protocol that codes and transforms qualitative interview data for statistical analysis is the Leeds Attributional Coding System (Munton, Silvester, Stratton, & Hanks, 1999), which assesses a participant's causal beliefs (see Causation Coding). Other interesting protocols to examine are the detailed categories in the "Coding Lexicon" files of the American Time Use Survey (www.bls.gov/tus/), and content analysis methodologist Kimberly A. Neuendorf's website collection of codebooks and coding forms at: http://academic.csuohio.edu/kneuendorf/content/.

Protocol Coding differs from Hypothesis Coding in that the former's set of codes has been developed by other researchers, while the latter's set of codes is generally developed by the researcher herself.

OCM (Outline of Cultural Materials) Coding

Sources

Bernard, 2011; DeWalt & DeWalt, 2011; Murdock et al., 2004 – the OCM website: http://www.yale.edu/hraf/Ocm_xml/traditionalOcm.xml

Description

The OCM (Outline of Cultural Materials) was developed in the mid-twentieth century by social scientists at Yale University as a topical index for anthropologists and archeologists. "The OCM provides coding for the categories of social life that have traditionally been included in ethnographic description: history, demography, agriculture" and is "a good starting point for the parts of field notes that deal with descriptions of cultural systems" (DeWalt & DeWalt, 2011, p. 184). The index, consisting of thousands of entries, serves to organize the database of the Human Relations Area Files (HRAF), a massive collection of ethnographic field notes and accounts about hundreds of world cultures. Each domain and subdomain of the OCM are assigned specific reference numbers, for example:

290 CLOTHING

   291 NORMAL GARB
   292 SPECIAL GARMENTS

Each index entry includes a description with cross-references to other relevant entries, for example:

292 SPECIAL GARMENTS Clothing of special occasions (e.g., festive apparel, rain gear, bathing costumes); headgear and footwear not ordinarily worn; costumes associated with special statuses and activities; special methods of wearing garments; etc.
  Ceremonial attire 796 ORGANIZED CEREMONIAL
  Dance costumes 535 DANCE
  Military uniforms 714 UNIFORM AND ACCOUTERMENT
  Dance and dramatic costumes 530 ARTS
  Drama costumes 536 DRAMA

Applications

OCM coding is appropriate for ethnographic studies (cultural and cross-cultural) and studies of artifacts, folk art, and human production.

The OCM is a specialized indexing system primarily for anthropologists, but the website is worth browsing by researchers from other disciplines to acquaint themselves with the breadth of possible topics about human experience for field note development. DeWalt and DeWalt (2011) note that "indexing is probably going to be more important than coding in the analysis of field notes. Coding is a more common activity when the researcher is working with interview transcripts and other documents" (p. 195). Database management software, particularly for artifact and document coding, is strongly recommended by Bernard (2011).

Example

The following is a descriptive field note excerpt of a Native American hoop dancer's garments. The four OCM numeric codes listed at the beginning apply to the entire excerpt. Portions of the codes' definitions and their included items are placed in square brackets for reader reference:

292 SPECIAL GARMENTS [costumes associated with special ... activities]
301 ORNAMENT [types of ornament worn ... mode of attachment]
535 DANCE [information on dance styles ... dance costumes and paraphernalia]
5311 VISUAL ARTS [material objects whose expressive dimension is primarily visual in nature ... information on genres in visual arts (e.g., beadwork, ...) ... design and pattern]

The Ho-chunk hoop dancer's long-sleeved shirt is almost lemon-yellow in color, full at the wrists, and appears to be made out of silk. His closed but loose-fitting vest has intricate reflective beading of triangular-shaped and jagged-edged motifs. This same beading pattern appears sewn as elbow patches on his shirt, headband, and skirt overlay. The bead colors are blue, dark red, light purple, and silver. A lemon-yellow silk neck scarf is tied once in front and hangs down to his stomach. The skirt appears to be constructed out of heavy rough leather but is also lemon-yellow in color. Eight-inch long and one-inch wide fringe strips follow along the edge of the skirt, which bounce freely and solidly as he stamps his feet and quickly rotates. A six-inch wide strip of fringe at the front and back of the skirt is dyed burnt orange. The skirt's sides are cut to his upper thigh while the front and back are knee-length. The oval-shaped beaded skirt overlay in front and back is also knee-length. His hoops are saffron-yellow with the same reflective beading patterns and colors at quarter portions of each one, which unifies his basic garments with the hoops.

OCM Codes can also be applied in the margins of field notes when the specific topic changes:

[1] Eight-inch long and one-inch wide fringe strips follow along the edge of [1] 292
the skirt, which bounce freely and solidly as [2] he stamps his feet and quickly [2] 535
rotates. [3] A six-inch wide strip of fringe at the front and back of the skirt is [3] 292
dyed burnt orange. The skirt's sides are cut to his upper thigh while the ...

Analysis

Bernard (2011) notes that context-specific studies may require highly specific topical codes that are not in the OCM, so decimals or words can be added after a number to adapt, customize, and extend the subdomains even further. For example, if SPECIAL GARMENTS is OCM Code 292, I can add extensions to "Drama Costumes" for quantitative applications and analysis such as:

292.1 PASTORELA COSTUMES
    292.11 SHEPHERDS' COSTUMES
    292.12 KINGS' COSTUMES
    292.13 DEVIL COSTUME

Bernard (2011) recommends predetermined hypotheses before drawing representative cross-cultural samples from the HRAF through OCM Codes, then administering appropriate statistical tests to confirm or disconfirm the hypotheses (pp. 300–4, 449–53). DeWalt and DeWalt (2011) offer non-quantitative display strategies such as quotes, vignettes, time flow charts, and decision modeling (pp. 196–203).

Some recommended ways to further analyze OCM Codes are (see Appendix B):

- content analysis (Krippendorff, 2003; Schreier, 2012; Weber, 1990; Wilkinson & Birmingham, 2003)
- cross-cultural content analysis (Bernard, 2011)
- data matrices for univariate, bivariate, and multivariate analysis (Bernard, 2011)

- descriptive statistical analysis (Bernard, 2011)
- domain and taxonomic analysis (Schensul et al., 1999b; Spradley, 1979, 1980)
- frequency counts (LeCompte & Schensul, 1999)
- memo writing about the codes/themes (Charmaz, 2006; Corbin & Strauss, 2008; Glaser, 1978; Glaser & Strauss, 1967; Strauss, 1987)
- mixed methods research (Creswell, 2009; Creswell & Plano Clark, 2011; Tashakkori & Teddlie, 2003)
- quick ethnography (Handwerker, 2001)

Notes

There are other established coding schemes developed by anthropologists for ethnographic studies, but the OCM is the largest and perhaps the most well known among several academic disciplines. DeWalt and DeWalt (2011), however, note that the OCM has an inherent bias that assumes universal, cross-cultural comparability. Contemporary ethnographies that focus more on their unique sites, sociopolitical-driven questions, and participatory social change agendas, rather than traditional, holistic cultural description, have made "the OCM less applicable for many researchers" (p. 184).

Domain and Taxonomic Coding

Sources

McCurdy et al., 2005; Spradley, 1979, 1980

Description

Domain and Taxonomic Coding is an ethnographic method for discovering the cultural knowledge people use to organize their behaviors and interpret their experiences (Spradley, 1980, pp. 30–1). "Every culture creates hundreds of thousands of categories by taking unique things and classifying them together" (p. 88), but this knowledge is mostly tacit. Hence, the ethnographer relies primarily on extensive interviews composed of strategic questions to discern these categories of meaning.

Domain and taxonomic analysis are separate steps combined into a single process:

> We call categories that categorize other categories *domains* and the words that name them *cover terms*. ... Taxonomies are simply [hierarchical] lists of different things that are classified together under a domain word by members of a microculture on the basis of some shared certain attributes. (McCurdy et al., 2005, pp. 44–5)

For example, the domain of this manual and its cover term might be labeled *Coding Methods*. The taxonomy begins under the cover term with two separate categories: **First Cycle Coding Methods** and **Second Cycle Coding Methods**. The taxonomy continues with subcategories since under each category is a more specific set of coding methods (see Figure 3.1 or this manual's Contents – those are taxonomies).

To obtain these cultural categories, it is presumed that

> knowledge, including shared cultural knowledge, is stored as a system of categories in the human brain. ... [If] we can find the words that name things when informants talk with other members of their microculture, we can infer the existence of the group's cultural categories. We call these informant-generated words *folk terms*. (McCurdy et al., 2005, pp. 35–6)

A verbatim data record to extract folk terms is mandatory for Domain and Taxonomic Coding. But when no specific folk terms are generated by participants, the researcher develops his or her own – called *analytic terms*.

To Spradley, nine possible *semantic relationships* exist within domains, which include these types (Spradley, 1979, p. 111), followed by examples related to codes and coding:

Form	Semantic Relationship
1 Strict inclusion	X is a kind of Y [*Process Coding* is a kind of *First Cycle coding method*]
2 Spatial	X is a place in Y, X is a part of Y [*Wide margin space* is a part of *hard-copy coding*]
3 Cause–effect	X is a result of Y, X is a cause of Y [*Analysis* is a result of *coding*]
4 Rationale	X is a reason for doing Y [*Transcribing interviews* is a reason for *coding them*]
5 Location for action	X is a place for doing Y [*A desk* is a place for *coding*]
6 Function	X is used for Y [*A computer* is used for *coding*]
7 Means–end	X is a way to do Y [*Reading data carefully* is a way to *code them*]
8 Sequence	X is a step (stage) in Y [*First Cycle Coding* is a stage in *coding data*]
9 Attribution	X is an attribute (characteristic) of Y [*Quotation marks* are an attribute of *In Vivo Codes*]

Strict inclusion forms are generally nouns in the data; *means–end* forms are generally verbs.

For analysis, a semantic relationship is chosen first. Data are then reviewed to find examples of the semantic relationship, and the related folk or analytic terms are listed in a worksheet. From this, a *folk taxonomy*, "a set of categories organized on the basis of a single semantic relationship," is developed. The taxonomy "shows the relationships among *all* the folk terms in a domain" (Spradley, 1979, p. 137).

Spradley did not recommend in his early published works specific codes or coding procedures for constructing domains and taxonomies. The search for folk terms or development of analytic terms was completed simply by reviewing the data, highlighting the terms, observing and interviewing participants further for verification or additional data collection, and compiling the information on separate worksheets. The methods outlined here adapt Spradley's procedures into a more code-based system for data organization and management and, if needed, further analysis.

Applications

Domain and Taxonomic Coding is appropriate for ethnographic studies and constructing a detailed topics list or index of major categories or themes in the data.

Domain and Taxonomic Coding is a thorough yet time-intensive method for organizing categories of meaning from participants, provided there are sufficient data for analysis. It is particularly effective for studying microcultures with a specific repertoire of folk terms – for example, homeless youth terms may include "street rat," "sp'ange," "make bank," "green," "squat," "schwillies" (Finley & Finley, 1999). The approach, however, may be perceived by some as imposing too much organization on the messiness of social life, as anthropologist Clifford Geertz (1973) cautioned:

> Nothing has done more, I think, to discredit cultural analysis than the construction of impeccable depictions of formal order in whose actual existence nobody can quite believe. ... [The] essential task of theory building here is not to codify abstract regularities but to make thick description possible, not to generalize across cases but to generalize within them. (pp. 157, 165)

Example

A field experiment in theatre of the oppressed (i.e., theatre for social change) with fourth- and fifth-grade children (Saldaña, 2005b) began by observing, interviewing, and surveying children about the types of oppressions they encountered in school and at home. The excerpts below are taken from group interviews and written, open-ended surveys, prompted by the researcher's inquiry of "what you've seen or heard of how kids hurt other kids – oppression." Folk terms within the verbatim text are coded by bolding them and noting them in quotes in the margin for organizational access. Researcher-generated analytic terms/codes are also noted in the margin. After initially reviewing the transcripts and survey responses, I noticed that oppressions occurred physically (PHY), verbally (VER), or a combination of both (PHY/VER). This was the beginning of a taxonomy, albeit a tentative one. Thus, the coding also classified the folk and analytic terms accordingly. Coding focuses *exclusively* on finding data that relate to the semantic relationship:

Semantic Relationship: Means–end [X is a way to do Y]: What children describe below are ways to "hurt" (oppress) others

Cover Term: Children's folk term for the Domain: "HURTING"; researcher's analytic term for the Domain: OPPRESSING

Taxonomy (major categories): Ways to hurt (oppress) others: PHYSICALLY, VERBALLY, and PHYSICALLY AND VERBALLY COMBINED

FIFTH-GRADE GIRLS [group interview]:

GIRL 1: There was this one boy, he was trying to
[1] **push** another boy into two other boys.

I: Yes?

GIRL 2: Some girls [2] **fight** and you can get
[3] **scratched** in the face, and they [4] **call you names**.

GIRL 3: This guy tried to do a [5] **wrestling** thing to his friend, and then they did it to another kid and he got hurt.

[1] PHY: "PUSH"

[2] PHY: "FIGHT"
[3] PHY: "SCRATCHED"
[4] VER: "CALL YOU NAMES"
[5] PHY: "WRESTLING"

FOURTH-GRADE BOY [group interview]:

Sometimes when we're playing games and stuff, and this one boy comes over and he says, "Can I play with you guys?", and people say, [6] **"No, you're not our kind of people, so [7] you better get out now."**

[6] PHY/VER: EXCLUDE
[7] VER: THREATEN

FIFTH-GRADE BOY [written survey response]: One day I was at schhol I was playing soccer then I came back inside and almost everybody started [8] **messing up** my hair when it was messed up everybody started [9] **laughing** and [10] **saying** your hair is messed up I got really made they were still messing with my hair I closed my fist and pretended like I was going to [11] **punch** him

[8] PHY: "MESSING UP MY HAIR"

[9] VER: "LAUGHING"
[10] VER: TEASING

[11] PHY: "PUNCH"

FIFTH-GRADE GIRL [written survey response]:

I was [12] **made fun of my fatness**. I was [13] **called** fat, huge fatso are you going to have a baby. I was sad all the time. I'm trying to luse wiaght but I just gain, gain and gain. Wiaght. I have not lose eney wight. I have not stoped being appresed.

[12] VER: "MADE FUN OF MY FATNESS"
[13] VER: NAME-CALLING

FIFTH-GRADE BOY [written survey response]:

Some times my brother [14] **calls me names**. And we don't play with each other. We get made at each other. Sometimes he is a poor sport when we play games.

[14] VER: "CALLS ME NAMES"

Analysis

The codes representing the domain (including repeated terms, which may suggest a major category rather than subcategory) are then assembled into their respective lists. Folk terms, if not uniquely a part of the microculture, can be modified into analytic terms (e.g., "push" becomes "pushing"):

WAYS TO HURT (OPPRESS) OTHERS

Physically	Verbally	Physically and Verbally
pushing	name-calling	excluding
fighting	threatening	
scratching	laughing	
wrestling	teasing	
messing up hair	making fun of fatness	
punching	name-calling	
	name-calling	

Since *name-calling* is a frequent category, the researcher can return to the field to ask participants (if they are willing to divulge, that is) the types of names children call each other and create a pool of subcategories – for example, "dork," "wuss," "fatso," etc.

As the study continued, more data were collected through other methods, and gender differences in children's perceptions and enactment of oppression became strikingly apparent. The taxonomy's initial three categories were eventually reduced to two, based on the children's folk categories that emerged and seemed to resonate with gender-based observations: oppression through physical *force* (primarily, but not exclusively, by boys) and oppression through hurting others' *feelings* (primarily, but not exclusively, by girls).

Taxonomic diagrams can be developed as a simple outline, box diagram, or tree diagram in the form of lines and nodes. Taxonomic analysis helps in finding data subsets and their relationships. Using some of the categories extracted above, together with additional data from the study, the terms are reorganized into a taxonomic tree diagram (excerpt), as illustrated in Figure 3.4.

Spradley's methods for domain and taxonomic analysis are the foundation for two advanced stages:

> *Componential analysis* involves a search for the attributes that signal differences among symbols in a domain. ... *Theme analysis* involves a search for the relationships among domains and how they are linked to the culture as a whole. ... All of these types of analysis lead to the discovery of cultural meaning. (Spradley, 1979, p. 94)

Componential and theme analysis do not necessarily require Second Cycle coding, but instead rely on synthesizing the analytic work from domains and taxonomies developed thus far, coupled with any necessary additional data collection to clarify and confirm the categories' relationships.

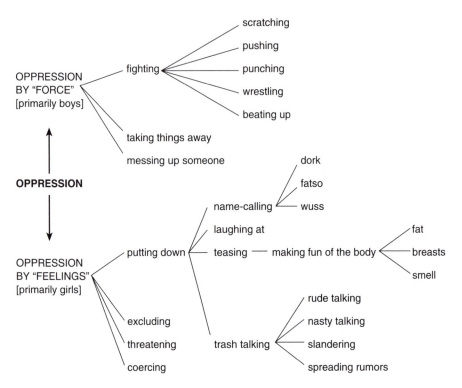

Figure 3.4 Excerpts from a taxonomic tree diagram of the ways children oppress others

Most CAQDAS programs include graphic capabilities to draw domains and taxonomies. Some programs, such as ATLAS.ti, can "calculate" and display a visual model that illustrates your codes' organizational arrangement based on their frequency and researcher-initiated linkages. CAQDAS programs can also arrange and manage your codes into hierarchies and trees, based on your input.

Some recommended ways to further analyze Domain and Taxonomic Codes are (see Appendix B):

- cognitive mapping (Miles & Huberman, 1994; Northcutt & McCoy, 2004)
- componential and cultural theme analysis (McCurdy et al., 2005; Spradley, 1979, 1980)
- content analysis (Krippendorff, 2003; Schreier, 2012; Weber, 1990; Wilkinson & Birmingham, 2003)
- cross-cultural content analysis (Bernard, 2011)
- domain and taxonomic analysis (Schensul et al., 1999b; Spradley, 1979, 1980)
- graph-theoretic techniques for semantic network analysis (Namey et al., 2008)
- illustrative charts, matrices, diagrams (Miles & Huberman, 1994; Morgan et al., 2008; Northcutt & McCoy, 2004; Paulston, 2000; Wheeldon & Åhlberg, 2012)
- memo writing about the codes/themes (Charmaz, 2006; Corbin & Strauss, 2008; Glaser, 1978; Glaser & Strauss, 1967; Strauss, 1987)

- meta-ethnography, metasummary, and metasynthesis (Finfgeld, 2003; Major & Savin-Baden, 2010; Noblit & Hare, 1988; Sandelowski & Barroso, 2007; Sandelowski, Docherty, & Emden, 1997)
- quick ethnography (Handwerker, 2001)
- situational analysis (Clarke, 2005)
- splitting, splicing, and linking data (Dey, 1993)
- thematic analysis (Auerbach & Silverstein, 2003; Boyatzis, 1998; Smith & Osborn, 2008)
- within-case and cross-case displays (Gibbs, 2007; Miles & Huberman, 1994; Shkedi, 2005)

Notes

Domain and Taxonomic Coding differs from In Vivo Coding in that the former method systematically searches for specific hierarchical organization of folk and analytic terms, while the latter is an open-ended coding method for grounded theory and other coding methods.

Causation Coding

Sources

Franzosi, 2010; Maxwell, 2012; Miles & Huberman, 1994; Morrison, 2009; Munton et al., 1999

Description

(Do not confuse Attribute Coding with *attribution* as it is used in this particular coding method. Attributes in Attribute Coding refer to descriptive variable information such as age, gender, ethnicity, etc. *Attribution* in Causation Coding refers to reasons or causal explanations.)

Causation Coding adopts yet adapts the premises of the Leeds Attributional Coding System (Munton et al., 1999), quantitative applications for narrative analysis outlined by Franzosi (2010), fundamental principles and theories of causation (Maxwell, 2012; Morrison, 2009), and selected explanatory analytic strategies of Miles and Huberman (1994). The goal is to locate, extract, and/or infer causal beliefs from qualitative data such as interview transcripts, participant observation field notes, and written survey responses. Causation Coding attempts to label the mental models participants use to uncover "what people believe about events and their causes. … An attribution is an expression of the way a person thinks about the relationship between a cause and an outcome," and an attribution can consist of an event, action, or characteristic (Munton et al., 1999, pp. 5–6).

At its most basic, an attribution answers the question "Why?", though Miles and Huberman (1994) caution, "there is a terrifying multitude of possible answers to any 'why' question" (p. 143). Munton et al. (1999) add, "Beliefs about causality can, and often do, involve multiple causes and multiple outcomes. ... In sequences of attributions, an outcome in one attribution can become a cause in the next" (p. 9). Morrison (2009) supports these principles and adds that we should carefully consider the nuanced differences between a cause, a reason, and a motive, and to keep our focus primarily on people's intentions, choices, objectives, values, perspectives, expectations, needs, desires, and agency within their particular contexts and circumstances: "It is individuals, not variables [like social class, sex, ethnicity, etc.], which do the acting and the causing" (p. 116).

Three sources for Causation Coding agree that there are three aspects to identify when analyzing causality. Munton et al. (1999) specify the three elements of an attribution as: the cause, the outcome, and the link between the cause and the outcome (p. 9). Miles and Huberman (1994) put forth a comparable model that documents: antecedent or start variables, mediating variables, and outcomes (p. 157). And Franzosi (2010) posits that "an action also has a reason and an outcome" (p. 26), a sequence he labels a "triplet." Thus, Causation Coding attempts to map a three-part process as a CODE 1 > CODE 2 > CODE 3 sequence. But since multiple causes and multiple outcomes can factor into the equation, the three-part process can include subsets such as: CODE 1A + CODE 1B > CODE 2 > CODE 3A + CODE 3B + CODE 3C.

Franzosi (2010) asserts that "narrative sequences imply causal sequences" (p. 13) and "a story grammar is nothing but a coding scheme and each constituent element of the grammar nothing but a coding category in the language of content analysis" (p. 35). But a linear sequence is not always apparently obvious or fully contained within narrative data. Certainly, we can first look for participant statements that identify factors or conditions that lead to a particular outcome. Sometimes such cluing words and phrases as "because," "so," "therefore," "since," "if it wasn't for," "as a result of," "the reason is," "and that's why," etc., will be used by participants. But analysts will also have to look for processes embedded within data narratives to storyline a three-part sequence. In other words, you will have to decode and piece together the process because participants may tell you the outcome first, followed by what came before or what led up to it, and sometimes explain the multiple causes and outcomes in a reverberative back-and-forth manner. Deducing these processes is like the childhood exercises in logic in which we had to determine from randomly arranged pictures what happened first, then second, then third. And, complicating the analysis is that sometimes participants may not overtly state the "mediating variable" or the details of what happened between the cause and the outcome (or the *agent* and *target*), and whether the effects were short term or long term (Hays & Singh, 2012, pp. 316, 329). In this case, the researcher will have to follow up participants for additional data or plausibly infer how CODE 1 led to CODE 3.

Munton et al. (1999) operationalized a set of dimensions to examine for the Leeds Attributional Coding System. Qualitative data do not have to be labeled as such for Causation Coding, but they may be helpful during analytic memo writing. The dimensions of causality are:

- internal/external – whether the cause is from self or others
- stable/unstable – an individual's prediction of successful outcome

- global/specific – the effect on a range of many or particular situations
- personal/universal – how unique the situation is to the individual or generalizable to most people
- controllable/uncontrollable – an individual's perception of control over the cause, outcome, and link

Applications

According to Munton et al. (1999):

> Attribution theory concerns the everyday causal explanations that people produce when they encounter novel, important, unusual or potentially threatening behaviour and events. According to attribution theorists, people are motivated to identify the causes of such events, because by doing so they render their environment more predictable and potentially more controllable. (p. 31)

And, when a researcher inquires into participants' rationale for why they think something is as it is, we obtain their speculations and perspectives on what they believe to be probable or "true" as they construct it.

Causation Coding is appropriate for discerning motives (by or toward something or someone), belief systems, worldviews, processes, recent histories, interrelationships, and the complexity of influences and affects (my qualitative equivalent for the positivist "cause and effect") on human actions and phenomena. The method may serve grounded theorists in meticulous searches for causes, conditions, contexts, and consequences. The method is also appropriate if you are trying to evaluate the efficacy of a particular program, or as preparatory work before diagramming or modeling a process through visual means such as decision modeling and causal networks (Miles & Huberman, 1994). Of course, Causation Coding is geared toward exploring "why" questions in research endeavors, but the method should not be considered a foolproof algorithm for deducing the "correct" answers. Instead, it should be used as a heuristic for considering or hypothesizing about *plausible* causes of particular outcomes, and potential outcomes from particular causes.

Miles and Huberman (1994) advise that analysts remain firmly grounded in the particulars of participants' experiences and perspectives since "causality is ultimately local, linked with specific nearby events in time" (p. 146). But as I reflect on the origins of some of my gestural habits and even thinking processes as a middle-aged adult, I realize they had familial and educational roots decades ago during childhood and adolescence. Also, today's global and interconnected world suggests that macro- and meso-levels of influence and affect from national government policies, international crises, and the ubiquitous impact of technology, can trickle down rapidly to the individual micro-level. Causation can range from actual people (e.g., a beloved high school teacher) to conceptual phenomena (e.g., the economy) to significant events (e.g., September 11, 2001) to natural phenomena (e.g., hurricanes) to personal ethos and agency (e.g., self-motivation to advance one's career), to a myriad of other factors in various combinations.

Both quantitative (e.g., regression and path analysis) and qualitative methods are available for discerning causation, but Morrison (2009) advocates that the latter may be more "ideal" for identifying causation's processes and mechanisms through action narratives and structural accounts (pp. 99, 105).

Example

Open-ended survey data were collected from adults of various ages who participated in high school speech/communication classes and related extracurricular activities (e.g., debate clubs, forensic tournaments). Participants responded to an e-mail questionnaire that solicited their memories and perceptions of their experiences (McCammon & Saldaña, 2011). Two of the prompts included: "Looking back, what do you think was the biggest challenge you overcame/faced in high school speech?" and "In what ways do you think your participation in speech as a high school student has affected the adult you have become?"

The researcher observed during initial coding and data analysis that several respondents mentioned specific causes and outcomes in their written reflections. Note how the participant narratives are not always linear in terms of storyline, but the coding sequences in the right-hand column rearrange the attributions and outcomes into a chronological sequence. Also, not all participants mentioned a three-part sequence – most provided only two. Multiple examples are included below to illustrate the possible coding variances and how an extensive number of codes are necessary for Causation Coding analysis. Maxwell (2012) emphasizes that coding for causation should not fragment the data but instead examine the processual links embedded within extended excerpts (p. 44):

[1] I was incredibly shy during high school, and the way I learned to think on my feet and to speak in front of other people helped me come out of my shell by the time I was a senior – so that I could do things like run organizations as president or editor of the high school paper and interview better for scholarships. [2] Without speech training, I may have been an anti-social mess. It also gave me the confidence I needed to start college on the right foot.	[1] SHY > "THINK ON MY FEET" + SPEAK IN FRONT OF OTHERS > "COME OUT OF MY SHELL" > LEADERSHIP SKILLS + INTERVIEW SKILLS [2] SPEECH TRAINING > CONFIDENCE > COLLEGE PREP
[1] A need to be accepted by my peers. Speech tournaments provided that to me every Saturday. Making friends from other schools; [2] competing and winning also tremendously	[1] SPEECH TOURNAMENTS > PEER ACCEPTANCE + FRIENDS [2] COMPETITION > WINNING >

helped build my staggering self-esteem issues that were completely related to school peer relationships.

SELF-ESTEEM

[1] Without a doubt, it was a fear of speaking in front of others. My ultimate career as an adult was in the field of journalism. Early fears I had about approaching strangers and speaking in front of a group of people were overcome due to involvement in speaking events. As I mentioned above, I think speech class and the events that I participated in due to taking that class, probably led directly to my choosing journalism as a career. My success in the field of journalism would have never come about without those speech classes in high school.

[1] "FEAR OF SPEAKING" > SPEAKING EVENTS + SPEECH CLASS > JOURNALISM CAREER + SUCCESS

[1] I have a measure of confidence and composure that would not exist were it not for speech. [2] I wouldn't have the same set of job skills and abilities. [3] I would not have the same set of friends and acquaintances (most of whom I met through speech and theatre). [4] I wouldn't have had the same influences that created my political ideologies and many of my individual beliefs. [5] I believe that my participation in speech and theatre in high school has influenced who I am as an adult more than any other single influence in my entire life. Of all the things that matter, it has mattered the most.

[1] SPEECH > CONFIDENCE + COMPOSURE
[2] SPEECH > JOB SKILLS
[3] SPEECH + THEATRE > FRIENDSHIPS
[4] SPEECH > PERSONAL ETHOS

[5] SPEECH + THEATRE > MAJOR INFLUENCE ON ADULTHOOD

Several things:
[1] Speaking skill set that has made it much easier for me to tackle, staff management, negotiating and business presentation.
[2] Built confidence through achieving success and experiencing the rewards of hard work (of course everyone did not have as good a coach as we did).

[1] SPEAKING SKILLS > BUSINESS SKILLS

[2] SUCCESS + HARD WORK REWARDS + GOOD COACH > CONFIDENCE

³ Increased skills in forming relationships since we were sort of a ready made group.

³ SENSE OF GROUP > INTERPERSONAL RELATIONSHIPS

¹ I went into speech-language pathology, partly because of the positive experience I had in speech competitions. ² When I became a professor, I relied heavily on what I learned from [my teacher] to get up in front of the class and perform. I've presented research all over the country and have had roles at my college where I had to give presentations to all-campus meetings with the faculty and administrators. I could not have done all of this if [my teacher] had not worked her magic on me.

¹ "POSITIVE EXPERIENCE" IN SPEECH COMPETITIONS > SPEECH-RELATED CAREER
² SPEECH TEACHER > TEACHER MODELING > PRESENTATION SKILLS

¹ The constant rehearsing and memorizing lines was difficult, especially when your teacher requires nothing less than perfection, but performing in front of the crowd was the scariest part to overcome, but it taught me to be a powerful leader.

¹ EXPECTATIONS OF PERFECTION + PERFORMANCE SKILLS > LEADERSHIP SKILLS

¹ We all also developed some close friends at competing schools. ² And, it's always fun when you're on a winning team and we won a lot. ³ Speech was my main source of positive feedback in school (looking back I was/am probably a bit ADD) and ⁴ I didn't live up to my my potential. Part of that is due to many of the faculty either being burned out or ambivalent about teaching. ⁵ Winning is among the fondest memories – ⁶ everybody needs to excel at something. This was the only group that most of us fit into and where some of us excelled. ⁷ Even those who were not the top performers were accepted unconditionally by our group and the groups from most of the other schools. Maybe it's part of the "nerd herd" mentality.

¹ SPEECH COMPETITIONS > FRIENDS
² WINNING > FUN
³ SPEECH > "POSITIVE FEEDBACK"
⁴ POOR FACULTY > STUDENTS NOT UP TO POTENTIAL

⁵ WINNING > FOND MEMORIES
⁶ BELONGING > EXCELLING

⁷ BELONGING > ACCEPTANCE

[8] The "popularity" that comes with winning also had its own rewards.

[8] WINNING > "POPULARITY"

[1] I am not worried about speaking persuasively to others and attempting to draw them into agreement with my position. I can also speak on an impromptu basis with little anxiety. I feel more confident if I am presenting something in a formal setting as a result of the experiences I had in high school.

[1] SPEECH EXPERIENCES > PERSUASIVE SPEAKING + IMPROMPTU SPEAKING + CONFIDENCE

[1] My work ethic was formed during that time; balancing academic work with the demands of speech required a lot of concentration and multitasking. [2] Of course the skills I learned in extemporaneous speaking have been invaluable in my work where quick thinking and entertaining presentation are essential. I have the capacity to talk to almost anyone. [3] In terms of entering college, I was a league ahead of many of my peers. I could speak confidently in front of a class, or quickly form my thoughts into structured and reasonable answers for essay questions.

[1] SPEECH > CONCENTRATION + MULTITASKING > WORK ETHIC

[2] EXTEMP SPEAKING > QUICK THINKING + PRESENTATION SKILLS + SOCIAL SKILLS

[3] SPEECH > CONFIDENT SPEAKING + QUICK THINKING

Analysis

After the corpus has been coded, one tactic to analyze the aggregate is to plot the attribution sequences into a chronological matrix or flow chart to assess what generally leads to what, according to participants and researcher inferences, and to categorize the codes accordingly based on similarity. A minimum of three columns to differentiate between antecedent and/or mediating variables (i.e., causes, conditions, contexts, actions) and outcomes (i.e., consequences) is strongly recommended. Below is the array of codes from the survey data examples above, reorganized manually into seven categories according to comparable variables and/or outcomes – a method and process educational researcher Howard Gardner once termed in a public lecture, "a sort of subjective factor analysis." Also note how the first survey example had a four-part code sequence, rather than three. Thus, both possible three-way combinations of codes were placed into the array below:

ANTECEDENT VARIABLES >	MEDIATING VARIABLES >	OUTCOMES
		Outcome Category: Career Skills
SPEECH TRAINING	CONFIDENCE SPEAKING SKILLS	COLLEGE PREP BUSINESS SKILLS
SPEECH		JOB SKILLS
SPEECH	CONCENTRATION + MULTITASKING	WORK ETHIC
"FEAR OF SPEAKING"	SPEAKING EVENTS + SPEECH CLASS	JOURNALISM CAREER + SUCCESS
	"POSITIVE EXPERIENCE" IN SPEECH COMPETITIONS	SPEECH-RELATED CAREER
		Outcome Category: Presentation Skills
SPEECH TEACHER	TEACHER MODELING EXTEMP SPEAKING	PRESENTATION SKILLS QUICK THINKING + PRESENTATION SKILLS
SPEECH		QUICK THINKING
	SPEECH EXPERIENCES	PERSUASIVE SPEAKING + IMPROMPTU SPEAKING
		Outcome Category: Leadership Skills
"THINK ON MY FEET" + SPEAK IN FRONT OF OTHERS	"COME OUT OF MY SHELL"	LEADERSHIP SKILLS + INTERVIEW SKILLS
	EXPECTATIONS OF PERFECTION + PERFORMANCE SKILLS	LEADERSHIP SKILLS
		Outcome Category: Confidence
SPEECH		CONFIDENCE+COMPOSURE
SPEECH EXPERIENCES		CONFIDENCE
	SUCCESS + HARD WORK REWARDS + GOOD COACH	CONFIDENCE
SPEECH		CONFIDENT SPEAKING

		Outcome Category: **Winning Payoffs**
COMPETITION	WINNING	SELF-ESTEEM
	WINNING	FUN
	WINNING	FOND MEMORIES
	WINNING	POPULARITY

		Outcome Category: **Social Belonging**
	EXTEMP SPEAKING	SOCIAL SKILLS
SPEECH + THEATRE		FRIENDSHIPS
	SPEECH TOURNAMENTS	FRIENDS
	SPEECH COMPETITIONS	FRIENDS
	BELONGING	EXCELLING
	BELONGING	ACCEPTANCE
	SPEECH TOURNAMENTS	PEER ACCEPTANCE
	SENSE OF GROUP	INTERPERSONAL RELATIONSHIPS

		Outcome Category: **Personal Affects**
SHY	"THINK ON MY FEET" + SPEAK IN FRONT OF OTHERS	"COME OUT OF MY SHELL"
SPEECH		PERSONAL ETHOS
SPEECH	"POSITIVE FEEDBACK"	
SPEECH + THEATRE		MAJOR INFLUENCE ON ADULTHOOD
POOR FACULTY	STUDENTS NOT UP TO POTENTIAL	

After initial categorizing, similar outcomes can be categorized even further. The researcher developed two major categories from the seven initially generated:

- **Workforce Preparation** (composed of **Career Skills**, **Presentation Skills**, and **Leadership Skills**)
- **Lifeforce Preparation** (composed of **Confidence**, **Winning Payoffs**, **Social Belonging**, and **Personal Affects**)

Analytic memos should now examine the researcher's assessment of the attributions that led to the outcomes. Codeweaving (see Chapter Two) is one tactic that insures the analyst is remaining grounded in the data and not relying too heavily on speculation. Language that incorporates chronological processes (first, initial, then, next, future, etc.) provides a sense of storylined influences and affects. Supportive evidence with participant quotes or field note excerpts also help make the case:

16 November 2010
ATTRIBUTIONS FOR WORKFORCE PREPARATION
An adolescent may first enter a SPEECH CLASS with an initial FEAR OF SPEAKING in front of others, but under the direction of an expert TEACHER with high EXPECTATIONS for SPEECH EXPERIENCES that shape not just the voice but the mind, the student gains the ability to mentally CONCENTRATE and MULTITASK. Survey respondents testify that EXTEMP/IMPROMPTU and PERSUASIVE SPEAKING tasks, particularly at speech COMPETITIONS with POSITIVE outcomes, establish QUICK THINKING and PRESENTATION SKILLS. These initial outcomes contribute to a strong WORK ETHIC for future COLLEGE and BUSINESS careers and, for some, LEADERSHIP roles: "My work ethic was formed during that time; balancing academic work with the demands of speech required a lot of concentration and multitasking. Of course the skills I learned in extemporaneous speaking have been invaluable in my work where quick thinking and entertaining presentation are essential."

Graphic models are another effective way to plot the flow of antecedent variables, mediating variables, and outcomes. Morrison (2009) posits that "an effect is a consequence of a net or network of conditions, circumstances, intentionality and agency that interact in a myriad of ways" (p. 12), and linear models are only one form of plotting causation. Figure 3.5 illustrates the **Lifeforce Preparation** codes and categories at work in the examples above.

CONFIDENCE emerged as the primary outcome from the majority of the 234 survey respondents in this particular study, but not every participant was involved in competitive speech events. Thus, the model illustrates the trajectories for those

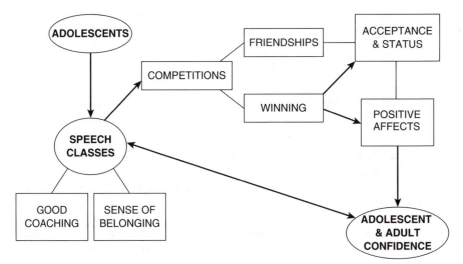

Figure 3.5   A causation model of speech classes as Lifeforce Preparation

who did and did not compete in forensics tournaments. The choice of connecting lines and arrows was also carefully considered, based on researcher assessment of interrelationship (indicated by a line) and influence and affect (indicated by one-way or two-way arrows), as suggested by the data corpus. A CAQDAS-coded set of data with its Simultaneous Coding feature can more intricately examine what types of interrelationships may exist among variables and outcomes.

But models do not speak for themselves. Since Causation Coding tackles a "why" question, you should tackle a "because" answer. An explanatory narrative from the full report of the study discusses not just how but *why* students gain confidence from speech classes, presentations, and competitive events:

> The most prominent outcome for most high school speech participants is life-long *confidence* – outgoing, independent expressiveness with an openness to ideas and people. The nature of speech programming demands that students physically, vocally, and mentally transcend their comfort zones and make themselves open to performance and presentation experiences with poise and composure. Confidence reverberates with the ability to excel at public speaking/communication, leadership, and cognitive/thinking affects. Along with confidence, or as a necessary antecedent, comes opportunities for one's potential and talent to be nurtured (if not "pushed" by a speech teacher with high expectations), to achieve significant accomplishment and "shine" on stage or at the forensic event, and to receive validation from peers and adults. Through these processes, a student discovers her voice, enhances her self-esteem, and expresses her evolving identity with passion. (McCammon & Saldaña, 2011, p. 100)

Explaining "why" something happens is a slippery task in qualitative inquiry (and even in some quantitative research). Gubrium and Holstein (1997) put forward that "the *whats* of the social world always inform our understanding of the *hows*. ... Taken together, these reciprocal *what* and *how* concerns offer a basis for answering a variety of *why* questions" (p. 196). During this cycle of coding and analysis, if you seem to have only a tentative explanation for why something is happening or has happened, return to the data to examine participant "whats" and "hows."

The data we collect may contain some sense of chronological order (even if the participant tells us his or her story in a fluid sequence), but we may not be able to always demarcate what happened *when*, specifically. Participants themselves are usually unable to recall specific dates, turning points, or periods, referring instead to changes or outcomes as gradual, evolutionary processes. The exception to this is if some sort of epiphanic or revelatory event occurred that enables a participant to pinpoint an exact moment or period of time (e.g., "That's a day I'll never forget, because it was from that point on that I vowed I would never, ever get myself into those kinds of situations again"; "I just turned 40, and I felt as if my life had suddenly kicked into mid-life crisis"). Franzosi's (2010) narrative methods encourage the specifications of time periods for causal analysis since "Narrative time has three aspects: order, duration, and frequency, dealing with three different questions:

When? For how long? And how often?" (p. 26). But such documentation is sparse in the data unless qualitative researchers can solicit more precise information from participants, or if they conduct a longitudinal fieldwork project that includes dated references that accompany participants' actions. If time is a critical component of your research study's questions, make sure that your data collection includes information that addresses when, for how long, and how often.

Finally, Munton et al. (1999) and Morrison (2009) also suggest that attributions can be dimensionalized or rated with such accompanying measures as Magnitude Coding, since the influence and affect of some causal factors and outcomes may be considered greater than others.

Some recommended ways to further analyze Causation Codes are (see Appendix B):

- action and practitioner research (Altrichter et al., 1993; Coghlan & Brannick, 2010; Fox et al., 2007; Stringer, 1999)
- assertion development (Erickson, 1986)
- case studies (Merriam, 1998; Stake, 1995)
- cognitive mapping (Miles & Huberman, 1994; Northcutt & McCoy, 2004)
- decision modeling (Bernard, 2011)
- discourse analysis (Gee, 2011; Rapley, 2007; Willig, 2008)
- grounded theory (Bryant & Charmaz, 2007; Charmaz, 2006; Corbin & Strauss, 2008; Glaser & Strauss, 1967; Stern & Porr, 2011; Strauss & Corbin, 1998)
- illustrative charts, matrices, diagrams (Miles & Huberman, 1994; Morgan et al., 2008; Northcutt & McCoy, 2004; Paulston, 2000; Wheeldon & Åhlberg, 2012)
- interrelationship (Saldaña, 2003)
- logic models (Knowlton & Phillips, 2009; Yin, 2009)
- memo writing about the codes/themes (Charmaz, 2006; Corbin & Strauss, 2008; Glaser, 1978; Glaser & Strauss, 1967; Strauss, 1987; Strauss & Corbin, 1998)
- phenomenology (Butler-Kisber, 2010; Giorgi & Giorgi, 2003; Smith et al., 2009; van Manen, 1990; Wertz et al., 2011)
- qualitative evaluation research (Patton, 2002, 2008)
- situational analysis (Clarke, 2005)
- splitting, splicing, and linking data (Dey, 1993)
- within-case and cross-case displays (Gibbs, 2007; Miles & Huberman, 1994; Shkedi, 2005)

Notes

Eatough and Smith (2006) take issue with "attribution approaches, with their reliance on matching cause with effect, [because they] are simply unable to explain the complexity of a person's meaning making" (p. 129). And, as discussed in other portions of this manual, qualitative data analysis should explore temporal processes or multifaceted influences and affects in human agency and interaction.

Causation Coding carries with it the risk of too easily assuming surface and positivist-driven causes and effects, most of which are actually human constructions and thus illusory (Packer, 2011, p. 142). Some solutions to this dilemma are gathering large amounts of data for enhancing credibility and trustworthiness through nuanced analysis and/or strategic, in-depth interviewing that explores with participants the subtle dynamics of attributions in action. Despite its slippery nature, do not be afraid to ask participants *why* they believe something is as it is. Some may reply, "I don't know"; some may venture only a guess; some may merely philosophize; and others may provide quite insightful answers.

For methods related to or for use in conjunction with Causation Coding, see Magnitude, Simultaneous, Process, Values, Evaluation, Dramaturgical, Hypothesis, and Focused Coding. Refer to the Analytic Storylining section in Chapter Six for time- and process-oriented vocabulary to employ in analytic memos and write-ups. Regardless of your discipline or field of study, read Morrison's (2009) outstanding work, *Causation in Educational Research*, for an extended discussion on the intricacies and nuances of the subject; and Maxwell's (2012) provocative thoughts on the nature of and search for causation in qualitative materials.

Themeing the Data

I stated in Chapter One that a theme is an *outcome* of coding, categorization, and analytic reflection, not something that is, in itself, coded. But several qualitative methodologists recommend labeling and thus analyzing portions of data with an extended thematic statement rather than a shorter code, as it is defined in this manual. Hence, "Themeing the Data" provides a brief profile of that process.

Sources

Auerbach & Silverstein, 2003; Boyatzis, 1998; Butler-Kisber, 2010; DeSantis & Ugarriza, 2000; Giorgi & Giorgi, 2003; Kvale & Brinkmann, 2009; Rubin & Rubin, 2012; Ryan & Bernard, 2003; Smith & Osborn, 2008; van Manen, 1990

Description

The definition and analytic function of a "theme" varies among the writers listed in the Sources above, but overall a theme is an *extended phrase* or *sentence* that identifies what a unit of data is *about* and/or what it *means*. Boyatzis (1998) explains that a theme "at a minimum describes and organizes possible observations or at the maximum interprets aspects of the phenomenon. A theme may be identified at the manifest level (directly observable in the information) or at the latent level (underlying the phenomenon)" (p. vii). DeSantis and Ugarriza (2000), after an extensive literature review on the use of theme in qualitative research, discovered that the term was often used interchangeably with such words as "category," "domain," "phrase," "unit of analysis," and others (p. 358). Ultimately, they proposed a more stable definition based on their content analysis: "A theme is an abstract entity that brings meaning and identity to a recurrent [patterned] experience and its variant manifestations. As such, a theme captures and unifies the nature or basis of the experience into a meaningful whole" (p. 362).

At its manifest level, a theme functions as a way to categorize a set of data into "an implicit topic that organizes a group of repeating ideas" (Auerbach & Silverstein, 2003, p. 38). This foundation work leads to the development of higher-level theoretical constructs when similar themes are clustered together. To Rubin and Rubin (2012), themes are statements *qua* (in the role of) ideas presented by participants during interviews that summarize what is going on, explain what is happening, or suggest why something is done the way it is (p. 118). Themes can also consist of descriptions of behavior within a culture, iconic statements, and morals from participant stories. These themes are discerned during data collection and initial analysis, and then examined further as interviews continue. The analytic goals are to winnow down the number of themes to explore in a report, and to develop an overarching theme from the data corpus, or an integrative theme that weaves various themes together into a coherent narrative.

At its latent level, themes serve phenomenology, "the study of the lifeworld – the world as we immediately experience it pre-reflectively rather than as we conceptualize, categorize, or reflect on it. … Phenomenology aims at gaining a deeper understanding of the nature or meaning of our everyday experiences" (van Manen, 1990, p. 9). Sandelowski (2008) clarifies that "phenomenological research questions tend to address what it is like to be, to have, or to live" (p. 787).

To van Manen, themes are interpretive, insightful discoveries – written attempts to get at the "notions" of data to make sense of them and give them shape. Overall, a theme is "the form of capturing the phenomenon one tries to understand" (p. 87), but the collective set of researcher-generated themes is not intended for systematic analysis; "themes are only fasteners, foci, or threads around which the phenomenological description is facilitated" (p. 91). Van Manen recommends the winnowing down of themes to what is "essential" rather than "incidental," the former making the phenomenon "what it is and without which the phenomenon could not be what it is" (p. 107). Butler-Kisber (2010, pp. 50–61) advises that this process consists of extracting verbatim "significant statements" from the data, "formulating meanings" about them through the researcher's interpretations, clustering these meanings into a series of organized themes, then elaborating on the themes through rich written description.

Applications

Themeing the Data is appropriate for virtually all qualitative studies, and especially for phenomenology and those exploring a participant's psychological world of beliefs, constructs, identity development, and emotional experiences (Giorgi & Giorgi, 2003; Smith & Osborn, 2008; Smith et al., 2009; Wertz et al., 2011). Kozinets (2010) advises that online research ("netnography") employs a blend of "analytic coding with a blend of hermeneutic interpretation" – that is, thematic analysis (p. 124). Themeing the Data is also a strategic approach for metasummary and metasynthesis studies (Major & Savin-Baden, 2010; Sandelowski & Barroso, 2007; see the discussion at the end of this profile). Unlike most approaches to content analysis, which often begin with predefined categories, thematic analysis allows categories to emerge from the data. Themeing the Data is not an expedient method of qualitative analysis. It is just as intensive as coding and requires comparable reflection on participant meanings and outcomes.

Like coding, thematic analysis or the search for themes in the data is a strategic choice as part of the research design that includes the primary questions, goals, conceptual framework, and literature review. Kvale and Brinkmann (2009) label this "thematizing" or describing the concept of the topic under investigation before interviews begin (p. 105). Kvale and Brinkmann, Rubin and Rubin, and van Manen attest that through carefully planned questioning techniques, participants construct the meanings of what the researcher is trying to explore. Themes should be stated as simple examples of something during the first cycle of analysis, then woven together during later cycles to detect processes, tensions, explanations, causes, consequences, and/or conclusions (Rubin & Rubin, 2012, p. 206).

Themeing the Data is perhaps more applicable to interviews and participant-generated documents and artifacts, rather than researcher-generated field notes.

Example

A phenomenological study is conducted on "belonging" – what it means "to belong." The question is posed to a middle-aged adult male. Note how the themes in the margin relate directly to the goal of the study. Some are manifest themes, others are latent, and some employ In Vivo Codes. There are also deliberate choices made between the phrases "Belonging is" and "Belonging means." The former generally refers to concrete details or action at the manifest level; the latter generally refers to conceptual ideas at the latent level:

[I: What does it mean to you to "belong"?]

Whoa, that's tough. To me, [1] it means to belong somewhere, a specific place and no place else.	[1] BELONGING MEANS A "SPECIFIC PLACE"

[I: What kind of place?]

New Orleans. [2] I feel so grounded in that city. This was before [Hurricane] Katrina, years before. [3] There's something about that place – the gentle decadence, the style, the robustness you can't find in any other city, even New York. There's a kind of sensuality about the	[2] BELONGING MEANS FEELING "GROUNDED" [3] BELONGING OCCURS IN A "UNIQUE" PLACE

city, a mix of food, music, stuff that's
unique, things you'll find no other place in
that combination … .

[4] I've got friends there, good friends, [5] good
memories, places to drink, places to eat. Every
time I go there, [6] I'm always in search of the
perfect jumbalaya. I still haven't found it yet,
but I'm still searching. I've found the perfect
red beans, rice and sausage, but no jumbalaya
yet.

[4] BELONGING IS WHERE THERE
ARE "GOOD FRIENDS"
[5] BELONGING IS WHERE
THERE ARE
"GOOD MEMORIES"
[6] BELONGING MEANS
THE SEARCH
FOR PERFECTION – UTOPIA

Oh, what else? [7] Sidewalk vendors and artists on
Jackson Square, those psychics, homeless kids,
tourists wearing those Mardi Gras beads. I have
them as décor all over my house, but I never
wear them in New Orleans because only
tourists do that when it's not Mardi Gras.
Yeah, [8] I'm not a tourist there. I belong there
even though I don't live there.

[7] BELONGING IS KNOWING
THE DETAILS OF THE CULTURE

[8] YOU CAN BELONG
SOMEWHERE WITHOUT
ACTUALLY BEING THERE

[9] If I could do it tomorrow, I'd sell my house
and move to New Orleans and live there 'til I die.
[10] I feel I've got some Cajun in me, and that's
where I belong.

[I: *Are* you part Cajun?]

[11] No, but I feel like I am.

[9] BELONGING IS A DRIVE TO
BE SOMEPLACE PERMANENT
[10] BELONGING MEANS HAVING
A SENSE OF ANCESTRY

[11] BELONGING MEANS
HAVING A SENSE OF
IDENTITY

Analysis

The Sources for Themeing the Data propose various ways of analyzing or reflecting
on themes after they have been generated. Basic categorization as an initial tactic is
the one most often prescribed, so it will be illustrated here. Generally, the researcher
looks for how various themes are similar, how they are different, and what kinds of
relationships may exist between them (Gibson & Brown, 2009, pp. 128–9).

The themes listed next to the transcript above are now categorized according to
commonality, and ordered in superordinate and subordinate outline format to
reflect on their possible groupings and relationships:

I. **Belonging means feeling "grounded"**

    A. Belonging means having a sense of ancestry
    B. Belonging means having a sense of identity
    C. Belonging is knowing the details of the culture

II. **Belonging is a drive to be someplace permanent**

    A. Belonging means a "specific place"
    B. Belonging occurs in a "unique" place
    C. You can belong somewhere without actually being there

III. **Belonging means the search for perfection – Utopia**

    A. Belonging is where there are "good friends"
    B. Belonging is where there are "good memories"

The three major theme headings (meta-themes or "elements" (Durbin, 2010)) suggest that "belonging" is: (1) an actual place; (2) a sense of self in that place; (3) an ideal place. A reflective analytic memo that builds on this initial categorization and weaves the thematic elements together might read:

> "Belonging" is both geographical and conceptual. It is an ideal place where we feel, as an overarching theme, *grounded* – grounded with a sense of ancestry and memory, grounded with a sense of culture and identity, and grounded with a sense of permanence and perfection.

A different approach to the themes would involve categorization in order to develop researcher-generated *theoretical constructs*. Note how the categorization of themes here is different from the way they were organized above:

Theoretical Construct 1: Belonging is Social

Supporting Themes:
Belonging means a "specific place"
Belonging occurs in a "unique" place
Belonging is knowing the details of the culture
Belonging is where there are "good friends"
Belonging means having a sense of identity

Theoretical Construct 2: Belonging is Memory

Supporting Themes:
Belonging is where there are "good memories"
Belonging means having a sense of ancestry
You can belong somewhere without actually being there

Theoretical Construct 3: Belonging is a Quest

Supporting Themes:
Belonging is a drive to be someplace permanent
Belonging means feeling "grounded"
Belonging means the search for perfection – Utopia

The write-up would then discuss each one of these constructs and how they integrate or relate with each other. The themes and their related data serve as illustrative examples to support the interpretation.

The same themes, organized and categorized in two ways, as illustrated above, generate somewhat different perspectives on what it means to "belong." Emerson et al. (2011) note that, aside from frequency, the themes ultimately developed and selected for analysis are those that resonate with personal or disciplinary concerns. Shaw (2010) also stresses the importance of situated embeddedness: "to understand people's experiences at a particular point in history, a particular time in their life, in [their] social, cultural, political and economic context" (p. 178). Keep in mind that this initial analysis is only of one excerpt from one participant's interview transcript. Additional participants may generate different as well as similar themes related to "belonging" that will be integrated into a fuller analysis. The themes developed thus far can be referenced as interviews continue to assess their validity and to shape the researcher's interview questions. Some themes from the particular example above may be dropped as more data are collected and analysis continues. Some may be subsumed under broader categories, and some themes may be retained. As a related thematic analysis, Madden (2010), reflecting on the meanings of "home," conceptualized and assembled a list that reads: home is familiar, parochial, discrete, habitual, permanent, birth, death, and ambivalence – the former meaning "a place I felt the need to leave, and to which I need to return" (pp. 45–6).

In Chapter One of this manual, I included a section titled "What Gets Coded?" For this particular method, one might ask, "What gets themed?" Ryan and Bernard (2003) recommend that themes can be found in the data by looking for such qualities as: repeating ideas, participant or indigenous terms, metaphors and analogies, transitions or shifts in topic, similarities and differences of participant expression, linguistic connectors ("because," "since," "then," etc.), theoretical issues suggested by the data (e.g., interpersonal relationships, social conflict and control), and even what is missing from – not discussed or present in – the data.

Themeing lends itself to selected CAQDAS programs, but themes are also intriguing to simply "cut and paste" in multiple arrangements on a basic word processor page to explore possible categories and relationships. Smith and Osborn (2008) use a three-column format for thematic analytic work. The center column of a page contains the interview transcript data; the left column provides working space for initial notes, key words, and shorter codes; while the right column contains the final themes for analysis.

Some recommended ways to further analyze themes are (see Appendix B):

- assertion development (Erickson, 1986)
- case studies (Merriam, 1998; Stake, 1995)

- discourse analysis (Gee, 2011; Rapley, 2007; Willig, 2008)
- memo writing about the themes (Charmaz, 2006; Corbin & Strauss, 2008; Glaser, 1978; Glaser & Strauss, 1967; Strauss, 1987)
- meta-ethnography, metasummary, and metasynthesis (Finfgeld, 2003; Major & Savin-Baden, 2010; Noblit & Hare, 1988; Sandelowski & Barroso, 2007; Sandelowski et al., 1997)
- metaphoric analysis (Coffey & Atkinson, 1996; Todd & Harrison, 2008)
- narrative inquiry and analysis (Clandinin & Connelly, 2000; Coffey & Atkinson, 1996; Cortazzi, 1993; Coulter & Smith, 2009; Daiute & Lightfoot, 2004; Holstein & Gubrium, 2012; Murray, 2003; Riessman, 2008)
- phenomenology (Butler-Kisber, 2010; Giorgi & Giorgi, 2003; Smith et al., 2009; van Manen, 1990; Wertz et al., 2011)
- poetic and dramatic writing (Denzin, 1997, 2003; Glesne, 2011; Knowles & Cole, 2008; Leavy, 2009; Saldaña, 2005a, 2011a)
- portraiture (Lawrence-Lightfoot & Davis, 1997)
- thematic analysis (Auerbach & Silverstein, 2003; Boyatzis, 1998; Smith & Osborn, 2008)
- vignette writing (Erickson, 1986; Graue & Walsh, 1998)

Notes

Packer (2011) cautions that "A theme never simply 'emerges'; it is the product of interpretation. ... [T]hemes that 'stand out' tell us more about the researcher than about the interviewee, and they should not be the starting point for analysis" (p. 70). His concern, however, is with themes that are simply nouns or incomplete phrases similar to categories, rather than complete sentences that elaborate on the researcher's interpretations of participants' meanings in more nuanced and/or complex ways.

Metasummary and metasynthesis

What follows is a brief overview of qualitative metasummary and metasynthesis, research enterprises that can employ unique combinations of coding *and* theme-ing qualitative data.

Metasummary and metasynthesis are methodological approaches that collect, compare, and synthesize the key findings of a number of related interpretive/quali-tative studies (Major & Savin-Baden, 2010; Noblit & Hare, 1988; Sandelowski & Barroso, 2007). A primary goal of these techniques is inductive and "systematic comparison of case studies to draw cross-case conclusions. ... It reduces the accounts while preserving the sense of the account through the selection of key metaphors and organizers" such as themes, concepts, ideas, and perspectives (Noblit & Hare, 1988, pp. 13–14). This is the qualitative cousin of quantitative research's meta-anal-ysis, and relies on the researcher's strategic collection and comparative analysis of phrases and sentences – that is, themes – that represent the essences and essentials of previous studies. The number of different yet related studies needed for such ventures varies among methodologists, ranging from as few as 2 to as many as 20, but Major and Savin-Baden (2010) recommend that "between 6 and 10 studies is optimal to provide sufficient yet manageable data" (p. 54).

Some researchers apply a mix of Descriptive, Holistic, and Simultaneous Codes, for example, to represent the gist of an entire study. These codes may be based on an a priori or emergent set of themes when reviewing a collected body of related studies for metasummary. Au (2007), for example, reviewed 49 qualitative educational studies and employed a six-code template to classify each study's site-specific curricular changes in response to high-stakes testing. Two of the six curriculum-based codes representing "dominant themes" were "PCT – Pedagogic change to teacher-centered" and "KCF – Form of knowledge changed, fractured" (p. 260).

Other researchers do not initially code but instead carefully search for and extract thematic statements and extended assertions from the collected studies' findings and, if necessary, abstract the statements for comparison and metasummary and metasynthesis. Sandelowski and Barroso (2003), for example, reviewed 45 qualitative studies on HIV-positive mothers and compiled an initial set of almost 800 thematic statements that represented the studies' major observations. These "raw data" themes were then compared and collapsed to 93 statements based on similarity, then coded and classified under 10 major emergent categories about the women, such as "stigma and disclosure" and "mothering the HIV-negative and HIV-positive child." Though not necessary for metasynthesis, both Au (2007) and Sandelowski and Barroso (2003, 2007) calculated percentages of selected data to assess such phenomena as participant effect sizes and major theme occurrences. Au's Simultaneous Coding system enabled him to infer "potentially significant relationships between dominant themes" (2007, p. 263).

But unlike codes and categories extracted in the studies above, Maher and Hudson (2007) metasynthesized 15 qualitative studies and identified "six key [meta-]themes that captured the nature and experience of women's participation in the illicit drug economy" (p. 812). The 15 studies' combined 60 summary themes were categorized into six key themes; then, like codeweaving (see Chapter Two), were "theme-woven" into an elegant concluding narrative. The key themes are bolded to highlight their integration into the text:

> The qualitative evidence reviewed here suggests that **the illicit drug economy and, in particular, street-based drug markets, are gender stratified and hierarchical** and that **women primarily access and sustain economic roles through their links with men** who act as gatekeepers, sponsors, and protectors. Within these markets, **female roles continue to be sexualized**, but **some women utilize "feminine" attributes and institutional sexism to their advantage.** Our metasynthesis also found that **family and kinship ties are important resources for women engaged in drug sales and that successful women dealers appear to have increased access to social capital.** Finally, our results suggest that **while women rely on a diverse range of income sources and juggle different roles**

both within the drug economy and in relation to dealing and domestic responsibilities, most women in most drug markets remain confined to low level and marginal roles. (p. 821)

Metasummary and metasynthesis can employ a unique combination of coding *and* themeing the data. This approach seems necessary since "Metasynthesis is not a method designed to produce oversimplification; rather, it is one in which differences are retained and complexity enlightened. The goal is to achieve more, not less. The outcome will be something like a common understanding of the nature of a phenomenon, not a consensual worldview" (Thorne, Jensen, Kearney, Noblit, & Sandelowski, 2004, p. 1346). Major and Savin-Baden (2010) code and theme at both the descriptive and interpretive levels to create new syntheses and perspectives on the issues, employing such First Cycle methods as Descriptive and Initial Coding, and Second Cycle methods such as Axial Coding, to find "bigger-picture" ideas through metaphors and concepts that link across several studies (pp. 62–3).

The following pages are provided for documenting additional First Cycle coding methods located in other sources or developed by the researcher.

_____ Coding

Source(s):

Description:

Application(s):

Example:

Analysis:

Notes:

_____ **Coding**

Source(s):

Description:

Application(s):

Example:

Analysis:

Notes:

_____ Coding

Source(s):

Description:

Application(s):

Example:

Analysis:

Notes:

FOUR

After First Cycle Coding

CHAPTER SUMMARY

This chapter reviews transitional processes after First Cycle coding. It begins with an Eclectic Coding methods profile, then illustrates two data management techniques: Code Mapping and Code Landscaping. A section on creating Operational Model Diagrams follows, and concludes with three additional transition methods.

Post-Coding Transitions

Transitions can be awkward. Whether it be physical or mental, the journey from one space to another can range from smooth and seamless to disruptive and disjointed. The transition from First Cycle coding to Second Cycle coding or other qualitative data analytic processes is no exception. This chapter examines those shifts after the initial review of the corpus and provides you with additional methods for reorganizing and reconfiguring your transformed work. The goal is not to "take you to the next level," but to cycle back to your first coding efforts so you can strategically cycle forward to additional coding and qualitative data analytic methods.

As you have been applying one or more coding methods to the data and writing analytic memos, you have hopefully been making new discoveries, insights, and connections about your participants, their processes, or the phenomenon under investigation. But after you have finished coding your data set, the primary question that may be running through your mind is, "Now what?" This chapter focuses on such analytic transitions as: selecting new coding methods for a reanalysis of your data; constructing categories from the classification of your codes; drawing preliminary models of the primary actions at work in your data; and reorganizing and reassembling the transformed data to better focus the direction of your study.

Remember Robert E. Stake's (1995) keen observation: "Good research is not about good methods as much as it is about good thinking" (p. 19). There are certainly new methods included in this chapter to guide you on your analytic journey, but techniques and examples can only take you so far. It is up to you to select and adapt the recommendations below for your own unique research project, and to exercise good thinking in your continued exploration of and reflection on the data. Lindof and Taylor (2011) remind us that our analytic ventures are a "blend of strategic mindfulness and unexpected discovery" (p. 242).

Eclectic Coding

Eclectic Coding is a method that is admittedly difficult to categorize. It meets selected criteria for Grammatical, Elemental, and Exploratory Methods, and can also be considered both a First and Second Cycle approach to the data. Though it best fits as an Exploratory Method, the profile is too important to be embedded in a category that may get overlooked. It seems appropriate, then, to include this hybrid profile separately in this particular chapter because it illustrates how an analyst can start with an array of coding methods for a "first draft" of coding, then transition to strategic "second-draft" recoding decisions based on the learnings of the experience.

Sources

All sources cited in First Cycle coding methods

Description

(Eclectic Coding could be considered a form of Open Coding, as it was originally conceived by Glaser & Strauss (1967). But I label this approach Eclectic Coding since it draws from the specific methods profiled in this book.)

Thus far, 25 First Cycle coding/themeing methods have been described, but each one has been profiled separately. There are many occasions when qualitative data can be appropriately coded using a repertoire of methods simultaneously. Eclectic Coding profiles the process, then demonstrates how it proceeds toward a Second Cycle of coding.

Eclectic Coding employs a select and compatible combination of two or more First Cycle coding methods. Ideally, the methods choices should not be random but purposeful to serve the needs of the study and its data analysis. Nevertheless, any "first-impression" responses from the researcher can serve as codes, with the understanding that analytic memo writing and Second Cycles of recoding will synthesize the variety and number of codes into a more unified scheme.

Applications

Eclectic Coding is appropriate for virtually all qualitative studies, but particularly for beginning qualitative researchers learning how to code data, and studies with a wide variety of data forms (e.g., interview transcripts, field notes, journals, documents, diaries, correspondence, artifacts, video). Eclectic Coding is also appropriate as: an initial, exploratory technique with qualitative data; when a variety of processes or phenomena are to be discerned from the data; or when combined First Cycle coding methods will serve the research study's questions and goals.

Example

A university research project is conducted with PhD students to assess their perceptions of their programs of study. A second-year doctoral student shares his thoughts on his degree plan in progress. The following illustrates how Eclectic Coding is applied to an interview transcript excerpt. For reference only, the specific First Cycle coding methods that relate to the codes are placed in square brackets:

PARTICIPANT'S GENDER: MALE [Attribute Code]
PARTICIPANT'S AGE: 27 [Attribute Code]
PARTICIPANT'S ETHNICITY: WHITE [Attribute Code]
PARTICIPANT'S DEGREE PROGRAM: PhD, SECOND YEAR [Attribute Code]

A SENSE OF URGENCY: "I'VE GOT TO" [Holistic/In Vivo Code]

[1] I'm 27 years old and I've got over $50,000 in student loans that I have to pay off, and that [2] scares the hell out of me. I've got to finish my dissertation next year because I can't afford to keep going to school. [3] I've got to get a job and start working.

[1] STUDENT DEBT [Descriptive Code]
[2] SCARED [Emotion Code]

[3] "I'VE GOT TO" [In Vivo Code]

[I: What kind of job do you hope to get?]
[4] A teaching job at a university someplace.
[I: Any particular part of the country?]
I'd like to go back to the east coast, work at one of the major universities there. But I'm keeping myself open to wherever there's a job.

[4] CAREER GOALS [Descriptive Code]

[5] It's hard listening to some of the others [in the current graduating class] like Jake and Brian interviewing for teaching jobs and being turned down. [6] As a white male, that lessens my chances of getting hired. [I: I think most employers really do look for the best person for the job, regardless of color.] [7] Maybe.

[5] WORRY [Emotion Code]

[6] PRIVILEGED STATUS VS. LIMITED JOB OPPORTUNITIES [Versus Code]

[7] DOUBT VS. HOPE [Versus Code]

[8] If I can get some good recs [letters of recommendation], that should help. My grades have been real good and I've been getting my name out there at conferences. [I: All of that's important.]	[8] TAC: SUCCESS STRATEGIES [Dramaturgical Code]
[9] The prospectus is the first step. Well, the IRB [Institutional Review Board approval] is the first step. I'm starting the lit review this summer, doing the interviews and participant observation in the fall, writing up as I go along, and being finished by spring. [I: What if more time is needed for the dissertation?]	[9] DISSERTATION PLANNING [Process Code]
[10] I've got to be finished by spring.	[10] MOTIF: "I'VE GOT TO" [Narrative/In Vivo Code]

Analysis

Recall that codes can serve as prompts or triggers for reflection through analytic memo writing on the deeper and complex meanings they evoke. Below is one such memo that initially interprets the eclectically coded interview excerpt, then a follow-up memo on the planned Second Cycle recoding of the data:

22 June 2011
EMERGENT PATTERNS, CATEGORIES, THEMES, CONCEPTS, ASSERTIONS: "I'VE GOT TO"

The participant's emotional state at this point in his doctoral program is negative (SCARED, WORRY, DOUBT). He has not yet even begun his capstone dissertation project, but is already worried about his future job prospects. "I'VE GOT TO" is his objective, his drive. He does not mention anything about the process of the dissertation's professional development experience, except in terms of time, just the end product.

With this pessimistic mind-set, he has set himself specific goals and even a compressed timetable to complete the work. The financial debt seems to be looming large in his mind. The Versus Codes suggest that he is torn within, and sees his white male identity as a liability, almost a self-defeating prophecy, for future employment. But he is problem/solution-oriented. When there's an obstacle, the doubt and fear can be lessened when he has a plan. He's not so much driven by fear as he is by urgency. Doubt vs. hope, past vs. future. He's not just accumulated debt, he's accumulated doubt. There's minimal talk of what he wants; the majority is what he has to do: "I've got" and "I've got to." Because he's got this, he's got to do that.

24 June 2011

FUTURE DIRECTIONS: DRAMATURGICAL CODING

After reflecting on this transcript, the content is filled with objectives, conflicts, emotions, and subtext – sounds like Dramaturgical Coding to me. Reapply it to the data as Second Cycle coding and see what I get.

Basic recoding, categorization, and/or analytic memo techniques described thus far can be applied to eclectically coded data to bring together what may seem richly diverse but disparately analyzed text. Below is a Second Cycle recoding of the same transcript excerpt with more focused First Cycle coding methods – Dramaturgical and In Vivo Coding – followed by an analytic memo. As a reminder, Dramaturgical Codes consist of:

1 OBJ: participant *objectives* or motives in the form of action verbs
2 CON: *conflicts* or *obstacles* confronted by the participant which prevent him or her from achieving his objectives
3 TAC: participant *tactics* or *strategies* to deal with conflicts or obstacles and to achieve his or her objectives
4 ATT: participant *attitudes* toward the setting, others, and the conflict
5 EMO: *emotions* experienced by the participant
6 SUB: *subtexts*, the participant's unspoken thoughts or impression management, in the form of gerunds

The *superobjective* is the overall or ultimate goal of the participant.

SUPEROBJECTIVE: "I'VE GOT TO GET A JOB"

[1] I'm 26 years old and I've got over $50,000 in student loans that [2] I have to pay off, and that [3] scares the hell out of me. [4] I've got to finish my dissertation next year because [5] I can't afford to keep going to school. [6] I've got to get a job and start working.	[1] CON: STUDENT DEBT [2] OBJ: REPAY LOANS [3] EMO: SCARED [4] OBJ: "FINISH MY DISSERTATION" [5] CON: LIMITED FINANCES [6] OBJ: "GET A JOB"
[I: What kind of job do you hope to get?] [7] A teaching job at a university someplace. [I: Any particular part of the country?] [8] I'd like to go back to the east coast, work at one of the major universities there. [9] But I'm keeping myself open to wherever there's a job.	[7] OBJ: TEACH AT A UNIVERSITY [8] OBJ: MOVE TO THE EAST COAST [9] TAC: "KEEPING MYSELF OPEN"
[10] It's hard listening to some of the others [in the current graduating class] [11] like Jake and Brian interviewing for teaching jobs and being turned down. [12] As a white male, [13] that lessens my chances of getting hired.	[10] EMO: ANXIETY [11] SUB: COMPARING AND PROJECTING [12] ATT: AFFIRMATIVE ACTION IS AGAINST ME

[I: I think most employers really do look for the best person for the job, regardless of color.]
[14] Maybe.

[15] If I can get some good recs [letters of recommendation], that should help. My grades have been real good and I've been getting my name out there at conferences. [I: All of that's important.]

[16] The prospectus is the first step. Well, the IRB [Institutional Review Board approval] is the first step. I'm starting the lit review this summer, doing the interviews and participant observation in the fall, writing up as I go along, and [17] being finished by spring.
[I: What if more time is needed for the dissertation?]
[18] I've got to be finished by spring.

[13] CON: NO JOB OPPORTUNITIES
[14] SUB: DOUBTING BUT HOPING

[15] TAC: SELF-PROMOTION

[16] TAC: TASKS AND TIMETABLE

[17] OBJ: FINISH BY SPRING

[18] SUB: DENYING AND INSISTING

Dramaturgical code array

SUPEROBJECTIVE: "I'VE GOT TO GET A JOB"
OBJECTIVES: REPAY LOANS, "FINISH MY DISSERTATION", "GET A JOB", TEACH AT A UNIVERSITY, MOVE TO THE EAST COAST, FINISH BY SPRING
CONFLICTS: STUDENT DEBT, LIMITED FINANCES, NO JOB OPPORTUNITIES
TACTICS: "KEEPING MYSELF OPEN", SELF-PROMOTION, TASKS AND TIMETABLE
ATTITUDES: AFFIRMATIVE ACTION IS AGAINST ME
EMOTIONS: SCARED, ANXIETY
SUBTEXTS: COMPARING AND PROJECTING, DOUBTING BUT HOPING, DENYING AND INSISTING

Analytic memo

24 June 2011
EMERGENT PATTERNS, CATEGORIES, THEMES, CONCEPTS, ASSERTIONS:
STAYING ON TRACK(S)

I'm reminded of a track and field race course in which multiple tracks lined in white are placed next to each other, but there's only one runner per track allowed. This student seems as if he's racing on all tracks simultaneously toward the finish line. The goal, the prize, is a university teaching position. But the multiple tracks consist of dealing with negative emotions such as anxiety about the future, limited financial resources, achieving good grades in current course work, soliciting letters of recommendation, attendance and self-promotion at professional conferences, and the dissertation itself, which could be further subdivided into tracks of IRB application, prospectus, field work, writing, etc.

To this student, the destination (a teaching job) rather than the journey seems more important. And the possibility of spreading oneself too thin exists, especially when pushing oneself at a rapid pace. There's not just multi-tasking here, there's MULTI-TRACKING, multi-worrying. Perhaps like the male that he is, there's a plan: procedural steps to achieve his goal. Never mind the fact that his peers don't seem to be getting jobs, or that the time to complete the dissertation is limited. Deny the failure of others, deny the possibility of additional semesters in school. (Maybe this is a horse race while wearing blinders so as not to be distracted?) There's a track of tasks to complete, all simultaneously and as quickly as possible.

Check with other doctoral students midway through their programs to see if MULTI-TRACKING is the process they experience. And see how men and women, and those from various disciplines, may perceive their experiences differently.

Side note: the root of "curriculum" is also a race track, a course to be run. Job hunting is a curriculum. Life is a curriculum. The question now is: What kind(s)?

The second coding example above utilized Dramaturgical Coding with a "dash" of In Vivo Coding. A different qualitative data analyst may have chosen a completely different method(s) after the first cycle of Eclectic Coding; or may have proceeded toward a categorization of the codes through Second Cycle coding; or may have discovered prominent themes and proceeded directly toward intensive analytic memo writing as preparation for a report. These options reinforce the principle that coding is not a precise science; it is primarily an interpretive act.

Since Eclectic Coding can employ a variety of methods, recommended ways to further analyze the coded data (aside from analytic memo writing) cannot be listed here. See the analytic recommendations for the specific coding methods you employ and refer to Appendix B.

Notes

Eclectic Coding differs from First Cycle Exploratory Methods and Initial Coding (a grounded theory method), in that the latter usually codes *and* tentatively categorizes data in detailed line-by-line analysis with preliminary attention to the categories' properties and dimensions. Eclectic Coding does not necessarily follow these recommended parameters. It is intended as a "first draft" or First Cycle of coding with multiple methods, followed by a "revised draft" or Second Cycle coding with a more purposeful and select number of methods.

Code Mapping and Landscaping

Before new Second Cycle methods are presented, let us explore two ways of organizing and assembling the codes developed from First Cycle processes: Code Mapping and Code Landscaping. These are just two techniques that you may find useful as preparatory work for preliminary analysis before or concurrent with Second Cycle coding, if needed.

Code mapping

Several qualitative data display strategies exist for enhancing the credibility and trustworthiness – not to mention the organization – of your observations as analysis proceeds toward and progresses during Second Cycle coding. Anfara (2008) cites the work of Brown (1999), who illustrates how a set of initial codes progresses through "iterations" of analysis – in other words, from the full set of codes, which is then reorganized into a selected list of categories, and then condensed further into the study's central themes or concepts.

The detailed example below is a way of illustrating one approach to how coding progresses from the First through Second Cycles "to bring meaning, structure, and order to data" (Anfara, 2008, p. 932). Versus Coding (see Chapter Three) was employed for a qualitative study of teachers responding to state-developed fine arts standards for educational achievement. Unfortunately, the process was rife with conflict, and participants we interviewed and observed resisted the new document, which was written with virtually no teacher input. In all, 52 Versus Codes were generated from and applied to individual interview transcripts, focus group transcripts, e-mail correspondence, participant observation field notes, documents, and artifacts. The 52 codes were extracted from the data set and listed randomly as the *First Iteration* of Code Mapping.

First iteration of versus coding:
A simple list of the 52 versus codes

STANDARDS VS. "WE KNOW WHAT WE WANT"
"GRASSROOTS" COMMITTEE VS. TEACHER INPUT
INTERDISCIPLINARY VS. PERFORMANCE/PRODUCTION
"KNOW AND BE ABLE TO DO" VS. "DIFFERENT STRENGTHS"
"TEACH TO THE TEST" VS. "FUN"
"TOP-DOWN" VS. BOTTOM-UP
PRODUCT VS. PROCESS
"WHO WROTE THIS?" VS. OWNERSHIP
ADMINISTRATOR VS. TEACHER
ENDORSEMENT VS. BOYCOTT

PRESCRIPTION VS. AUTONOMY

US VS. THEM

YOU KNOW VS. "WE KNOW"

PERFORMANCE OBJECTIVES VS. "WORK BACKWARDS"

ASSESSMENT VS. "HOW DO YOU TEST THAT?"

BENCHMARKS VS. "I'M NOT GOING TO"

ROADMAP VS. "CHOOSE YOUR OWN ADVENTURE"

AIMS TEST VS. CREDITS

IVORY TOWER VS. INNER CITY

CLASSROOM VS. EXTRA-CURRICULAR

SPECIFIC VS. VAGUE

ADVOCACY VS. "DON'T MEAN A THING TO ME"

CONFORMITY VS. INDIVIDUALITY

YOUR WAY VS. OUR WAY

THEATRE CONFERENCES VS. THESPIAN SOCIETY

REQUIRED VS. "CHOSEN NOT TO"

CONSERVATIVE VS. LIBERAL

WRITERS' GOALS VS. TEACHERS' GOALS

URBAN VS. RURAL

"A FAIR AMOUNT OF WRITING" VS. CONSENSUS

DISCIPLINE-BASED VS. "LIFE SKILLS"

REPUBLICAN VS. DEMOCRAT

AMBITIOUS VS. REALITIES

DISTRICT VS. SCHOOL

"RUSHED" VS. TAKING TIME

ELITISM VS. MEDIOCRITY

FUNDING VS. "NOT ONE DOLLAR"

QUANTITATIVE VS. QUALITATIVE

STATE VS. DISTRICT

ART FORM VS. LIFE FORM

GRADUATION REQUIREMENT VS. ELECTIVE

PROGRESSIVE LEVEL DESIGN VS. MULTIPLE DISTRICTS

INFORMED VS. "?"

LANGUAGE ARTS VS. THEATRE STANDARDS

"BASICS" VS. THE ARTS

MANDATES VS. LOCAL GOVERNMENT

PERFORMANCE OBJECTIVES VS. "STRICTLY UP TO YOU"

FIRST PRIORITY VS. SECOND PRIORITY

REVISION VS. RATIONALIZATION

ATP (Arizona Teacher Proficiency) EXAM VS. COLLEGE CREDIT

RUBRICS VS. PERSONAL JUDGMENT

STATE SCHOOL BOARD VS. ARIZONA UNIVERSITIES

The *Second Iteration* of Code Mapping now categorizes the initial codes. The categories in this particular study range from the real (**People**) to the conceptual (**Political Ideologies**). The eight categories and their labels that emerged came from nothing more difficult than simply comparing and sorting (i.e., cutting and pasting on a word processor page) all 52 codes to determine which ones seemed to go together, a task that is sometimes quite easy and sometimes quite slippery.

Second iteration of versus coding:
Initial categorization of the 52 versus codes

Category 1: People

Related Codes:
US VS. THEM
ADMINISTRATOR VS. TEACHER

Category 2: Institutions

Related Codes:
DISTRICT VS. SCHOOL
STATE VS. DISTRICT
STATE SCHOOL BOARD VS. ARIZONA UNIVERSITIES
URBAN VS. RURAL
THEATRE CONFERENCES VS. THESPIAN SOCIETY

Category 3: Political Ideologies

Related Codes:
REPUBLICAN VS. DEMOCRAT
CONSERVATIVE VS. LIBERAL
IVORY TOWER VS. INNER CITY

Category 4: Curricula

Related Codes:
YOUR WAY VS. OUR WAY
LANGUAGE ARTS VS. THEATRE STANDARDS
"BASICS" VS. THE ARTS
PERFORMANCE OBJECTIVES VS. "WORK BACKWARDS"
"KNOW AND BE ABLE TO DO" VS. "DIFFERENT STRENGTHS"
INTERDISCIPLINARY VS. PERFORMANCE/PRODUCTION
CLASSROOM VS. EXTRA-CURRICULAR
PRODUCT VS. PROCESS
ART FORM VS. LIFE FORM

Category 5: Arts Standards Development

Related Codes:
SPECIFIC VS. VAGUE

REVISION VS. RATIONALIZATION
"RUSHED" VS. TAKING TIME
DISCIPLINE-BASED VS. "LIFE SKILLS"
PROGRESSIVE LEVEL DESIGN VS. MULTIPLE DISTRICTS
MANDATES VS. LOCAL GOVERNMENT

Category 6: Testing and Graduation Requirements

Related Codes:
GRADUATION REQUIREMENT VS. ELECTIVE
ATP EXAM VS. COLLEGE CREDIT
AIMS TEST VS. CREDITS
"TEACH TO THE TEST" VS. "FUN"
ASSESSMENT VS. "HOW DO YOU TEST THAT?"
RUBRICS VS. PERSONAL JUDGMENT
QUANTITATIVE VS. QUALITATIVE

Category 7: Exclusion and Marginalization

Related Codes:
FIRST PRIORITY VS. SECOND PRIORITY
AMBITIOUS VS. REALITIES
ELITISM VS. MEDIOCRITY
INFORMED VS. "?"
"TOP-DOWN" VS. BOTTOM-UP
"GRASSROOTS" COMMITTEE VS. TEACHER INPUT
WRITERS' GOALS VS. TEACHERS' GOALS
"A FAIR AMOUNT OF WRITING" VS. CONSENSUS
FUNDING VS. "NOT ONE DOLLAR"

Category 8: Teacher Resistance

Related Codes:
CONFORMITY VS. INDIVIDUALITY
PRESCRIPTION VS. AUTONOMY
ENDORSEMENT VS. BOYCOTT
"WHO WROTE THIS?" VS. OWNERSHIP
YOU KNOW VS. "WE KNOW"
STANDARDS VS. "WE KNOW WHAT WE WANT"
REQUIRED VS. "CHOSEN NOT TO"
ADVOCACY VS. "DON'T MEAN A THING TO ME"
BENCHMARKS VS. "I'M NOT GOING TO"
PERFORMANCE OBJECTIVES VS. "STRICTLY UP TO YOU"
ROADMAP VS. "CHOOSE YOUR OWN ADVENTURE"

The *Third Iteration* of Code Mapping now *categorizes the categories* even further from eight to three. Notice that new category names are applied.

Third iteration of versus coding:
Recategorizing the eight initial categories

Category 1: Human and Institutional Conflicts – The "Fighters"

Subcategories:
People
Institutions
Political Ideologies

Category 2: Standards and Curriculum Conflicts – The "Stakes"

Subcategories:
Curricula
Arts Standards Development
Testing and Graduation Requirements

Category 3: Results of Conflicts – The "Collateral Damage"
Subcategories:
Exclusion and Marginalization
Teacher Resistance

Now that three major categories have been constructed, Versus Coding explores how they fit into the concept of "moieties" – as one of two, and only two, divisions within a group – for the *Fourth Iteration* of Code Mapping, transforming the categories into an X **vs.** Y format.

Fourth iteration of versus coding:
Three "moiety" concepts phrased in versus terms

Concept 1: US VS. THEM [teachers vs. all other personnel, such as principals, school districts, the state department of education, state universities, etc.]

Concept 2: YOUR WAY VS. OUR WAY [mandated yet poorly written state standards vs. experienced educators working at the local level who know their art and their students]

Concept 3: CON-FORM VS. ART-FORM [conformity to prescribed and standardized curricula vs. creative expression in the subject area and its practice]

Code Mapping, as illustrated above, also serves as part of the auditing process for a research study. It documents how a list of codes gets categorized, recategorized, and conceptualized throughout the analytic journey. Not all Second Cycle coding methods may employ Code Mapping, but it is a straightforward technique that gives you a condensed textual view of your study, and potentially transforms your codes first into organized categories and then into higher-level concepts.

Figure 4.1 A Wordle graphic of the content of Chapter Four (created from www.wordle.net)

Code landscaping

A lack of sophisticated CAQDAS or content analysis software does not prevent you from using simple but innovative ways to organize and examine your codes through basic word processing programs. Code Landscaping integrates textual and visual methods to see both the forest and the trees. It is based on the visual technique of "tags" in which the most frequent word or phrase from a text appears larger than the others. As the frequency of particular words or phrases decreases, so does its visual size.

Internet tools such as Wordle (www.wordle.net) enable you to cut and paste large amounts of text into a field. The online software then analyzes its word count frequencies and displays the results in a randomized "cloud" design with the more frequent words in a larger font size. Figure 4.1 illustrates the results for the text from this chapter of the manual.

Wordle also provides a detailed word count of your entered text, but the program does not analyze data beyond this descriptive level. Nevertheless, this initial data entry gives you a "first-draft" visual look of your text's most salient words and thus potential codes and categories. The CAQDAS programs NVivo 9 and QDA Miner 4.0 feature such comparable methods as Tag Clouds and Cluster Analyses. Code Landscaping is a manual yet systematic method that replicates these ideas in a similar way.

Basic outlining formats enable you to organize codes into subcodes and sub-subcodes as needed. Figure 4.2 illustrates an array of codes assigned to portions of 234 qualitative survey responses that asked participants, "My participation in high school speech and/or theatre has affected the adult I am now. In what ways do you think your participation in speech and/or theatre as a high school student has affected the adult you have become?" (McCammon & Saldaña, 2011).

FRIENDSHIPS+4

SOCIAL
INTERACTION WITH PEOPLE
CONNECTING WITH PEOPLE
FAMILY RELATIONSHIPS
NETWORKING (WITH OTHER GAY PEOPLE)
RECREATE COMMUNITY
TALKATIVE
HUMAN AWARENESS
OPEN-MINDEDNESS / TOLERANCE
CULTURAL AWARENESS
TRUSTING OTHERS
LISTENING
BELONGING
ACCEPTANCE

IDENTITY
DISCOVERY OF TALENTS / STRENGTHS
ENTERTAINING
SENSE OF PURPOSE / FOCUS
WISH FULFILLMENT
WHAT MATTERS
BELIEF SYSTEMS
EMPATHY
EMOTIONAL INTELLIGENCE / GROUNDING
HAPPINESS
PASSION
JOY
HAVE FUN
SENSE OF HUMOR
PRIDE
LOVABLE
SELF-ESTEEM / SELF-WORTH
"HIGHS"
"ALIVE AS A HUMAN BEING"
MOTIVATING FOR LIFE / ADVENTURE
SECURITY
SELF-AWARENESS
MATURITY / CHARACTER
FACE SITUATIONS
CHALLENGING SELF
RESILIENCY
VULNERABILITY
BODY AWARENESS
RELAXATION
NO CHANGE

Figure 4.2   Code Landscaping of a major category and its sub- and sub-subcategories

One of the major categories developed from their responses was **Lifelong Living and Loving**, and Figure 4.2 spatially outlines the category's related codes. Notice how font size is used to convey the frequency of codes and thus their magnitude. The font size of a code was increased once for each time it appeared in the data corpus. The number of times FRIENDSHIPS was mentioned by survey respondents was so large that I had to use "+4" after the code because my word processing program's font size could only go up so far. The font size and +4 to the FRIENDSHIPS code means that 18 people in total mentioned this as an outcome of their high school experiences. The SOCIAL code font size indicates eight responses; INTERACTION WITH PEOPLE seven responses; CONNECTING WITH PEOPLE five responses; and FAMILY RELATIONSHIPS one response.

Simple outlining methods through indents organized the major codes and their related sub- and sub-subcodes further. The words with no indents (FRIENDSHIPS, SOCIAL, and IDENTITY) suggested that these were the major elements for discussion in my analytic memos and final report. The indented words and phrases under them enabled me to "flesh out" the meanings of the primary codes further with detail and nuance. Of course, quotes from the data themselves lend evidentiary support to your assertions. The code landscape serves as a thumbnail sketch, of sorts, for the final write-up. An excerpt from the related report based on Figure 4.2 reads (and notice how many of the code words themselves are woven into the analytic narrative):

Lifelong Living and Loving

> Even though I'm not currently doing theatre, I still feel an element of the theatrical in my bones. It comes out in my personality from time to time. Working in theatre in high school actually helped me become alive as a human being as well as a student. (Male, Adjunct Professor of Art, High School Class of 1978)

This category is composed of the affective, intra-, and interpersonal domains of learning. Like earlier survey findings, some respondents noted the lifelong friendships that were initiated during their high school years. But also prominent here is the formation of one's personal identity. Theatre and speech were opportunities to discover one's talents and strengths, and thus to find one's focus or purpose:

> During my time in the theatre, I became the person I always wanted to be. Throughout my life I was struggling to find my niche, as well as finding who I truly was. Theatre, and all the people involved, helped me find these two things. Theatre made me. (Female, University Theatre Design Major, High School Class of 2009)

Selected respondents attest that they experienced emotional growth through such conceptual processes as self-esteem, self-worth, values clarification, maturity, and personal character development. For some, speech and theatre were conduits for discovering "what matters," particularly in domains of human awareness and social interaction:

> Theatre created me. It's almost impossible to think of who I might have been without it. I honestly don't know that I could have survived without the outlet. I learned how to express myself in the only environment I ever felt accepted into. With that, my confidence grew, my mind opened, and I was pushed to explore more of myself. (Female, Flight Attendant, High School Class of 1992)

Code Landscaping is recommended if you have no access to CAQDAS and particularly if you code as a "splitter" (see Chapter One). Code Landscaping will also help you transition from First to Second Cycle coding, if needed. Also, I caution in this book that simple code frequency is not always a trustworthy indicator of what may be significant in the data. Use this technique as an exploratory heuristic for *qualities*, not as an algorithm for mere *quantities*.

Operational Model Diagramming

Miles and Huberman's (1994) sage advice to "think display" can assist our concurrent coding, categorizing, and analytic memo-writing efforts. Dey (1993) notes that when "we are dealing with complex and voluminous data, diagrams can help us disentangle the threads of our analysis and present results in a coherent and intelligible form" (p. 192). Friese (2012) adds that diagrams in the form of networks display not only our analytic categories, but the answers to our research questions (p. 214). Aside from manual pencil and paper sketches, which work well as first drafts, CAQDAS programs enable you to map or diagram the emergent sequences or networks of your codes and categories related to your study in sophisticated ways, and permit related comments and memos linked to the visual symbols for explanatory reference.

A few operational model diagrams are included in this book (see Figures 1.1, 2.1, 2.2, 3.3, 3.5, and 5.5). This section includes a more complex operational model diagram (see Figure 4.3) from the author's ethnographic study of a White female theatre teacher at an inner city, grades K–8 magnet school for the arts (Saldaña, 1997). It is provided here to demonstrate how participants, codes, categories, phenomena, processes, and concepts can be mapped for the researcher's analytic synthesis and the reader's visual grasp of the study. Notice how the bins or nodes (both plain and bolded and in various shapes and masses), connecting lines or links (both solid and dashed), and arrows (both one-way and two-directional) illustrate not only the space and flow, and the stream and convergence of action/reaction/interaction, but also suggest a sense of quality and magnitude.

The diagram illustrates the key participants in rectangular nodes: *Martinez School's Children and Staff* (a cultural group) and *Nancy*, the theatre instructor. Their convergence created the phenomenon of *cultural shock* (DeWalt & DeWalt, 2011; Winkelman, 1994) for Nancy. The salient categories of Martinez School culture most difficult for her to deal with as a beginning teacher were the Hispanic children's

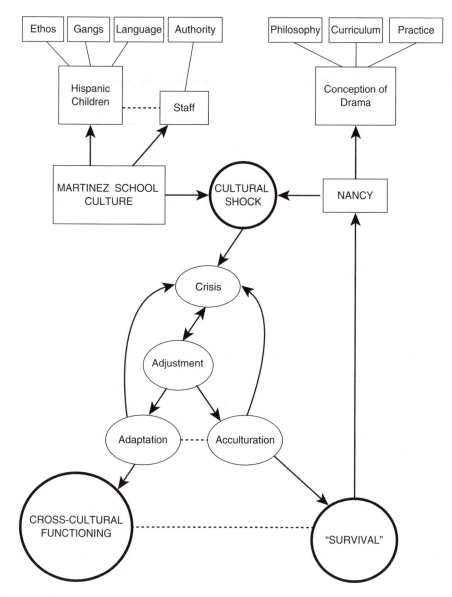

Figure 4.3 An operational model diagram of an inner city teacher's cultural shock and survival processes

ethos (value, attitude, and belief systems), *gang* subculture, and Spanish *language*. From the *staff*, Nancy had to submit to older and tenured faculty colleagues' presumed *authority* over her as a novice educator.

Nancy's actions, reactions, and interactions to function in the school adhered to the processual and cyclical patterns of cultural shock and adaptation outlined by DeWalt and DeWalt and Winkelman, and represented in the diagram with oval nodes. In one example of cultural shock, Nancy dealt with a *crisis* (e.g., not being able to speak Spanish) by *adjusting* to it (e.g., learning a few key Spanish words and phrases). A successful *adaptation* to the crisis (e.g., Spanish language oral fluency) would have led to what multicultural education scholar James A. Banks (1994) labels *cross-cultural functioning*. But half-hearted or insufficient coping strategies (e.g., overreliance on student translators, a small Spanish language vocabulary, accepting the limitations of classroom communication) were *acculturation*, not adaptation, to her teaching context. This process was not as effective as cross-cultural functioning; it was merely *"survival"* (note that the three major concepts of the study are in bolded circular nodes). During Nancy's first two years as a teacher, new crises led to new adjustments; once she adapted successfully to something, a new crisis would emerge, and so on.

Whether Nancy successfully adapted and exhibited cross-cultural functioning, or whether she acculturated and exhibited mere survival, across time the process influenced and affected her *conception of drama* with Hispanic children, which changed her teaching *philosophy*, *curriculum*, and *practice*. For example, rather than having them read plays from a Eurocentric canon, as she had done in her first year, Nancy later chose material with more cultural relevance to the population (see the examples in Verbal Exchange Coding and Holistic Coding). Some veteran staff members made unreasonable demands on her program with stage performance expectations. Nancy's cultural shock and adaptation processes to this led to poor theatre production work in her first year of teaching ("survival"), but more successful outcomes in her second year (cross-cultural functioning).

This diagram was not created at the beginning of the ethnographic study. Its development emerged across three years of literature reviews, fieldwork, data analysis, and writing. I have observed in my research methods courses that students new to qualitative data analysis tend to diagram their conceptual bins in basic linear or circular arrangements. Though nothing is wrong with this as an initial tactic, social interaction is rarely linear or perfectly circular. Review some of the intricately detailed diagram displays in Knowlton and Phillips (2009), Miles and Huberman (1994), Wheeldon and Åhlberg (2012), and the user manuals of CAQDAS programs to heighten your awareness of complex interaction, interplay, and interrelationship among participants and phenomena. Access "A Periodic Table of Visualization Methods" for a fascinating online overview of representing data in various visual forms (http://www.visual-literacy.org/periodic_table/periodic_table.html), and explore free downloadable software for constructing concept maps from CmapTools (http://cmap.ihmc.us/download/).

Regardless of the length or scope of your study, think display. Explore how your codes, categories, themes, and concepts can be represented visually to supplement your analysis, clarify your thoughts, and enhance your written presentation.

Additional Transition Methods

Below are a few practical suggestions from my research methods course and dissertation supervision that students have found most helpful as they transition from coding to more conceptual levels of analysis.

Tabletop categories

One exercise in my qualitative research methods course involves the literal spatial arrangement on a table of coded and categorized data. We first code the data in the margins of hard copy, cut each coded "chunk" of data into separate pieces of paper, pile them together into appropriate categories, staple each category's pile of coded data together, label each pile with its category name, then explore how they can be arranged on a tabletop to map the categories' processes and structures.

Depending on the data we use, some category piles are arranged in a single column from top to bottom according to numeric frequency of their codes. Sometimes the categories are grouped together in superordinate and subordinate arrangements, like an outline or taxonomy on paper. Other times selected categories may be clustered together in separate piles because they share a broader theme or concept. Yet at other times the categories may be placed in linear, circular, or networked arrangements on the tabletop because they suggest a sequence or process of influences and affects. And at other times some category piles overlap each other in Venn diagram-like fashion because they share some similar traits while retaining their unique features.

Students remark that "touching the data" and physically moving categories on a tabletop in multiple arrangements helps them better discover and understand such organizational concepts as hierarchy, process, interrelationship, themeing, and structure. Ironically, this manual method is faster and more flexible than CAQDAS software's modeling functions. You can manipulate paper with two hands quicker than you can computer graphics with one mouse.

If you are encountering difficulty with how your emergent or final sets of categories, themes, or concepts work together, try this tabletop technique and spatially arrange the items (written on index cards or separate half sheets of paper) in various combinations until a structure or process emerges that "feels right" and can be supported by the data. Use the layout as a visual template for your writing. If possible, adapt the layout into an accompanying operational model diagram for the study. More on this topic is discussed and illustrated in the Categories of Categories section in Chapter Six.

From codes to themes

If you have coded your data with only words or short phrases and feel that the resultant codes are elusive, transform the final set of codes or categories into longer-phrased themes (see Themeing the Data in Chapter Three). Themeing may allow you to draw out a code's truncated essence by elaborating on its meanings.

For example, a Process Code from your analysis might be NEGOTIATING. Though the word might indeed identify the general types of social actions you observed among participants, the term is too broad (and overused nowadays) to provide any analytic utility. Two recommended strategies for Themeing the Data add the verbs "is" and "means" after the phenomenon under investigation. Thus, expanding on "Negotiating is ..." and "Negotiating means ..." keeps you grounded in the data as you transcend them. By rereading and reflecting on the data categorized under

NEGOTIATING, you may observe, for example, that "Negotiating is the path of least resistance," or "Negotiating means manipulating others." These are more substantive and evocative prompts for further analysis and writing.

"Shop talking" through the study

Talk regularly with a trusted peer, colleague, advisor, mentor, expert, or even a friend about your research and data analysis. This person can ask provocative questions the researcher has not considered, discuss and talk through the analytic dilemmas you are facing, and offer fresh perspectives on future directions with the study. If we are lucky, the person may also intentionally or inadvertently say that one thing to us that pulls everything together.

Many of my students working on their dissertation projects tell me that our one-on-one conversations about their studies are most productive because they have to verbally articulate for the first time "what's going on" with their data and analysis. Through our "shop talk" exchanges, they often arrive at some sense of focus and clarity about their analytic work, enabling them to better write about the studies.

Some inquiry approaches, such as action and feminist research, encourage participant ownership of the data. Talking with the people you observed and interviewed about your analytic reflections can also provide a "reality check" for you and possibly stimulate additional insights.

Transitioning to Second Cycle Coding Methods

Remember that data are not coded – they are *re*coded. A second cycle of coding does not necessarily have to utilize one of the six methods profiled in the next chapter. You may find that, like Eclectic Coding, a recoding of your data with a First Cycle method will suffice to tighten or condense the number of codes and categories into a more compact set for analysis. So, depending on which First Cycle coding method(s) you have chosen, and how your preliminary data analyses have progressed, you may or may not need to proceed to Second Cycle coding. But do not let that stop you from reading the profiles, for you may discover that one of the methods, like Pattern or Focused Coding, may help you categorize and crystallize your analytic work even further. If your project involves constructing grounded theory, building on previous researchers' work, or exploring longitudinal change in participants or systems, then Second Cycle coding is necessary to explore the complexity at work in the corpus.

Good thinking through analytic memos, coupled and concurrent with the processes of coding and categorizing, can lead toward higher-level themes, concepts, assertions, and theory. The next two chapters are intended to map that journey with some recommended pathways, but it is up to you to decide which road(s) to take. *Be prepared to cycle back to this chapter's methods after Second Cycle coding because some of these strategies may still be helpful during the latter stages of analysis.*

FIVE

Second Cycle Coding Methods

CHAPTER SUMMARY

This chapter first reviews the goals of Second Cycle coding, then profiles six particular methods for further or more complex analytic work. Each profile contains the following: Sources, Description, Applications, Example, Analysis, and Notes.

The Goals of Second Cycle Methods

Second Cycle coding methods, if needed, are advanced ways of reorganizing and reanalyzing data coded through First Cycle methods. They each require, as Morse (1994, p. 25) puts it, "of linking seemingly unrelated facts logically, of fitting categories one with another" to develop a coherent metasynthesis of the data corpus. Before categories are assembled, your data may have to be recoded because more accurate words or phrases were discovered for the original codes; some codes will be merged together because they are conceptually similar; infrequent codes will be assessed for their utility in the overall coding scheme; and some codes that seemed like good ideas during First Cycle coding may be dropped altogether because they are later deemed "marginal" or "redundant" after the data corpus has been fully reviewed (Lewins & Silver, 2007, p. 100).

The primary goal during Second Cycle coding is to develop a sense of categorical, thematic, conceptual, and/or theoretical organization from your array of First Cycle codes. But some of the methods outlined in this chapter may occur during the initial as well as latter coding periods. Basically, your First Cycle codes (and their associated coded data) are reorganized and reconfigured to eventually develop a smaller and more select list of broader categories, themes, concepts, and/or assertions. For example, if you generated 50 different codes for your data corpus during First Cycle coding, those 50 codes (and their associated coded data) are then recoded as needed, then categorized according to similarity during Second Cycle coding, which might result in 25 codes for one category, 15 codes for a second category, and the remaining 10 codes for a third category. These three categories then become the major components of your research study and write-up. Keep in mind that this is a very simple and clean example. Your actual process might generate different numbers or even different approaches altogether. Plus, methodologist Ruthellen

Josselson astutely reminds us that "Categories that are too separate are artificial. Human life is of a piece, multilayered, contradictory, and multivalent, to be sure, but the strands are always interconnected" (in Wertz et al., 2011, p. 232).

The goal is not necessarily to develop a perfectly hierarchical bullet-pointed outline or list of permanently fixed coding labels during and after this cycle of analysis. Let me offer an analogy. Imagine buying a large piece of furniture like a table that comes unassembled in a box which says "assembly required." The instructions state that you take out all of the packaged items, such as the bolts, washers, nuts, table legs, and tabletop, then gather the necessary tools, such as a wrench and screwdriver. The instructions recommend that you *inventory all parts* to make certain everything you need is there, and that you *arrange the parts appropriately on the floor before assembling*. You have probably determined by now where this analogy is going. The individual pieces of inventoried hardware and wood are the First Cycle coded data; and their appropriate arrangement into organized categories on the floor, the tools, and the assembly process are the Second Cycle coding methods of how everything fits together.

The analogy fails in one regard, however. There is a *specific and prescribed* set of instructions for how the table is to be assembled. Any deviation from the directions or substitution of materials and the integrity of the furniture is compromised. In qualitative data analysis, some interpretive leeway is necessary – indeed, imagination and creativity are essential to achieve new and hopefully striking perspectives about the data. A bolt is a bolt, a wrench is a wrench, and a tabletop is a tabletop. But after assembly, consider what would happen if you brought in an electric sander to reshape or smooth the wood's edges, or a brush and varnish to change the table's finish, or various tablecloths and centerpieces to experiment with and capture a certain "look." The methods profiled in this chapter are neither prescriptive nor inflexible. They are guidelines for basic assembly with opportunities for the researcher's elaboration. Wolcott (1994) and Locke (2007) remind us that our ultimate analytic goal is not just to transform data, but to transcend them – to find something else, something more.

Acknowledge that with each successive cycle of coding, the number of codes should become less, not more. Figure 1.1 illustrates that codes and subcodes are eventually transformed into categories (and subcategories, if needed), which then progress toward major themes or concepts, and then into assertions or possibly a new theory. Second Cycle coding is reorganizing and condensing the vast array of initial analytic details into a "main dish." To propose another analogy: When I grocery shop (i.e., visit a site for fieldwork), I can place up to 20 different food items (data) in my shopping cart (field note journal). When I go to the cashier's stand (computer) and get each item (datum) with a bar code scanned (First Cycle coding), the bagger (analyst) will tend to place all frozen foods in one bag (category one), fresh produce in another bag (category two), meats in another bag (category three), and so on. As I bring my food items home, I think about what I might prepare (reflection and analytic memo writing). I unpack the food items (Second Cycle coding), and organize them appropriately in the kitchen refrigerator (concept one), pantry (concept two), freezer (concept three), and so on. And when I am ready to make that one special dish (a key assertion or theory), I take out only what I need (the essence and essentials of the data corpus) out of everything I bought (analyzed) to cook it (write-up).

Like First Cycle methods, some Second Cycle methods can be compatibly mixed and matched. Depending on the study, for example, Pattern Coding could be used as the sole Second Cycle method, or serve in conjunction with Elaborative or Longitudinal Coding. Those interested in developing grounded theory might begin this cycle with Focused Coding, then progress toward Axial and/or Theoretical Coding.

Overview of Second Cycle Coding Methods

Pattern Coding develops the "meta-code" – the category label that identifies similarly coded data. Pattern Codes not only organize the corpus but attempt to attribute meaning to that organization.

Focused Coding, Axial Coding, and Theoretical Coding are the latter stages toward developing grounded theory – the former stages being a combination of In Vivo, Process, and Initial Coding.

Focused Coding categorizes coded data based on thematic or conceptual similarity. Axial Coding describes a category's properties and dimensions and explores how the categories and subcategories relate to each other. Theoretical Coding progresses toward discovering the central/core category that identifies the primary theme of the research. In these three methods, reflective analytic memo writing is both a code- and category-generating heuristic.

Elaborative Coding builds on a previous study's codes, categories, and themes while a current and related study is underway. This method employs additional qualitative data to support or modify the researcher's observations developed in an earlier project.

Longitudinal Coding is the attribution of selected change processes to qualitative data collected and compared across time. Matrices organize fieldwork observations, interview transcripts, and document excerpts into similar temporal categories that permit researcher analysis and reflection on their similarities and differences from one time period through another.

Second Cycle Coding Methods

Pattern Coding

Source

Miles & Huberman, 1994

Description

Pattern Codes are

> explanatory or inferential codes, ones that identify an emergent theme, configuration, or explanation. They pull together a lot of material into a more meaningful and parsimonious unit of analysis. They are a sort of meta-code. ... Pattern Coding is a way of grouping those summaries into a smaller number of sets, themes, or constructs. (Miles & Huberman, 1994, p. 69)

Applications

According to Miles and Huberman, Pattern Coding is appropriate for:

- the second cycle of coding, after Initial Coding, for example
- development of major themes from the data
- the search for rules, causes, and explanations in the data
- examining social networks and patterns of human relationships
- the formation of theoretical constructs and processes (e.g., "negotiating," "bargaining")

Example

Five staff members of a small office were interviewed separately about their administrative leadership. Each one remarked how internal communications from their director were occasionally haphazard, incomplete, or non-existent. Each passage below was initially Descriptive Coded or In Vivo Coded. Note that one sentence is bolded because, during coding, it struck the researcher as a strong statement:

SECRETARY: [1] I often have to go back to her and get more information about what she wants done because her first set of instructions weren't clear.	[1] UNCLEAR INSTRUCTIONS
RECEPTIONIST: [2] It's kind of hard working for her, because she rushes in, tells you what needs to be done, then goes into her office. [3] After she's gone you start doing the job, and then you find out there's all these other things she didn't think of to tell you.	[2] RUSHED DIRECTIONS [3] INCOMPLETE DIRECTIONS
ADMINISTRATIVE ASSISTANT: [4] Sometimes I think she expects you to read her mind and know what she wants, or that she expects you to know everything that's going on without her having to tell you. [5] **I can't do my job effectively if she doesn't communicate with me.**	[4] EXPECTATIONS OF INFO [5] "SHE DOESN'T COMMUNICATE"

BUSINESS MANAGER: [6] I hate it when she tells me in the hallway or in a conversation what to do. I need it written in an e-mail so there's documentation of the transaction for the operations manager and the auditor.

[6] WRITTEN DIRECTIONS NEEDED

FACILITIES MANAGER: [7] Sometimes she doesn't always tell me what she needs, and then she gets upset later when it hasn't been done. Well, that's because you never told me to do it in the first place.

[7] "YOU NEVER TOLD ME"

Similar codes were assembled together (see Figure 5.1) to analyze their commonality and to create a Pattern Code.

Several ideas were then brainstormed for the Pattern Code, among them:

"SHE DOESN'T COMMUNICATE" [an In Vivo Code from the Initial Coding cycle that seemed to hold summative power for the remaining codes]

MISS-COMMUNICATION [a title reference to the female administrator – a flip yet sexist code]

But after researcher reflection, the final Pattern Code created and selected for the above data was:

DYSFUNCTIONAL DIRECTION [a Pattern Code that suggests action with consequences]

Analysis

These interview excerpts contain consequential words and phrases such as "if," "and then," and "because," which alert the researcher to infer what Miles and Huberman state are "rules, causes, and explanations" in the data. Finally, the bolded sentence, "**I can't do my job effectively if she doesn't communicate with me**," seems to holistically capture the spirit of the dysfunction theme at work.

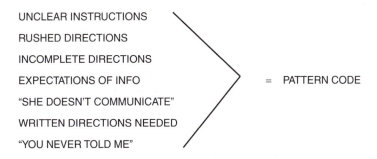

UNCLEAR INSTRUCTIONS

RUSHED DIRECTIONS

INCOMPLETE DIRECTIONS

EXPECTATIONS OF INFO   = PATTERN CODE

"SHE DOESN'T COMMUNICATE"

WRITTEN DIRECTIONS NEEDED

"YOU NEVER TOLD ME"

Figure 5.1 Assembly of codes to determine their Pattern Code

The Pattern Code, in concert with the "if–then" actions and bolded statement, led the researcher to construct the assertion, *"Poor communication from administrative leadership results in staff members who feel not just frustrated but personally unsuccessful at their jobs."* The explanatory narrative continues with evidence to support the claim, then describes the dysfunctional workplace dynamics for the reader.

For Second Cycle Pattern Coding, collect similarly coded passages from the data corpus. CAQDAS searches, queries, and retrievals will assist greatly with this process. Review the First Cycle codes to assess their commonality and assign them various Pattern Codes. Use the Pattern Code as a stimulus to develop a statement that describes a major theme, a pattern of action, a network of interrelationships, or a theoretical construct from the data.

Gibson and Brown (2009, p. 143) recommend an analytic process related to and useful for Pattern Coding called "Super Coding" (also found in most CAQDAS programs), which finds relationships between codes. Super Coding searches for these relationships among coded data using Boolean search terms (*and, or, not, and/or*). Thus, if you wanted to pool the data units from the corpus coded INCOMPLETE DIRECTIONS *and* UNCLEAR INSTRUCTIONS *and* RUSHED DIRECTIONS, you would enter these three codes for a CAQDAS Boolean search, then examine what possible relationship might exist between the three sets of coded data to develop a new Super Code. In this case, DIRECTIONS and INSTRUCTIONS would be considered synonymous, but the goal is to determine what INCOMPLETE, UNCLEAR, and RUSHED have in common. Perhaps the Super Code that represents all three and emerges after analytic reflection would be labeled INEFFECTIVE INSTRUCTIONS or VAGUE GUIDANCE.

"Many codes – especially pattern codes – are captured in the form of metaphors ('dwindling efforts,' 'interactive glue'), where they can synthesize large blocks of data in a single trope" (Miles & Huberman, 1994, p. 302). Several Pattern Codes can emerge from Second Cycle analysis of qualitative data. Each one may hold merit as a major theme to analyze and develop, but Miles and Huberman also caution that "pattern codes are hunches: Some pan out, but many do not" (p. 72).

Some recommended ways to further analyze Pattern Codes are (see Appendix B):

- action and practitioner research (Altrichter et al., 1993; Coghlan & Brannick, 2010; Fox et al., 2007; Stringer, 1999)
- assertion development (Erickson, 1986)
- content analysis (Krippendorff, 2003; Schreier, 2012; Weber, 1990; Wilkinson & Birmingham, 2003)
- decision modeling (Bernard, 2011)
- grounded theory (Bryant & Charmaz, 2007; Charmaz, 2006; Corbin & Strauss, 2008; Glaser & Strauss, 1967; Stern & Porr, 2011; Strauss & Corbin, 1998)
- interactive qualitative analysis (Northcutt & McCoy, 2004)
- logic models (Knowlton & Phillips, 2009; Yin, 2009)
- mixed methods research (Creswell, 2009; Creswell & Plano Clark, 2011; Tashakkori & Teddlie, 2003)
- qualitative evaluation research (Patton, 2002, 2008)
- situational analysis (Clarke, 2005)

- splitting, splicing, and linking data (Dey, 1993)
- thematic analysis (Auerbach & Silverstein, 2003; Boyatzis, 1998; Smith & Osborn, 2008)

Notes

See Focused, Axial, and Theoretical Coding for comparable analytic processes to Pattern Coding.

Focused Coding

Source

Charmaz, 2006

Description

Focused Coding follows In Vivo, Process, and/or Initial Coding, First Cycle grounded theory coding methods, but it can also be applied with other coding methods to categorize the data. Focused Coding searches for the most frequent or significant codes to develop "the most salient categories" in the data corpus and "requires decisions about which initial codes make the most analytic sense" (Charmaz, 2006, pp. 46, 57).

Applications

Focused Coding is appropriate for virtually all qualitative studies, but particularly for studies employing grounded theory methodology, and the development of major categories or themes from the data.

Focused Coding, as a Second Cycle analytic process, is a streamlined adaptation of classic grounded theory's Axial Coding. The goal of this method is to develop categories without distracted attention at this time to their properties and dimensions. Dey (1999), however, cautions that categories, particularly in qualitative inquiry, do not always have their constituent elements sharing a common set of features, do not always have sharp boundaries, and that "there are different degrees of belonging" (pp. 69–70).

Example

The interview transcript excerpt from the Initial Coding profile in Chapter Three is used again to show how the codes transformed from the First to the Second Cycles; refer to that first before proceeding. In the example below, data similarly (not necessarily exactly) coded are clustered together and reviewed to create tentative category names with an emphasis on process through the use of gerunds ("-ing" words; see Process Coding). Note that just one coded excerpt is the only one in its category:

Category: DEFINING ONESELF AS A FRIEND

I think people, [31] people define me as popular	[31] DEFINING SELF THROUGH OTHERS: "POPULAR"

Category: MAINTAINING FRIENDSHIPS

[1] I hang out with everyone. Really.	[1] "HANGING OUT WITH EVERYONE"
[3] I can look back to kindergarten, and at some point I was	[3] RECALLING FRIENDSHIPS
[4] best friends with everybody who's been here And so there are	[4] "BEST FRIENDS WITH EVERYBODY"
[7] certain people that I've just been	[7] FRIENDS WITH "CERTAIN PEOPLE"
[8] friends with since forever	[8] FRIENDS WITH "SINCE FOREVER"

Category: LABELING THE GROUPS

[10] really super popular pretty girls are all mean	[10] LABELING: "REALLY SUPER POPULAR PRETTY GIRLS"
[14] geeky people	[14] LABELING: "GEEKY PEOPLE"
[16] strange-psycho-killer-geek-people-who-draw-swastikas-on-their-backpacks	[16] LABELING: "STRANGE-PSYCHO-KILLER-GEEK"
[23] jocks	[23] LABELING: "JOCKS"

Category: QUALIFYING THE GROUPS

[5] practically	[5] QUALIFYING: "PRACTICALLY"
[6] Almost everybody in my grade	[6] QUALIFYING: "ALMOST"
[15] Some of them though	[15] QUALIFYING: "SOME OF THEM"
[17] kind of geeks	[17] QUALIFYING: "KIND OF"
[18] some of them are kind of	[18] QUALIFYING: "SOME OF THEM"
[19] But then again	[19] QUALIFYING: "BUT THEN …"
[21] not all of them are completely, like	[21] QUALIFYING: "NOT ALL OF THEM"

Category: DISPELLING STEREOTYPES OF THE GROUPS

[9] not fair of me to stereotype either	[9] "NOT FAIR TO STEREOTYPE"
[11] they're all snobby and they all talk about each other	[11] IDENTIFYING STEREOTYPES

[12] 'cause they don't. Some of them, some of them don't	[12] DISPELLING STEREOTYPES
[20] there's not the complete stereotype	[20] DISPELLING STEREOTYPES
[24] not all of the guys are idiots	[24] DISPELLING STEREOTYPES

Category: SETTING CRITERIA FOR FRIENDSHIPS

[2] I choose.	[2] "CHOOSING" WHO YOU HANG OUT WITH
[13] those are the ones I'm friends, friends with	[13] CHOOSING FRIENDS: "SUPER POPULAR PRETTY GIRLS"
[22] I'm friends with those people	[22] CHOOSING FRIENDS: "GEEKS"
[25] I'm friends with the ones who can carry on a conversation	[25] CHOOSING FRIENDS: JOCKS "WHO CAN CARRY ON A CONVERSATION"
[26] I'm friends with someone because of who they are,	[26] CRITERIA FOR FRIENDSHIP: "WHO THEY ARE"
[27] not because of what group they, they hang out in basically. 'Cause I think	[27] CRITERIA FOR FRIENDSHIP: NOT GROUP MEMBERSHIP
[28] that's really stupid to be, like,	[28] ETHICS OF FRIENDSHIP
[29] "What would people think if they saw me walking with this person?" or something. [I: So you wouldn't define yourself with any specific group?]	[29] NOT CONCERNED WITH WHAT OTHERS THINK
[30] No. I would rather hang out with someone who's [32] good hearted but a little slow, compared to someone	[30] MAINTAINING INDIVIDUALITY [32] CRITERIA FOR FRIENDSHIP: "GOOD HEARTED BUT SLOW"
[33] very smart but very evil	[33] CRITERIA FOR FRIENDSHIP: NOT THOSE "VERY SMART BUT VERY EVIL"

Analysis

The codes *qua* (in the role of) categories are now listed for a review:

DEFINING ONESELF AS A FRIEND
MAINTAINING FRIENDSHIPS
LABELING THE GROUPS
QUALIFYING THE GROUPS
DISPELLING STEREOTYPES OF THE GROUPS
SETTING CRITERIA FOR FRIENDSHIPS

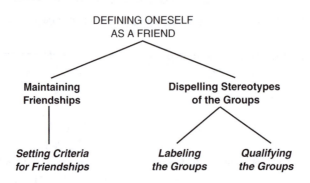

Figure 5.2 A tree diagram from categories and subcategories

Rubin and Rubin (2012) recommend that simple organizational or hierarchical outlining of the categories and subcategories gives you a handle on them. Using the major categories from above, the outline might read:

I. DEFINING ONESELF AS A FRIEND

    A. Maintaining Friendships
       1. Setting Criteria for Friendships

    B. Dispelling Stereotypes of the Groups
       1. Labeling the Groups
       2. Qualifying the Groups

The same categories and subcategories can also be plotted as a tree diagram for a visual "at-a-glance" representation of the phenomena or process (see Figure 5.2).

An analytic memo reveals the researcher's thinking process about the codes and categories developed thus far. Notice that *memo writing also serves as a code- and category-generating method*. The deliberate linking or weaving of codes and categories within the narrative is a heuristic to integrate them semantically and systematically (see Chapter Two). Dey (2007) reminds us of the integrated nature of the theory-building process by advising that we "do not categorize and then connect; we connect by categorizing" (p. 178):

31 May 2011
CODING: FOCUSING THE CATEGORIES
    After reviewing the categories, I feel that QUALIFYING THE GROUPS can be subsumed under DISPELLING THE STEREOTYPES OF THE GROUPS. Tiffany provides exceptions to the stereotypes through her use of qualifiers. DEFINING ONESELF AS A FRIEND seems to have some connection with how adolescents go about MAINTAINING FRIENDSHIPS. Perhaps DEFINING ONESELF AS A FRIEND might be more accurately recoded as PERCEIVING ONESELF AS A FRIEND. According to

Tiffany, others perceive her as "popular," so that's how she may perceive herself, which in turn influences and affects how she goes about MAINTAINING FRIENDSHIPS both in the past and present.

Students in high school culture adopt the social group labels and stereotypes passed on to them from oral tradition, influences of media, and personal observation. Tiffany seems very aware of the social group names and how the group becomes stereotyped with particular attributes. But she negates the stereotyped images by finding exceptions to them. And it is those in the exceptions category who become her friends. She seems to be ACCEPTING THROUGH EXCEPTING. She acknowledges that some of her friends belong to the social groups with subcultural labels and that they carry stereotypical baggage with them. Labels are for baggage, not for friends.

The earlier Initial Coding memo on DISCRIMINATING as a process seems to still hold during this cycle of coding. Once I get more data from other students, I can see if this category does indeed hold.

Focused Coding enables you to compare newly constructed codes during this cycle across other participants' data to assess comparability and transferability. The researcher can ask other high school participants how they construct friendships, then compare their coded data with Tiffany's. "Your study fits the empirical world when you have constructed codes and developed them into categories that crystallize participants' experience" (Charmaz, 2006, p. 54). Also note that categories are constructed emergently from the reorganization and categorization of participant data: "Data should not be forced or selected to fit pre-conceived or pre-existent categories or discarded in favor of keeping an extant theory intact" (Glaser, 1978, p. 4).

CAQDAS programs lend themselves very well to Focused Coding since they simultaneously enable coding, category construction, and analytic memo writing.

Some recommended ways to further analyze Focused Codes are (see Appendix B):

- Axial Coding and Theoretical Coding
- grounded theory (Bryant & Charmaz, 2007; Charmaz, 2006; Corbin & Strauss, 2008; Glaser & Strauss, 1967; Stern & Porr, 2011; Strauss & Corbin, 1998)
- interactive qualitative analysis (Northcutt & McCoy, 2004)
- memo writing about the codes/themes (Charmaz, 2006; Corbin & Strauss, 2008; Glaser, 1978; Glaser & Strauss, 1967; Strauss, 1987)
- situational analysis (Clarke, 2005)
- splitting, splicing, and linking data (Dey, 1993)
- thematic analysis (Auerbach & Silverstein, 2003; Boyatzis, 1998; Smith & Osborn, 2008)

Notes

See Themeing the Data and Pattern Coding as methods related to Focused Coding.

Axial Coding

Sources

Boeije, 2010; Charmaz, 2006; Glaser, 1978; Glaser & Strauss, 1967; Strauss, 1987; Strauss & Corbin, 1998

Description

Axial Coding extends the analytic work from Initial Coding and, to some extent, Focused Coding. The goal is to strategically reassemble data that were "split" or "fractured" during the Initial Coding process (Strauss & Corbin, 1998, p. 124). Boeije (2010) succinctly explains that Axial Coding's purpose is "to determine which [codes] in the research are the dominant ones and which are the less important ones ... [and to] reorganize the data set: synonyms are crossed out, redundant codes are removed and the best representative codes are selected" (p. 109).

The "axis" of Axial Coding is a *category* (like the axis of a wooden wheel with extended spokes) discerned from First Cycle coding. This method "relates categories to subcategories [and] specifies the properties and dimensions of a category" (Charmaz, 2006, p. 60). Properties (i.e., characteristics or attributes) and dimensions (the location of a property along a continuum or range) of a category refer to such components as the contexts, conditions, interactions, and consequences of a process – actions that let the researcher know "if, when, how, and why" something happens (p. 62).

Applications

Axial Coding is appropriate for studies employing grounded theory methodology, and studies with a wide variety of data forms (e.g., interview transcripts, field notes, journals, documents, diaries, correspondence, artifacts, video).

Grouping similarly coded data reduces the number of Initial Codes you developed while sorting and relabeling them into conceptual categories. During this cycle, "the code is sharpened to achieve its best fit" (Glaser, 1978, p. 62), and there can be more than one Axial Code developed during this process. Axial Coding is the transitional cycle between the Initial and Theoretical Coding processes of grounded theory, though the method has become somewhat contested in later writings (see Notes at the end of this profile).

Example

The categories from the Focused Coding example in this chapter will be used here; refer to that first before proceeding. Keep in mind that only one participant's data are analyzed as an example, along with the experiential data (i.e., personal knowledge and experiences) of the researcher. The analytic memo is an uncensored and permissibly messy opportunity to let thoughts flow and ideas emerge. Also notice that *memo writing serves as a code- and category-generating method*. The deliberate linking or weaving of codes and categories within the narrative is a heuristic to integrate them semantically and systematically (see Chapter Two).

There are two Axial Codes explored below: SOCIALIZING and ACCEPTING THROUGH EXCEPTING. These two new codes emerged from pooling the six major categories developed during Focused Coding:

1 DEFINING ONESELF AS A FRIEND
2 MAINTAINING FRIENDSHIPS
3 LABELING THE GROUPS
4 QUALIFYING THE GROUPS
5 DISPELLING STEREOTYPES OF THE GROUPS
6 SETTING CRITERIA FOR FRIENDSHIPS

Figure 5.3 illustrates how SOCIALIZING and ACCEPTING THROUGH EXCEPTING became the two Axial Codes around which the other six revolve.

30 May 2011
AXIAL CODE: BEING SOCIALLY ACCEPTABLE/EXCEPTABLE
   The high school as social system is, to both adults and adolescents, a place to *socialize*. SOCIALIZING by adults happens when they indoctrinate young people to the cultural knowledge and ethos of the country, while SOCIALIZING by adolescents is an opportunity to establish and maintain possibly lifelong friendships. I remember reading an article that said adolescents who participate in extracurricular athletics and arts activities like first and foremost the opportunities these activities provide to socialize with friends – check out the specific reference and log it in a memo later. (I could have used an Axial Code labeled FRIENDING instead of SOCIALIZING, but that's traditionally associated with online Facebook interaction, and the participant's referring to her in-school and live experiences.)
   ACCEPTING THROUGH EXCEPTING was one of the Focused Codes that could possibly transform into a category during this cycle of memo writing and analysis. ACCEPTING is a bit broader as a code and category, but I feel ACCEPTING THROUGH EXCEPTING has a conceptual "ring" to it.
   BEING SOCIALLY ACCEPTABLE is not just adhering to expected norms of behavior. To adolescents, BEING SOCIALLY ACCEPTABLE/EXCEPTABLE are the action/interaction patterns of friendships – who's in and who's out.
   The *Properties* [characteristics or attributes] of BEING SOCIALLY ACCEPTABLE:

- Adolescents accept peers with whom they find *perceived similarities*.
- Adolescents accept those with whom they feel *compatible*.
- Adolescents accept those with whom they feel *safe*, or at least *secure*.
- Adolescents accept those with whom they have *shared interests*.

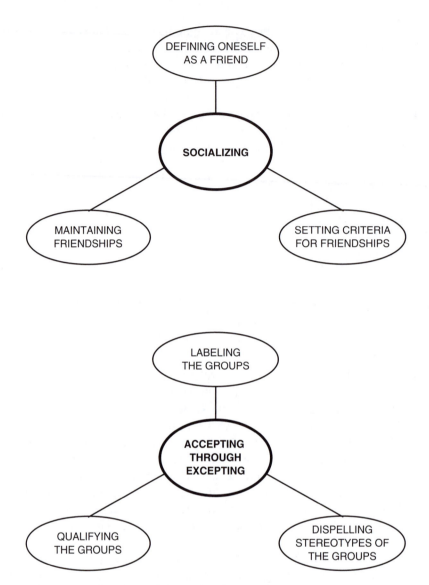

Figure 5.3 Two Axial Codes and their related categories

- Adolescents accept those who are *doing something they want to get into* (e.g., drugs, sports).
- Adolescents accept those with whom they have *fun*.
- If you're none of the above, you're most likely SOCIALLY EXCEPTABLE.

The *Dimensions* [the location of a property along a continuum or range; the conditions, causes, and consequences of a process that tell if, when, how, and why something happens] of BEING SOCIALLY ACCEPTABLE/EXCEPTABLE:

- Popularity: You can be perceived as popular by some people, and disliked by others (e.g., some people admire Charlie Sheen while others feel he is "socially unacceptable").
- Popularity: Teens perceived as popular can come from several subcultures/cliques, not just the "popular pretty girls" and "jocks" – e.g., a popular goth, even a popular geek.
- Popularity: Some gravitate toward the popular because it builds their own self-esteem; others gravitate toward the popular because they're trendy; others gravitate toward the popular because "there's just something about them" – charisma?
- Acceptability: We can accept some people but not be their friends – we except them.
- Exceptability: Even the "outcasts" seem to find a group somewhere.
- Acceptable while Exceptable: Some groups will let "that one kid" hang out with them even though he may not be particularly well liked.
- Stereotypes: We can acknowledge the stereotypes, but can find exceptions to the rule. "They're usually like this. But … ."

My psychologist buddy shared with me that the human need to BELONG is to be part of something (like clubs, organizations). But to be ACCEPTED means to be validated, that I am OK, that I am a person, I have worth. *If somebody belongs to something they are being accepted. If you are excepted, you do not belong. But even the excepted can find acceptance somewhere.* I know that I am ACCEPTED by some and EXCEPTED by others for such SOCIAL CATEGORIES as my ethnicity, sexual orientation, age, size, etc. But it is being with your own kind, like with like, that makes me feel comfortable, compatible. However, I can physically BELONG to a group without feeling fully ACCEPTED by them – I feel EXCEPTED by them.

Analysis

As with Initial and Focused Coding, analytic memo writing is a critical component of Axial Coding. The focus, however, is placed on the emergent and emerging codes themselves, along with the categories' properties and dimensions. Glaser and Strauss (1967) advise that "categories should not be so abstract as to lose their sensitizing aspect, but yet must be abstract enough to make [the emerging] theory a general guide to multi-conditional, ever-changing daily situations" (p. 242). Northcutt and McCoy (2004), in their signature qualitative analytic system, observe that a participant will sometimes unknowingly do the analytic work for the researcher when participant quotes in interview transcripts that lend themselves as Axial Codes are found: "Respondents will often describe how one [category] relates to another in the process of discussing the nature of one [category]" (p. 242).

Also note that analytic memos during Axial Coding explicate or "think through" four additive elements of process or causation suggested by the data (Boeije, 2010, pp. 112–113; Richards, 2009, p. 78):

- the *contexts* – settings and boundaries in which the action or process occurs ("The high school as social system is, to both adults and adolescents, a place to *socialize*"); plus

- the *conditions* – routines and situations that happen (or do not) within the contexts ("SOCIALIZING by adolescents is an opportunity to establish and maintain possibly lifelong friendships"); plus
- the *interactions* – the specific types, qualities, and strategies of exchanges between people in these contexts and conditions ("adolescents who participate in extracurricular athletics and arts activities like first and foremost the opportunities these activities provide to socialize with friends"); equals
- the *consequences* – the outcomes or results of the contexts, conditions, and interactions ("*If somebody belongs to something they are being accepted. If you are excepted, you do not belong*")

One of the ultimate goals during Axial Coding (along with continued qualitative data gathering and analysis) is to achieve saturation – "when no new information seems to emerge during coding, that is, when no new properties, dimensions, conditions, actions/interactions, or consequences are seen in the data" (Strauss & Corbin, 1998, p. 136).

Diagrams of the phenomena at work are also encouraged during the Axial Coding process (see Figure 5.4). These displays can be as simple as tables, charts, or matrices, or as complex as flow diagrams.

These illustrative techniques bring codes and analytic memos to life and help the researcher see where the story of the data is going. One of Strauss's students shared that her "diagramming process would begin with a phrase of single code, perhaps even a hunch about what was important in the analysis at that point in time [with] arrows and boxes showing connections of temporal progression" (Strauss, 1987, p. 179). Clarke's (2005) relational analysis, social worlds/arenas, and positional maps are highly advised as heuristics to explore the complexity of relationships among the major elements of the study.

To appreciate the breadth and depth of Strauss's (1987) and Strauss and Corbin's (1998) discussion of Axial Coding, readers are referred to *Qualitative Analysis for Social Scientists* and *Basics of Qualitative Research* for a full explanation on such matters as action/interaction; structure and process; and causal, intervening, and contextual conditions (also discussed for longitudinal qualitative research studies in Saldaña, 2003).

ACCEPTABLE ⟵───────────────────⟶ **EXCEPTABLE**

Acknowledging Exceptions to the Stereotypes -------------------- Accepting the Stereotypes

Those with Common Interests -------------------------------- Those with Uncommon Interests

"Popular" and Liked by Some -------------------------------- "Popular" Yet Not Liked By Others

Belonging and Accepted ---- Belonging but Not Accepted ---- Not Belonging or Accepted

Accepted and Belonging ---- Accepted but Not Belonging ---- Not Accepted or Belonging

---

Figure 5.4 A simple properties and dimensions table derived from Axial Coding

Some recommended ways to further analyze Axial Codes are (see Appendix B):

- Theoretical Coding
- grounded theory (Bryant & Charmaz, 2007; Charmaz, 2006; Corbin & Strauss, 2008; Glaser & Strauss, 1967; Stern & Porr, 2011; Strauss & Corbin, 1998)
- interrelationship (Saldaña, 2003)
- longitudinal qualitative research (Giele & Elder, 1998; McLeod & Thomson, 2009; Saldaña, 2003, 2008)
- memo writing about the codes/themes (Charmaz, 2006; Corbin & Strauss, 2008; Glaser, 1978; Glaser & Strauss, 1967; Strauss, 1987)
- meta-ethnography, metasummary, and metasynthesis (Finfgeld, 2003; Major & Savin-Baden, 2010; Noblit & Hare, 1988; Sandelowski & Barroso, 2007; Sandelowski et al., 1997)
- situational analysis (Clarke, 2005)
- splitting, splicing, and linking data (Dey, 1993)
- thematic analysis (Auerbach & Silverstein, 2003; Boyatzis, 1998; Smith & Osborn, 2008)

Notes

Charmaz (2006) and Dey (1999) take issue with Axial Coding. Charmaz perceives it as a cumbersome step that may stifle analytic progress achieved from previous Initial Coding toward Theoretical Coding. Dey feels the logics of categorization and process have not been fully developed by grounded theory's originators. Even as grounded theory evolved, the methodological utility of Axial Coding became a controversial issue between Glaser, Strauss, and Corbin (Kendall, 1999). Corbin herself downplays the method in her later edition of grounded theory's procedures (Corbin & Strauss, 2008). All sources are worth examining as supplemental references before and during Axial Coding.

Theoretical Coding

Sources

Charmaz, 2006; Corbin & Strauss, 2008; Glaser, 1978, 2005; Stern & Porr, 2011; Strauss, 1987; Strauss & Corbin, 1998

Description

(Some publications in grounded theory refer to Theoretical Coding as "Selective Coding" or "Conceptual Coding." The former term will be used in this manual since it more appropriately labels the outcome of this analytic cycle.)

A Theoretical Code functions like an umbrella that covers and accounts for all other codes and categories formulated thus far in grounded theory analysis. Integration begins with finding the primary theme of the research – what is called in grounded theory the *central* or *core category* – which "consists of all the products of analysis condensed into a few words that seem to explain what 'this research is all about'" (Strauss & Corbin, 1998, p. 146). Stern and Porr (2011) add that the central/core category identifies the major conflict, obstacle, problem, issue, or concern to participants. In Theoretical Coding, all categories and subcategories now become systematically linked with the central/core category, the one "that appears to have the greatest explanatory relevance" for the phenomenon (Corbin & Strauss, 2008, p. 104). The theoretical code – as a few examples: SOCIAL ARENA, BALANCING, CREDENTIALIZING, PERSONAL PRESERVATION WHILE DYING, and so on – is not the theory itself, but an abstraction that models the integration (Glaser, 2005, p. 17).

If Kathy Charmaz calls codes the "bones" that form the "skeleton" of our analysis, then think of the central or core category as the *spine* of that skeleton, the "backbone" which supports the corpus and aligns it. Strauss (1987) expands the metaphor by noting that continuous and detailed coding cycles eventually put "analytic meat on the analytic bones" (p. 245). Glaser (2005) asserts that development of a Theoretical Code is not always necessary for every grounded theory study, and it is better to have none at all rather than a false or misapplied one.

Applications

Theoretical Coding is appropriate as the culminating step toward achieving grounded theory (but see the Notes at the end of this profile for theory-building caveats).

Theoretical Coding integrates and synthesizes the categories derived from coding and analysis to now create a theory. At this cycle, categories developed thus far from Initial, Focused, and Axial Coding "have relevance for, and [can] be applicable to, all cases in the study. It is the details included under each category and subcategory, through the specifications of properties and dimensions, that bring out the case differences and variations within a category" (Glaser, 1978, p. 145). A Theoretical Code specifies the possible relationships between categories and moves the analytic story in a theoretical direction (Charmaz, 2006, p. 63). In dramaturgical parlance, the central/core category identifies the major conflict that initiates trajectories of action by its character/participants to (hopefully) resolve the conflict (Stern & Porr, 2011).

Original theory development, however, is not always necessary in a qualitative study. Hennink et al. (2011) note that research that applies pre-existing theories in different contexts or social circumstances, or that elaborates or modifies earlier theories, can be just as substantive. But most important during this cycle of theory building is to address the "how" and "why" questions to explain the phenomena in terms of how they work, how they develop, how they compare to others, or why they happen under certain conditions (pp. 258–61, 277).

Example

The example content from the Initial, Focused, and Axial Coding profiles will be applied here; refer to those first before proceeding. A well-developed analytic memo about theory can extend for pages, but only an excerpt is provided below. Notice that *memo writing serves as a code- and category-generating method; and it is from carefully sorted memos themselves that the theoretical code is derived and the theory articulated* (Glaser, 2005, p. 8). By this cycle of Theoretical Coding, the primary shift in narrative is toward the confirmed central/core category and its related categories.

As a reminder, the major categories outline derived from the Focused Coding example included:

I. DEFINING ONESELF AS A FRIEND

    A. Maintaining Friendships
       1. Setting Criteria for Friendships

    B. Dispelling Stereotypes of the Groups
       1. Labeling the Groups
       2. Qualifying the Groups

And some of the major Axial Codes illustrated in the analytic profile included:

1 SOCIALIZING
2 BEING SOCIALLY ACCEPTABLE/EXCEPTABLE
3 ACCEPTING THROUGH EXCEPTING
4 EXCEPTING THROUGH ACCEPTING

The researcher now reflects on all of these major codes and categories to determine the central/core process, theme, or problem. The central/core idea may lie in the name of one of the codes or categories developed thus far, but it may also emerge as a completely new word or phrase that subsumes all of the above (see Pattern Coding). Previously written analytic memos become key pieces to review for possible guidance and synthesizing ideas. Graphics-in-progress that illustrate the central/core category and its related processes are also most helpful. Figure 5.5 shows the model for this particular case.

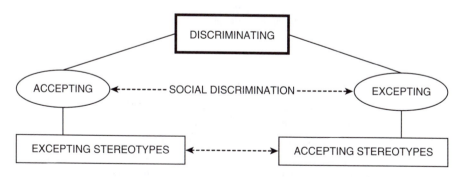

Figure 5.5   A diagram for a central/core category and its major processes

In the analytic memo below, the categories and subcategories are capitalized to emphasize their woven integration into the narrative:

5 June 2007
CENTRAL/CORE CATEGORY: DISCRIMINATING

The central/core category of this study is: DISCRIMINATING. Adolescents DISCRIMINATE when they choose their friends. They DISCRIMINATE through a process of ACCEPTING AND EXCEPTING. Adolescents SOCIALLY DISCRIMINATE as an action, and *are* SOCIALLY DISCRIMINATE in their choice of friendships.

We have generally constructed the term DISCRIMINATION as an abhorrent quality in ourselves and in others. The term in negative contexts suggests racism, sexism, and other "-isms" based on learned yet STEREOTYPING attitudes, values, and beliefs about others. But to DISCRIMINATE also means to distinguish by examining differences, to carefully select based on quality. When adolescents DISCRIMINATE (as a verb) they carefully select their friendships from a spectrum of peers BELONGING to various SOCIAL GROUP IDENTITIES. They are also DISCRIMINATE (as an adjective) when they observe the distinguishing SOCIAL SIMILARITIES AND DIFFERENCES between themselves and others.

ACCEPTING AND EXCEPTING suggests a continuum, ranging from full admission of an individual into one's personal confidence or SOCIAL GROUP; to neutrality or indifference about the individual; through overt exclusion, rejection, or avoidance of the individual. Adolescents ACCEPT others when the conditions for FRIENDSHIP are positive, including such properties as *compatibility* and *shared interests*. Adolescents EXCEPT others when the conditions for FRIENDSHIP lie on the opposite side of the spectrum. But regardless of where a teenager's choices about peers lie on the continuum, he or she is actively DISCRIMINATING. We DISCRIMINATE when we ACCEPT and we DISCRIMINATE when we EXCEPT. We DISCRIMINATE when we EXCEPT the STEREOTYPES of selected adolescent SOCIAL GROUPS (e.g., dumb jocks, killer geeks) and ACCEPT them as FRIENDS. But we can also ACCEPT the STEREOTYPES of these same SOCIAL GROUPS and EXCEPT them as candidates for FRIENDSHIP.

So, after all this, what's my theory? At this time I'll put forth the following: *An adolescent's inclusion and exclusion criteria for friendships are determined by the young person's ability to discriminate both positively and negatively among socially constructed peer stereotypes.*

Analysis

In some published grounded theory research, authors neglect to explicitly state, "The central/core category of this study is ..." and "The theory proposed is ... ." Make certain that your analytic memos and final report include these phrases; overtly name the category and state the theory in one sentence with an accompanying narrative. If you cannot, then you most likely have not constructed a grounded theory. (More on theory development is discussed in Chapter Six.)

The central or core category may appear frequently in the data coded and recoded thus far, and is phrased as an abstract concept that permits it to "explain variation as well as the main point made by the data" (Strauss & Corbin, 1998, p. 147). By this cycle, "If all data cannot be coded, the emerging theory does not fully fit or work for the data and must be modified" (Glaser, 1978, p. 56). Analytic memos and the final written report should explain and justify – with references to the data themselves – how categories and subcategories relate to the central/core category. The narrative also describes its related components (e.g., contexts, conditions, interactions, and consequences) for the reader.

Additional or selective sampling of new or existing participant data is encouraged to identify any variations within the developing theory. Morse (2007) recommends that researchers ask participants themselves to title their own stories after an interview to capture analytic leads toward a "supercode" or "core variable" (p. 237). Diagram refinement of the categories, process, and theory (begun during Axial Coding) is encouraged during this cycle to develop an operational model of the phenomenon or process and to map the complexity of the story, though Glaser (2005) discourages graphic representation and feels a Theoretical Code should be emergently constructed from analytic memos and explained solely through narrative.

Again, I caution that mere numeric frequency of a code or category from data analysis and memos is not necessarily a reliable and valid indicator of a central/core category. In one of my ethnographic studies (Saldaña, 1997), the In Vivo Code "SURVIVAL" appeared only four times in 20 months' worth of field notes and interview transcripts. Yet the code held summative power for all major and minor categories in the corpus and became the through-line for the study. So be conscious of a code's *qualities* as well as its quantity. In some cases, less is more (Saldaña, 2003, p. 115), for the criteria of a theory are its "elegance, precision, coherence, and clarity" (Dey, 2007, p. 186).

In Glaser's (1978) early work, he listed 18 "coding families" (pp. 73–82) to guide researchers labeling data at the conceptual level. These families were intended to sensitize the analyst to the many ways a category could be examined and included such things to consider as: *unit* (e.g., family, role, organization), *degree* (e.g., amount, possibility, intensity), *strategy* (e.g., techniques, tactics, means), and *cutting point* (e.g., boundary, benchmark, deviance). The "bread and butter" coding families for sociologists are what he labels "*The Six C's*: Causes, Contexts, Contingencies, Consequences, Covariances and Conditions" (p. 74). In his later work (2005), Glaser provides additional examples of Theoretical Code families such as *symmetry–asymmetry, micro–macro, social constraints, levels,* and *cycling.*

Glaser also noted in his early work that one type of core category could be a sociological "basic social process" (BSP), which includes such examples as *becoming, career,* and *negotiating.* BSPs "are theoretical reflections and summarizations of the patterned, systematic uniformity flows of social life" (1978, p. 100). BSPs are processual, meaning that they occur over time and involve change over time, most often demarcated in stages. If emergent as a central/core category, BSPs should also exhibit properties and dimensions with a particular emphasis on the temporal aspects of action/interaction. Conversely, Strauss and Corbin (1998) caution that "one can usefully code for *a* basic social or psychological process, but to organize every study around the idea of steps, phases, or social-psychological processes limits creativity" (p. 294).

Some recommended ways to further analyze Theoretical Codes are (see Appendix B):

- assertion development (Erickson, 1986)
- grounded theory (Bryant & Charmaz, 2007; Charmaz, 2006; Corbin & Strauss, 2008; Glaser & Strauss, 1967; Stern & Porr, 2011; Strauss & Corbin, 1998)
- illustrative charts, matrices, diagrams (Miles & Huberman, 1994; Morgan et al., 2008; Northcutt & McCoy, 2004; Paulston, 2000; Wheeldon & Åhlberg, 2012)
- longitudinal qualitative research (Giele & Elder, 1998; McLeod & Thomson, 2009; Saldaña, 2003, 2008)
- memo writing about the codes/themes (Charmaz, 2006; Corbin & Strauss, 2008; Glaser, 1978; Glaser & Strauss, 1967; Strauss, 1987)
- situational analysis (Clarke, 2005)
- thematic analysis (Auerbach & Silverstein, 2003; Boyatzis, 1998; Smith & Osborn, 2008)

Notes

To appreciate the breadth and depth of Strauss's (1987), Strauss and Corbin's (1998), and Corbin and Strauss's (2008) discussion of central/core categories, memos, and process, readers are referred to *Qualitative Analysis for Social Scientists* and *Basics of Qualitative Research* for a full explanation and thorough examples of memo development and grounded theory explained in narrative (storyline) format, respectively. Glaser's (2005) monograph on Theoretical Coding presents a more in-depth discussion of the subject from his perspective, while Stern and Porr (2011) provide an elegant overview of "classic" grounded theory development with an excellent description of Theoretical Coding.

Analysts should also examine Adele E. Clarke's *Situational Analysis: Grounded Theory After the Postmodern Turn* (2005), which presents "a radically different conceptual infrastructure" (p. xxii) of grounded theory that does not approach data analysis as a reductive act, but as one that intentionally maps the complexity of it:

> I propose that we complicate our stories, represent not only difference(s) but even contradictions and incoherencies in the data, note other possible readings, and at least note some of our anxieties and omissions. ... We need to address head-on the inconsistencies, irregularities, and downright messiness of the empirical world – not scrub it clean and dress it up for the special occasion of a presentation or a publication. (p. 15)

Researchers should also note postmodern perspectives on theory building. Though Clarke (2005) is an advocate of grounded theory's initial analytic methods and constructions, ultimately she feels that "the era of grand or formal theory is long over. ... Life on the planet is changing too quickly to claim permanence much less transcendence" (p. 293).

Finally, examine Ian Dey's (1999) *Grounding Grounded Theory: Guidelines for Qualitative Inquiry*, which critiques the method and takes issue with finding a central/core category: "[T]he problem arises that data suggesting alternatives may be ignored. By focusing on a single core variable, the research agenda may become one-dimensional rather than multi-dimensional" (p. 43).

Elaborative Coding

Source

Auerbach & Silverstein, 2003

Description

Elaborative Coding "is the process of analyzing textual data in order to develop theory further" (Auerbach & Silverstein, 2003, p. 104). The method is called "top-down" coding because

> one begins coding with the theoretical constructs from [a] previous study in mind. This contrasts with the coding one does in an initial study (bottom-up), where relevant text is selected without preconceived ideas in mind (to develop grounded theory). In elaborative coding where the goal is to refine theoretical constructs from a previous study, relevant text is selected with those constructs in mind. (p. 104)

Hence, a minimum of two different yet related studies – one completed and one in progress – is necessary for Elaborative Coding. Theoretical constructs emerge from the coded data's themes that are then grouped together into categories or "meaningful units" (p. 105).

Applications

Elaborative Coding is appropriate for qualitative studies that build on or corroborate previous research and investigations. Basically, the second study elaborates on the major theoretical findings of the first, even if there are slight differences between the two studies' research concerns and conceptual frameworks. Different participants or populations can also be used for the second study. This method can support, strengthen, modify, or disconfirm the findings from previous research.

Example

In the first project, a longitudinal case study was conducted with a boy named Barry as he progressed from ages 5 through 18. During childhood, Barry developed a strong interest in classroom improvisational drama and formal theatre production that continued into his teenage years. Key adults in his life – his mother and theatre teachers – cultivated this interest because they perceived him as a talented and gifted performer. The presentation of this first life course study was constructed as an ethnodramatic performance with Barry portraying himself (Saldaña, 1998). Each play script scene represented a major theme in his life course development. In Vivo Codes were used for the eight scene titles, but more traditional descriptions to recognize the themes are listed in parentheses:

1 "I DEVELOPED MY PASSION" (CHILDHOOD EXPERIENCES AND INFLUENCES)
2 "I WAS COMPLETELY EMPTY" (TROUBLED AND EPIPHANIC EARLY ADOLESCENCE)
3 "I NEVER FOUND IT IN SPORTS" (EXTRACURRICULAR/CAREER OPTIONS)
4 "I THINK A GOOD ACTOR ..." (DEVELOPMENT OF CRAFT)
5 "LOVE THE ART IN YOURSELF" (DEVELOPMENT OF ARTISTRY)
6 "THE SUPPORT OF PEOPLE" (INFLUENTIAL ADULTS)
7 "THEATRE'S A VERY SPIRITUAL THING" (PERSONAL MEANING DERIVED FROM THEATRE)
8 "I WANT THIS" (FUTURE CAREER/LIFE GOALS)

The magnitude of this case study is too complex to even summarize in this description, but for purposes of the method profile, one of the intended findings was the development of the participant's *through-line*, a statement "that captures the essence and essentials of a participant's journey and change (if any) through time" in longitudinal studies (Saldaña, 2003, p. 170). Barry's family church played a significant role in his life course, but during adolescence he became disenchanted with several congregational matters. Since Barry's most influential period of artistic development clustered during his high school years, the through-line *qua* (in the role of) key assertion from the first study reads:

> From his sophomore through senior years in high school, Barry gradually interchanged the insufficient spiritual fulfillment he received at church with the more personal and purposeful spiritual fulfillment he experienced through theatre. (Saldaña, 2003, p. 154)

The major theoretical construct for this first study was "PASSION," derived from an In Vivo Code that captured Barry's self-described affinity for his chosen art form: "I developed my passion for the arts and began seeing them as something as an idealistic career, an almost – a romantic, bigger than life – you know, *passion* – I don't know how else to put it – a *passion* for the arts!" (Saldaña, 1998, p. 92).

After this first study's presentation and completion, periodic contact with Barry was maintained from ages 18 through 26. During that period, I continued to collect data related to his life course, and his trajectory thus far – even with its multiple directions – appeared to harmonize with previous research in human developmental trends (Giele & Elder, 1998). But this period was also one of revelation for the researcher. Not only did I learn about current problems in

Barry's life, but I also learned about problems from his past not shared with me during the first study – among them, a late diagnosis of bipolar disorder and two unsuccessful suicide attempts.

Auerbach and Silverstein (2003) advise that, for Elaborative Coding:

> Sometimes the relevant text that you select [from your second study] will fit with your old theoretical constructs [from the first study]. This is helpful because it will lead you to develop your constructs further. On other occasions, however, the relevant text will not fit with one of your old theoretical constructs, but instead will suggest new ones. This is also helpful, because it will increase your understanding of your research concerns. (p. 107)

The original eight themes from the first study represent not only categories but roughly overlapping time periods – phases and stages in Barry's life course development up through age 18. The second study would profile his life from ages 18 through 26 (our mutually agreed stopping point for the study). Would the original eight themes endure as his life story progressed? Obviously, the past cannot be changed, but the past can be reinterpreted in new contexts as one's life progresses forward and new experiences accumulate.

Analysis

For the second study (Saldaña, 2008), the first theme, CHILDHOOD EXPERIENCES AND INFLUENCES, endured as a period that primarily included his theatrical and religious experiences and influences. But the second theme, TROUBLED AND EPIPHANIC EARLY ADOLESCENCE, would now become the first phase of a cycle that generated a new theme for the second cycle: TROUBLED AND EPIPHANIC EARLY ADULTHOOD. Both of these periods included Barry's suicide attempts, but it was not until after the second attempt that the late diagnosis of bipolar disorder was made, placing the original second theme in a new context.

The third theme, EXTRACURRICULAR/CAREER OPTIONS, included football as a possible avenue of interest for Barry, but in retrospect the category was a minor theme during the first study and was thus deleted as an influence on his life course.

The original fourth and fifth themes, DEVELOPMENT OF CRAFT and DEVELOPMENT OF ARTISTRY, were condensed into one theme for the second study: ARTISTIC DEVELOPMENT. Differentiation for the first study was made to show his progression from technician to artisan.

The first study's sixth theme, INFLUENTIAL ADULTS, is a "given" in life course research and endured for the second study.

The seventh theme, PERSONAL MEANING DERIVED FROM THEATRE (or its In Vivo Code, "THEATRE'S A VERY SPIRITUAL THING"), was not deleted but modified as the second study progressed and its data were coded, which placed this theme in a new context (more on this below).

After high school, Barry's opportunities for performance waned due to such contextual and intervening conditions as higher-education priorities and full- and part-time work for income needs. He majored in social work with a minor in religious studies, opting not to pursue theatre because of its limited chances for financial success. There were still times, though, when he felt (as In Vivo Coded) "I'M FEELING KIND OF LOST".

The Descriptive Code THEATRE PARTICIPATION decreased significantly during his college and university years, while the code YOUTH MINISTRY appeared with more frequency. In his mid-twenties, another epiphany occurred that altered the eighth and final original theme, FUTURE LIFE/CAREER GOALS. During the second study, Barry received a spiritual calling from God to pursue the ministry. The theme took on new direction and meaning, for he no longer had "career goals" but a LIFE CALLING. Nevertheless, he felt his theatrical experiences and training benefited his youth ministry's informal drama projects and his preaching skills. Though it was my In Vivo field note code, not Barry's, I inverted the original study's "THEATRE'S A VERY SPIRITUAL THING" to become SPIRITUALITY'S A VERY THEATRICAL THING.

To recap, the new seven thematic periods in Barry's life for the second study (ages 5–26) emerged as:

1 CHILDHOOD EXPERIENCES AND INFLUENCES ("I DEVELOPED MY PASSION")
2 TROUBLED AND EPIPHANIC EARLY ADOLESCENCE ("I WAS COMPLETELY EMPTY")
3 ARTISTIC DEVELOPMENT ("LOVE THE ART IN YOURSELF")
4 INFLUENTIAL ADULTS ("THE SUPPORT OF PEOPLE")
5 PERSONAL MEANING DERIVED FROM THEATRE ("THEATRE'S A VERY SPIRITUAL THING")
6 TROUBLED AND EPIPHANIC EARLY ADULTHOOD ("I'M FEELING KIND OF LOST")
7 LIFE CALLING (SPIRITUALITY'S A VERY THEATRICAL THING)

The second study also sought a through-line *qua* (in the role of) key assertion to capture Barry's life course development. The first through-line focused on just three years of his adolescence. This final one, however, now needed to place his entire life thus far in a longitudinal context. Barry's life consisted of such successes as high academic achievement, recognition for his artistic accomplishments, leadership service roles, and spiritual fulfillment. But his life also consisted of a period of drug abuse, years of undiagnosed bipolar disorder, an alcoholic father once arrested for drug use, frequent bouts with depression, and two unsuccessful suicide attempts. Barry's life course now had new meaning, new direction, and the through-line needed to reflect that. The key assertion and accompanying narrative for the second study reads:

He ascends. From ages five through twenty-six, Barry has sought ascension in both lit- eral and symbolic ways to compensate for and transcend the depths he has experienced throughout his life course. He has excelled in academics, towered above peers, stood up for victims of bullying, gotten high on drugs, performed up on stage, surpassed teammates on the football field, lifted weights, climbed rocks, risen above drug use, appeared upbeat, looked up to his teachers as father figures, surmounted bipolarity, lived up to his mother's expectations, exhibited higher levels of intra- and interpersonal intelligence, empowered church youth to reach new heights, sought advanced degrees, received a higher calling, grew in his faith, mounted the pulpit, uplifted others with his sermons, and exalted his God.

The primary theoretical construct for this case, which derived from the first study, would endure but take on new interpretive and ironic meaning for the second study. "PASSION" refers not only to a drive out of love for something, but also means suffering and outbreaks of intense, uncontrollable emotion. Barry experienced all of these passions in one form or another throughout his life course. His ups and downs, highs and lows, ascents and descents were the consistent yet erratic rhythms before his diagnosis of bipolarity. Even after receiving prescribed medication, he prefers not to take it when possible, relying instead on more natural aids for self-control, though he admits "some days are more difficult than others."

This example profiled the development and evolution of themes, through-lines, and the meaning of a major theoretical construct from one longitudinal period (ages 5–18) of a case study through the next (ages 18–26). The elaboration of codes and themes would obviously evolve across time for a life course project. But collection, comparison, and coding of these two major pools of data made the changes that did occur more apparent and generated a more provocative analysis.

Elaborative Coding is a method applicable to qualitative metasummary and metasynthesis (see Themeing the Data in Chapter Three). Heaton (2008) also suggests that secondary analysis of qualitative data – which includes such approaches as the reanalysis of data from a former study, the aggregation of two or more separate studies' data, and so on – might use Elaborative Coding for initial exploration.

Some recommended ways to further analyze Elaborative Codes are (see Appendix B):

- action and practitioner research (Altrichter et al., 1993; Coghlan & Brannick, 2010; Fox et al., 2007; Stringer, 1999)
- assertion development (Erickson, 1986)
- grounded theory (Bryant & Charmaz, 2007; Charmaz, 2006; Corbin & Strauss, 2008; Glaser & Strauss, 1967; Stern & Porr, 2011; Strauss & Corbin, 1998)
- longitudinal qualitative research (Giele & Elder, 1998; McLeod & Thomson, 2009; Saldaña, 2003, 2008)
- memo writing about the codes/themes (Charmaz, 2006; Corbin & Strauss, 2008; Glaser, 1978; Glaser & Strauss, 1967; Strauss, 1987)
- meta-ethnography, metasummary, and metasynthesis (Finfgeld, 2003; Major & Savin-Baden, 2010; Noblit & Hare, 1988; Sandelowski & Barroso, 2007; Sandelowski et al., 1997)
- situational analysis (Clarke, 2005)
- thematic analysis (Auerbach & Silverstein, 2003; Boyatzis, 1998; Smith & Osborn, 2008)
- within-case and cross-case displays (Gibbs, 2007; Miles & Huberman, 1994; Shkedi, 2005)

Notes

Elaborative Coding is more fully explained in Auerbach and Silverstein's (2003) elegant text, *Qualitative Data: An Introduction to Coding and Analysis*. In their book, the researchers adopt and adapt grounded theory methodology for their studies on fathers and fatherhood among various populations. Readers are also advised to examine Layder (1998) for his "adaptive theory," which builds on grounded theory's principles yet "combines the use of prior theory to lend order and pattern to research data while simultaneously adapting to the order and pattern contained in [the] emerging data" (p. viii). Layder's framework is a construct-based variant of Elaborative Coding.

(For those concerned about the personal welfare of the case study described in this profile, as of April 2012, Barry is now married, holds a masters degree in divinity, and serves as an associate pastor for a mainstream denomination church.)

Longitudinal Coding

Sources

Giele & Elder, 1998; LeGreco & Tracy, 2009; McLeod & Thomson, 2009; Saldaña, 2003, 2008

Description

(For brevity and clarity, this method profile focuses on life course studies. See the Notes for recommended references in anthropology, sociology, and education.)

Longitudinal Coding is the attribution of selected change processes to qualitative data collected and compared across time. Holstein and Gubrium (2000), in *Constructing the Life Course*, conceptualize that:

> The life course and its constituent parts or stages are not the objective features of experience that they are conventionally taken to be. Instead, the constructionist approach helps us view the life course as a social form that is constructed and used to make sense of experience. ... The life course doesn't simply unfold before and around us; rather, we actively organize the flow, pattern, and direction of experience in developmental terms as we navigate the social terrain of our everyday lives. (p. 182)

Long-term quantitative analysis of change examines statistical increase, decrease, constancy, and so on in selected measured variables of interest. Yet there can also be *qualitative* increase, decrease, constancy, and so on within data gathered from participants through time. Longitudinal Coding categorizes researcher observations into a series of matrices (Saldaña, 2008; see Figure 5.6) for comparative analysis and interpretation to generate inferences of change – if any.

LONGITUDINAL QUALITATIVE DATA SUMMARY MATRIX

DATA TIME POOL/POND: FROM ___/___/_____ THROUGH ___/___/_____
STUDY:_____
RESEARCHER(S):_____

(when possible or if relevant, note specific days, dates, times, periods, etc. below; use appropriate DYNAMIC descriptors)

INCREASE/ EMERGE	CUMULATIVE	SURGE/EPIPH/ TURN POINT	DECREASE/ CEASE	CONSTANT/ CONSISTENT	IDIOSYN- CRATIC	MISSING

DIFFERENCES ABOVE FROM PREVIOUS DATA SUMMARIES

CONTEXTUAL/INTERVENING CONDITIONS INFLUENCING/AFFECTING CHANGES ABOVE

INTERRELATIONSHIPS	CHANGES THAT OPPOSE/ HARMONIZE WITH HUMAN DEV/SOCIAL PROCESSES	PARTIC/CONCEPT RHYTHMS (phases, stages, cycles, etc. in progress)

PRELIMINARY ASSERTIONS AS DATA ANALYSIS PROGRESSES
(refer to previous matrices)

THROUGH-LINE
(in progress)

Figure 5.6 A longitudinal qualitative data summary matrix (from Saldaña, 2003, courtesy of Rowman and Littlefield Publishing Group/AltaMira Press)

The analytic template in Figure 5.6 provides a method for summarizing vast amounts of qualitative data collected from long-term research projects:

> Imagine that one matrix page holds summary observations from three months' worth of fieldwork. And if the study progresses through two years, then there would be eight pages total of longitudinal qualitative data. ... Think of each three-month page as an animator's cartoon cell, whose artwork changes subtly or overtly with each successive drawing to suggest movement and change. Or, imagine that each matrix sheet is a monthly page from a calendar, which suggests a chronological progression of time and change as each page is turned. Or, imagine that each matrix page is a photograph of the same child taken at different intervals across time, so that each successive photo reveals growth and development. (Saldaña, 2008, p. 299)

During the First Cycle of collection and analysis, qualitative data collected through an extended period of time may have been coded descriptively, processually, etc., with a possible focus on participant emotions, values, and so on. In Longitudinal Coding, the data corpus is reviewed categorically, thematically, and comparatively across time to assess whether participant change may have occurred. Seven descriptive categories first organize the data into matrix cells during Second Cycle coding (Saldaña, 2003, 2008). Briefly explained, they are:

1 **Increase and Emerge**: This cell includes both quantitative and qualitative summary observations that answer *What increases or emerges through time?* An increase in a participant's income is an example of quantitative change, but accompanying qualitative increases/emergences may include such related factors as "job responsibilities," "stress," and "reflection on career goals." This code documents change that occurs in smooth and average trajectories, unlike the next two codes.

2 **Cumulative**: This cell includes summary observations that answer *What is cumulative through time?* Cumulative affects result from *successive* experiences across a span of time. Examples include: a pianist's improved technique after a year of private lessons and independent practice, and acquired knowledge about interpersonal relationships after a few years of social activity and dating.

3 **Surges, Epiphanies, and Turning Points**: This cell includes summary observations that answer *What kinds of surges, epiphanies, or turning points occur through time?* These types of changes result from experiences of sufficient magnitude that they significantly alter the perceptions and/or life course of the participant. Examples include: graduation from high school, the terrorist attacks on the USA on September 11, 2001, and unexpected termination from employment.

4 **Decrease and Cease**: This cell includes summary observations that answer *What decreases or ceases through time?* Like increases, qualitative decrease cells can include both quantitative and qualitative summary observations. Examples include: a decline in workplace morale after a new incompetent administrator is hired, and a decrease and eventual cessation of illegal drug use.

5 **Constant and Consistent**: This cell includes summary observations that answer *What remains constant or consistent through time?* The "recurring and often regularized fea-

tures of everyday life" (Lofland et al., 2006, p. 123) compose most data sets. Examples include: daily operations in a fast-food restaurant, and a participant's long-term marriage to the same spouse.

6 **Idiosyncratic**: This cell includes summary observations that answer *What is idiosyncratic through time?* These are events that are not of magnitude, such as epiphanies, but rather the "inconsistent, ever-shifting, multidirectional and, during fieldwork, unpredictable" actions in life (Saldaña, 2003, p. 166). Examples include: a teenager's experiments with an alternative wardrobe, a series of problematic automobile repairs, and occasional non-life-threatening illnesses.

7 **Missing**: This cell includes summary observations that answer *What is missing through time?* During fieldwork, the researcher should note not only what is present but also what is possibly and plausibly absent or missing so as to influence and affect participants. Examples include: a teacher's lack of knowledge on working with children with disabilities, no sexual activity during an adult's mid-life years, and incomplete standard operating procedures for an organization to run efficiently.

Throughout data entry, the researcher is encouraged to use *dynamic* descriptors. These are carefully selected verbs, adjectives, and adverbs that most "accurately" describe phenomena and change, even though the act is, at best, "approximate and highly interpretive" (Saldaña, 2003, p. 89). Dynamic descriptors extend beyond linear continua, such as "less" and "more" of something, and focus instead on the essential qualities of phenomena. For example, one might substitute a phrase such as "getting more conservative" with "adopting conservative ideologies." A global observation such as "growing older" becomes more specific with such descriptive phrases as "salt-and-pepper hair, soft grunts as he sits down and rises, arthritic bones that ache dully in humid weather."

Applications

A person's perceptions in relation to the social world around him or her evolve throughout the lifespan (Sherry, 2008, p. 415). Thus, Longitudinal Coding is appropriate for longitudinal qualitative studies that explore change and development in individuals, groups, and organizations through extended periods of time. Studies in identity lend themselves to this method since identity is conceptualized as a fluid rather than static construct. "Qualitative longitudinal research enables us to capture personal processes that are socially situated, capturing psychological depth and emotional poignancy" (McLeod & Thomson, 2009, p. 77). And for studies that explore broader social processes, "including the facilitation of change and the institution of new routines" across micro-, meso-, and macro-levels, *discourse tracing* examines chronologically emergent and transformative themes and issues (LeGreco & Tracy, 2009, p. 1516).

Giele and Elder (1998) note that recent life course study research has broken away from composing patterned models of general human development to acknowledge the unique character, unpredictable and diverse trajectories, and complex interrelationship of the gendered individual exercising agency within varying social contexts through particular eras of time. Life history extends beyond the sequential reporting of factual events, such as graduation from college, full-time employment, marriage, the birth of a first child, and so on, and now considers participant *transition* and *transformation* in such domains as worldview, life satisfaction, and personal values. Reporting the life course can be structured and mapped thematically and narratively as well as chronologically in unique analytic blends (Clausen, 1998). The coding and categorizing method presented here is just one of several qualitative and mixed methods models available for longitudinal data analysis.

Example

The example content presented here relates to the case profiled in Elaborative Coding; refer to that first before proceeding.

Longitudinal Qualitative Data Summary Matrix pages do not have to be apportioned into standardized time blocks (e.g., each page holding six months of data). Each matrix can hold a portion (a large "pool" or smaller "pond") of data from the life course that adopts a traditional period we often allocate in social life, such as the elementary school years, secondary school years, university education, etc. The periods can also be separated by major turning points in the life course whenever they may occur (Clausen, 1998). Sometimes a division must be necessarily artificial, such as periods between scheduled follow-up interviews.

In the longitudinal study with Barry (Saldaña, 2008), the first data pool and matrix for ages 5–12 collected his major elementary school INCREASES/EMERGENCES:

- additional theatre-viewing experiences beyond the treatment
- parental involvement in nurturing his theatre interest
- at ages 11–12, victim of bullying by peers
- at age 12, reflecting on career choices (actor, writer, "think tank")
- at age 12, counseling for withdrawal and depression

Barry was not formally tracked from ages 12 through 16, but in retrospective accounts during later years, he recalled two key epiphanies – an unsuccessful suicide attempt and his first formal stage performance experience. Related INCREASES/EMERGENCES data from the second matrix included:

- new: smoking, illegal drug use
- hair length
- at ages 12–14, anxiety from peer bullying
- age 14, attitude "renaissance" from first and future performance opportunities

Follow-up and direct participant observation was initiated during Barry's secondary school years. The third matrix, representing ages 16–18, listed the following INCREASES/EMERGENCES:

- new: mentorship from theatre teachers
- new: questioning his spiritual faith/belief system
- roles in theatre productions
- concentration during performance work
- "passion" for the art form
- leadership skills

The fourth matrix, at ages 18–23, included the following as INCREASES/EMERGENCES:

- new: personal credit card
- new: prescription medication for bipolarity
- attending community college for general studies
- learning American Sign Language
- exploring drama therapy as a career
- service as a summer camp counselor for special populations
- attending a different church but same faith
- searching for "artful living"

The fifth matrix, during age 23, listed the following as his INCREASES/EMERGENCES in actions:

- new: eyebrow piercing, facial hair, spiked hair style
- deciding between social work and urban sociology as possible majors at the university
- providing urban ministry for youth

The sixth and final matrix, during ages 24–26, listed as his INCREASES/EMERGENCES:

- new: rock climbing as a hobby
- new: disclosure of his father's past spiritual abuse
- new: tattoo on left arm – "fight, race, faith" (from 2 Timothy 4:7)
- university education: pursuing a bachelor's degree in social work with a minor in religious studies
- preaching occasionally at Sunday worship services
- working for "social justice"

The portions of data listed above are just small excerpts from one data cell category summarizing 21 years of participant observation, interviews, and document collection about one human being whose life had been a relatively tumultuous journey thus far. A chronological scan from start to finish of salient aspects that increased and emerged in Barry's life has an almost narrative and foreshadowing flow to it. Not included in this category, of course, are those data coded as SURGES, EPIPHANIES, AND TURNING POINTS in Barry's life course, such as his two unsuccessful suicide attempts, his diagnosis of bipolarity, and his call to serve in the ministry.

Analysis

What follows after the coding and categorization of data into the matrices? Each of the seven descriptive coding cells are then chronologically compared to comparable cells from other longitudinal matrices (e.g., increases from the third matrix are compared to increases in the first and second matrices). Any differences inferred and interpreted are noted in the *Differences Above from Previous Data Summaries* cells. There is also no need to keep analyses of Increases completely separate from Decreases, for example, or the Cumulative completely separate from the Idiosyncratic. As analysis continues, your observations and interpretations of interaction and interplay between these categories will become sharpened as you reflect on their possible overlap and complex connections.

The next row of cells, *Contextual/Intervening Conditions Influencing/Affecting Changes Above*, asks you to think how, how much, in what ways, and why the descriptive observations and noted differences may be present. Contextual Conditions refer to social life's routine activities and daily matters, such as attending school, working, parenting, etc. Contextual Conditions also refer to the "givens" of one's social identity or personal patterns, such as gender, ethnicity, and habits. Intervening Conditions refer to those events or matters that can play a more substantive and significant role in activating change, such as a hostile work environment, the enactment of new laws, or writing a dissertation. Whether something is interpreted as a Contextual or Intervening Condition is admittedly a matter of researcher perception. A hostile work environment might be a "given" Contextual Condition for some occupations, but if it activates participant change, such as deteriorating self-esteem, then the Contextual becomes Intervening.

Again, the columns of change processes do not have to remain isolated. In fact, by this time there should be an intricate weaving of the actions and phenomena inspected thus far for the next items of analysis.

The *Interrelationships* cell notes observations and interpretations of direct connection or influences and affects (my qualitative equivalent for the positivist "cause and effect") between selected matrix items. For example, Increases may correlate with Decreases, the Cumulative may correlate with the Constant and Consistent. Caution should be exercised here, as the cognitive constructions of data connections can run amok. This is testimony to the general observation that social life is complexly interconnected, but evidence from the data corpus should support any assertions of interrelationship.

Changes that Oppose/Harmonize with Human Development/Social Processes refers to the particulars of the case compared to previous studies and literature reviews in related areas. For example, does the case's life course seem to follow what might be generalized developmental trends or does it suggest alternative pathways? Does the participant's unique occupations throughout the life course suggest reconceptualizing a basic social process, such as "career"?

Participant/Conceptual Rhythms refers to observations of patterned periodicities of action, such as phases, stages, cycles, and other time-based constructs. If sequential observations of change seem to cluster together in somewhat distinct ways, this may suggest the apportionment of action into phases (separate but chronological action clusters), stages (cumulative action clusters across time), and cycles (repetitive action clusters through time). Attention should also be paid to analyzing the transitional processes in between these clusters, reminiscent of anthropologist Victor Turner's now-classic study of "liminal" social spaces.

Preliminary Assertions as Data Analysis Progresses are statements that "bullet point" the various observations about the participants or phenomenon based on the analysis thus far. This is a large critical space in the matrix for the researcher to reflect on the data and their synthesis. Analytic memos written elsewhere are necessary, but the matrix is the place where salient observations are summarized and listed. Researchers should be particularly attuned to noticeable repetitive motifs throughout the data corpus.

The *Through-Line* (see Elaborative Coding for examples) is comparable to a key assertion (Erickson, 1986) or a central/core category (Corbin & Strauss, 2008), though it is not necessarily the ultimate analytic goal for a longitudinal qualitative study. The through-line is generally a thematic statement that captures the totality of change processes in the participant.

CAQDAS programs become indispensable for longitudinal qualitative studies. The software's ability to manage massive amounts of data in organized files, and to maintain and permit complex coding changes as a project progresses, are beneficial advantages for the researcher. The ATLAS.ti program also features "Snapshot Coding," which represents a "situation at a particular moment in time" (Lewins & Silver, 2007, p. 218), enabling the analyst to create a progression of documented snapshot moments to assess participant change (if any).

By default, a discussion of longitudinal processes is lengthy. A complete illustration of all the principles tersely summarized above could easily fill several volumes. Observations and assertions of participant change can be credibly assumed only from long-term immersion in the field, extensive and reflective interviews with participants, and astute recognition of differences in data collected through time about the life course. Patton (2008), however, notes that in contemporary society and especially within organizations, "Rapid change is the norm rather than the exception" (p. 198).

Some recommended ways to further analyze Longitudinal Codes are (see Appendix B):

- assertion development (Erickson, 1986)
- case studies (Merriam, 1998; Stake, 1995)
- grounded theory (Bryant & Charmaz, 2007; Charmaz, 2006; Corbin & Strauss, 2008; Glaser & Strauss, 1967; Stern & Porr, 2011; Strauss & Corbin, 1998)
- illustrative charts, matrices, diagrams (Miles & Huberman, 1994; Morgan et al., 2008; Northcutt & McCoy, 2004; Paulston, 2000; Wheeldon & Åhlberg, 2012)
- interrelationship (Saldaña, 2003)
- life course mapping (Clausen, 1998)
- logic models (Knowlton & Phillips, 2009; Yin, 2009)
- longitudinal qualitative research (Giele & Elder, 1998; McLeod & Thomson, 2009; Saldaña, 2003, 2008)

- memo writing about the codes/themes (Charmaz, 2006; Corbin & Strauss, 2008; Glaser, 1978; Glaser & Strauss, 1967; Strauss, 1987)
- narrative inquiry and analysis (Clandinin & Connelly, 2000; Coffey & Atkinson, 1996; Cortazzi, 1993; Coulter & Smith, 2009; Daiute & Lightfoot, 2004; Holstein & Gubrium, 2012; Murray, 2003; Riessman, 2008)
- portraiture (Lawrence-Lightfoot & Davis, 1997)
- situational analysis (Clarke, 2005)
- thematic analysis (Auerbach & Silverstein, 2003; Boyatzis, 1998; Smith & Osborn, 2008)
- within-case and cross-case displays (Gibbs, 2007; Miles & Huberman, 1994; Shkedi, 2005)

Notes

To learn more about Longitudinal Coding and research, refer to Giele and Elder (1998) and Saldaña (2003, 2008) for more procedural and analytic details about life course and longitudinal research, respectively. The best theoretical and epistemological discussions of life course research are Holstein and Gubrium (2000) and McLeod and Thomson (2009), while Bude (2004) proposes a "generation" as a reconceptualization of the "birth cohort" as a longitudinal unit of study. Reports on long-term fieldwork in anthropology – some studies lasting up to 50 years – can be accessed from Kemper and Royce (2002). Educational change studies are masterfully profiled in Fullan (2001) and Hargreaves, Earl, Moore, and Manning (2001), while theories of change in organizations, institutions, and systems are dynamically profiled in Patton (2008, Chapter 10). Calendar and time diary methods for long-term data collection, management, and analysis (of primarily "quantitized" qualitative data) are described in Belli, Stafford, and Alwin (2009). For information on "Timescapes," promoted as the first major funded longitudinal qualitative study of personal and family relationships in the UK, access: www.timescapes.leeds.ac.uk.

The following pages are provided for documenting additional Second Cycle coding methods located in other sources or developed by the researcher.

_____ Coding

Source(s):

Description:

Application(s):

Example:

Analysis:

Notes:

_____ **Coding**

Source(s):

Description:

Application(s):

Example:

Analysis:

Notes:

_____ Coding

Source(s):

Description:

Application(s):

Example:

Analysis:

Notes:

SIX

After Second Cycle Coding

CHAPTER SUMMARY

This chapter reviews transitional processes after Second Cycle coding, yet most of these can be applied after First Cycle coding as well. Strategies for focusing, theorizing, formatting, writing, ordering, networking, and mentorship are provided. The chapter concludes with reflections on our goals as qualitative researchers.

Post-Coding and Pre-Writing Transitions

If you have diligently applied First Cycle coding methods to your data (several times) and – if needed – transitioned those codes through Second Cycle methods (again, several times), concurrently maintained a substantive corpus of insightful analytic memos, and employed one or more additional analytic approaches to the data, if all has gone well you should now have several major categories, themes, or concepts, or at least one theory (or through-line, key assertion, primary narrative, etc.). That, of course, is the ideal scenario. But what if you are not yet there? Or, what if you are already there and do not know how to proceed?

This closing chapter offers a few recommendations for what might be labeled post-coding and pre-writing – the transitional analytic processes between coding cycles and the final write-up of your study. *And refer back to the methods in Chapter Four since they may also be useful and applicable at this stage of your analysis.* Where you are in your analytic journey does, to some degree, depend on which coding method(s) you have applied to your data. Versus Coding, for example, encourages you to find three major "moieties"; Themeing the Data and organizational techniques such as Code Landscaping recommend listing the outcomes in outline format; Axial Coding prescribes that you specify the properties and dimensions of a major category. But some find it difficult to make those final confirmatory assertions. Fear gets the better of us as we sometimes wonder after our analytic work is almost completed, "Have I got it right?", "Did I learn anything new?", "Now what do I do?"

I do not discuss how to craft and write the final report itself, for there are so many genres, styles, and formats of research reporting possible – ethnography, narrative short story, ethnotheatrical performance, academic journal article, dissertation, dedicated Internet site, etc. – that I cannot adequately address them all (for expert guidance see Gibbs, 2007; Richards, 2009; Wolcott, 1994, 2009; Woods, 2006). Anthropologist Clifford Geertz (1983) charmingly mused, "Life is just a bowl of strategies" (p. 25). So, I offer a bowl of strategies below that will hopefully crystallize your analytic work thus far and provide a template or springboard for your written document or mediated report. Pick one or more to guide you toward the final stages of your study's write-up. Glesne (2011) astutely reminds us that "The proof of your coding scheme is, literally, in the pudding of your manuscript" (p. 197).

Focusing Strategies

Sometimes we become overwhelmed by the magnitude of our studies and thus need to intentionally focus the parameters of our investigation in progress to find its core. Forcing yourself to select a limited number of various ideas that have emerged from your study encourages you to prioritize the multiple observations and reflect on their essential meanings.

The "top 10" list

Regardless of codes applied to them, extract no more than 10 quotes or passages (preferably no longer than half a page in length each) from your field notes, interview transcripts, documents, analytic memos, or other data that strike you as the most vivid and/or representational of your study. Print each excerpt on a separate page of paper.

Reflect on the content of these 10 items and arrange them in various orders: chronologically, hierarchically, telescopically, episodically, narratively, from the expository to the climactic, from the mundane to the insightful, from the smallest detail to the bigger picture, etc. I cannot predict what you may find since each study's data are unique. But you may discover different ways of structuring or outlining the write-up of your research story by arranging and rearranging the most salient ideas from the data corpus.

The study's "trinity"

If you feel you are unable to identify the key issues of your study after Second Cycle coding, ask yourself: What are the three (and only three) major codes, categories, themes, and/or concepts generated thus far that strike you, which stand out in your study?

Write each item in a separate bin on a piece of paper (or use CAQDAS graphics on a monitor) and arrange the three bins in a triangle. Which one of the three items, to you, is the apex or dominant item and why? In what ways does this apex influence and affect or interrelate with the other two codes, categories, themes, and/or concepts? Explore other possible three-way combinations with other major items from the study.

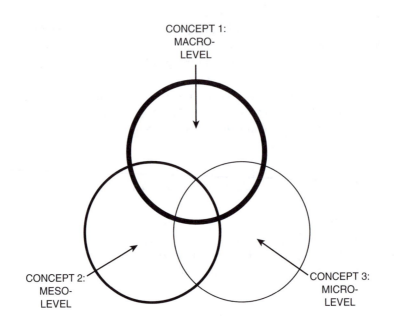

Figure 6.1 A trinity of concepts as a Venn diagram (based on Soklaridis, 2009)

Another trinity configuration is to plot three major codes, categories, themes, and/ or concepts within overlapping circles as a Venn diagram (see Figure 6.1). Reflect on what labels or properties can be attributed to the overlapped areas of two of the three items, and the label and properties for the center area that represents all three items. Soklaridis (2009) developed three themes from her qualitative study and attributed not just labels but dimensions or *magnitude* to her trinity. The first was an organizational theme at the *macro*-level; the second was an intergroup theme at the *meso*-level; and the third was an individual theme at the *micro*-level. Explore whether your over-lapped trinity also possesses comparable dimensions or magnitude.

Codeweaving

In Chapter Two I noted that one of the most critical outcomes of qualitative data analysis is to interpret how the individual components of the study weave together. Codeweaving is the actual integration of key code words and phrases into narrative form to see how the puzzle pieces fit together. The technique may, at first, create a forced and seemingly artificial assertion, but use it as a heuristic to explore the possible and plausible interaction and interplay of your major codes.

Codeweave the primary codes, categories, themes, and/or concepts of your analy-sis into as few sentences as possible. Try writing several variations to investigate how the items might interrelate, suggest causation, indicate a process, or work holistically to create a broader theme. Search for evidence in the data that supports your summary statements, and/or disconfirming evidence that suggests a revision of those statements. Use the codewoven assertion as a topic sentence for a paragraph or extended narrative that explains the observations in greater detail (see Causation Coding in Chapter Three and Code Landscaping in Chapter Four for extended examples).

The "touch test"

Sometimes an emergent set of codes or categories might seem uninspiring – a set of nouns that reveals only surface, descriptive patterns. The "touch test" is a strategy for progressing from topic to concept, from the real to the abstract, and from the particular to general. I tell my students that you can literally touch someone who is a mother, but you cannot physically touch the concept of "motherhood." You can touch an old house in poor disrepair, but you cannot touch the phenomenon of "poverty." And you can touch a painting an artist has rendered, but you cannot physically touch the artist's "creative process." Those things that cannot literally be touched are conceptual, phenomenological, and processual, and represent forms of abstraction that most often suggest higher-level thinking.

Examine the latter-developed set of codes and categories from your study. Can you physically touch what they represent? If so, then explore how those codes and categories can be reworded and transformed into more abstract meanings to transcend the particulars of your study. For example, one category from an adolescent case study might be the use and abuse of **Drugs**. But through richer Descriptive and/ or Process Code language, the higher-level concepts, phenomena, and processes might emerge as: *dependency, addiction, coping mechanism, searching for "highs"*, or *escaping from*.

I do advise caution, however, in transcending too high with your conceptual ideas, lest you lose sight of their important and perhaps more insightful origins. At the time of this writing, the worldwide economic crisis was attributed, in part, to some people in influential corporate, financial, and political positions possessing what some called "a sense of entitlement" leading them to "an abuse of power." These are phenomenological ideas or conceptual constructs, but they do not zero in on the *base motives and needs* that propelled these people's actions. Also "a sense of entitlement" and "an abuse of power" are about something in retrospect – noun phrases rather than current verbs or drives. To me, "a sense of entitlement" is not as meaningful as something like *arrogant hoarding of wealth* or even a basic "deadly sin" such as *greed*. And "an abuse of power" has become a phrase so overused these days that it is almost trite. More clearly defined financial drives such as *unethical manipulation* or *exploiting with impunity* more closely delineate what is at work within humans. The lesson here is that once you have a word or phrase that you believe captures the conceptual or theoretical in your study, think again. For every choice there are many sacrifices. Think not only of what words you have chosen, but what related words you have not.

From Coding to Theorizing

Theoretical Coding (see Chapter Five) profiles methods for progressing from codes toward a central/core category that suggests a grounded theory at work in the data.

But Theoretical Coding is not the sole method that must be utilized to develop theory. This topic is very complex, yet I offer a few salient strategies that may assist you with what some perceive as a necessary outcome of qualitative inquiry. I myself believe that it is good when a researcher develops a theory, but it is all right if it does not happen.

Elements of a theory

From my perspective, a social science theory has three main characteristics, as it is traditionally conceived: it predicts and controls action through an if–then logic; explains how and/or why something happens by stating its cause(s); and provides insights and guidance for improving social life:

> At its most practical, a theory is an elegant statement that proposes a way of living or working productively. In education, a theory for teachers is: *The more that students are engaged with the content of the lesson, the less management and discipline problems that may occur in the classroom.* In psychotherapy, a practitioner's theory is: *A parent with clinical depression will tend to raise clinically depressed children.* (Saldaña, 2011b, p. 114; emphasis in original)

Many theories are provisional; thus, language should be included that supports the tentative nature of our proposals (e.g., "may occur," "tend to"). Also, I have observed that what is a sound theoretical proposition to one person may be perceived as a weak statement to another. "Like beauty, theory is in the eye of the beholder" (p. 114). A theory is not so much a story as much as it is a proverb. It is a condensed lesson of wisdom we formulate from our experiences that we pass along to other generations. Aesop's fables have morals; our research tales have theories.

Categories of categories

From my own research experiences, the stage at which I seem to find a theory emerging in my mind is when I create *categories of categories*. For example, in the Code Mapping illustration in Chapter Four, 52 codes were clustered into eight categories, which were then reorganized into three "meta" categories. It is at this point that a level of abstraction occurs which transcends the particulars of a study, enabling generalizable transfer to other comparable contexts.

How multiple categories become condensed into fewer and more streamlined categories does have a repertoire of interrelationship arrangements from which I tend to draw, discussed in the Tabletop Categories strategy in Chapter Four. First, I look for possible *structures* such as:

- **Superordinate and Subordinate Arrangement**: Categories and their subcategories are arranged in outline format as a form of structural organization, suggesting discrete linearity and classification:

I. **Category 1**

    A. *Subcategory 1A*
    B. *Subcategory 1B*
    C. *Subcategory 1C*

II. **Category 2**

    A. *Subcategory 2A*
    B. *Subcategory 2B*

- **Taxonomy**: Categories and their subcategories are grouped but without any inferred hierarchy; each category seems to have equal weight:

Category 1	**Category 2**	**Category 3**
Subcategory 1A	*Subcategory 2A*	*Subcategory 3A*
Subcategory 1B	*Subcategory 2B*	*Subcategory 3B*
	Subcategory 2C	

- **Hierarchy**: Categories are ordered from most to least in some manner – frequency, importance, impact, etc.:

    Category 1 – most
    Category 2 – some
    Category 3 – least

- **Overlap**: Some categories share particular features with others while retaining their unique properties:

    Category 1 ◄ - - - - - - - - **Category 2** - - - - - - - - ► **Category 3**

Second, I look for *processes* – the action-oriented influences and affects of one or more categories on another, such as:

- **Sequential Order**: The action suggested by categories progresses in a linear manner:

    Category 1 ──────► **Category 2** ──────► **Category 3**

- **Concurrency**: Two or more categories operate simultaneously to influence and affect a third:

- **Domino Effects**: Categories cascade forward in multiple pathways:

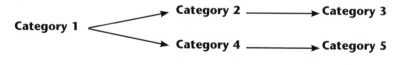

- **Networks**: Categories interact and interplay in complex pathways to suggest interrelationship:

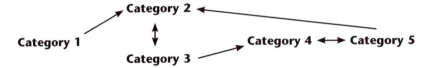

I do not mean to suggest that these are formulaic ways of constructing theory from categories, and these are not the only arrangements available to you. I present these oft-cited structures and processes as possible heuristics to explore with your own analytic work to determine whether anything "clicks" on paper or in your head. See Lyn Richards' (2009) *Handling Qualitative Data: A Practical Guide* for a more thorough discussion of category development and interrelationship.

Categories and analytic memos as sources for theory

Codes and coding are ways to progress toward a theory because they develop categories. And in your analytic memo writings of how these categories interrelate and transcend to themes or concepts, you build a foundation for theory development (see Figure 1.1). Since a theory is a rich statement with accompanying narrative to expand on its meaning, your ultimate goal is to write one sentence, based on the totality of your analysis, that captures insightful if–then and how/why guidance for as many relevant contexts as possible. If that seems like a formidable and daunting task, it is. To my knowledge, there is no magic algorithm that leads to a new theory. It is more likely accomplished through deep reflection on the categories and the categories of categories you have constructed, which symbolically represent particular patterns of human action derived from your data and codes.

Just as all research projects begin with a one-sentence statement – "The purpose of this study is …" – some research projects culminate with another one-sentence statement – "The theory constructed from this study is … ." Since I am a task- and goal-oriented researcher, I devote some analytic memo-writing time throughout the project to reflect on how I can complete that latter sentence, based on the analytic journey I am undertaking. But good ideas, like good coffee and good tea, need time to brew and steep. Sometimes I actively pursue how can I brew a theoretical statement; other times I simply let my mind steep in the data, codes, categories, and analytic memos thus far to see if there is serendipitous theoretical crystallization. Most of the time, the struggle is finding just the right words from the corpus and putting them in just the right order that pulls everything together for a theory. Codeweaving is just one way of integrating these categories together.

If I cannot develop a theory, then I will be satisfied with my construction of a *key assertion* (Erickson, 1986), a summative and data-supported statement about the *particulars* of a research study, rather than the suggested generalizable and transferable meanings of my findings to other settings and contexts. McCammon and Saldaña (2011) conducted an e-mail mixed methods survey of 234 adults ranging in age from 18 to 70+. Respondents provided testimony about their secondary school theatre and speech classes and extracurricular programming and how that may have made an impact on their adult careers and lives. We felt we could not credibly put forth a generalizable theory since we used purposive sampling and limited our survey to North Americans. But based on the evidentiary warrant and analysis of this database, we asserted that "Quality high school theatre and speech experiences can not only significantly influence but even accelerate adolescent development and provide residual, positive, lifelong impacts throughout adulthood" (p. 5). This key assertion meets the if–then criterion of a theory, and even suggests how social life can be improved, but it does not include or infer "how" or "why." The accompanying analytic narrative with its related assertions and subassertions must do that job.

Formatting Matters

Text is visual. Hence, we can use simple formats and cosmetic devices available to us to highlight what matters most in a written account.

Rich text emphasis

I strongly recommend that *key assertions and theories should be italicized or bolded for emphasis in a final report*. The same advice holds for the first time significant **codes**, **themes**, and **concepts** are addressed. This simple but rich text formatting better guarantees that salient and important ideas do not escape the reader's notice, especially if the reader should be scanning the report to quickly search for major findings, or conducting a metasummary or metasynthesis. Also, the tactic is a way of confirming for yourself that your data analysis has reached a stage of synthesis and crystallization. Non-print formats such as Internet pages and CD-ROM files can also explore such cosmetic devices as font size, color, and, of course, accompanying pictorial content for emphasizing what matters (Saldaña, 2011b, p. 144).

Headings and subheadings

Use code, category, theme, and concept labels themselves as headings and subheadings frequently in your written report. In a way, these italicized, bolded, left-justified, or centered devices are also forms of coding and categorizing the sections of your text. They serve as organizing frames for your own development of the research story, and using them often keeps the reader on track with the linear units of your write-up.

When I review a lengthy journal article manuscript or dissertation chapter undivided by headings and subheadings, I soon become lost without these cognitive signposts to help guide me on my private reading journey. I slyly note in the margin for the writer, "Subheadings are your friend." Review this chapter alone and notice how frequently headings and subheadings are used to organize the post-coding and pre-writing recommendations. Imagine how difficult it would have been to read and stay focused had this chapter been written as one lengthy narrative.

Subheadings are your friend.

Findings "at a glance"

One-page visual displays help immensely with mapping a process or phenomenon, but they can only contain so many words. A simple text chart in as few pages as possible that outlines your findings and their connections provides an executive summary of sorts for you as the researcher and possibly for your readers as well. Henwood and Pidgeon (2003) recommend matrix data displays consisting of a major code or theme in one column, followed by an example (or two) of a datum that supports the major code or theme in the second column, then a short interpretive summary of how the major code or theme relates to the overall analytic scheme, or contributes to the study's conclusions. An example of such a display might read:

COLUMN 1 Code or Theme	COLUMN 2 Datum Supporting the Code or Theme	COLUMN 3 Researcher's Interpretive Summary
RESISTANCE	"And I thought, 'OK, if that's the way you're going to treat me, I'm not budging one inch on this'."	Employee RESISTANCE will be linked to ENTITLEMENT, based on his or her SENIORITY in the company.
DEFEATISM	"I wasn't going to raise a stink. It just wasn't worth the effort to get him to see it my way."	DEFEATISM interrelates strongly with the participant's total number of years working in the company, not necessarily his or her AGE. Selected employees ranging from their late 20s to early 50s were actively searching for other jobs during fieldwork.

Writing About Coding

Due to manuscript length restrictions in print journal articles, a discussion about codes and coding methods utilized for a study is usually brief – approximately two full paragraphs at most. But longer documents such as theses, dissertations, and technical reports can include more detailed descriptions of a researcher's analytic processes. Throughout your research study, document your coding and data analytic processes in analytic memos, yet integrate only the most relevant and salient portions of them into your final written report. Below are a few considerations for your write-ups.

Researchers provide brief storied accounts of what happened "backstage" at computer terminals and during intensive work sessions. After a description of the participants and the particular data collected for a study, descriptions of coding and analysis procedures generally include: references to the literature that guided the analytic work; qualitative data organization and management strategies for the project; the particular coding and data analytic methods employed and their general outcomes; and the types of CAQDAS programs and functions used. Some authors may include accompanying tables or figures that illustrate the codes or major categories constructed. Collaborative projects usually explain team coding processes and procedures for reaching intercoder agreement or consensus. Some authors may also provide brief confessional anecdotes that highlight any analytic dilemmas they may have encountered. These passages are intended to demonstrate researcher accountability and trustworthiness (i.e., knowledge of acceptable procedures within a field) and to inform the readers of data analytic methods which may help them in their own future work.

As one example of a write-up, McCammon and Saldaña (2011) addressed how accessible software was used for their coding and mixed methods data analysis, including references to specific program functions and techniques, which may provide little-known yet useful information for readers:

> Completed surveys were e-mailed or forwarded to Saldaña who cut-and-pasted and maintained the data in Excel spread sheets for qualitative coding and quantitative calculations (Hahn, 2008; Meyer & Avery, 2009). Descriptive information (e.g., date received, e-mail address of respondent, gender of respondent), quantitative ratings, and open-ended comments each received their own cells in a matrix, enabling comparison and analytic induction as rows and columns were scanned and later rearranged for queries. An eclectic combination of attribute, structural, descriptive, in vivo, process, initial, emotion, values, pattern, and elaborative coding were applied to the qualitative data (Saldaña, 2009). Cells were color-coded and narratives were given rich text features to enhance analysis "at-a-glance" (e.g., data rows of respondents not involved in theatre-related professions were highlighted in yellow; significant passages were bolded or assigned a red font for later citation).
>
> Descriptive statistics were calculated by Excel's AVERAGE function … ; inferential statistic gathering employed the TTEST application. Qualitative codes were manually assigned, organized, categorized, and assembled into hierarchical landscapes and formats for content analysis and pattern detection (Krippendorff & Bock, 2009) for the first 101 cases as a preliminary analysis, then later merged with Excel's CONCATENATE function for codes from cases 102–234. … Microsoft Word's functions such as SORT and FONT SIZE enhanced coding organization and management. Erickson's (1986) interpretive heuristics were employed to compose assertions and to search for confirming and disconfirming evidence in the data corpus. Quotes from respondents that supported the assertions were extracted from the data base for the evidentiary warrant. (pp. 19–20)

Since important points can get overlooked or lost when embedded in narrative, simple tables and figures, in addition to rich text features, headings, and subheadings, can highlight the resultant codes and/or categories for "at a glance" or "quick look" reader review (see Figure 6.2).

What advice would you give a university student about to become a high school speech or theatre teacher?

Lifelong Passion – love what you do, maintain energy, enthusiasm and passion; make experiences fun; the job requires commitment and sacrifice

Lifelong Challenges – challenge students as artists, maintain high standards for excellence, set up rich creative experiences, tackle issues, challenge the status quo

Lifelong Relationships – develop an ethic of care, connect with students (encourage, respect, inspire); create inclusive, equitable, student focused "safe haven," community, and ensemble, especially for marginalized students; look beyond the immediate because a teacher can impact a student's future

Lifelong Learning – need broad range of content knowledge and organized teaching; find and explore challenging scripts; keep learning and find a balance between process and product

Lifelong Resilience – because the job is hard work and time consuming, teachers should maintain physical and mental health, patience and perseverance, especially for political "battles"; remember that "less is more" and have a back-up teaching plan

Figure 6.2   A sample table listing major categories and descriptions (derived from codes) from a research study (McCammon & Saldaña, 2011, p. 64)

Finally, emphasize for readers through introductory phrases and italicized text, if necessary, the major outcomes of your analysis: "The three major categories constructed from transcript analysis are _____", "The core category that led to the grounded theory is _____", "The key assertion of this study is _____", "A theory I propose is _____", and so on. Overt labeling such as this is not sterile writing but helpful, time-saving guidance for readers to grasp the headlines of your research story, particularly if they are conducting literature reviews or qualitative metasummaries or metasyntheses. McCammon and Saldaña (2011) put forth the following three-category conclusion at the beginning and end of their report:

> According to survey respondent testimony, high school theatre and speech experiences: (1) empower one to *think and function improvisationally* in dynamic and ever-changing contexts; (2) deepen and accelerate development of an individual's *emotional and social intelligences*; and (3) expand one's verbal and non-verbal *communicative dexterity* in various presentational modes. (p. 6)

Ordering and Reordering

A small list of just two to seven major codes, categories, themes, and/or concepts – or even just one new theory – can seem formidable when it comes to writing about them in a report. The recommendations and strategies offered below are a few ways to plot (i.e., structure) their discussion.

Analytic storylining

A plot in dramatic literature is the overall structure of the play. The storyline is the linear sequence of the characters' actions, reactions, interactions, and episodic events within the plot. Kathy Charmaz (2001, 2008) is a masterful writer of process, or what playwrights call *storylining*, in grounded theory. Her analytic narratives include such active processual words and phrases as "it means," "it involves," "it reflects," "when," "then," "by," "shapes," "affects," "necessitates," "happens when," "occurs if," "occurs when," "shifts as," "contributes to," "varies when," "especially if," "is a strategy for," "because," "differs from," "does not … but instead," "subsequently," "consequently," "hence," "thus," and "therefore." Notice how these words and phrases suggest an unfolding of events through time. Charmaz (2010) also strategically chooses analytic "words that reproduce the tempo and mood of the [researched] experience," along with experiential rhythms that are reproduced within her writing (p. 201).

Not all qualitative reporting is best told through a storyline, and remember that the positivist construction of "cause and effect" can force limited parameters around detailed descriptions of complex social action (see Causation Coding in Chapter Three). Nevertheless, if there is a story with conditions and consequences to be told from and about your data, explore how the words and phrases quoted above can be integrated into your own written description of what is *happening* to your participants or what is *active* within the phenomenon (Saldaña, 2011b, pp. 142–3).

One thing at a time

If you have constructed several major categories, themes, concepts, or theories from your data, start by writing about them *one at a time*. After your exhaustive qualitative data analysis you may have come to the realization of how intricately everything interrelates, and how difficult it is to separate ideas from their contexts. But rest assured that discussing one thing at a time keeps you focused as a writer, and keeps us focused as readers. After you have discussed each element separately, then you can begin your reflections on how these items may connect and weave complexly together.

But which item do you discuss first, then second, then third, and so on? Remember that numeric frequency of data related to a code, category, theme, or concept is not necessarily a reliable indicator of its importance or significance, so the item with the highest tally does not always merit first place in the write-up. Various ordering strategies exist for your analytic discussion: from major to minor, minor to major, particular to general, initiating incident to final consequence, etc. The sequence you choose will vary depending on the nature of your work and its audience, but I appreciate being told early in a report what the "headline" of the research news is, followed by the story's details.

When it comes to "one thing at a time," here is another small nugget that has helped me tremendously in my own professional career, particularly when I became anxious about the magnitude of a research project: Write and edit at least one page a day, and in a year, you have a book.

Begin with the conclusion

One of my dissertation students was a terrible procrastinator and suffered from severe writer's block. She told me after her fieldwork was completed and the formal writing stage began that she did not know where or how to start. I facetiously but strategically replied, "Then start by writing the conclusion." That advice actually triggered the development of a solid chapter that summarized the major outcomes of her study. All she had to do was now write the material leading up to those conclusions.

The same strategy may work for you. If you find yourself unable to start at the beginning, then begin with the conclusion. The final chapter of a longer work most often includes such conventional items as: a recap of the study's goals and research design; a review of the major outcomes or findings from fieldwork (albeit tentative if you start by writing the conclusion); recommendations for future research in the topic; and a reflection on how the researcher him- or herself has been influenced and affected by the project. This thumbnail sketch of the study's details may provide you with better direction for writing the full-length report.

Assistance from Others

A counseling folk saying I often pass along to others goes, "You can't see the frame when you're in the picture." Sometimes we need an outside pair of eyes or ears to respond to our work in progress.

Peer and online support

Aside from local colleagues with whom you can converse about your study and analysis in progress, explore the ever-growing international network of peer support available through online sites such as Sage Publications (www.methodspace. com and www.socialsciencespace.com). Organizational list-serves are also ways in which you might connect with peers or mentors to get quick feedback on questions you may have about your study. If possible, arrange private one-on-one meetings or tutorials ahead of time at conferences with a colleague who has some knowledge about your subject area or research methodology. I have received several e-mails and made follow-up telephone calls to "shop-talk" with some wonderful doctoral scholars conducting exciting studies.

Self-help sites such as Sage Research Methods Online (http://srmo.sagepub. com), QDA Online (http://onlineqda.hud.ac.uk/), Text Analysis Info Page (www. textanalysis.info), and Phenomenology Online (www.phenomenologyonline. com) are also available for resource support with such features as textbook excerpts, references, and, on QDA Online, video clips of research methods class lectures. Nova Southeastern University's *The Weekly Qualitative Report* (www. nova.edu/ssss/QR/WQR/index.html) keeps readers apprised of current conference events, related news items, and recently published journal articles of interest.

Forum: Qualitative Social Research (www.qualitative-research.net/index.php/fqs) is an international, peer-reviewed, online journal with a breadth of articles, book reviews, and informational resources in several languages.

Searching for "buried treasure"

When I read later drafts of my students' dissertations, I am always on the lookout for what I call "buried treasure." In their analysis chapters, they sometimes make statements that, to me, demonstrate remarkable analytic insight about the study. But these statements are often embedded in the middle of a paragraph or section when they should be placed as a topic sentence or summarizing idea. I circle the sentence in red ink and write in the margin such notes as, "This is brilliant!" or "A major idea here," and "Italicize this and move it to the beginning of the paragraph." Perhaps the students have been so immersed in their studies' data that they cannot see the forest for the trees. Perhaps they wrote what was, to them, just another part of the analytic story, but were unaware that they had developed an insight of relative magnitude.

When a substantive portion of your research is written, show it to a mentor or advisor and ask him or her to be on the lookout for "buried treasure" in the report.

Closure

Researchers are offered varied yet sometimes contradictory advice in qualitative inquiry. We are told by some scholars that coding is an essential and necessary step in qualitative data analysis, while others tell us that the method is outdated, colonial, and incompatible with newer genres of research. We are told to capture the essence of our study's data, yet also told to write about the intricate complexity of what we observed in the field. We are advised to "reduce" our data to an elegant set of well-codified themes, yet also advised to render our accounts with thick description. We are cautioned to maintain a sense of scientific rigor in an era of evidence-based accountability, yet also encouraged to explore more progressive forms of academic research reporting such as poetic and autoethnographic representations. We are charged to contribute productively to the knowledge bases of our disciplines, yet also advised to leave our readers with more questions than answers through evocative ambiguity and uncertainty enhancement.

We do not need to reconcile the contradictions; we only need to acknowledge the multiplicity of them and become well versed in various methods and modes of working with qualitative (and quantitative) data. I am a pragmatic, eclectic researcher, and I sincerely feel everyone else should be one as well. Coding is just *one* way of analyzing qualitative data, not *the* way. There are times when coding the data is absolutely necessary, and times when it is most inappropriate for the study at hand. There are times when we need to write a 30-page article for an academic journal, and times when we need to write a 30-minute performance ethnography for the stage. There are times when we must crunch the numbers, and times when we must compose a poem. And there are times when it is more powerful to end a presentation with tough questions, and times when it is more powerful to end with thoughtful answers. But to be honest, we need much more of the latter.

My personal belief is: It is not the questions that are interesting, it is the *answers* that are interesting. As a student and teacher of qualitative inquiry, what remains with me after I read a report or experience a presentation, regardless of form or format, is its demonstration of the researcher's analytic prowess. When I silently think or verbally whisper "Wow ..." at the conclusion of someone's work, I know that I have been given not just new knowledge but new *awareness*, and am now the better for it.

Permit me to close with a poetic adaptation and weaving of anthropologist Harry F. Wolcott's sage advice from his various writings (permission for use granted by the author), which I feel should serve as our ideal goals as qualitative researchers:

Only understanding matters.

We must not just transform our data,
    we must transcend them.

Insight is our forté.

The whole purpose of the enterprise is
    discovery and
    revelation.

We do it to be profound ... .

APPENDIX A

A Glossary of Coding Methods

Below are summaries of First and Second Cycle coding categories and methods. See the methods profiles for additional information (Sources, Descriptions, Applications, Examples, Analyses, and Notes).

Affective Methods   Investigates participant emotions, values, conflicts, and other subjective qualities of human experience. See: Emotion Coding, Values Coding, Versus Coding, and Evaluation Coding.

Attribute Coding   Notation, usually at the beginning of a data set rather than embedded within it, of basic descriptive information such as the fieldwork setting, participant characteristics or demographics, data format, and other variables of interest for qualitative and some applications of quantitative analysis. Appropriate for virtually all qualitative studies, but particularly for those with multiple participants and sites, and studies with a wide variety of data forms. Provides essential participant information for future management, reference, and contexts for analysis and interpretation. Examples: PARTICIPANTS – 5th GRADE CHILDREN; DATA FORMAT – P.O. FIELD NOTES/SET 14 OF 22; DATE – 6 OCTOBER 2011.

Axial Coding   Extends the analytic work from Initial Coding and, to some extent, Focused Coding. Describes a category's properties (i.e., characteristics or attributes) and dimensions (the location of a property along a continuum or range) and explores how the categories and subcategories relate to each other. Properties and dimensions refer to such components as the contexts, conditions, interactions, and consequences of a process. Appropriate for studies employing grounded theory methodology (as the transitional cycle between Initial and Theoretical Coding processes) and studies with a wide variety of data forms. Example: BEING SOCIALLY ACCEPTABLE/EXCEPTABLE; Sample Property: Adolescents accept peers with whom they find perceived similarities; Sample Dimension: Acceptability – We can accept some people but not be their friends – we except them.

Causation Coding   Extracts attributions or causal beliefs from participant data about not just how but why particular outcomes came about. Searches for combinations of antecedent and mediating variables that lead toward certain pathways. Attempts to map a three-part process as a CODE 1 > CODE 2 > CODE 3 sequence. Appropriate for discerning motives, belief systems, worldviews, processes, recent histories, interrelationships, and the complexity of influences and affects on human actions and phenomena. May serve grounded theorists in searches for causes, conditions, contexts, and consequences. Also appropriate to evaluate the efficacy of a particular program, or as preparatory work before diagramming or modeling a process through visual means such as decision modeling and causation networks. Examples: SPEECH TRAINING > CONFIDENCE > COLLEGE PREP; COMPETITION > WINNING > SELF-ESTEEM; SUCCESS + HARD WORK REWARDS + GOOD COACH > CONFIDENCE.

Code   Most often a researcher-generated word or short phrase that symbolically assigns a summative, salient, essence-capturing, and/or evocative attribute for a portion of language-based or visual data. The data and thus coding processes can range in magnitude from a single word to a full paragraph to an entire page of text to a stream of moving images. Attributes specific meaning to each individual datum for purposes of pattern detection, categorization, and other analytic processes. Examples: SENSE OF SELF-WORTH; STABILITY; "COMFORTABLE".

Descriptive Coding   Assigns labels to data to summarize in a word or short phrase – most often as a noun – the basic topic of a passage of qualitative data. Provides an inventory of topics for indexing and categorizing. Appropriate for virtually all qualitative studies, but particularly for beginning qualitative researchers learning how to code data, ethnographies, and studies with a wide variety of data forms. Perhaps more appropriate for social environments rather than social action. Examples: BUSINESSES; HOUSES; GRAFFITI.

Domain and Taxonomic Coding   The systematic search for and categorization of cultural terms. An ethnographic method for discovering the cultural knowledge people use to organize their behaviors and interpret their experiences. Categories that categorize other categories are domains. Taxonomies are hierarchical lists of things classified together under a domain. A verbatim data record to extract folk terms is mandatory, but when no specific folk terms are generated by participants, the researcher develops his or her own analytic terms. Appropriate for ethnographic studies and constructing a detailed topics list or index of major categories or themes in the data. Particularly effective for studying microcultures with a specific repertoire of folk terms. Examples: Domain – TRASH TALKING; Taxonomy – RUDE TALKING, NASTY TALKING, SLANDERING, and SPREADING RUMORS.

Dramaturgical Coding   Applies the terms and conventions of character, play script, and production analysis to qualitative data. For character, these terms include such items as participant objectives (OBJ), conflicts (CON), tactics (TAC), attitudes (ATT), emotions (EMO), and subtexts (SUB). Appropriate for exploring intrapersonal and interpersonal participant experiences and actions in case studies, power relationships, and the processes of human motives and agency. Examples: OBJ: CONFRONT; TAC: ADMONISH; ATT: IRONIC.

Eclectic Coding   Employs a purposeful and compatible combination of two or more First Cycle coding methods, with the understanding that analytic memo writing and Second

Cycles of recoding will synthesize the variety and number of codes into a more unified scheme. Appropriate for virtually all qualitative studies, but particularly for beginning qualitative researchers learning how to code data, and studies with a wide variety of data forms. Also appropriate as an initial, exploratory technique with qualitative data; when a variety of processes or phenomena are to be discerned from the data; or when combined First Cycle coding methods will serve the research study's questions and goals. Examples: A few First Cycle eclectic codes may consist of SCARED [Emotion Code], "I'VE GOT TO" [In Vivo Code], and DOUBT VS. HOPE [Versus Code]. Second Cycle recoding of the same data set employs Dramaturgical Codes throughout: OBJ: "FINISH MY DISSERTATION"; TAC: TASKS AND TIMETABLE.

Elaborative Coding   Builds on a previous study's codes, categories, and themes while a current and related study is underway to support or modify the researcher's observations developed in an earlier project. Hence, a minimum of two different yet related studies are necessary. Appropriate for qualitative studies that build on or corroborate previous research and investigations, even if there are slight differences between the two studies' research concerns, conceptual frameworks, and participants. Example: A case study's FUTURE CAREER/LIFE GOALS from the first study becomes a LIFE CALLING in the second study.

Elemental Methods   Foundation approaches to coding qualitative data. Basic but focused filters for reviewing the corpus to build a foundation for future coding cycles. See: Structural Coding, Descriptive Coding, In Vivo Coding, Process Coding, and Initial Coding.

Emotion Coding   Labels the emotions recalled and/or experienced by the participant, or inferred by the researcher about the participant. Appropriate for virtually all qualitative studies, but particularly for those that explore intrapersonal and interpersonal participant experiences and actions. Provides insight into the participants' perspectives, worldviews, and life conditions. Examples: "TEARING ME APART"; MILD SURPRISE; RELIEF.

Evaluation Coding   Application of (primarily) non-quantitative codes to qualitative data that assign judgments about the merit, worth, or significance of programs or policy. Appropriate for policy, critical, action, organizational, and evaluation studies, particularly across multiple sites and extended periods of time. Selected coding methods profiled can be applied to or supplement Evaluation Coding, but the method is also customized for specific studies. Examples: + SERMONS: USED TO BE "POWERFUL"; – OPENING MUSIC: TOO LONG; REC: SHORTER SERVICES.

Exploratory Methods   Open-ended investigation and preliminary assignments of codes to the data before more refined coding systems are developed and applied. Can serve as preparatory work before more specific First Cycle or Second Cycle coding methods. See: Holistic Coding, Provisional Coding, Hypothesis Coding, and Eclectic Coding.

Focused Coding Follows In Vivo, Process, and/or Initial Coding. Categorizes coded data based on thematic or conceptual similarity. Searches for the most frequent or significant Initial Codes to develop the most salient categories in the data corpus. Appropriate for virtually all qualitative studies, but particularly for studies employing grounded theory methodology, and the development of major categories or themes from the data. Develops categories without attention at this time to Axial Coding's properties and dimensions. Examples: Category: MAINTAINING FRIENDSHIPS; Category: SETTING CRITERIA FOR FRIENDSHIPS.

Grammatical Methods Refers not to the grammar of language but to the basic grammatical principles of coding techniques. These enhance the organization, nuances, and texture of qualitative data. See: Attribute Coding, Magnitude Coding, Subcoding, and Simultaneous Coding.

Holistic Coding Applies a single code to a large unit of data in the corpus, rather than line-by-line coding, to capture a sense of the overall contents and the possible categories that may develop. A preparatory approach to a unit of data before a more detailed coding or categorization process through First or Second Cycle methods. The coded unit can be as small as one-half a page in length, to as large as an entire completed study. Appropriate for beginning qualitative researchers learning how to code data, and studies with a wide variety of data forms. Applicable when the researcher has a general idea of what to investigate in the data. Example: For a 140-word interview excerpt, the entire passage receives the code, CAUTIONARY ADVICE.

Hypothesis Coding Application of a researcher-generated, predetermined list of codes to qualitative data specifically to assess a researcher-generated hypothesis. The codes are developed from a theory/prediction about what will be found in the data before they have been collected or analyzed. Statistical applications, if needed, can range from simple frequency counts to more complex multivariate analyses. Appropriate for hypothesis testing, content analysis, and analytic induction of the qualitative data set, particularly the search for rules, causes, and explanations in the data. Can also be applied midway or later in a qualitative study's data collection or analysis to confirm or disconfirm any assertions or theories developed thus far. Examples: It is hypothesized that the responses to a particular question about language issues in the USA will generate one of four answers from participants: RIGHT – We have the right to speak whatever language we want in America; SAME – We need to speak the same language in America – English; MORE – We need to know how to speak more than one language; and NR – No Response or "I don't know."

In Vivo Coding Uses words or short phrases from the participant's own language in the data record as codes. May include folk or indigenous terms of a particular culture, subculture, or microculture to suggest the existence of the group's cultural categories. Appropriate for virtually all qualitative studies, but particularly for beginning qualitative researchers learning how to code data, and studies that prioritize and honor the participant's voice. Part of and employed in other grounded theory methods (Initial, Focused, Axial, and

Theoretical Coding). In Vivo Codes are placed in quotation marks. Examples: "HATED SCHOOL", "STOPPED CARING", "I DON'T KNOW".

Initial Coding   The first major open-ended stage of a grounded theory approach to the data. Can incorporate In Vivo and Process Coding, plus other methods. Breaks down qualitative data into discrete parts, closely examines them, and compares them for similarities and differences. Appropriate for virtually all qualitative studies, but particularly for beginning qualitative researchers learning how to code data, grounded theory studies, ethnographies, and studies with a wide variety of data forms. Examples: DISPELLING STEREOTYPES; QUALIFYING: "KIND OF"; LABELING: "GEEKY PEOPLE".

Literary and Language Methods   Borrows from established approaches to the analysis of literature and oral communication to explore underlying sociological, psychological, and cultural constructs. See: Dramaturgical Coding, Motif Coding, Narrative Coding, and Verbal Exchange Coding.

Longitudinal Coding   The attribution of selected change processes to qualitative data collected and compared across time. Matrices organize data from fieldwork observations, interview transcripts, and document excerpts into similar temporal categories that permit researcher analysis and reflection on their similarities and differences from one time period through another to generate inferences of change – if any. Appropriate for studies that explore identity, change, and development in individuals, groups, and organizations through extended periods of time. Examples of change processes: INCREASE AND EMERGE; CONSTANT AND CONSISTENT; CUMULATIVE.

Magnitude Coding   Consists of and adds a supplemental alphanumeric or symbolic code or subcode to an existing coded datum or category to indicate its intensity, frequency, direction, presence, or evaluative content. Magnitude Codes can be qualitative, quantitative, and/or nominal indicators to enhance description. Appropriate for mixed methods and qualitative studies in social science and health care disciplines that also support quantitative measures as evidence of outcomes. Examples: STRONGLY (STR); 1 = LOW; + = PRESENT.

Motif Coding   Application to qualitative data of previously developed or original index codes used to classify types and elements of folk tales, myths, and legends. A motif as a literary device is an element that appears several times within a narrative work, yet in Motif Coding the element might appear several times or only once within a data excerpt. Appropriate for exploring intrapersonal and interpersonal participant experiences and actions in case studies, particularly those leading toward narrative or arts-based presentational forms, together with identity studies and oral histories. Examples: CRUEL FATHER; TRANSFORMATION; MOTHER AND SON.

Narrative Coding   Applies the conventions of (primarily) literary elements and analysis to qualitative texts most often in the form of stories. Appropriate for exploring intrapersonal and interpersonal participant experiences and actions to understand the human condition through narrative. Suitable for such inquiries as identity development, critical/feminist studies, documentation of the life course, and narrative inquiry. Examples: FLASHBACK; ASIDE; CODA.

OCM (Outline of Cultural Materials) Coding   Uses the OCM, an extensive numbered index of cultural topics developed by anthropologists for the classification of fieldwork data from ethnographic studies. A systematic coding system which has been applied to the Human Relations Area Files, a massive collection of ethnographic field notes and accounts about hundreds of world cultures. OCM coding is appropriate for ethnographic studies (cultural and cross-cultural) and studies of artifacts, folk art, and human production. Examples: 292 SPECIAL GARMENTS; 301 ORNAMENT; 535 DANCE.

Pattern Coding   A category label ("meta-code") that identifies similarly coded data. Organizes the corpus into sets, themes, or constructs and attributes meaning to that organization. Appropriate for Second Cycle coding; development of major themes from the data; the search for rules, causes, and explanations in the data; examining social networks and patterns of human relationships; or the formation of theoretical constructs and processes. Example: DYSFUNCTIONAL DIRECTION as the Pattern Code for the following related codes: UNCLEAR INSTRUCTIONS; RUSHED DIRECTIONS; "YOU NEVER TOLD ME"; etc.

Procedural Methods   Prescriptive, pre-established coding systems or very specific ways of analyzing qualitative data. See: Protocol Coding, OCM (Outline of Cultural Materials) Coding, Domain and Taxonomic Coding, and Causation Coding.

Process Coding   Uses gerunds ("-ing" words) exclusively to connote observable and conceptual action in the data. Processes also imply actions intertwined with the dynamics of time, such as things that emerge, change, occur in particular sequences, or become strategically implemented. Appropriate for virtually all qualitative studies, but particularly for grounded theory research that extracts participant action/interaction and consequences. Part of and employed in other grounded theory methods (Initial, Focused, Axial, and Theoretical Coding). Examples: TELLING OTHERS; REJECTING RUMORS; STICKING BY FRIENDS.

Protocol Coding   The coding of qualitative data according to a pre-established, recommended, standardized, or prescribed system. The generally comprehensive lists of codes and categories provided to the researcher are applied after his or her own data collection. Some protocols also recommend specific qualitative (and quantitative) data analytic techniques with the coded data. Appropriate for qualitative studies in disciplines with previously developed and field-tested coding systems. Examples: ALCOH = alcoholism or drinking; DRUG = drug use; MONEY = lack of money or financial problems.

Provisional Coding   Begins with a "start list" of researcher-generated codes based on what preparatory investigation suggests might appear in the data before they are collected and analyzed. Provisional Codes can be revised, modified, deleted, or expanded to include new codes. Appropriate for qualitative studies that build on or corroborate previous research and investigations. Examples: Language arts and drama research suggest the following may be observed in child participants during classroom work: VOCABULARY DEVELOPMENT; ORAL LANGUAGE FLUENCY; STORY COMPREHENSION; DISCUSSION SKILLS.

Simultaneous Coding The application of two or more different codes to a single qualitative datum, or the overlapped occurrence of two or more codes applied to sequential units of qualitative data. Appropriate when the data content suggests multiple meanings (e.g., descriptively and inferentially) that necessitate and justify more than one code. Examples: INEQUITY simultaneously coded to a datum with SCHOOL DISTRICT BUREAUCRACY; the hierarchical code FUNDRAISING with four nested codes: DELEGATING, MOTIVATING, PROMOTING, and TRANSACTING.

Structural Coding Applies a content-based or conceptual phrase to a segment of data that relates to a specific research question to both code and categorize the data corpus. Similarly coded segments are then collected together for more detailed coding and analysis. Appropriate for virtually all qualitative studies, but particularly for those employing multiple participants, standardized or semi-structured data-gathering protocols, hypothesis testing, or exploratory investigations to gather topics lists or indexes of major categories or themes. Example: Research Question – What types of smoking cessation techniques (if any) have participants attempted in the past? Structural Code: UNSUCCESSFUL SMOKING CESSATION TECHNIQUES.

Subcoding A second-order tag assigned after a primary code to detail or enrich the entry. Appropriate for virtually all qualitative studies, but particularly for ethnographies and content analyses, studies with multiple participants and sites, and studies with a wide variety of data forms. Also appropriate when general code entries will later require more extensive indexing, categorizing, and subcategorizing into hierarchies or taxonomies, or for nuanced qualitative data analysis. Can be employed after an initial yet general coding scheme has been applied and the researcher realizes that the classification scheme may have been too broad, or added to primary codes if particular qualities or interrelationships emerge. Examples: HOUSES-YARDS; HOUSES-DÉCOR; HOUSES-SECURITY.

Theme, Themeing the Data Unlike a code, a theme is an extended phrase or sentence that identifies what a unit of data is about and/or what it means. A theme may be identified at the manifest level (directly observable in the information) or at the latent level (underlying the phenomenon). Themes can consist of such ideas as descriptions of behavior within a culture; explanations for why something happens; iconic statements; and morals from participant stories. The analytic goals are to develop an overarching theme from the data corpus, or an integrative theme that weaves various themes together into a coherent narrative. Appropriate for virtually all qualitative studies, especially for phenomenology and those exploring a participant's psychological world of beliefs, constructs, identity development, and emotional experiences. Also a strategic approach for metasummary and metasynthesis studies. Examples: For a study exploring what it means "to belong":

BELONGING IS KNOWING THE DETAILS OF THE CULTURE; BELONGING MEANS FEELING "GROUNDED"; YOU CAN BELONG SOMEWHERE WITHOUT ACTUALLY BEING THERE.

Theoretical Coding Functions like an umbrella that covers and accounts for all other codes and categories formulated thus far in grounded theory analysis. Progresses toward discovering the central/core category that identifies the primary theme or major conflict, obstacle, problem, issue, or concern to participants. The code is not the theory itself, but an abstraction that models the integration of all codes and categories. Appropriate as the culminating step toward achieving a grounded theory. Examples: BALANCING; DISCRIMINATING; PERSONAL PRESERVATION WHILE DYING.

Values Coding The application of codes to qualitative data that reflect a participant's values, attitudes, and beliefs, representing his or her perspectives or worldview. A value (V:) is the importance we attribute to oneself, another person, thing, or idea. An attitude (A:) is the way we think and feel about oneself, another person, thing, or idea. A belief (B:) is part of a system that includes values and attitudes, plus personal knowledge, experiences, opinions, prejudices, morals, and other interpretive perceptions of the social world. Appropriate for virtually all qualitative studies, but particularly for those that explore cultural values, identity, intrapersonal and interpersonal participant experiences and actions in case studies, appreciative inquiry, oral history, and critical ethnography. Examples: V: SUCCESS; A: FUTURE IS SCARY; B: PERSEVERANCE NETS SUCCESS.

Verbal Exchange Coding A signature ethnographic approach to analyzing conversation through reflection on social practices and interpretive meanings. Requires verbatim transcript analysis and interpretation of the types of conversation of key moments in the exchanges. Appropriate for a variety of human communication studies, studies that explore cultural practices, and the analysis of pre-existing ethnographic texts such as autoethnographies. Examples (of verbal exchanges): *Skilled Conversation, Routines and Rituals, Surprise-and-Sense-Making Episodes*.

Versus Coding Identifies in dichotomous or binary terms the individuals, groups, social systems, organizations, phenomena, processes, concepts, etc., in direct conflict with each other, a duality that manifests itself as an X VS. Y code. Appropriate for policy studies, discourse analysis, critical ethnography, action and practitioner research, and qualitative data sets that suggest strong conflicts, injustice, power imbalances, or competing goals within, among, and between participants. Examples: "IMPOSSIBLE" VS. REALISTIC; CUSTOM VS. COMPARISON; STANDARDIZATION VS. "VARIANCES".

APPENDIX B
A Glossary of Analytic Recommendations

Below are one-sentence descriptors of the coding methods profiles' recommendations for further analytic work with coded qualitative data. See the References for additional information and a discussion of procedures.

action and practitioner research   (Altrichter et al., 1993; Coghlan & Brannick, 2010; Fox et al., 2007; Stringer, 1999) – a proactive research project geared toward constructive and positive change in a social setting by investigating one's own practice or participants' conflicts and needs (see In Vivo, Process, Emotion, Values, Versus, Evaluation, Verbal Exchange, Holistic, Causation, Pattern, Elaborative Coding).

assertion development   (Erickson, 1986) – the interpretive construction of credible and trustworthy observational summary statements based on confirming and disconfirming evidence in the qualitative data corpus (see Magnitude, Values, Versus, Evaluation, Hypothesis, Causation, Pattern, Theoretical, Elaborative, Longitudinal Coding; Themeing the Data).

case studies   (Merriam, 1998; Stake, 1995) – focused in-depth study and analysis of a unit of one – one person, one group, one organization, one event, etc. (see Attribute, In Vivo, Process, Values, Evaluation, Dramaturgical, Motif, Narrative, Causation, Longitudinal Coding; Themeing the Data).

cognitive mapping   (Miles & Huberman, 1994; Northcutt & McCoy, 2004) – the detailed visual representation and presentation, most often in flow chart format, of a cognitive process (negotiating, decision making, etc.) (see Process, Emotion, Domain and Taxonomic, Causation Coding).

componential and cultural theme analysis   (McCurdy et al., 2005; Spradley, 1979, 1980) – the search for attributes of and relationships among domains (categories) for the discovery of cultural meaning (see Domain and Taxonomic Coding).

content analysis   (Krippendorff, 2003; Schreier, 2012; Weber, 1990; Wilkinson & Birmingham, 2003) – the systematic qualitative and quantitative analysis of the contents of a data corpus (documents, texts, videos, etc.) (see Attribute, Magnitude, Subcoding, Simultaneous, Structural, Descriptive, Values, Provisional, Hypothesis, OCM, Domain and Taxonomic, Pattern Coding).

cross-cultural content analysis (Bernard, 2011) – a content analysis that compares data from two or more cultures (see Attribute, Subcoding, Descriptive, Values, OCM, Domain and Taxonomic Coding).

data matrices for univariate, bivariate, and multivariate analysis (Bernard, 2011) – the tabular layout of variable data for inferential analysis (e.g., histograms, ANOVA, factor analysis) (see Magnitude, Hypothesis, OCM Coding).

decision modeling (Bernard, 2011) – the graphic flow chart layout or series of if–then statements of choices participants will make under particular conditions (see Process, Evaluation, Causation, Pattern Coding).

descriptive statistical analysis (Bernard, 2011) – the computation of basic descriptive statistics such as the median, mean, correlation coefficient, etc., for a set of data (see Magnitude, Subcoding, OCM Coding).

discourse analysis (Gee, 2011; Rapley, 2007; Willig, 2008) – the strategic examination of speech or texts for embedded and inferred sociopolitical meanings (see In Vivo, Process, Values, Versus, Evaluation, Dramaturgical, Narrative, Verbal Exchange, Causation Coding; Themeing the Data).

domain and taxonomic analysis (Schensul et al., 1999b; Spradley, 1979, 1980) – the researcher's organizational and hierarchical arrangement of participant-generated data into cultural categories of meaning (see Subcoding, Descriptive, In Vivo, OCM, Domain and Taxonomic Coding).

framework policy analysis (Ritchie & Spencer, 1994) – a signature, multistage analytic process (e.g., indexing, charting, mapping) with qualitative data to identify key issues, concepts, and themes from social policy research (see Values, Versus, Evaluation Coding).

frequency counts (LeCompte & Schensul, 1999) – basic descriptive statistical summary information such as totals, frequencies, ratios, percentages, etc., about a set of data (see Attribute, Magnitude, Subcoding, Structural, Descriptive, In Vivo, Emotion, Values, Evaluation, Hypothesis, OCM Coding).

graph-theoretic techniques for semantic network analysis (Namey et al., 2008) – statistics-based analyses (e.g., hierarchical clustering, multi-dimensional scaling) of texts to identify associations and semantic relationships within the data (see Attribute, Magnitude, Simultaneous, Structural, Descriptive, Evaluation, Domain and Taxonomic Coding).

grounded theory (Bryant & Charmaz, 2007; Charmaz, 2006; Corbin & Strauss, 2008; Glaser & Strauss, 1967; Stern & Porr, 2011; Strauss & Corbin, 1998) – a systematic methodological approach to qualitative inquiry that generates theory "grounded" in the data themselves (see Descriptive, In Vivo, Process, Initial, Versus, Evaluation, Causation, Pattern, Focused, Axial, Theoretical, Elaborative, Longitudinal Coding; also see Chapter Two).

illustrative charts, matrices, diagrams   (Miles & Huberman, 1994; Morgan et al., 2008; Northcutt & McCoy, 2004; Paulston, 2000; Wheeldon & Åhlberg, 2012) – the visual representation and presentation of qualitative data and their analysis through illustrative summary (see Attribute, Magnitude, Simultaneous, Structural, Process, Evaluation, Domain and Taxonomic, Causation, Theoretical, Longitudinal Coding; also see Chapter Four).

interactive qualitative analysis   (Northcutt & McCoy, 2004) – a signature method for facilitated and participatory qualitative data analysis and the computation of the data's frequencies and interrelationships (see In Vivo, Values, Versus, Evaluation, Pattern, Focused Coding).

interrelationship   (Saldaña, 2003) – qualitative "correlation" that examines possible influences and affects within, between, and among categorized data (see Subcoding, Simultaneous, Structural, Emotion, Causation, Axial, Longitudinal Coding).

life course mapping   (Clausen, 1998) – a chronological diagrammatic display of a person's life course with emphasis on the range of high and low points within various time periods (also see Longitudinal Coding in Chapter Five) (see Emotion, Values, Motif, Narrative, Longitudinal Coding).

logic models   (Knowlton & Phillips, 2009; Yin, 2009) – the flow diagramming of a complex, interconnected chain of events across an extended period of time (see Process, Evaluation, Hypothesis, Causation, Pattern, Longitudinal Coding).

longitudinal qualitative research   (Giele & Elder, 1998; McLeod & Thomson, 2009; Saldaña, 2003, 2008) – the collection and analysis of qualitative data from long-term fieldwork (also see Longitudinal Coding in Chapter Five) (see Attribute, Magnitude, Values, Evaluation, Hypothesis, Axial, Theoretical, Elaborative, Longitudinal Coding).

memo writing about the codes/themes   (Charmaz, 2006; Corbin & Strauss, 2008; Glaser, 1978; Glaser & Strauss, 1967; Strauss, 1987; Strauss & Corbin, 1998) – the researcher's written reflections on the study's codes/themes and complex meanings of patterns in the qualitative data (see In Vivo, Process, Initial, Evaluation, Holistic, OCM, Domain and Taxonomic, Causation, Focused, Axial, Theoretical, Elaborative, Longitudinal Coding; Themeing the Data; also see Chapter Two).

meta-ethnography, metasummary, and metasynthesis   (Finfgeld, 2003; Major & Savin-Baden, 2010; Noblit & Hare, 1988; Sandelowski & Barroso, 2007; Sandelowski et al., 1997) – an analytic review of multiple and related qualitative studies to assess their commonalities and differences of observations for summary or synthesis (see Domain and Taxonomic, Axial, Elaborative Coding; Themeing the Data).

metaphoric analysis   (Coffey & Atkinson, 1996; Todd & Harrison, 2008) – examination of how participant language is used figuratively (e.g., metaphor, analogy, simile) (see In Vivo, Emotion, Motif, Narrative, Verbal Exchange Coding; Themeing the Data).

mixed methods research (Creswell, 2009; Creswell & Plano Clark, 2011; Tashakkori & Teddlie, 2003) – a methodological research approach that compatibly combines quantitative and qualitative methods for data collection and analysis (see Attribute, Magnitude, Descriptive, Evaluation, Provisional, Hypothesis, OCM, Pattern Coding).

narrative inquiry and analysis (Clandinin & Connelly, 2000; Coffey & Atkinson, 1996; Cortazzi, 1993; Coulter & Smith, 2009; Daiute & Lightfoot, 2004; Holstein & Gubrium, 2012; Murray, 2003; Riessman, 2008) – qualitative investigation, representation, and presentation of the participants' lives through the use of story (see In Vivo, Emotion, Values, Versus, Dramaturgical, Motif, Narrative, Verbal Exchange, Longitudinal Coding; Themeing the Data).

performance studies (Madison, 2012; Madison & Hamera, 2006) – a discipline that acknowledges "performance" in its broadest sense as an inherent quality of social interaction and social products (see Dramaturgical, Narrative, Verbal Exchange Coding).

phenomenology (Butler-Kisber, 2010; Giorgi & Giorgi, 2003; Smith et al., 2009; van Manen, 1990; Wertz et al., 2011) – the study of the nature or meaning of everyday or significant experiences (see In Vivo, Emotion, Values, Dramaturgical, Motif, Narrative, Verbal Exchange, Causation Coding; Themeing the Data).

poetic and dramatic writing (Denzin, 1997, 2003; Glesne, 2011; Knowles & Cole, 2008; Leavy, 2009; Saldaña, 2005a, 2011a) – arts-based approaches to qualitative inquiry and presentation using poetry and drama as expressive literary genres (see In Vivo, Emotion, Dramaturgical, Motif, Narrative, Verbal Exchange Coding; Themeing the Data).

political analysis (Hatch, 2002) – a qualitative approach that acknowledges and analyzes the "political" conflicts and power issues inherent in social systems and organizations such as schools, bureaucracies, etc. (see Values, Versus, Evaluation Coding).

polyvocal analysis (Hatch, 2002) – a qualitative approach that acknowledges and analyzes the multiple and sometimes contradictory perspectives of participants, giving voice to all (see In Vivo, Versus, Evaluation, Narrative Coding).

portraiture (Lawrence-Lightfoot & Davis, 1997) – a signature approach to qualitative inquiry that renders holistic, complex, and dimensional narratives of participants' perspectives and experiences (see In Vivo, Emotion, Values, Dramaturgical, Motif, Narrative, Longitudinal Coding; Themeing the Data).

qualitative evaluation research (Patton, 2002, 2008) – an approach that collects and analyzes participant and programmatic data to assess merit, worth, effectiveness, quality, value, etc. (see Attribute, Magnitude, Subcoding, Descriptive, In Vivo, Values, Versus, Evaluation, Holistic, Provisional, Hypothesis, Causation, Pattern Coding).

quick ethnography (Handwerker, 2001) – an approach to fieldwork in which the research parameters (questions, observations, goals, etc.) are tightly focused and efficient when time is limited (see Magnitude, Structural, Descriptive, Holistic, Provisional, Hypothesis, OCM, Domain and Taxonomic Coding).

situational analysis (Clarke, 2005) – a signature approach to qualitative data analysis (with foundations in grounded theory) that acknowledges and visually maps the contexts and complexities of social life (see Simultaneous, Initial, Emotion, Versus, Evaluation, Domain and Taxonomic, Causation, Pattern, Focused, Axial, Theoretical, Elaborative, Longitudinal Coding).

splitting, splicing, and linking data (Dey, 1993) – a systematic approach to the categorization and interrelationship construction of units of qualitative data, most often assisted through CAQDAS (see Magnitude, Subcoding, Simultaneous, Structural, Process, Evaluation, Domain and Taxonomic, Pattern, Causation, Focused, Axial Coding).

survey research (Fowler, 2001; Wilkinson & Birmingham, 2003) – standardized approaches and instrument formats, most often in written form, for gathering quantitative and qualitative data from multiple participants (see Attribute, Magnitude, Structural, Values, Provisional Coding).

thematic analysis (Auerbach & Silverstein, 2003; Boyatzis, 1998; Smith & Osborn, 2008) – summary and analysis of qualitative data through the use of extended phrases and/or sentences rather than shorter codes (see Structural, Descriptive, In Vivo, Process, Initial, Values, Evaluation, Motif, Narrative, Verbal Exchange, Holistic, Provisional, Domain and Taxonomic, Pattern, Focused, Axial, Theoretical, Elaborative, Longitudinal Coding; Themeing the Data).

vignette writing (Erickson, 1986; Graue & Walsh, 1998) – the written presentation and representation of a small scene of social action that illustrates and supports a summary assertion (see Process, Dramaturgical, Motif, Narrative, Verbal Exchange Coding; Themeing the Data).

within-case and cross-case displays (Gibbs, 2007; Miles & Huberman, 1994; Shkedi, 2005) – visual summaries of qualitative data and analysis into tables, charts, matrices, diagrams, etc., that illustrate the contrasts and ranges of observations (see Attribute, Magnitude, Subcoding, Structural, Descriptive, Versus, Evaluation, Domain and Taxonomic, Causation, Elaborative, Longitudinal Coding).

APPENDIX C

Field Note, Interview Transcript, and Document Samples for Coding

The following samples of qualitative data are provided as content for individual or classroom coding exercises. An interesting approach for classes is to have one-third of the group code the data using one method, another third code with a different method, and the final third of the group code with a third method. Compare findings and discuss how each method may have generated different outcomes. Also, the recommendations for coding are from the repertoire of First Cycle methods. Explore how the analysis progresses by applying a Second Cycle coding method afterward, such as Pattern Coding or Focused Coding.

Field Note Sample – Observations at a University Weight Room

In this field note excerpt, participant observation takes place at a university sports and recreation complex's weight room on a February afternoon. The male participants are assigned descriptors in place of names (e.g., WORK BOOTS, GOATEE). Observer's Comments (OC), in addition to the descriptive detail, are deliberately included as part of the sample. Code the following excerpt in the right-hand margin using Process Coding, Initial Coding, or Values Coding, then write an analytic memo based on the codes. If Process Coding is chosen, diagram the social action at work here. (For an example of how these field notes were taken through Erickson's (1986) assertion development heuristics, see Saldaña, 2011b, pp. 119–27.)

> The prominent odor in the room can be described as "musky, sweaty clothes." The ceiling height is approximately twelve feet and has air conditioning vents to maintain a comfortable temperature, and speakers where rock music from a radio station is playing at a moderate volume.
>
> The east side handweight floor is covered with black, rectangular, rubber mats. The designated area for this observation has three weight benches: metal frames with adjustable, dark red, patent leather, padded platforms that

can accommodate a person sitting on and/or leaning against them. Benches are spaced to allow people to work by them while others work on them. Weight and accessory racks, holding various sizes and pounds of round metal disks, are located against the east wall and central pillar.

The north wall has large windows providing sunlight to complement the florescent lighting. The south wall also has windows with a view of the Center's hall and towel booth. Laminated or plated signs on the east wall state "Weight Room Policies" such as "Collars are Required" and "Repack your Weights."

Prominent on the east side are seven foot high mirrors extending across the length of the wall.

OC: It's like a voluntary, contemporary torture chamber; only the serious need apply. With all the metal and glass there's a feeling of coldness, hardness, massiveness in the environment.

A white twenty-ish man in baggy jeans, a loose white t-shirt, and tan WORK BOOTS is seated on a weight bench. He rises, grips two handweights, one in each hand, and lifts them simultaneously in arm curls. His face clenches in an expression that looks like pain as he raises the weights to neck level. Throughout this exercise he is standing about three feet from and facing the wall length mirror. His medium-length hair is honey blonde.

OC: His dress is not typical of what most men wear in this weight room. Most wear shorts and athletic shoes. Through his loose fitting clothes and by the size of his forearms I sensed that he was fairly muscular.

WORK BOOTS is still seated at the bench but the weights are on the floor. He leans back, his hands interlocked behind his head, his legs spread apart. He looks at himself in the mirror. He then looks to the side, breathes in, stretches his arms, stands, and talks to a THIN MAN next to him. WORK BOOTS picks up the same weights as before and continues his arm curls for approximately twenty "reps" (repetitions). Throughout this he looks at himself in the mirror, smiles, then grimaces his face, looks down, then looks at himself in the mirror.

OC: The man thinks he's hot. That classic leaning-back-with-your-arms-behind-your-head-legs-spread-apart pose is just too suggestive of stereotypical male sexuality ("I'm a fuckin' man"). He was checking out his muscles – the breathing in to expand his chest was a personal pleasure sensation to feel himself. The continuous looks and smiles he gives himself in the mirror make him look like an arrogant S.O.B. His self-esteem seems very high and he seems pleased with his own physical appearance.

A fairly large but somewhat muscular man with a GOATEE, green ball cap, grey t-shirt, and blue shorts sits on a weight bench close to WORK BOOTS and arm curls one weight over and behind his head. His feet are not flat on the floor, but on "tiptoe." GOATEE does approximately seven reps with one arm, then switches to another. He, too, faces the mirror but is now approximately ten feet away from it.

OC: The "tiptoe" seemed so out of place – a stereotypical feminine action in juxtaposition with his large body frame. Weight lifting ballet – "masculine dance." Dancers rehearse with mirrors, too.

WORK BOOTS, standing, makes eye contact with himself in the mirror for approximately fifteen seconds. His mouth twitches. He picks up the handweights and continues his reps, continually looking at himself in the mirror as he does so.

Interview Transcript Sample – a School Principal Talks About Her School's Neighborhood

In the following interview transcript, a White female principal of an inner city grades K–8 school with a predominantly Hispanic population, describes to the interviewer the cultural conditions surrounding the site and the social services provided by the school to its students and families. Code the following excerpt in the right-hand margin using Descriptive Coding, In Vivo Coding, or Versus Coding, then write an analytic memo based on the codes:

We're helping people with rent, helping them get jobs, giving them emergency food, getting their power turned back on when it's been shut down, um, families that are in jail, um, bringing in a police resource officer, dealing with all of those agencies. We have someone in our social services office from Helping House, we have community police in that center, we have a migrant resource person in there. Yeah, that's not so much Hispanic culture as the culture of poverty, and, you know, all of the children here are on free lunch and free breakfast. And it *is* different.

This year is the first time that I have really seen a junior high teacher make the assignment that all kids have to do research at the library and see the kids take their parents to the main branch of the public library on First Street and Main. It's, the difference is I think that the gangs are not as active as they have been. They're active in a different way, perhaps, but for awhile there the kids couldn't step across Main Street without taking the chance of being shot.

And there's all the, the territoriality of the Hispanic gangs, plus the, the, uh, economic motives of the gangs that moved in from Chicago and L.A. If you look at this little area around the school, if you walk across Juarez Street that's *campito*, and that's the campground where the migrant workers used to live when they worked the crops that were on this field where the school is. And then *(laughs)*, OK? And, the migrant workers coming up from Mexico used to, uh, put stakes in the corners of the fields that they were working and mark them as their territory. So we have several generations of families here who are parts of gangs that were territorial gangs in the sense of, this is where we work, which have now been corrupted by the drugs and the money coming in for the Crips and the Bloods.

Um, and the grandparents think it's perfectly all right if a child joins a gang and has his first communion in the same week, because that gang was like being part of a labor union for them. So, that's a mix of the economic thing, the culture of poverty, and the culture of the Mexican field worker.

Document Sample – How to Construct
a Successful "Thank You" Letter

The following document excerpt is a standard form letter included with a personalized letter to a university student notifying her of a scholarship. The document was created by a development office in charge of securing funds from private and corporate donors and administrating scholarships. All rich text features (bolding, italicizing) are kept intact from the original one-page document (written in 12 pt. Times New Roman font). Code the following text in the right-hand margin using Initial Coding, Values Coding, or through Themeing the Data, then write an analytic memo based on the codes. Or, write your open-ended impressions about the document first, then code your written notes:

How to Construct a Successful *Thank You* Letter

Here is a suggested guide to help you create your *Thank You* letter:
NOTE: Be sure to use a warm yet professional tone in your letter.
Proofread and spell-check your letter. Keep a copy for your files.

Date

Your Name
Street Address
City, State, Zip Code

Name of Scholarship Donor
Person's Job Title, if applicable
Name of Organization, if applicable
Street Address
City, State, Zip Code

Dear Mr./Mrs./Dr./Professor/Whatever:

Thank your scholarship donor personally for the scholarship by its title. Explain **how** it will help you; give a **relevant example** of the scholarship's benefit to your academic career.

Let the scholarship donor know **what** you have done and **why** you are in school. Briefly highlight any **skills/accomplishments** you have achieved at this point in your education. **Be specific**: List examples by title.

Indicate your **educational or professional goal** and explain **how this scholarship helps** you in attaining this goal.

Thank the scholarship donor once more.

Sincerely,

Your Signature
Your Typed Name

APPENDIX D

Exercises and Activities for Coding and Qualitative Data Analytic Skill Development

These activities can be conducted by oneself or with classmates in a qualitative research methods course. These exercises are intended to attune the researcher to basic principles of coding, pattern development, categorization, and qualitative data analysis.

Know Thyself

Who are you? Empty your purse, wallet, backpack, or briefcase and place all items on a table. Arrange, organize, and cluster those items that share similar characteristics (e.g., all writing instruments in one pile, all credit cards in one pile, all makeup in one pile). Give each pile its own label or category name. Write an analytic memo on yourself that explores the assertion, "our identities are supported and altered by various forms of identification" (Prior, 2004, p. 88). Also address the higher-order analytic question: What do all the piles (categories) have in common? What is the Pattern Code?

The Pattern of Patterns

Patterns are ubiquitous in social and natural environments. Humans have a need and propensity to create patterns for order, function, or ornamentation, and those needs and thus skills transfer into our analysis of qualitative data. In a classroom or other average-size indoor environment (such as an office, small restaurant, or bedroom), look for and list all patterns observed. These can range from patterns in the architecture or décor (e.g., rows of fluorescent lighting tubes, slats in air-conditioning vents) to patterns in furnishings and their arrangements (e.g., desks lined up in rows, vertically arranged cabinet drawers). Next, organize the individual items in your master list into categories – a "pattern of patterns." For example:

- *decorative patterns*: those patterns that are purely ornamental or aesthetic, such as stripes on upholstery fabric, painted marbling on a wall
- *functional patterns*: those patterns that have a utilitarian purpose, such as four legs on a chair, three hinges connecting a door to its frame
- *organizational patterns*: those patterns that bring order to the environment or its artifacts, such as books of similar topics shelved together, various office supplies in appropriate bins
- *other types of patterns you construct*

Conduct the same exercise above in an outdoor/natural environment. However, create a different classification system for the individual patterns you observe (e.g., petals on a flower, leaves on a tree, clusters of cacti).

T-shirt Codes

Visit a clothing store, or have all members of a class wear a favorite t-shirt to a session. Address the following:

- What is the t-shirt made of? Look at the label (if any) sewn into the garment. That label, with information on the fabric composition and country of manufacture, is like an *Attribute Code* for the clothing item's contents. The label – the code – summarizes the entire t-shirt's basic contents.
- What size is the t-shirt? Again, look at the label (or better still, try it on). The symbols S, M, L, XL, XXL, XXXL are *Magnitude Codes*. The experience of trying it on yourself gives you a better understanding of what that size code actually means. These days, what passes for "medium" in one brand of clothing may be labeled "large" by another manufacturer's line. If there is no label that specifies the t-shirt's size, use observation and comparison with other t-shirts to assess its probable size.
- What words and/or images (if any) are on the front or back of the t-shirt? Those words and images are both textual and non-verbal *In Vivo Codes* for the garment. Cluster together with others wearing similarly coded shirts (a form of *Focused Coding*) and discuss not only what the messages have in common but also what the people wearing them have in common. What you identify for each cluster or category of people might be called a *Pattern Code*, based on the collective values, attitudes, and beliefs of the wearers – a form of *Values Code*.

Board Games

Several commercial board/DVD and electronic games actually provide valuable experience with exercising necessary analytic skills for the qualitative researcher, such as pattern recognition, coding and categorizing, and inductive and deductive reasoning:

- Three for All!
- The $100,000 Pyramid
- Scattergories
- Simon

Also see Waite (2011) for a clever classroom exercise in sorting a deck of playing cards to stimulate student discussion about categories and discrepant cases.

Popular Film Viewing

Selected popular films include scenes that illustrate the characters in analytic life-dilemmas (Saldaña, 2009). These conflicts are artistic metaphors, comparable to what the qualitative researcher encounters when coding and analyzing data. View and reflect on relevant scenes from the titles below to assess how certain principles of qualitative inquiry are depicted and can transfer to your own work.

Research genres

- Case studies: *The Final Cut, The Truman Show, 49 Up* (and the entire *Up* series)
- Survey research: *Kinsey*
- Quantitative (and qualitative) research: π [*pi*], *A Beautiful Mind*
- Longitudinal research/change: *The Truman Show, 49 Up, Half Nelson*
- Action research: *Dangerous Minds, Kindergarten Cop*
- Life course research: *The Final Cut, 49 Up*
- Phenomenology: *The Silence of the Lambs*
- Field experiments: *Super Size Me*
- Critical ethnography: *Bowling for Columbine*
- Performance ethnography/ethnodrama: *Twilight: Los Angeles, The Laramie Project, The Exonerated, United 93, Howl*

Research methodology and methods

- Epistemology and ontology: *The Matrix, Inception, Source Code*
- Research design: *Super Size Me*
- Research ethics: *The Truman Show, Krippendorf's Tribe, Miss Evers' Boys*
- Participant observation/fieldwork: *The Truman Show, Gorillas in the Mist, Looking for Comedy in the Muslim World, Kitchen Stories, WALL*E, Avatar*

- Interview techniques: *Kinsey, 49 Up, The Laramie Project, The Guys, Looking for Comedy in the Muslim World, The Help*
- Inductive and deductive reasoning: *Memento, Fargo, π [pi], The Silence of the Lambs*
- Codes and categories: *The Final Cut*
- Triangulation: *Minority Report*
- Cause and effect, influences and affects: *The Butterfly Effect*
- Correlation/interrelationship: *An Inconvenient Truth, The Number 23*
- Data analysis: *A Beautiful Mind, Contact, The Final Cut, The Silence of the Lambs*
- Mixed methods: *Super Size Me*

References

Abbott, A. (2004). *Methods of discovery: Heuristics for the social sciences*. New York: W.W. Norton.

Adler, P. A., & Adler, P. (1987). *Membership roles in field research*. Newbury Park, CA: Sage.

Agar, M. (1994). *Language shock: Understanding the culture of conversation*. New York: Quill-William Morrow.

Agar, M. H. (1996). *The professional stranger: An informal introduction to ethnography*. San Diego, CA: Academic Press.

Alderson, P. (2008). Children as researchers: Participation rights and research methods. In P. Christensen & A. James (Eds.), *Research with children: Perspectives and practices* (2nd ed.) (pp. 276–90). New York: Routledge.

Altheide, D. L. (1996). *Qualitative media analysis*. Thousand Oaks, CA: Sage.

Altrichter, H., Posch, P., & Somekh, B. (1993). *Teachers investigate their work: An introduction to the methods of action research*. London: Routledge.

Andrews, M., Squire, C., & Tamboukou, M. (Eds.) (2008). *Doing narrative research*. London: Sage.

Anfara, V. A., Jr. (2008). Visual data displays. In L. M. Given (Ed.), *The Sage encyclopedia of qualitative research methods* (Vol. 2, pp. 930–4). Thousand Oaks, CA: Sage.

Angus, L., Levitt, H., & Hardtke, K. (1999). The narrative processes coding system: Research applications and implications for psychotherapy practice. *Journal of Clinical Psychology, 55*(10), 1255–70.

Au, W. (2007). High-stakes testing and curricular control: A qualitative metasynthesis. *Educational Researcher, 36*(5), 258–67.

Auerbach, C. F., & Silverstein, L. B. (2003). *Qualitative data: An introduction to coding and analysis*. New York: New York University Press.

Back, M. D., Küfner, A. C. P., & Egloff, B. (2010). The emotional timeline of September 11, 2001. Psychological Science. Accessed 30 March 2012 from: http://pss.sagepub.com/content/21/10/1417

Bamberg, M. (2004). Positioning with Davie Hogan: Stories, tellings, and identities. In C. Daiute & C. Lightfoot (Eds.), *Narrative analysis: Studying the development of individuals in society* (pp. 135–57). Thousand Oaks, CA: Sage.

Banks, J. A. (1994). *Multiethnic education: Theory and practice* (3rd ed.). Boston: Allyn and Bacon.

Barone, T. (2000). *Aesthetics, politics, and educational inquiry: Essays and examples*. New York: Peter Lang.

Basit, T. N. (2003). Manual or electronic? The role of coding in qualitative data analysis. *Educational Research, 45*(2), 143–54.

Bazeley, P. (2003). Computerized data analysis for mixed methods research. In A. Tashakkori & C. Teddlie (Eds.), *Handbook of mixed methods in social & behavioral research* (pp. 385–422). Thousand Oaks, CA: Sage.

Bazeley, P. (2007). *Qualitative data analysis with NVivo*. London: Sage.

Behar, R., & Gordon, D. A. (Eds.). (1995). *Women writing culture*. Berkeley, CA: University of California Press.

Belli, R. F., Stafford, F. P., & Alwin, D. F. (Eds.). (2009). *Calendar and time diary methods in life course research*. Thousand Oaks, CA: Sage.

Berg, B. L. (2001). *Qualitative research methods for the social sciences* (4th ed.). Boston: Allyn and Bacon.

Berger, A. A. (2009). *What objects mean: An introduction to material culture*. Walnut Creek, CA: Left Coast Press.

Berger, A. A. (2012). *Media analysis techniques* (4th ed.). Thousand Oaks, CA: Sage.

Bernard, H. R. (2011). *Research methods in anthropology: Qualitative and quantitative approaches* (5th ed.). Walnut Creek, CA: AltaMira Press.

Bernard, H. R., & Ryan, G. W. (2010). *Analyzing qualitative data: Systematic approaches*. Thousand Oaks, CA: Sage.

Bettelheim, B. (1976). *The uses of enchantment: The meaning and importance of fairy tales*. New York: Alfred A. Knopf.

Birks, M., Chapman, Y., & Francis, K. (2008). Memoing in qualitative research: Probing data and processes. *Journal of Research in Nursing, 13*(1), 68–75.

Birks, M., & Mills, J. (2011). *Grounded theory: A practical guide*. London: Sage.

Boal, A. (1995). *The rainbow of desire: The Boal method of theatre and therapy*. London: Routledge.

Boeije, H. (2010). *Analysis in qualitative research*. London: Sage.

Bogdan, R. C., & Biklen, S. K. (2007). *Qualitative research for education: An introduction to theories and methods* (5th ed.). Boston, MA: Pearson Education.

Booth, W. C., Colomb, G. G., & Williams, J. M. (2003). *The craft of research* (2nd ed.). Chicago: University of Chicago Press.

Boyatzis, R. E. (1998). *Transforming qualitative information: Thematic analysis and code development*. Thousand Oaks, CA: Sage.

Brent, E., & Slusarz, P. (2003). "Feeling the beat": Intelligent coding advice from meta-knowledge in qualitative research. *Social Science Computer Review, 21*(3), 281–303.

Brown, K. M. (1999). Creating community in middle schools: Interdisciplinary teaming and advisory programs. Unpublished doctoral dissertation, Temple University, Philadelphia.

Bryant, A., & Charmaz, K. (Eds.). (2007). *The Sage handbook of grounded theory*. London: Sage.

Bude, H. (2004). Qualitative generation research (B. Jenner, Trans.). In U. Flick, E. von Kardoff, & I. Steinke (Eds.), *A companion to qualitative research* (pp. 108–12). London: Sage. (Original work published 2000.)

Burant, T. J., Gray, C., Ndaw, E., McKinney-Keys, V., & Allen, G. (2007). The rhythms of a teacher research group. *Multicultural Perspectives, 9*(1), 10–18.

Butler-Kisber, L. (2010). *Qualitative inquiry: Thematic, narrative, and arts-informed perspectives*. London: Sage.

Cahnmann-Taylor, M., & Siegesmund, R. (2008). *Arts-based research in education: Foundations for practice*. New York: Routledge.

Chang, H. (2008). *Autoethnography as method*. Walnut Creek, CA: Left Coast Press.

Charmaz, K. (2001). Grounded theory. In R. M. Emerson (Ed.), *Contemporary field research: Perspectives and formulations* (2nd ed.) (pp. 335–52). Prospect Heights, IL: Waveland Press.

Charmaz, K. (2002). Qualitative interviewing and grounded theory analysis. In J. F. Gubrium & J. A. Holstein (Eds.), *Handbook of interview research: Context & method* (pp. 675–94). Thousand Oaks, CA: Sage.

Charmaz, K. (2006). *Constructing grounded theory: A practical guide through qualitative analysis*. Thousand Oaks, CA: Sage.

Charmaz, K. (2008). Grounded theory. In J. A. Smith (Ed.), *Qualitative psychology: A practical guide to research methods* (2nd ed.) (pp. 81–110). London: Sage.

Charmaz, K. (2009). Example: The body, identity, and self: Adapting to impairment. In J. M. Morse et al., *Developing grounded theory: The second generation* (pp. 155–91). Walnut Creek, CA: Left Coast Press.

Charmaz, K. (2010). Grounded theory: Objectivist and constructivist methods. In W. Luttrell (Ed.), *Qualitative educational research: Readings in reflexive methodology and transformative practice* (pp. 183–207). New York: Routledge.

Clandinin, D. J., & Connelly, F. M. (2000). *Narrative inquiry: Experience and story in qualitative research*. San Francisco: Jossey-Bass.

Clark, C. D. (2011). *In a younger voice: Doing child-centered qualitative research*. New York: Oxford.

Clarke, A. E. (2005). *Situational analysis: Grounded theory after the postmodern turn*. Thousand Oaks, CA: Sage.

Clausen, J. A. (1998). Life reviews and life stories. In J. Z. Giele & G. H. Elder, Jr. (Eds.), *Methods of life course research: Qualitative and quantitative approaches* (pp. 189–212). Thousand Oaks, CA: Sage.

Coffey, A., & Atkinson, P. (1996). *Making sense of qualitative data: Complementary research strategies*. Thousand Oaks, CA: Sage.

Coghlan, D., & Brannick, T. (2010). *Doing action research in your own organization* (3rd ed.). London: Sage.

Constas, M. A. (1992). Qualitative analysis as a public event: The documentation of category development procedures. *American Educational Research Journal, 29*(2), 253–66.

Corbin, J., & Strauss, A. (2008). *Basics of qualitative research: Techniques and procedures for developing grounded theory* (3rd ed.). Thousand Oaks, CA: Sage.

Cortazzi, M. (1993). *Narrative analysis*. London: Falmer Press.

Coulter, C. A., & Smith, M. L. (2009). The construction zone: Literary elements in narrative research. *Educational Researcher, 38*(8), 577–90.

Creswell, J. W. (2009). *Research design: Qualitative, quantitative, and mixed methods approaches* (3rd ed.). Thousand Oaks, CA: Sage.

Creswell, J. W. (2012). *Qualitative inquiry and research design: Choosing among five approaches* (3rd ed.). Thousand Oaks, CA: Sage.

Creswell, J. W., & Plano Clark, V. L. (2011). *Designing and conducting mixed methods research* (2nd ed.). Thousand Oaks, CA: Sage.

Crossley, M. (2007). Narrative analysis. In E. Lyons & A. Coyle (Eds.), *Analysing qualitative data in psychology* (pp. 131–44). London: Sage.

Daiute, C., & Lightfoot, C. (Eds.). (2004). *Narrative analysis: Studying the development of individuals in society*. Thousand Oaks, CA: Sage.

Davidson, J., & di Gregorio, S. (2011). Qualitative research, technology, and global change. In N. K. Denzin & M. D. Giardina (Eds.), *Qualitative inquiry and global crises* (pp. 79–96). Walnut Creek, CA: Left Coast Press.

DeCuir-Gunby, J. T., Marshall, P. L., & McCulloch, A. W. (2011). Developing and using a codebook for the analysis of interview data: An example from a professional development research project. *Field Methods, 23*(2), 136–55.

Denzin, N. (1997). *Interpretive ethnography: Ethnographic practices for the 21st century*. Thousand Oaks, CA: Sage.

Denzin, N. (2003). *Performance ethnography: Critical pedagogy and the politics of culture*. Thousand Oaks, CA: Sage.

Denzin, N. K., & Lincoln, Y. S. (Eds.). (2011). *The Sage handbook of qualitative research* (4th ed.). Thousand Oaks, CA: Sage.

DeSantis, L., & Ugarriza, D. N. (2000). The concept of theme as used in qualitative nursing research. *Western Journal of Nursing Research, 22*(3), 351–72.

DeWalt, K. M., & DeWalt, B. R. (2011). *Participant observation: A guide for fieldworkers* (2nd ed.). Lanham, MD: AltaMira Press.

Dey, I. (1993). *Qualitative data analysis: A user-friendly guide for social scientists*. London: Routledge.

Dey, I. (1999). *Grounding grounded theory: Guidelines for qualitative inquiry*. San Diego, CA: Academic Press.

Dey, I. (2007). Grounding categories. In A. Bryant & K. Charmaz (Eds.), *The Sage handbook of grounded theory* (pp. 167–90). London: Sage.

Dobbert, M. L., & Kurth-Schai, R. (1992). Systematic ethnography: Toward an evolutionary science of education and culture. In M. D. LeCompte, W. L. Millroy, & J. Preissle (Eds.), *The handbook of qualitative research in education* (pp. 93–159). San Diego, CA: Academic Press.

Drew, P. (2008). Conversation analysis. In J. A. Smith (Ed.), *Qualitative psychology: A practical guide to research methods* (2nd ed.) (pp. 133–59). London: Sage.

Durbin, D. J. (2010). Using multivoiced poetry for analysis and expression of literary transaction. Paper presented at the American Educational Research Association Annual Conference, Denver, CO.

Eatough, V., & Smith, J. A. (2006). I feel like a scrambled egg in my head: An idiographic case study of meaning making and anger using interpretative phenomenological analysis. *Psychology and Psychotherapy: Theory, Research and Practice, 79*, 115–35.

Edhlund, B. M. (2011). *NVivo 9 Essentials*. Stallarholmen, Sweden: Form & Kunskap.

Emerson, R. M., Fretz, R. I., & Shaw, L. L. (2011). *Writing ethnographic fieldnotes* (2nd ed.). Chicago: University of Chicago Press.

Erickson, F. (1986). Qualitative methods in research on teaching. In M. C. Wittrock (Ed.), *Handbook of research on teaching* (3rd ed.) (pp. 119–61). New York: Macmillan.

Erickson, K., & Stull, D. (1998). *Doing team ethnography: Warnings and advice*. Thousand Oaks, CA: Sage.

Ezzy, D. (2002). *Qualitative analysis: Practice and innovation*. London: Routledge.

Faherty, V. E. (2010). *Wordcraft: Applied qualitative data analysis (QDA): Tools for public and voluntary social services*. Thousand Oaks, CA: Sage.

Feldman, M. S. (1995). *Strategies for interpreting qualitative data*. Thousand Oaks, CA: Sage.

Fetterman, D. M. (2008). Ethnography. In L. M. Given (Ed.), *The Sage encyclopedia of qualitative research methods* (Vol. 1, pp. 288–92). Thousand Oaks, CA: Sage.

Fetterman, D. M. (2010). *Ethnography: Step-by-step* (3rd ed.). Thousand Oaks, CA: Sage.

Fielding, N. (2008). The role of computer-assisted qualitative data analysis: Impact on emergent methods in qualitative research. In S. N. Hesse-Biber & P. Leavy (Eds.), *Handbook of emergent methods* (pp. 675–95). New York: Guilford.

Fiese, B. H., & Spagnola, M. (2005). Narratives in and about families: An examination of coding schemes and a guide for family researchers. *Journal of Family Psychology, 19*(1), 51–61.

Finfgeld, D. L. (2003). Metasynthesis: The state of the art – so far. *Qualitative Health Research, 13*(7), 893–904.

Finley, S., & Finley, M. (1999). Sp'ange: A research story. *Qualitative Inquiry, 5*(3), 313–37.

Flick, U. (2009). *An introduction to qualitative research* (4th ed.). London: Sage.

Fowler, F. J., Jr. (2001). *Survey research methods*. Thousand Oaks, CA: Sage.

Fox, M., Martin, P., & Green, G. (2007). *Doing practitioner research*. London: Sage.

Frank, A. W. (2012). Practicing dialogical narrative analysis. In J. A. Holstein & J. F. Gubrium (Eds.), *Varieties of narrative analysis* (pp. 33–52). Thousand Oaks, CA: Sage.

Franzosi, R. (2010). *Quantitative narrative analysis*. Thousand Oaks, CA: SAGE.

Freeman, M. (2004). Data are everywhere: Narrative criticism in the literature of experience. In C. Daiute & C. Lightfoot (Eds.), *Narrative analysis: Studying the development of individuals in society* (pp. 63–81). Thousand Oaks, CA: Sage.

Freeman, M., & Mathison, S. (2009). *Researching children's experiences*. New York: Guilford.

Friese, S. (2012). *Qualitative data analysis with ATLAS.ti*. London: Sage.

Fullan, M. (2001). *The new meaning of educational change* (3rd ed.). New York: Teachers College Press.

Gable, R. K., & Wolf, M. B. (1993). *Instrument development in the affective domain: Measuring attitudes and values in corporate and school settings* (2nd ed.). Boston, MA: Kluwer Academic.

Gallagher, K. (2007). *The theatre of urban: Youth and schooling in dangerous times*. Toronto: University of Toronto Press.

Galman, S. C. (2007). *Shane, the lone ethnographer: A beginner's guide to ethnography*. Walnut Creek, CA: AltaMira Press.

Gee, J. P. (2011). *How to do discourse analysis: A toolkit*. New York: Routledge.

Gee, J. P., Michaels, S., & O'Connor, M. C. (1992). Discourse analysis. In M. D. LeCompte, W. L. Millroy, & J. Preissle (Eds.), *The handbook of qualitative research in education* (pp. 227–91). San Diego, CA: Academic Press.

Geertz, C. (1973). Thick description: Toward an interpretive theory of culture. In Y. S. Lincoln & N. K. Denzin (Eds., 2003), *Turning points in qualitative research: Tying knots in a handkerchief* (pp. 143–68). Walnut Creek, CA: AltaMira Press.

Geertz, C. (1983). *Local knowledge: Further essays in interpretive anthropology*. New York: Basic Books.

Gibbs, G. R. (2002). *Qualitative data analysis: Explorations with NVivo*. Maidenhead: Open University Press.

Gibbs, G. R. (2007). *Analysing qualitative data*. London: Sage.

Gibson, W. J., & Brown, A. (2009). *Working with qualitative data*. London: Sage.

Giele, J. Z., & Elder, G. H., Jr. (Eds.). (1998). *Methods of life course research: Qualitative and quantitative approaches*. Thousand Oaks, CA: Sage.

Gilligan, C., Spencer, R., Weinberg, M. K., & Bertsch, T. (2006). On the Listening Guide: A voice-centered relational method. In S. N. Hesse-Biber & P. Leavy (Eds.), *Emergent methods in social research* (pp. 253–71). Thousand Oaks, CA: Sage.

Giorgi, A. P., & Giorgi, B. M. (2003). The descriptive phenomenological psychological method. In P. M. Camic, J. E. Rhodes, & L. Yardley (Eds.), *Qualitative research in psychology: Expanding perspectives in methodology and design* (pp. 243–73). Washington, DC: American Psychological Association.

Glaser, B. G. (1978). *Theoretical sensitivity*. Mill Valley, CA: Sociology Press.

Glaser, B. G. (2005). *The grounded theory perspective III: Theoretical coding*. Mill Valley, CA: Sociology Press.

Glaser, B. G., & Holton, J. (2004). Remodeling grounded theory. Forum: Qualitative Social Research, 5(2), art. 4. Accessed 29 January 2012 from: http://www.qualitative-research.net/index.php/fqs/article/view/607/1315.

Glaser, B. G., & Strauss, A. L. (1967). *The discovery of grounded theory: Strategies for qualitative research*. New York: Aldine de Gruyter.

Glesne, C. (2011). *Becoming qualitative researchers: An introduction* (4th ed.). Boston, MA: Pearson Education.

Goffman, E. (1959). *The presentation of self in everyday life*. New York: Anchor Books.

Goffman, E. (1963). *Stigma: Notes on the management of spoiled identity*. Englewood Cliffs, NJ: Prentice-Hall.

Goleman, D. (1995). *Emotional intelligence*. New York: Bantam Books.

Goodall, H. L., Jr. (2000). *Writing the new ethnography*. Walnut Creek, CA: AltaMira Press.

Goodall, H. L., Jr. (2008). *Writing qualitative inquiry: Self, stories, and academic life*. Walnut Creek, CA: Left Coast Press.

Gordon-Finlayson, A. (2010). QM2: Grounded theory. In M. A. Forrester (Ed.), *Doing qualitative research in psychology* (pp. 154–76). London: Sage.

Graue, M. E., & Walsh, D. J. (1998). *Studying children in context: Theories, methods, and ethics*. Thousand Oaks, CA: Sage.

Grbich, C. (2007). *Qualitative data analysis: An introduction*. Thousand Oaks, CA: Sage.

Greene, S., & Hogan, D. (Eds.). (2005). *Researching children's experience: Approaches and methods*. London: Sage.

Greig, A., Taylor, J., & MacKay, T. (2007). *Doing research with children* (2nd ed.). London: Sage.

Gubrium, J. F., & Holstein, J. A. (1997). *The new language of qualitative method*. New York: Oxford University Press.

Gubrium, J. F., & Holstein, J. A. (2009). *Analyzing narrative reality*. Thousand Oaks, CA: Sage.

Guest, G., & MacQueen, K. M. (2008). *Handbook for team-based qualitative research*. Lanham, MD: AltaMira Press.

Guest, G., MacQueen, K. M., & Namey, E. E. (2012). *Applied thematic analysis*. Thousand Oaks, CA: Sage.

Hager, L., Maier, B. J., O'Hara, E., Ott, D., & Saldaña, J. (2000). Theatre teachers' perceptions of Arizona state standards. *Youth Theatre Journal, 14*, 64–77.

Hahn, C. (2008). *Doing qualitative research using your computer: A practical guide*. London: Sage.

Hakel, M. (2009). How often is often? In K. Krippendorff & M.A. Bock (Eds.), *The content analysis reader* (pp. 304–5). Thousand Oaks, CA: Sage.

Hammersley, M. (1992). *What's wrong with ethnography? Methodological explorations*. London: Routledge.

Hammersley, M., & Atkinson, P. (2007). *Ethnography: Principles in practice* (3rd ed.). London: Routledge.

Handwerker, W. P. (2001). *Quick ethnography*. Walnut Creek, CA: AltaMira Press.

Hargreaves, A., Earl, L., Moore, S., & Manning, S. (2001). *Learning to change: Teaching beyond subjects and standards*. San Francisco: Jossey-Bass.

Harré, R., & van Langenhove, L. (1999). *Positioning theory: Moral contexts of intentional action*. Oxford: Blackwell.

Harry, B., Sturges, K. M., & Klingner, J. K. (2005). Mapping the process: An exemplar of process and challenge in grounded theory analysis. *Educational Researcher, 34*(2), 3–13.

Hatch, J. A. (2002). *Doing qualitative research in education settings*. Albany, NY: SUNY Press.

Hatch, J. A., & Wisniewski, R. (Eds.). (1995). *Life history and narrative*. London: Falmer Press.

Haw, K., & Hadfield, M. (2011). *Video in social science research: Functions and forms*. London: Routledge.

Hays, D. G., & Singh, A. A. (2012). *Qualitative inquiry in clinical and educational settings*. New York: Guilford.

Heath, C., Hindmarsh, J., & Luff, P. (2010). *Video in qualitative research: Analysing social interaction in everyday life*. London: Sage.

Heaton, J. (2008). Secondary analysis of qualitative data. In P. Alasuutari, L. Bickman, & J. Brannen (Eds.), *The Sage handbook of social research methods* (pp. 506–19). London: Sage.

Heiligman, D. (1998). *The New York public library kid's guide to research*. New York: Scholastic Reference.

Hendry, P. M. (2007). The future of narrative. *Qualitative Inquiry, 13*(4), 487–98.

Hennink, M., Hutter, I., & Bailey, A. (2011). *Qualitative research methods*. London: Sage.

Henwood, K., & Pidgeon, N. (2003). Grounded theory in psychological research. In P. M. Camic, J. E. Rhodes, & L. Yardley (Eds.), *Qualitative research in psychology: Expanding perspectives in methodology and design* (pp. 131–55). Washington, DC: American Psychological Association.

Hitchcock, G., & Hughes, D. (1995). *Research and the teacher: A qualitative introduction to school-based research* (2nd ed.). London: Routledge.

Hochschild, A. R. (2003). *The managed heart: Commercialization of human feeling* (2nd ed.). Berkeley, CA: University of California Press.

Holstein, J. A., & Gubrium, J. F. (2000). *Constructing the life course* (2nd ed.). Dix Hills, NY: General Hall.

Holstein, J. A., & Gubrium, J. F. (Eds.). (2012). *Varieties of narrative analysis*. Thousand Oaks, CA: Sage.

Hruschka, D. J., Schwartz, D., St. John, D. C., Picone-Decaro, E., Jenkins, R. A., & Carey, J. W. (2004). Reliability in coding open-ended data: Lessons learned from HIV behavioral research. *Field Methods, 16*(3), 307–31.

Hubbard, R. S., & Power, B. M. (1993). *The art of classroom inquiry: A handbook for teacher-researchers*. Portsmouth, NH: Heinemann.

Janesick, V. J. (2011). "Stretching" exercises for qualitative researchers (3rd ed.). Thousand Oaks, CA: Sage.

Jones, E., Gallois, C., Callan, V., & Barker, M. (1999). Strategies of accommodation: Development of a coding system for conversational interaction. *Journal of Language and Social Psychology, 18*(2), 123–52.

Kemper, R. V., & Royce, A. P. (Eds.). (2002). *Chronicling cultures: Long-term field research in anthropology*. Walnut Creek, CA: AltaMira Press.

Kendall, J. (1999). Axial coding and the grounded theory controversy. *Western Journal of Nursing Research, 21*(6), 743–57.

Knowles, J. G., & Cole, A. L. (2008). *Handbook of the arts in qualitative research: Perspectives, methodologies, examples, and issues*. Thousand Oaks, CA: Sage.

Knowlton, L. W., & Phillips, C. C. (2009). *The logic model guidebook: Better strategies for great results*. Thousand Oaks, CA: Sage.

Kozinets, R. V. (2010). *Netnography: Doing ethnographic research online*. London: Sage.

Krippendorff, K. (2003). *Content analysis: An introduction to its methodology*. Thousand Oaks, CA: Sage.

Krippendorff, K. (2009). Testing the reliability of content analysis data: What is involved and why. In K. Krippendorff & M. A. Bock (Eds.), *The content analysis reader* (pp. 350–7). Thousand Oaks, CA: Sage.

Krippendorff, K., & Bock, M. A. (Eds.). (2009). *The content analysis reader*. Thousand Oaks, CA: Sage.

Kuckartz, U. (2007). *MAXQDA: Professional software for qualitative data analysis*. Berlin & Marburg, Germany: VERBI Software.

Kvale, S., & Brinkmann, S. (2009). *Interviews: Learning the craft of qualitative research interviewing* (2nd ed.). Thousand Oaks, CA: Sage.

La Pelle, N. (2004). Simplifying qualitative data analysis using general purpose software tools. *Field Methods, 16*(1), 85–108.

Lawrence-Lightfoot, S., & Davis, J. H. (1997). *The art and science of portraiture.* San Francisco: Jossey-Bass.

Layder, D. (1998). *Sociological practice: Linking theory and research.* London: Sage.

Leavy, P. (2009). *Method meets art: Arts-based research practice.* New York: Guilford.

LeCompte, M. D., & Preissle, J. (1993). *Ethnography and qualitative design in educational research* (2nd ed.). San Diego, CA: Academic Press.

LeCompte, M. D., & Schensul, J. J. (1999). *Analyzing & interpreting ethnographic data.* Walnut Creek, CA: AltaMira Press.

Leech, N. L., & Onwuegbuzie, A. J. (2005). Qualitative data analysis: Ways to improve accountability in qualitative research. Paper presented at the American Educational Research Association Annual Conference, Montreal.

LeGreco, M., & Tracy, S. J. (2009). Discourse tracing as qualitative practice. *Qualitative Inquiry, 15*(9), 1516–43.

Lewins, A., & Silver, C. (2007). *Using software in qualitative research: A step-by-step guide.* London: Sage.

Liamputtong, P. (2009). *Qualitative research methods* (3rd ed.). Melbourne: Oxford University Press.

Liamputtong, P., & Ezzy, D. (2005). *Qualitative research methods* (2nd ed.). Melbourne: Oxford University Press.

Lichtman, M. (2010). *Qualitative research in education: A user's guide* (2nd ed.). Thousand Oaks, CA: Sage.

Lieblich, A., Zilber, T. B., & Tuval-Mashiach, R. (2008). Narrating human actions: The subjective experience of agency, structure, communion, and serendipity. *Qualitative Inquiry, 14*(4): 613–31.

Lincoln, Y. S., & Denzin, N. K. (Eds.). (2003). *Turning points in qualitative research: Tying knots in a handkerchief.* Walnut Creek, CA: AltaMira Press.

Lincoln, Y. S., & Guba, E. G. (1985). *Naturalistic inquiry.* Newbury Park, CA: Sage.

Lindlof, T. R., & Taylor, B. C. (2011). *Qualitative communication research methods* (3rd ed.). Thousand Oaks, CA: Sage.

Locke, K. (2007). Rational control and irrational free-play: Dual-thinking modes as necessary tension in grounded theorizing. In A. Bryant & K. Charmaz (Eds.), *The Sage handbook of grounded theory* (pp. 565–79). London: Sage.

Lofland, J., Snow, D., Anderson, L., & Lofland, L. H. (2006). *Analyzing social settings: A guide to qualitative observation and analysis* (4th ed.). Belmont, CA: Thomson Wadsworth.

MacQueen, K. M., & Guest, G. (2008). An introduction to team-based qualitative research. In G. Guest & K. M. MacQueen (Eds.), *Handbook for team-based qualitative research* (pp. 3–19). Lanham, MD: AltaMira Press.

MacQueen, K. M., McLellan, E., Kay, K., & Milstein, B. (2009). Codebook development for team-based qualitative analysis. In K. Krippendorff & M. A. Bock (Eds.), *The content analysis reader* (pp. 211–19). Thousand Oaks, CA: Sage.

MacQueen, K. M., McLellan-Lemal, E., Bartholow, K., & Milstein, B. (2008). Team-based codebook development: Structure, process, and agreement. In G. Guest &

K. M. MacQueen (Eds.), *Handbook for team-based qualitative research* (pp. 119–35). Lanham, MD: AltaMira Press.

Madden, R. (2010). *Being ethnographic: A guide to the theory and practice of ethnography.* London: Sage.

Madison, D. S. (2012). *Critical ethnography: Method, ethics, and performance* (2nd ed.). Thousand Oaks, CA: Sage.

Madison, D. S., & Hamera, J. (Eds.). (2006). *The Sage handbook of performance studies.* Thousand Oaks, CA: Sage.

Maher, L., & Hudson, S. L. (2007). Women in the drug economy: A metasynthesis of the qualitative literature. *Journal of Drug Issues, 7*(4), 805–26.

Major, C. H., & Savin-Baden, M. (2010). *An introduction to qualitative research synthesis: Managing the information explosion in social science research.* London: Routledge.

Mason, J. (1994). Linking qualitative and quantitative data analysis. In A. Bryman & R. G. Burgess (Eds.), *Analyzing qualitative data* (pp. 89–110). London: Routledge.

Mason, J. (2002). *Qualitative researching* (2nd ed.). London: Sage.

Maxwell, J. A. (2004). Using qualitative methods for causal explanation. *Field Methods, 16*(3): 243–64.

Maxwell, J. A. (2012). *A realist approach for qualitative research.* Thousand Oaks, CA: Sage.

Maycut, P., & Morehouse, R. (1994). *Beginning qualitative research: A philosophic and practical guide.* London: Falmer Press.

McCammon, L. A., & Saldaña, J. (2011). Lifelong impact: Adult perceptions of their high school speech and/or theatre participation. Unpublished report.

McCurdy, D. W., Spradley, J. P., and Shandy, D. J. (2005). *The cultural experience: Ethnography in complex society* (2nd ed.). Long Grove, IL: Waveland Press.

McIntosh, M. J., & Morse, J. M. (2009). Institutional review boards and the ethics of emotion. In N. K. Denzin & M. D. Giardina (Eds.), *Qualitative inquiry and social justice* (pp. 81–107). Walnut Creek, CA: Left Coast Press.

McLeod, J., & Thomson, R. (2009). *Researching social change.* London: Sage.

Mears, C. L. (2009). *Interviewing for education and social science research: The gateway approach.* New York: Palgrave Macmillan.

Mello, R. A. (2002). Collocation analysis: A method for conceptualizing and understanding narrative data. *Qualitative Research, 2*(2), 231–43.

Merriam, S. B. (1998). *Qualitative research and case study applications in education.* San Francisco: Jossey-Bass.

Meyer, D. Z., & Avery, L. M. (2009). Excel as a qualitative data analysis tool. *Field Methods, 21*(1), 91–112.

Miles, M. B., & Huberman, A. M. (1994). *Qualitative data analysis* (2nd ed.). Thousand Oaks, CA: Sage.

Miller, P. J., Hengst, J. A., & Wang, S. (2003). Ethnographic methods: Applications from developmental cultural psychology. In P. M. Camic, J. E. Rhodes, & L. Yardley (Eds.), *Qualitative research in psychology: Expanding perspectives in methodology and design* (pp. 219–42). Washington, DC: American Psychological Association.

Morgan, D., Fellows, C., & Guevara, H. (2008). Emergent approaches to focus group research. In S. N. Hesse-Biber & P. Leavy (Eds.), *Handbook of emergent methods* (pp. 189–205). New York: Guilford.

Morner, K., & Rausch, R. (1991). *NTC's dictionary of literary terms*. New York: NTC.

Morrison, K. (2009). *Causation in educational research*. London: Routledge.

Morse, J. M. (1994). "Emerging from the data": The cognitive processes of analysis in qualitative inquiry. In J. M. Morse (Ed.), *Critical issues in qualitative research methods* (pp. 22–43). Thousand Oaks, CA: Sage.

Morse, J. M. (2007). Sampling in grounded theory. In A. Bryant & K. Charmaz (Eds.), *The Sage handbook of grounded theory* (pp. 229–44). London: Sage.

Morse, J. M., Niehaus, L., Varnhagen, S., Austin, W., & McIntosh, M. (2008). Qualitative researchers' conceptualizations of the risks inherent in qualitative interviews. In N. K. Denzin & M. D. Giardina (Eds.), *Qualitative inquiry and the politics of evidence* (pp. 195–217). Walnut Creek, CA: Left Coast Press.

Mukherji, P., & Albon, D. (2010). *Research methods in early childhood: An introductory guide*. London: Sage.

Munton, A. G., Silvester, J., Stratton, P., & Hanks, H. (1999). *Attributions in action: A practical approach to coding qualitative data*. Chichester: Wiley.

Murdock, G. P. et al. (2004). Outline of cultural materials (5th ed.). Accessed 29 January 2012 from: http://www.yale.edu/hraf/Ocm_xml/traditionalOcm.xml.

Murray, M. (2003). Narrative psychology and narrative analysis. In P. M. Camic, J. E. Rhodes, & L. Yardley (Eds.), *Qualitative research in psychology: Expanding perspectives in methodology and design* (pp. 95–112). Washington, DC: American Psychological Association.

Murray, M. (2008). Narrative psychology. In J. A. Smith (Ed.), *Qualitative psychology: A practical guide to research methods* (2nd ed.) (pp. 111–32). London: Sage.

Namey, E., Guest, G., Thairu, L., & Johnson, L. (2008). Data reduction techniques for large qualitative data sets. In G. Guest & K. M. MacQueen (Eds.), *Handbook for team-based qualitative research* (pp. 137–61). Lanham, MD: AltaMira Press.

Narayan, K., & George, K. M. (2002). Personal and folk narrative as cultural representation. In J. F. Gubrium & J. A. Holstein (Eds.), *Handbook of interview research: Context & method* (pp. 815–31). Thousand Oaks, CA: Sage.

Nathan, R. (2005). *My freshman year: What a professor learned by becoming a student*. New York: Penguin Books.

Noblit, G. W., & Hare, R. D. (1988). *Meta-ethnography: Synthesizing qualitative studies*. Newbury Park, CA: Sage.

Northcutt, N., & McCoy, D. (2004). *Interactive qualitative analysis: A systems method for qualitative research*. Thousand Oaks, CA: Sage.

O'Connor, P. (2007). Reflection and refraction – the dimpled mirror of process drama: How process drama assists people to reflect on their attitudes and behaviors associated with mental illness. *Youth Theatre Journal, 21*, 1–11.

O'Kane, C. (2000). The development of participatory techniques: Facilitating children's views about decisions which affect them. In P. Christensen & A. James (Eds.), *Research with children: Perspectives and practices* (pp. 136–59). London: Falmer Press.

Olesen, V., Droes, N., Hatton, D., Chico, N., & Schatzman, L. (1994). Analyzing together: Recollections of a team approach. In A. Bryman & R. G. Burgess (Eds.), *Analyzing qualitative data* (pp. 111–28). London: Routledge.

Packer, M. (2011). *The science of qualitative research*. Cambridge: Cambridge University Press.

Patterson, W. (2008). Narratives of events: Labovian narrative analysis and its limitations. In M. Andrews, C. Squire, & M. Tamboukou (Eds.), *Doing narrative research* (pp. 22–40). London: Sage.

Patton, M. Q. (2002). *Qualitative research & evaluation methods* (3rd ed.). Thousand Oaks, CA: Sage.

Patton, M. Q. (2008). *Utilization-focused evaluation* (4th ed.). Thousand Oaks, CA: Sage.

Paulston, R. G. (Ed.). (2000). *Social cartography: Mapping ways of seeing social and educational change*. New York: Garland.

Pitman, M. A., & Maxwell, J. A. (1992). Qualitative approaches to evaluation: Models and methods. In M. D. LeCompte, W. L. Millroy, & J. Preissle (Eds.), *The handbook of qualitative research in education* (pp. 729–70). San Diego, CA: Academic Press.

Poland, B. D. (2002). Transcription quality. In J. F. Gubrium & J. A. Holstein (Eds.), *Handbook of interview research: Context & method* (pp. 629–49). Thousand Oaks, CA: Sage.

Polkinghorne, D. E. (1995). Narrative configuration in qualitative analysis. In J. A. Hatch & R. Wisniewski (Eds.), *Life history and narrative* (pp. 5–23). London: Falmer Press.

Poulos, C. N. (2008). *Accidental ethnography: An inquiry into family secrecy*. Walnut Creek, CA: Left Coast Press.

Prior, L. (2004). Doing things with documents. In D. Silverman (Ed.), *Qualitative research: Theory, method and practice* (2nd ed.) (pp. 76–94). London: Sage.

Prus, R. (1996). *Symbolic interaction and ethnographic research: Intersubjectivity and the study of human lived experience*. Albany, NY: SUNY Press.

Punch, S. (2009). Case study: Researching childhoods in Bolivia. In E. K. M. Tisdall, J. M. Davis, & M. Gallagher (Eds.), *Researching with children & young people* (pp. 89–96). London: Sage.

Rallis, S. F., & Rossman, G. B. (2003). Mixed methods in evaluation contexts: A pragmatic framework. In A. Tashakkori & C. Teddlie (Eds.), *Handbook of mixed methods in social & behavioral research* (pp. 491–512). Thousand Oaks, CA: Sage.

Rapley, T. (2007). *Doing conversation, discourse and document analysis*. London: Sage.

Richards, L. (2009). *Handling qualitative data: A practical guide* (2nd ed.). London: Sage.

Richards, L., & Morse, J. M. (2007). *Readme first for a user's guide to qualitative methods* (2nd ed.). Thousand Oaks, CA: Sage.

Riessman, C. K. (2002). Narrative analysis. In A. M. Huberman & M. B. Miles (Eds.), *The qualitative researcher's companion* (pp. 217–70). Thousand Oaks, CA: Sage.

Riessman, C. K. (2008). *Narrative methods for the human sciences*. Thousand Oaks, CA: Sage.

Ritchie, J., & Spencer, L. (1994). Qualitative data analysis for applied policy research. In A. Bryman & R. G. Burgess (Eds.), *Analyzing qualitative data* (pp. 173–94). London: Routledge.

Rossman, G. B., & Rallis, S. F. (2003). *Learning in the field: An introduction to qualitative research* (2nd ed.). Thousand Oaks, CA: Sage.

Rubin, H. J., & Rubin, I. S. (2012). *Qualitative interviewing: The art of hearing data* (3rd ed.). Thousand Oaks, CA: Sage.

Ryan, G. W., & Bernard, H. R. (2003). Techniques to identify themes. *Field Methods, 15*(1), 85–109.

Saldaña, J. (1992). Assessing Anglo and Hispanic children's perceptions and responses to theatre: A cross-ethnic pilot study. *Youth Theatre Journal, 7*(2), 3–14.

Saldaña, J. (1995). "Is theatre necessary?": Final exit interviews with sixth grade participants from the ASU longitudinal study. *Youth Theatre Journal, 9*, 14–30.

Saldaña, J. (1997). "Survival": A white teacher's conception of drama with inner city Hispanic youth. *Youth Theatre Journal, 11*, 25–46.

Saldaña, J. (1998). "Maybe someday, if I'm famous …": An ethnographic performance text. In J. Saxton & C. Miller (Eds.), *Drama and theatre in education: The research of practice, the practice of research* (pp. 89–109). Brisbane: IDEA.

Saldaña, J. (2003). *Longitudinal qualitative research: Analyzing change through time.* Walnut Creek, CA: AltaMira Press.

Saldaña, J. (Ed.). (2005a). *Ethnodrama: An anthology of reality theatre.* Walnut Creek, CA: AltaMira Press.

Saldaña, J. (2005b). Theatre of the oppressed with children: A field experiment. *Youth Theatre Journal, 19*, 117–33.

Saldaña, J. (2008). Analyzing longitudinal qualitative observational data. In S. Menard (Ed.), *Handbook of longitudinal research: Design, measurement, and analysis* (pp. 297–311). Burlington, MA: Academic Press.

Saldaña, J. (2009). Popular film as an instructional strategy in qualitative research methods courses. *Qualitative Inquiry, 15*(1), 247–61.

Saldaña, J. (2010). Writing ethnodrama: A sampler from educational research. In M. Savin-Baden & C. H. Major (Eds.), *New approaches to qualitative research: Wisdom and uncertainty* (pp. 61–79). London: Routledge.

Saldaña, J. (2011a). *Ethnotheatre: Research from page to stage.* Walnut Creek, CA: Left Coast Press.

Saldaña, J. (2011b). *Fundamentals of qualitative research.* New York: Oxford University Press.

Salovey, P., Detweiler-Bedell, B. T., Detweiler-Bedell, J. B., & Mayer, J. D. (2008). Emotional intelligence. In M. Lewis, J. M. Haviland-Jones, & L. F. Barrett (Eds.), *Handbook of emotions* (3rd ed.) (pp. 533–47). New York: Guilford.

Sandelowski, M. (2008). Research question. In L. M. Given (Ed.), *The Sage encyclopedia of qualitative research methods* (Vol. 2, pp. 786–7). Thousand Oaks, CA: Sage.

Sandelowski, M., & Barroso, J. (2003). Creating metasummaries of qualitative findings. *Nursing Research, 52*(4), 226–33.

Sandelowski, M., & Barroso, J. (2007). *Handbook for synthesizing qualitative research.* New York: Springer.

Sandelowski, M., Docherty, S., & Emden, C. (1997). Qualitative metasynthesis: Issues and techniques. *Research in Nursing & Health, 20*(4), 365–71.

Schensul, J. J., LeCompte, M. D., Nastasi, B. K., & Borgatti, S. P. (1999a). *Enhanced ethnographic methods: Audiovisual techniques, focused group interviews, and elicitation techniques.* Walnut Creek, CA: AltaMira Press.

Schensul, S. L., Schensul, J. J., & LeCompte, M. D. (1999b). *Essential ethnographic methods: Observations, interviews, and questionnaires.* Walnut Creek, CA: AltaMira Press.

Schreier, M. (2012). *Qualitative content analysis in practice*. London: Sage.

Schwalbe, M. L., & Wolkomir, M. (2002). Interviewing men. In J. F. Gubrium & J. A. Holstein (Eds.), *Handbook of interview research: Context & method* (pp. 203–19). Thousand Oaks, CA: Sage.

Schwarz, N., Kahneman, D., & Xu, J. (2009). Global and episodic reports of hedonic experience. In R. F. Belli, F. P. Stafford, & D. F. Alwin (Eds.), *Calendar and time diary methods in life course research* (pp. 157–74). Thousand Oaks, CA: Sage.

Seidman, I. (2006). *Interviewing as qualitative research: A guide for researchers in education and the social sciences* (3rd ed.). New York: Teachers College Press.

Shank, G. D. (2002). *Qualitative research: A personal skills approach*. Upper Saddle River, NJ: Merrill Prentice-Hall.

Shaw, M. E., & Wright, J. M. (1967). *Scales for the measurement of attitudes*. New York: McGraw-Hill.

Shaw, R. (2010). QM3: Interpretative phenomenological analysis. In M. A. Forrester (Ed.), *Doing qualitative research in psychology* (pp. 177–201). London: Sage.

Sherry, M. (2008). Identity. In L. M. Given (Ed.), *The Sage encyclopedia of qualitative research methods* (Vol. 1, p. 415). Thousand Oaks, CA: Sage.

Shkedi, A. (2005). *Multiple-case narrative: A qualitative approach to studying multiple populations*. Amsterdam: John Benjamins.

Shrader, E., & Sagot, M. (2000). *Domestic violence: Women's way out*. Washington, DC: Pan American Health Organization.

Silverman, D. (2006). *Interpreting qualitative data: Methods for analyzing talk, text and interaction* (3rd ed.). London: Sage.

Sipe, L. R., & Ghiso, M. P. (2004). Developing conceptual categories in classroom descriptive research: Some problems and possibilities. *Anthropology and Education Quarterly, 35*(4), 472–85.

Smith, J. A., Flowers, P., & Larkin, M. (2009). *Interpretative phenomenological analysis: Theory, method and research*. London: Sage.

Smith, J. A., & Osborn, M. (2008). Interpretative phenomenological analysis. In J. A. Smith (Ed.), *Qualitative psychology: A practical guide to research methods* (2nd ed.) (pp. 53–80). London: Sage.

Soklaridis, S. (2009). The process of conducting qualitative grounded theory research for a doctoral thesis: Experiences and reflections. *The Qualitative Report, 14*(14), 719–34. Accessed 29 January 2012 from: http://www.nova.edu/ssss/QR/QR14-4/soklaridis.pdf.

Sorsoli, L., & Tolman, D. L. (2008). Hearing voices: Listening for multiplicity and movement in interview data. In S. N. Hesse-Biber & P. Leavy (Eds.), *Handbook of emergent methods* (pp. 495–515). New York: Guilford.

Spencer, S. (2011). *Visual research methods in the social sciences: Awakening visions*. London: Routledge.

Spindler, G., & Spindler, L. (1992). Cultural process and ethnography: An anthropological perspective. In M. D. LeCompte, W. L. Millroy, & J. Preissle (Eds.), *The handbook of qualitative research in education* (pp. 53–92). San Diego, CA: Academic Press.

Spradley, J. P. (1979). *The ethnographic interview*. Fort Worth, TX: Harcourt Brace Jovanovich.

Spradley, J. P. (1980). *Participant observation*. Fort Worth, TX: Harcourt Brace Jovanovich.

Stake, R. E. (1995). *The art of case study research*. Thousand Oaks, CA: Sage.

Stanfield, J. H., II, & Dennis, R. M. (Eds.). (1993). *Race and ethnicity in research methods*. Newbury Park, CA: Sage.

Stern, P. N. (2007). On solid ground: Essential properties for growing grounded theory. In A. Bryant & K. Charmaz (Eds.), *The Sage handbook of grounded theory* (pp. 114–26). London: Sage.

Stern, P. N., & Porr, C. J. (2011). *Essentials of accessible grounded theory*. Walnut Creek, CA: Left Coast Press.

Stewart, A. (1998). *The ethnographer's method*. Thousand Oaks, CA: Sage.

Strauss, A., & Corbin, J. (1998). *Basics of qualitative research: Techniques and procedures for developing grounded theory* (2nd ed.). Thousand Oaks, CA: Sage.

Strauss, A. L. (1987). *Qualitative analysis for social scientists*. Cambridge: Cambridge University Press.

Stringer, E. T. (1999). *Action research* (2nd ed.). Thousand Oaks, CA: Sage.

Sullivan, P. (2012). *Qualitative data analysis using a dialogical approach*. London: Sage.

Sunstein, B. S., & Chiseri-Strater, E. (2007). *FieldWorking: Reading and writing research* (3rd ed.). Boston, MA: Bedford/St. Martin's Press.

Tashakkori, A., & Teddlie, C. (1998). *Mixed methodology: Combining qualitative and quantitative approaches*. Thousand Oaks, CA: Sage.

Tashakkori, A., & Teddlie, C. (Eds.) (2003). *Handbook of mixed methods in social & behavioral research*. Thousand Oaks, CA: Sage.

Tesch, R. (1990). *Qualitative research: Analysis types and software tools*. New York: Falmer Press.

Thompson, S. (1977). *The folktale*. Berkeley, CA: University of California Press.

Thomson, P. (Ed.). (2008). *Doing visual research with children and young people*. London: Routledge.

Thorne, S., Jensen, L., Kearney, M. H., Noblit, G., & Sandelowski, M. (2004). Qualitative metasynthesis: Reflections on methodological orientation and ideological agenda. *Qualitative Health Research, 14*(10), 1342–65.

Tisdall, E. K. M., Davis, J. M., & Gallagher, M. (2009). *Researching with children & young people*. London: Sage.

Todd, Z., & Harrison, S. J. (2008). Metaphor analysis. In S. N. Hesse-Biber & P. Leavy (Eds.), *Handbook of emergent methods* (pp. 479–93). New York: Guilford.

Trede, F., & Higgs, J. (2009). Framing research questions and writing philosophically: The role of framing research questions. In J. Higgs, D. Horsfall, & S. Grace (Eds.), *Writing qualitative research on practice* (pp. 13–25). Rotterdam: Sense.

Turner, B. A. (1994). Patterns of crisis behaviour: A qualitative inquiry. In A. Bryman & R. G. Burgess (Eds.), *Analyzing qualitative data* (pp. 195–215). London: Routledge.

Van de Ven, A. H., & Poole, M. S. (1995). Methods for studying innovation development in the Minnesota Innovation Research Program. In G. P. Huber & A. H. Van de Ven (Eds.), *Longitudinal field research methods: Studying processes of organizational change* (pp. 155–85). Thousand Oaks, CA: Sage.

van Maanen, J. (2011). *Tales of the field: On writing ethnography* (2nd ed.). Chicago: University of Chicago Press.

---

van Manen, M. (1990). *Researching lived experience: Human science for an action sensitive pedagogy*. Albany, NY: SUNY Press.

Wagner, B. J. (1998). *Educational drama and language arts: What research shows*. Portsmouth, NH: Heinemann.

Waite, D. (2011). A simple card trick: Teaching qualitative data analysis using a deck of playing cards. *Qualitative Inquiry, 17*(10), 982–5.

Walsh, D. J., Bakin, N., Lee, T. B., Chung, Y., Chung, K., & Colleagues. (2007). Using digital video in field-based research with children: A primer. In J. A. Hatch (Ed.), *Early childhood qualitative research* (pp. 43–62). New York: Routledge.

Warren, S. (2000). Let's do it properly: Inviting children to be researchers. In A. Lewis & G. Lindsay (Eds.), *Researching children's perspectives* (pp. 122–34). Buckingham: Open University Press.

Weber, R. P. (1990). *Basic content analysis* (2nd ed.). Newbury Park, CA: Sage.

Wertz, F. J., Charmaz, K., McMullen, L. M., Josselson, R., Anderson, R., & McSpadden, E. (2011). *Five ways of doing qualitative analysis: Phenomenological psychology, grounded theory, discourse analysis, narrative research, and intuitive inquiry*. New York: Guilford.

Weston, C., Gandell, T., Beauchamp, J., McAlpine, L., Wiseman, C., & Beauchamp, C. (2001). Analyzing interview data: The development and evolution of a coding system. *Qualitative Sociology, 24*(3), 381–400.

Wheeldon, J., & Åhlberg, M. K. (2012). *Visualizing social science research: Maps, methods, & meaning*. Thousand Oaks, CA: Sage.

Wilkinson, D., & Birmingham, P. (2003). *Using research instruments: A guide for researchers*. London: Routledge Farmer.

Willig, C. (2008). Discourse analysis. In J. A. Smith (Ed.), *Qualitative psychology: A practical guide to research methods* (2nd ed.) (pp. 160–85). London: Sage.

Winkelman, M. (1994). Cultural shock and adaptation. *Journal of Counseling and Development, 73*(2), 121–6.

Wolcott, H. F. (1994). *Transforming qualitative data: Description, analysis, and interpretation*. Thousand Oaks, CA: Sage.

Wolcott, H. F. (1999). *Ethnography: A way of seeing*. Walnut Creek, CA: AltaMira Press.

Wolcott, H. F. (2003). *Teachers versus technocrats: An educational innovation in anthropological perspective*. Walnut Creek, CA: AltaMira Press.

Wolcott, H. F. (2009). *Writing up qualitative research* (3rd ed.). Thousand Oaks, CA: Sage.

Woods, P. (2006). *Successful writing for qualitative researchers* (2nd ed.). London: Routledge.

Yin, R. K. (2009). *Case study research: Design and methods* (4th ed.). Thousand Oaks, CA: Sage.

Zoppi, K. A., & Epstein, R. M. (2002). Interviewing in medical settings. In J. F. Gubrium & J. A. Holstein (Eds.), *Handbook of interview research: Context & method* (pp. 355–83). Thousand Oaks, CA: Sage.

Zwiers, M. L., & Morrissette, P. J. (1999). *Effective interviewing of children: A comprehensive guide for counselors and human service workers*. Philadelphia: Accelerated Development.

Index

CAQDAS *cont.*
  and simultaneous coding, 69, 83, 173
  and themes, 180
  Transana, 28, 28 *(fig)*, 29, 56
  unit divisions, 18
  Weft QDA, 29
  Wordle, 199, 199 *(fig)*
case study, 229
category, categories, 14, 216 *(fig)*
  in analytic memos, 45, 226
  of categories, 197–8, 250–2
  central/core, 52, 117, 223–4, 225, 225
    (fig), 226–7
  from codes, 8, 79, 216, 218
  construction of, 6, 9–12, 196–8, 217
  metacategory, 250
  properties and dimensions of, 52, 76, 93,
    101, 103–4, 213, 218, 219–21, 224
  subcategories, 12, 25, 79, 161, 208, 216,
    218, 227
  tabletop, 205, 250
causality, causation, 164–5, 172 *(fig)*, 221–2
  see also coding, causation
Causation in Educational Research, 175
change, see longitudinal
Charmaz, Kathy, 1, 42, 51, 223
Clarke, Adele E., 51, 56
codable moments, 19
code
  definition, 3–4
  landscaping, 12, 80, 199–202, 200 *(fig)*,
    246, 249
  mapping, 12, 119, 194–8, 250
  operational definition, 44–5
  quantities, 24
  see also coding
codebook, 24–5, 148
codeweaving, 45, 46 *(fig)*, 145, 171, 182, 201,
  216, 219, 248–9, 252
codifying, 9, 12
coding
  action, 96
  affective methods, 53, 58, 67, 105
  of analytic memos, 50
  attribute, 64, 69–72, 163, 280
  axial, 51–2, 62, 84, 96, 104, 183, 209, 213,
    217, 218–23, 220 *(fig)*, 224, 225, 227, 246
  and categories, 213
  causation, 15, 61, 82, 99, 100, 151, 154,
    163–75, 249, 257
  collaboratively, 34–5
  conceptual, 223
  as craft, 40
  critiques against, 2, 38–40
  Davis Observation System, 3
  decision criteria, 64–6

coding *cont.*
  decoding, 5
  descriptive, 4, 7, 15, 61, 64, 70, 74, 78, 79,
    83, 87–91, 108, 119, 120, 182, 183,
    210, 232, 249
  domain and taxonomic, 12, 15, 61, 80, 83,
    90, 91, 151, 157–63
  dramaturgical, 61, 100, 115, 123–7, 136,
    175, 191–3
  eclectic, 5, 19, 44, 60, 61, 63, 64, 105, 120,
    127, 141, 147, 188–93, 206
  elaborative, 62, 147, 153, 209, 229–34,
    238, 241
  elemental methods, 53, 58, 67 83–4
  emic, 91
  emotion, 15, 61, 63, 77, 105–10, 115
  encoding, 5
  evaluation, 61, 63, 77, 80, 105, 119–22, 175
  exploratory methods, 58, 67, 141–2, 193
  families, 227
  fear, 66
  filters, 7–8
  first cycle overview, 58, 66–7, 188
  focused, 9, 12, 51–2, 61, 62, 64, 84, 90,
    96, 104, 130, 175, 206, 209, 213,
    213–17, 218, 221, 224, 225, 280
  frequency, 39, 69, 73, 76, 77, 80, 86, 147,
    148, 162, 180, 199, 201, 202, 205,
    227, 251
  generic methods, 64
  grammatical methods, 53, 58, 67, 69
  as heuristic, 8
  hierarchical, 81
  holistic, 23, 64, 78, 87, 141, 142–4,
    182, 204
  hybrid, 64
  hypothesis, 62, 63, 76, 77, 90, 142, 147–50,
    154, 175
  in vivo, 4, 7, 23, 51, 61, 62, 64, 76, 84,
    91–6, 100, 106, 109, 117, 143, 163,
    177, 191, 193, 209, 210, 213, 230,
    232, 280
  indigenous, 91
  inductive, 91
  initial, 12, 51–2, 61, 62, 64, 80, 84, 96, 100–5,
    183, 193, 209, 213, 218, 221,
    223, 224
  intercoder agreement, 35, 39, 255
  interpretive convergence, 35
  jottings, 20–1
  lean, 24, 144
  Leeds Attributional Coding System, 154,
    163, 164
  literal, 91
  literary and language methods, 58,
    67, 123

coding *cont.*
    longitudinal, 61, 80, 100, 209, 234–42, 235 *(fig)*
    lumping, 22–4, 78, 142
    magnitude, 63, 64, 69, 72–7, 75 *(fig)*, 80, 108, 119, 120, 121, 174, 175, 280
    manually, 25–8
    motif, 123, 128–31, 136
    narrative, 123, 127, 130, 131, 131–6
    Narrative Processes System, 3
    necessary personal attributes for, 36–7
    necessity for, 2
    nested, 31, 77, 80, 81
    open, 51, 100, 188
    outline of cultural materials (OCM), 131, 151, 154–7
    pattern, 9, 15, 61, 64, 76, 90, 206, 209, 209–13, 211 *(fig)*, 217, 225, 277, 280
    perspectives on, 60
    pre-coding, 19–20
    procedural methods, 58, 67, 150–1
    process, 5–6, 15, 51, 61, 62, 82, 83, 84, 96–100, 108, 175, 205, 209, 213, 214, 249
    protocol, 62, 80, 131, 150, 151, 151–4
    provisional, 24, 62, 111, 141, 144–7
    questions to consider, 21–2
    recoding, 10, 11–12, 22, 37, 39, 58, 206
    researcher data, 16
    scheme, 9
    second cycle overview, 58, 188, 207–9
    selective, 51, 223
    setting/context, 70
    simultaneous, 6, 63, 69, 80–3, 108, 175, 182
    snapshot, 241
    solo, 35–6
    splitting, 22–4, 78, 103, 142, 202
    strategy, 124
    structural, 62, 64, 84–7, 144
    subcode, subcoding, sub-subcoding, 12, 23, 51, 69, 76, 77–80, 83, 90, 108, 135, 152, 199, 201, 208
    super coding, 212, 227
    theoretical, 51–2, 62, 84, 209, 213, 217, 218, 223, 223–9, 249–50
    topic, 88
    utilitarian, 84
    values, 7, 15, 61, 63, 64, 77, 105, 108, 110–15, 119, 127, 175, 280
    verbal exchange, 123, 136–41, 204
    verbatim, 91
    versus, 15, 61, 105, 108, 115–19, 194–8, 246
    writing about, 37–8, 254–6
concept, 13, 45, 249
conceptual framework, 2, 4, 61, 144, 177, 229

concurrency, 251
conditions (for grounded theory), 165, 169, 218, 220, 222, 224, 227
consequences, 15, 96, 99, 103, 165, 169, 172, 177, 218, 220, 222, 227, 257
context, contexts, 2, 14, 22, 34, 38, 60, 70, 99, 108, 118, 122, 134, 146, 150–1, 164, 165, 169, 218, 221–2, 224, 227, 231–2, 238, 240, 252
Constructing Grounded Theory, 1
Constructing the Life Course, 234
Corbin, Juliet, 51
credibility, 152, 174
culture, cultural, 71, 91, 124, 132, 136, 137–8, 139, 140, 154–5, 157, 158, 159, 161, 176
cultural shock, 81, 202–4

data
    amounts to code, 16–17
    layout, 17–19
decision modeling, 152, 156, 165
demographics, 70, 71
diagram, 45, 98, 161, 165, 172, 222, 225, 227
    operational model, 202–4, 203 *(fig)*
    resources, 204
    trinity, 247–8
    Venn, 205, 248, 248 *(fig)*
differential association, 113
discourse tracing, 237
documents, 20, 52, 54, 128, 155, 177
domino effects, 251

emotional ambivalence, 109
empathy, 39, 40, 43–4, 106, 109
ethics, 37, 47, 109
ethnography, 53, 78, 88, 138, 202
ethos, 130, 165, 203

field notes, 7, 16–17, 20–1, 42, 51, 90, 101, 123, 124, 154–6, 177
fieldwork, 7, 16, 17, 22, 26, 52, 55, 70, 88, 90, 136, 146, 242
film, 281–2
fluid inquiry, 134
folk and indigenous terms, 91, 158, 159, 161, 163
Fundamentals of Qualitative Research, 2

Gardner, Howard, 169
Geertz, Clifford, 159, 247
Gibbs, Graham, 1
Glaser, Barney, 51
Goffman, Erving, 127
Goodall, H. L. (Bud), 123
grounded theory, 42, 53 *(fig)*, 134, 234

research questions, 44, 60–1
rich text, 20, 92, 201, 253
Richards, Lyn, 252

Sage Handbook of Grounded Theory, The, 51
salience score, 76
saturation, 222
Science of Qualitative Research, The, 2
semantic
  differential, 114
  network analysis, 87
  relationship, 158, 159–60
semiotics, 4
sequence, 32, 96, 98, 166, 169, 202, 205,
    251, 257
shop–talk, 35, 206, 258–9
situated embeddedness, 180
Situational Analysis, 56, 228
Smith, Anna Deavere, 94
social drama, 123, 127
SPSS, 63
Spindler, George and Louise, 58–9
Spradley, James P., 151
Stake, Robert E., 41, 187
stanzas, 17–19, 106, 107, 124
statistics, 63, 73, 76, 83, 86–7, 114, 147, 153,
    156, 234
story-line, 98, 107, 164, 166, 172
Strauss, Anselm L., 2, 51
structures, 250–1
subcategory, *see* category
subcoding, *see* coding, subcode
superobjective, 126–7, 191
survey, 26, 31, 63, 85, 114, 121, 159, 163
symbol, 46
sympathy, 39, 43, 106, 109

tables, 255, 256 *(fig)*
taxonomies, 78, 79, 152, 158, 162 *(fig)*,
    205, 251
Teachers versus Technocrats, 115
theme
  definition, 13, 14, 175–6
  differences between code and, 14

theme *cont.*
  meta-theme, 179, 182
  see also themeing the data
themeing the data, 14, 58, 61, 67, 136, 175–83,
    205–6, 217, 233, 246
theoretical construct, 179–80
theory, 224, 226, 249–50
  in analytic memos, 46, 252–3
  attribution, 165
  from codes and categories, 12–13, 13 *(fig)*
  elements of, 250
  positioning, 118
  see also coding, theoretical
Thomson Motif-Index, 128, 129, 131
Thomson, Stith, 130, 131
through-line, 20, 230, 232–3, 241
  see also coding, longitudinal
Timescapes, 242
transformation, 63, 71, 128–9, 134, 154, 238
trustworthiness, 24, 36, 111, 150, 152, 174,
    194, 202, 255
Turner, Victor, 241

units of social organization, 15
Uses of Enchantment, The, 130

validity, 152, 180
values, attitudes, beliefs
  see coding, values
visual
  analysis, 52–7, 101
  approaches, 37, 52–3
  data, 52–7
  display, 199, 202–4, 254
  literacy, 57
voiceprints, 135

Wolcott, Harry F., 24, 260
writing
  about coding, 37–8, 254–6
  final report, 48–9, 246–7, 252, 257–8, 259
  formatting, 253
  headings, subheadings, 253
  vignette, 126, 142

978-1-4462-4918-5

978-1-4462-0046-9

978-1-84920-303-6

978-1-4129-6557-6

978-0-8570-2914-0

978-1-8486-0034-8

978-1-4129-7854-5

978-1-4129-9530-6

978-1-4129-9120-9

Find out more about these titles and our wide range of books for students and researchers at **www.sagepub.co.uk**

EXCITING RESEARCH METHODS TEXTS FROM SAGE

QUALITATIVE DATA ANALYSIS

Practical Strategies

Patricia Bazeley *Research Support Pty Limited, Australia*

Written by an experienced researcher in the field of qualitative methods, this dynamic new book provides a definitive introduction to analysing qualitative data.

It is a clear, accessible and practical guide to each stage of the process, including:

- Designing and managing qualitative data for analysis
- Working with data through interpretive, comparative, pattern and relational analyses
- Developing explanatory theory and coherent conclusions, based on qualitative data.

The book pairs theoretical discussion with practical advice using a host of examples from diverse projects across the social sciences. It describes data analysis strategies in actionable steps and helpfully links to the use of computer software where relevant.

This is an exciting new addition to the literature on qualitative data analysis and a must-read for anyone who has collected, or is preparing to collect, their own data.

CONTENTS

PART ONE: PREPARING THE WAY: LAYING THE FOUNDATIONS FOR ANALYSIS \ Foundations for thinking and working qualitatively \ Designing for analysis \ Managing and preparing data for analysis \ PART TWO: WORKING WITH DATA: A PATHWAY INTO ANALYSIS \ DATA SAMPLES - BECOMING \ BEING A RESEARCHER \ Read, reflect and connect-initial explorations of data \ Codes and coding: principles and practice \ Naming, organising, and refining codes \ Alternative approaches to breaking open and connecting data \ PART THREE: DESCRIBE, COMPARE, AND RELATE: MOVING ON FROM CODES AND THEMES \ Describing, evolving and theorising concepts \ Comparative analyses as a means of furthering analysis \ Relational analyses \ PART FOUR: BRINGING IT TOGETHER-MOVING TOWARD CLIMAX AND CLOSURE \ If...then...is it because? Developing explanatory models and theories \ Developing coherent understanding \ Defending and extending: issues of quality and significance

READERSHIP

Researchers and students across the social sciences

February 2013 • 320 pages
Cloth (978-1-84920-302-9) • £75.00
Paper (978-1-84920-303-6) • £26.99

ALSO FROM SAGE

GROUNDED THEORY FOR QUALITATIVE RESEARCH

A Practical Guide

Cathy Urquhart *Manchester Metropolitan University Business School*

Based on the author's own wealth of experience this timely, engaging book helps first-time researchers to discover the excitement of grounded theory method.

Fresh, innovative and clear this book traces the history and development of grounded theory method, and examines how the method is evolving for new contexts today. It sets out the principles involved in using grounded theory method and explains the process and theory associated with coding in grounded theory.The book introduces us to the practicalities of research design, theory building, coding and writing up and gives us the tools to tackle key questions:

- What is grounded theory?
- How do we code and theorize using grounded theory?
- How do we write up a grounded theory study?

This is an exciting new text for students and researchers across the social sciences who want to use grounded theory method.

CONTENTS

Introduction \ Understanding Analysis \ Grounded Theory Method (GTM) \ Research Design using GTM \ Coding and Conceptualizing \ Building the Theory \ Scaling up the Theory \ Writing up a Grounded Theory Study \ The Contribution of Grounded Theory: Some Reflections

READERSHIP

Students and researchers across the social sciences

November 2012 • 172 pages
Cloth (978-1-84787-053-7) • £70.00
Paper (978-1-84787-054-4) • £23.99

ALSO FROM SAGE